JACK THE RIPPER

RIPPER

The Final Chapter

Paul H. Feldman

The quotations from the original journal which inspired the research that has gone into this book are reproduced by the kind permission of the copyright holders, Smith Gryphon Ltd.

The journal was first published as part of *The Diary of Jack the Ripper* which was written by Shirley Harrison and first published in 1993 by Smith Gryphon Ltd, 12 Bridge Wharf, 156 Caledonian Road, London N1 9UU.

Paul Feldman would like to thank Shirley Harrison and Smith Gryphon Ltd for their generous co-operation.

This edition published in Great Britain in 2005 by
Virgin Books Ltd
Thames Wharf Studios
Rainville Road
London
W6 9HA

Published in Great Britain in 1998, 2002 by Virgin Books Ltd

A catalogue record for this book is available from the British Library.

ISBN 0 7535 0637 8

The paper used in this book is a natural, recyclable product made from wood grown in sustainable forests. The manufacturing process conforms to the regulations of the country of origin.

Typeset by TW Typesetting, Plymouth, Devon

Printed and bound in Great Britain by Mackays of Chatham PLC, Chatham, Kent

I dedicate this book to

my wonderful children, Gary, Naomi and Joshua

and to the memories of

William (Billy) Ernest Graham, without whom it may not have been worthwhile

Robert Alan Johnson, who became a friend first and foremost

and

Brian Maybrick, honest and always sincere

My sincerest thanks to:

Keith Skinner, who headed up my research team of Melvyn Fairclough, Martine Rooney and Carol Emmas, all of whom were invaluable to me

Michael H. Marx, whose perception and knowledge put me on the right road

Paul Begg, for all his assistance

Anne Elizabeth Graham, for acknowledging that the truth had to be told

Michael Kenley and David Franks, for being there

Jeremy Beadle, for his suggestion to include the Glossary of Characters in this edition

CONTENTS

ACKNOWLEDGEMENTS

I should like to thank the following people for their invaluable help and cooperation in producing this book:

Paula Adamick, Andy Aliffe, Mark Angus, Hilary Bailey, Vivienne Bales (Public Record Office), Richard Bark-Jones, Lynne Barrett, Michael Barrett, Robert Barrett, Jeremy Beadle, Marie Bierau, Barbara Bills (Parkinson), Alan Bond, Gerald Brierley, Jo Brooks, Harold Brough, Andrew Brown (Metropolitan Police Archives), Carol Cain, Professor David Canter, Muriel Cheeseman, Alex Chisholm, Lars B. Clausen, Alan Cox, Edwin Crick and family, Jonathan Cross, Paul Daniel, Alice Dean, Direct Communications Design, Paul Dodd, Mark Duffy, Tony Duffy, Timothy Dundas, Clive Dyall, Dr Nicholas Eastaugh, Carol Emmas, Stewart Evans, Rick Ewigh, Melvyn Fairclough, Nicholas Farrell, Carol Feldman, Gary Feldman, Maurice Feldman, Martin and Karen Fido, Janice Flint, Dr David Forshaw, Gerald and Connie Freed, Jean Overton Fuller, Barry Gold, Jim and Jeanette Grady, Anne Elizabeth Graham, Caroline Graham, Mary Graham, William Graham, Alan Gray, Rod Green, Shani Grossman, Judge Richard Hamilton, John Hanks, Melvin Harris, John Harrison, Paul Harrison, Shirley Harrison, Mary S. Hartman, Ethel Hartnett, Reed Hayes, Ellie Haynes (New Scotland Yard Library), Phyllis Head, William Hopkin, John Hostettler, Martin Howells, Tamara Huddle, Sue Iremonger, Peter Jepson, Albert and Valerie Johnson, Eric and Audrey Johnson, Judy Johnson, Robert Johnson, Traccy Johnson, Alice Jones, Allan Jones, Fergus Hugh Graham Kell, Michele Kimche, Hannah

Koren, Ellen May Lackner, Damian Lalley, Loretta Lay, Christopher McLaren, Rod McNeill, Patsy Martin, Peggy Martin, Annie Maybrick, Brian and Faye Maybrick, Vincent Maybrick Ellison, Mrs Maybury, Norma Meagher, Tony Miall, Jean Miles, Terry Morland, John Morrison, Mr and Mrs Murphy, Richard Nicholas, Sheelesh Patel, Andrew Perry, Nick Pinto (Public Record Office), Bill Pollard, Kenneth Rendell, Julia Ridout (Selfridges), Irene Riley, Laurence Ronson, Martine Rooney, John Ross (Metropolitan Police Crime 'Black' Museum), Janice and Paul Roughton, Donald Rumbelow, Bernard Ryan, Richard Sharp (Metropolitan Police Archives), Chris Short, Joseph Sickert, Sam Sinclair, Robert Smith, Ray Smyth, Frank Spiering, Nancy Steele, Gay Steinbach, Edith Stonehouse, Philip Sugden, Brian Tapley, Sgt Colin 'Bones' Thomas, Freda and Stuart Thomson, Tess Tippling, Val Traylen (Public Record Office), Alec Voller, Bill and Marjorie Waddell, Olga Walls, Nick Warren, Pamela West, Richard and Molly Whittington-Egan, Gary Wickes, John Wilding, Roger Wilkes, Colin and Joy Wilson, Jeannette Wilson, Camille Wolff, Barbara Young

INTRODUCTION

In December 1992, when I became involved in this project, I had no intention of writing this book, nor did I want to. As the research I had undertaken developed, I realised that I had to.

I had always been fascinated by Jack the Ripper, not because of his crimes, but because the mystery was unsolved.

The stories of a royal connection, a Freemasonry link and a cover-up were frequent and fascinating. If there was nothing to these rumours, how did they start? And why?

I wondered why so many of the Home Office and police files had been 'destroyed'. Whether such destruction was common or otherwise, what significant information did those files carry, if any?

As my research developed, I realised that the Florence Maybrick trial of 1889 filled up nearly as many newspaper columns as the Ripper crimes had in the previous autumn. Florence Maybrick was the first American woman to be charged with murder in this country. This pretty twenty-six-year-old was said to have poisoned her forty-nine-year-old husband with arsenic. Although the prosecution may have proved her promiscuity, the public did not believe they had proved her guilt. The jury did.

Florence Maybrick was sentenced to death.

The Maybrick trial would continue to fascinate many throughout the twentieth century.

Bernard Ryan, Nigel Morland and Trevor Christie all investigated the case between 1940 and 1969. In each case their work resulted in publication of a book.

However, Frederick Bowman had quite another objective in mind, following twenty years of research and study. In August 1965, he claimed that he now had 'enough evidence to prove Florence Maybrick was not guilty of the crime she was charged with'. He continued: 'the new evidence uncovered is enough to persuade the Home Secretary to reopen the case'.

Frederick claimed that Florence Maybrick should be posthumously acquitted. The Home Secretary was duly petitioned. The new evidence that Frederick Bowman had was never published. The result of the petition was never reported.

While Bowman awaited the outcome of his efforts, he died. Alone and without family. The police removed all papers and documents from his home.

The petition? As the Home Office informed me, it no longer exists. It has also been destroyed.

You will learn, while reading this book, of Dr Thomas Dutton: a man who was intrigued by the Ripper crimes and reported to be a good friend of Inspector Abberline. He was known to the Duke of Clarence. He died alone. His personal papers and documents were removed by the police.

In my possession now is the largest collection of papers and documents about the Maybrick trial that exists anywhere in the world. While I may not be able to say the same of my Jack the Ripper collection, it is, nevertheless, quite extensive.

I, like many of my research team, had become more and more frustrated at the superficial way in which the cynics had dealt, and were dealing, with the document purported to have been written by James Maybrick/Jack the Ripper.

'Cynics Incorporated', as I would sometimes refer to them, would ignore scientific evidence that they could not explain, or consider such scientific evidence to have been produced by somebody incompetent.

I had for some time believed that the diary was genuine. I now know it is. I also know that I have proved it beyond any reasonable doubt.

Throughout my investigation, I had consistently requested that my research team play devil's advocate. I asked them to guess how the diary could have been forged, and by whom, taking in all of the facts we had unearthed. By the end of our investigation, not one could construct anything remotely sensible.

This book is not like any other Jack the Ripper book. It is not a historical précis of events and was not intended to be. It is, primarily, about people. People who are alive today and do all the things that you or I do. They are people who I came to like, respect and admire.

I am confident that, ultimately, common sense will prevail.

Enjoy.

FOREWORD

When Paul Feldman asked me to write the introduction to this book, I agreed without hesitation. I had seen the Maybrick Journal – even held it in my hands – long before Paul even knew of its existence and in a way I – and Keith Skinner – were inadvertently responsible for introducing it to Paul. In a sense, then, this book is our fault. I make no apologies. What you are about to read, whether you agree with it or not, is a remarkable achievement.

This book is both a beginning and an end. It is an end in the sense of being the culmination of years of extraordinarily dedicated research by Paul Feldman. It is a beginning because it is the very long-awaited opportunity for us to look at and assess Paul's evidence and arguments. I say 'us' because, although Paul has consulted with me many times during the writing of this book and I am familiar with much of the evidence he presents, this will also be my first real opportunity to assess Paul's arguments as a coherent whole.

I feel privileged to have been party to much of the on-going research for this book, initially as a founder-draftee to Paul's research team and later as an interested onlooker off whom Paul would sometimes bounce his ideas. We have disagreed, sometimes heatedly, but the theories and ideas have always been interesting and have without fail caused me to stop and think.

The story began when a Liverpudlian named Michael Barrett received the 'Diary' from a man named Tony Devereux. Both men would pop into a pub called the Saddle and they would chat as regulars in a pub often will. When Mr Devereux became ill, Barrett would run a few errands for him. In return Devereux gave him the 'Diary', telling him to do something with it. Barrett managed to work out that the supposed author of the document was James Maybrick – whose death in 1889 had resulted in a *cause célèbre* when his wife, Florence, was charged with and convicted of his murder – and early in 1992 Barrett took the 'Diary' to the offices of the Rupert Crew Literary Agency. Agent Doreen Montgomery was sufficiently intrigued to ask two of her clients, Shirley Harrison and Sally Evemy (who together comprise the writing/research Word Team), to undertake some preliminary research into the document. They did so and were impressed enough for a book project to go ahead. In June 1992 the publishing rights for the projected book were bought by Robert Smith of Smith Gryphon publishers (*The Diary of Jack the Ripper*, London: Smith Gryphon, 1993) and that is how I came to be involved.

Robert has formerly been editorial director of Sidgwick and Jackson and has been responsible for commissioning *The Ripper Legacy* by Martin Howells and Keith Skinner. He now turned to Keith Skinner and asked him to take a look at the 'Diary'. Keith in turn brought in Martin Fido and myself, his co-authors on *The Jack the Ripper A–Z*.

Keith supplied me with photocopies of the 'Diary' along with a photocopy of James Maybrick's will. The handwriting clearly wasn't the same and I wasn't very impressed. Then one day I accompanied Keith to the offices of Doreen Montgomery at Rupert Crew and there saw the 'Diary' in the flesh. It was odd holding that document in my hands and I'd like to say I felt some sort of vibes emanating from the pages, but I didn't. I left uninspired and I remember that on our return journey I demonstrated to Keith how the letter shapes differed between the will and the 'Diary'.

A short time later Paul Feldman contacted me. A video maker, Paul was keen to make a video about Jack the Ripper and wanted to get the views and opinions of as many Ripper authors as he could. An opportunity came for us to meet a little while later when I was in London filming an episode of the American TV series *Sightings*. Paul met Keith and I, we talked and later Paul hired me to advise him during the preliminary work on his video. Keith didn't join us because by that time he'd been hired by Shirley Harrison to help with the early stages of research into James Maybrick.

Paul learned about the existence of the 'Diary', but neither Keith nor I could tell him the name of the author because we were tied to a confidentiality agreement with Robert Smith. But from various bits of information Paul worked out Maybrick's identity and one day I received a phone call. Paul didn't introduce himself or engage in any preliminary chit-chat. He just gruffly said 'Spring is a good time for building houses' (or some such phrase). I thought I had a nutter on the line. Then I realised it was Paul and he explained what he meant – springtime = May. Building houses = bricks. I laughed.

Thus I came to get more closely involved with the 'Diary' and became highly intrigued by some of the information being unearthed – such as a hitherto unsuspected link between James Maybrick and the East End. Was this all coincidence or had somebody done a lot of research? And if somebody had done research, who was that somebody? None of those involved seemed at all likely. I was still of the opinion that the 'Diary' was a forgery, but I wondered when it had been forged – was it possible that it was forged by somebody who knew the Maybrick family? Did it possibly reflect a genuine tradition linking Maybrick to the crimes? I didn't know and it soon became clear that nobody else cared. Two camps had emerged. One believed the 'Diary' was genuine, the other believed that it was a modern forgery. Neither camp was asking when it was written. I asked three questions: when was this document composed, why was it composed and who composed it? As you read this book, ask those questions.

By 1993 my active involvement with the project was diminishing. At that time I lived in Leeds in Yorkshire, too far away to undertake any worthwhile research in London, and I was under pressure with other demanding work. But Keith Skinner's work for Shirley Harrison had ended and in April 1993 he had joined Paul's 'team' – and in speaking of a 'team', don't imagine that it was composed of people who all shared Paul's total conviction that the 'Diary' is genuine. It didn't and doesn't. In fact, one of the most remarkable things about Paul is that he . . . well, I once had a cat which seemed to sense and make a beeline for people who didn't like cats. Paul is a bit like that. If he found someone who didn't believe as he did, he targeted them, listening to their objections and tried to overcome them. Some people closed their minds like a steel trap against Paul's ideas. It was discouraging. But some didn't. Keith was one. Keith didn't think the 'Diary' was genuine either – and he has made that clear in private and in public – but he was willing to surrender his time and ability to find out who did write it and when.

A word about Keith Skinner. Critics of the 'Diary' have accused Keith of being Paul Feldman's 'paid henchman' and of suppressing information in Paul Feldman's interest. I can say without hesitation – and I know Martin Fido would agree – that from our close association with Keith for over a decade we know without a shadow of a doubt that he would not have continued to probe the journal's origins if he knew – or even suspected – that information was being deliberately suppressed. I also know that Paul Feldman has given Keith an absolutely free hand with his research and has trusted him to explore those areas which might be productive. At any time Keith could have found a piece of information that damned the Journal as a modern forgery. Paul knew, as I knew, that Keith would have wanted that information made known and would have walked away from the project if it had not been.

Work distanced me even further from the journal and for a while took me out of contact with Keith and the on-going research. During that time Keith came to question the prevailing modern forgery claim of the most vociferous critics of the 'Diary' and, like me, began to wonder if it was an old forgery. I wonder what your opinion will be.

It has seemed a little odd talking about the 'Diary' as a forgery in the introduction to a book which will at least advance the proposition that it is genuine, but I am frankly bewildered by the sheer weight of research which Paul Feldman has guided over several years. I have been faced with a seemingly unending sequence of names and dates and photographs and all manner of claims and suggestions and evidence. I simply haven't been able to grasp hold of it all. That's why I will value this book as a sequential narrative of Paul Feldman's years of research. Perhaps when you have read the book, you will share his beliefs. Perhaps you won't. But I hope you will all recognise that this book is a remarkable achievement. And if at any time you stop and think and wonder if the 'Diary' could be genuine, the book will have succeeded.

Paul Begg
February 1997

with interest ... ... the chapters
West Germany, the ... ... Europe, ... The Hitler
Diaries had not been ... ... it, had some
... ... with the ... ...

CHAPTER

1

'WE SIMPLY CAN'T SHAKE IT'

ON 22 APRIL 1993, a story broke in the local Liverpool press that a diary had been found, purported to have been written by the infamous Jack the Ripper. The autumn of 1888, from 30 August until 9 November, had been the time when the Ripper's horrific crimes had been committed. He had never been caught.

The clues in the diary made it clear that the real name of the Whitechapel Murderer was James Maybrick, a Liverpool Cotton Merchant who died on 11 May 1889. James Maybrick was, in fact, the star of another late-Victorian scandal. His adulterous wife, Florence, American by birth, was arrested and charged with murdering him by poisoning him with arsenic. At that time, James was forty-nine years old, his beautiful young spouse was not quite twenty-six.

In September 1993, just before Smith Gryphon published *The Diary of Jack the Ripper*, the *Sunday Times* published a story claiming the diary was a hoax, relying in the main on 'expert' opinion, particularly from authors with different theories on the subject of Jack the Ripper. Most certainly, the lingering memory of the 'Hitler Diaries' had not been forgotten and, no doubt, had some influence with the thought process of many.

That was unfortunate for them because the Maybrick diary is, remarkably, genuine. This is my belief – and this book sets out to say why.

However, my belief didn't start with James Maybrick and his young wife . . .

* * *

Montague John Druitt was Jack the Ripper.

From the books that have been written and the suspects nominated, my hunch was that M.J. was our man. He was, after all, one of three suspects mentioned in memoranda from a retired assistant commissioner at Scotland Yard, Sir Melville Macnaghten.[1]

I had always felt that, whoever the Whitechapel murderer was, he was first and foremost a 'gentleman'. The last of his known victims, Mary Kelly, had been murdered on 9 November 1888, in a manner that does not bear thinking about. I believed that the man who had killed her was the man that she had entertained in her rented room, 13 Miller's Court, Dorset Street, when she was heard singing 'Only a violet I plucked from my mother's grave'. Mary Kelly was different from the other victims: she had her own room. They, on the other hand rented lodging-house beds for the night. Mary did not need fourpence for her bed. She would not have taken one of the locals back to her own place. Whoever she entertained that night would have appeared to her to have been a little different, a little bit special, a cut above the local riff-raff.

The Ripper had always been of interest to me primarily because it was an 'unsolved crime'. As I read more, I became fascinated by the connection with the royal family and Masons. I asked myself how such a rumour had unfolded. After all, the royal family had not been associated with any other serial killer – had it?

My primary concern in business at the time was to produce hour-long videos. In the late 1980s and very early 1990s I created the Pathé *Year to Remember* series. I had also created various sports videos and believe I was the prime mover in the feature film *The Krays*.

---

[1] Assistant Chief Constable, Scotland Yard CID 1890–1903; Chief Constable 1903–13; Assistant Commissioner, CID, 1908. There are two versions of the memoranda: one in Scotland Yard file and a copy shown to Daniel Farson by Macnaghten's daughter, Lady Aberconway in 1959.

I was asked at the time what my next feature film project would be. 'I don't have one,' I said, 'but Jack the Ripper appeals to me.' Little did I know.

They had been the good times, but by the summer of 1992 I had recently experienced bad times. For various reasons I found myself starting up in business all over again, and Jack the Ripper had been identified by me as a worthwhile project. My partner was not so sure. It had been done before. I argued that there were few good documentaries and no programme had ever revealed new information. We compromised, as good partners do. I promised that I would research into the subject before any decision was made to finance the new project.

With this in mind, I contacted Patsy Martin, an agent I knew, and asked her if she could get hold of Don Rumbelow, who'd written a Ripper book in the 1970s. Patsy managed to set up a meeting at my house in Hertfordshire.

I had asked for Don because his book appeared to be the most balanced of all that I had read. I do not claim that at that point I had read nearly anything like what was available. Don and I discussed the subject in great detail. I learnt a lot that day and Don and I discussed the evidence that was available. I had told him who my suspect was and he agreed that, of all known suspects, M.J. Druitt was most likely, although he reiterated the lack of evidence against him.

The Ripper Legacy by Martin Howells and Keith Skinner had been the book that had most influenced me, and I wanted Don's opinion of it. Don had told me he was bored with the subject and I really should contact the authors of *The Jack the Ripper A–Z*. 'They are the new experts,' Don told me. 'I've lost touch.'

The authors were Paul Begg, Martin Fido and Keith Skinner. As Keith was considered a co-author of *The Ripper Legacy*, I asked Don to give me his written opinion on this book.

Before he left my home, he mentioned something to me that I dealt with as flippantly as he had asked it. 'Have you heard about this diary that's been found in Liverpool?' It was supposed to have been written by Jack the Ripper, he told me. My reaction was no surprise to him: 'Oh, yeah?'

'That's exactly what I think,' he said.

Don produced his report for me on *The Ripper Legacy*. He also offered to contact Keith Skinner for me. One autumn day in late October 1992, Keith called me. A meeting was arranged instantly. I told Keith that I would be bringing Gary Wickes, a producer of considerable ability, with me. There was no objection.

We were all to meet at my office in Baker Street. Paul Begg was the first to arrive and immediately informed me that Martin Fido would not be able to make it. Keith arrived a little later, and we went to a Chinese restaurant for lunch, accompanied by my assistant, Martine. Gary was already there.

For two hours we dined and debated. I asked Keith, or maybe even told him, that he seemed to believe M.J. Druitt to be the Ripper. Keith denied this. He made it clear that he had done all the research for *The Ripper Legacy* with Martin Howells and despite the fact that he wanted the jacket credit merely to say 'With research by . . .' Martin had generously insisted otherwise.

Keith made it clear he did not favour anybody in particular as a Ripper suspect. He did, however, feel that revelations made in Martin Fido's book, *The Crimes, Detection and Death of Jack the Ripper*, concerning one Aaron Kosminski were most important. Kosminski was a Polish Jew who lived in Whitechapel, and was named in the Macnaghten memoranda. He was said to have become insane owing to his indulgence in solitary vices. He was also known to have had a great hatred of women, especially prostitutes. Kosminski was incarcerated in an asylum about March 1889. There were several circumstances connected with him that made him a strong suspect, as we'll see later.

Paul Begg also had an open mind but, as I was to learn later when I read his book, Kosminski was favoured by him, too. I pointed out why I did not believe that the

Ripper was a poor Polish Jew, the very reasons I gave at the beginning of this chapter. I felt like a star when Keith responded that my point was valid. He explained that he had always felt that if you understood the death of Mary Kelly then you would discover the truth of Jack the Ripper.

As lunch was ending I asked if they knew about the diary that Don had told me about at my home in Hertfordshire. They did, but were bound by a letter of confidentiality with Robert Smith, who was considering its publication. I hadn't heard of Robert Smith, but Gary told us he had. Robert is chairman and managing director of Smith Gryphon, the family-owned publishing house in Northdown Street, founded in 1990.

Back at the office – minus Gary – Paul Begg suggested that the project I had outlined should not be affected by the diary. One could almost see cynicism in his smile. Keith did not disagree. I wondered if the Ripper could really be found if finance was available for research, and Paul said finance had never been made available for this subject, that one author had often relied upon another.

I was in two minds: logic said don't bother with this project, but I decided I would take it one stage further. We decided that both Paul and Keith would arrange a meeting with me and Martin Fido next time Fido travelled to London from his home in Cornwall.

The meeting took place a few days later in an Italian restaurant near my office. It was not long before I worked out what had taken place since Martin's colleagues had met me. They'd told him that somebody was prepared to finance research, and that he should not lose any time. During my meeting with Paul and Keith they had clearly respected each other's views on Jack the Ripper, but Martin was different: he was on his own, and it seemed that he could not wait to put forward *his* views.

I had read Martin's book, *The Crimes, Detection and Death of Jack the Ripper*, in the few days before I met him. Martin was looking for Kosminski as the culprit but

5

concluded with David Cohen, another Polish Jew. However, I didn't think Cohen was anything more than John Doe is to Americans: just another anonymous man. My view had been that Martin had researched a specific individual, had not found what he was looking for, and had changed horses, because if he hadn't there would have been no book. But Martin did not so much debate the point with me as *tell* me. He even made me lie down on the floor to demonstrate how the Ripper murders took place. (Don Rumbelow had also reconstructed the crimes, but for him I'd had to stand up.) As my project was only beginning, I decided humouring Martin was important. It would also amuse the restaurant's clientele.

After this impromptu performance I managed to question Martin about the diary. He repeated his colleagues' confidentiality claims regarding detail, but added that it was rubbish. 'Don't waste your time with it.' At the end of our conversation, I concluded that nobody believed in the diary and, indeed, put it out of my mind. I did, however, decide to continue researching for my documentary and informed Paul and Keith accordingly.

Although my initial research was directed through Keith, I was soon deflected to Paul Begg, in Leeds. Every journey home from Baker Street to Potters Bar at the end of a day would be filled with communication by car phone on the topic of Jack the Ripper. I was hooked.

I don't know what Paul thought of our debates in these early days, but without question I was still very naive about the subject. Once or twice, however, Paul would say, 'You may have a point there. I'll pass it on to Keith.' One such observation, I recall, was about whether Walter Ernest Boultbee[1] was Sir Melville Macnaghten's 'private info'.[2]

---

[1] Private secretary to Sir Charles Warren, Chief of Police at the time of the murders. Boultbee was connected by marriage to the Druitt family.

[2] Macnaghten memoranda: 'He was sexually insane and from private info I have little doubt that his own family believed him to have been the murderer.'

Six weeks into my research, and after several marathon conversations with Paul, he rang me one day at the office. I was intrigued because our conversations had previously been confined to the evenings. Had Keith found something?

He'd been talking to Keith and Martin and they'd concluded that it was only fair to tell me that they didn't believe I could continue to finance research into Jack the Ripper or make a documentary without taking into account the diary found in Liverpool.

'We simply can't shake it,' he said.

Couldn't shake it? Did they believe it? Well, yes and no. One thing was for certain: they couldn't find anything historically that would prove that the diary could *not* have been written by Jack the Ripper – 'and to the best of our knowledge no scientific test has either.' Paul said it would be irresponsible of them to let me continue my project without knowing this.

I was astounded. I had not given the diary a thought since the meeting with Martin Fido. But now the experts were telling me they were confused. I could not ignore this any longer. If there was to be a project, then I had to know more.

I phoned my producer friend, Gary Wickes. At our meeting in the Chinese restaurant he had chipped in that he knew the Robert Smith who was planning to publish the diary. I quickly filled him in on the events of the past few weeks, and asked him if he could set up a meeting between me and Smith.

Gary duly obliged and even accompanied me to my first meeting. The offices of Smith Gryphon were in a side street just north of King's Cross Station.

Robert had agreed to see me as I had expressed an interest in making a film around the diary. As the conversation continued, Robert learnt that there was no significant money available at this stage of the game. He soon made it very clear that he would not part with any rights until after the book was published. He was clearly excited about this project – and his enthusiasm would result in my obtaining precisely what I wanted.

Robert spoke of the diary without revealing, of course, the identity of the author. He did reveal that it was a 'love story'. He also spoke of a connection with another case after the last Ripper victim was killed. Many crime historians would probably have guessed who the author was from this information alone, but I was not a historian and neither was Gary Wickes. I returned home, later that evening, empty-handed and frustrated. I telephoned Paul Begg and told him just that. I said that I believed the only way I could acquire the film rights would be to work out who must have written the diary. I think Paul thought I was asking him, because he was apologetic when he repeated to me that he was tied to a letter of confidentiality. The conversation over, I sat in silence in my study. The grey matter got to work.

Could the Ripper have been involved in a different murder case that had nothing to do with the Whitechapel murders? Robert Smith's words kept coming back: 'love story . . . another case'.

In a bookcase opposite my desk was a complete set of the Marshall Cavendish part work, *Murder Casebook*, all filed neatly in its black binders. I took them all out and slammed them on my desk. I started with volume one and turned the pages vigorously. I could ignore most of it: I was, after all, looking for a murder that had happened after 1888.

I went through every volume but found nothing. Had I missed something? I started again. I began to think that I was wasting my time when I saw a picture of a man with a top hat and moustache. At the bottom of the picture were the words 'arsenic eater' in bold red. A shiver went up my spine but I did not know why. I turned the page slowly: there was a picture of a house and a woman. I had missed this the first time, because the victim of this particular murder had been a man. The perpetrator of the crime was a woman.

Then I focused on the words.

'Liverpool' (I remembered Don Rumbelow and his revelation about the diary); 'murdered in May 1889' (just a few months after Mary Kelly's death the previous November); 'famous trial' (Robert Smith's words echoed in my head: 'another case').

Then the clincher! This mustachioed gentleman, James Maybrick, had met one Florence Chandler on a boat travelling from New York to Liverpool in 1880. I had the love story that Robert had referred to.

I had never even heard of the Maybrick case. But, whoever James Maybrick was, I felt this was the purported author of the diary. I felt chuffed with myself. I was sure I had found the key to help me obtain the rights I wanted.

I phoned Paul Begg. I knew he could not confirm or deny what I had just found and I had, therefore, spent the previous half-hour trying to find a way not to embarrass him. 'Paul, would "Springtime for building houses" be a good cryptic clue?' Paul hesitated and then burst into laughter. I almost sang and put down the phone without his saying a word. I had the confirmation I needed.

I read the Marshall Cavendish article over and over again. When I looked at my watch, it was 2 a.m. I was wide awake. I couldn't sleep now. I went through to my library and started digging out any information I could find on this James Maybrick, but had very little. I kept looking at his picture. His eyes were haunting and it disturbed me. Martin had said it was rubbish, but Paul Begg's words kept lifting my spirits: 'We simply can't shake it.'

I did finally fall asleep. I was woken up by my eight-year-old daughter. My head was resting on my hands. I was still in the study. James Maybrick stared back at me.

As soon as I arrived at the office I telephoned Robert and told him that I knew who had written the diary, without mentioning Maybrick's name. His immediate suspicion was that someone must have told me. No, I said: the clues had come from him.

Robert was curious and agreed to meet me at my office

later that day. He was taken into the boardroom and I joined him clutching my copy of the *Murder Casebook*, which I had hidden behind an A4 notepad.

'Robert,' I said, 'I'm in the middle of making a documentary and want to include the diary.' I wanted to change the focus of the documentary, to put the diary centre stage. I wanted the documentary to be released at the same time as the book for maximum impact, and I wanted the chance to make a film.

I patted my notepad and looked Robert in the eye. I told him that under my pad was a picture of the man I believed wrote the diary. If I was wrong I would bother him no further. But if I was right, could we negotiate a deal?

Meaningfully, I added, 'I have to make a telephone call from my office, and when I get back, if you're not here, I'll know I've made a mistake.'

I'd decided earlier that Robert would give me an honest response if I allowed him time to reflect on the situation. So I had invented the need for a phone call. A white lie, nothing more.

When I returned to the boardroom, Robert's face was scarlet. I felt a big grin cross my face. He put out his hand to shake mine. 'OK,' he said, 'what's the deal?'

We agreed terms, subject to my bringing in an expert to validate the document.

I confess that, without knowing the scientific or historical arguments that might – or might not – support this diary, I had to consider the probability that it was a hoax. If I could prove it was by bringing in my expert, then I could continue with my original project and knock the diary on its head. If, however, my expert considered it genuine, then I would own the very lucrative visual rights.

In the meantime, Robert arranged for me to read the diary on condition I signed a letter of confidentiality.

The very next day I returned to his offices. Robert filled me in on the little he knew about the diary's background. He told me it had been taken to a literary agent in London by a man who lived around the corner from Liverpool

Football Club. That man had claimed he received it from a friend who had recently died. Robert conceded that the origins of the diary were unclear and unsatisfactory.

He then showed me a report on the diary that had been prepared by Dr Nicholas Eastaugh, a scientist who had examined the constituent parts of the ink. The charts and explanations he produced were difficult to take in at a glance, but one of the conclusions made exciting reading: 'There is nothing in the ink that is inconsistent with the Victorian date.'

The diary was then produced for me to read.

I was immediately struck by the fact that it was not a diary at all. It was a leather-bound book, eight by ten inches or thereabouts, with no dates or printed material inside. It was clear that some pages had been cut out at the beginning and there was a black substance resembling soot caught up in the spine. The diary appeared to start mid-sentence. The writing was difficult to read but I persevered. And as I did so my emotions were very mixed.

I could not yet quite believe that this really was Jack the Ripper's diary, and yet there was something about it that was frighteningly honest. What struck me was that the document was sixty-three pages long and contained a lot of information – and yet the three authors of *The Jack the Ripper A–Z* could not fault it.

At this point I was still relatively uneducated in the world of Ripperology and had been impressed by recent arguments that Elizabeth Stride – said to have been the Ripper's third victim – was not a Ripper victim after all. I had also believed the authors who suggested that the letter dated 25 September 1888, signed 'Jack the Ripper' and sent to the Central News Agency, was a hoax. Yet the author of the diary clearly claimed ownership of both. These entries bothered me most.

I went on to read about the author's emotions. How he wanted to kill himself but was too much of a coward, about his feelings for his children, his anger at his wife's infidelity. There was something very personal and very real about this. I was confused.

Now I had signed the letter of confidentiality, I could,

for the first time, discuss the diary with Paul Begg. I told him of the points I felt uncomfortable with and much to my surprise he said he felt the same – about the same points. But he also felt that there were personal observations that appeared to be beyond the scope of a hoaxer. I told him I wanted to bring in an expert to look at the diary. Could he suggest anyone?

'What do you want to test?' I was stumped. What *did* I want to test. I assumed that Paul, having more experience in these matters, would have some ideas. But he just said he would think about it.

One of my closest friends is a man by the name of Michael Marx. Our friendship developed in the late 1980s and grew stronger as we visited Arsenal each fortnight together to watch football matches.

At the time, Michael was finance director of a large international corporation. Michael is one of the most intelligent men I have met, and also one of the most cautious. He has an extremely good instinct but will still test it by using experts who specialise in fields where he has a limited knowledge.

Without discussing specific details or breaching my confidentiality agreement, I told Michael about the events that had occurred over the previous few weeks and he was immediately impressed. He would later explain to me the reasons why:

- the historians had not been able to prove the diary inaccurate;
- its origins would appear to be from very ordinary people;
- the few scientific tests that had been done could not disprove it;
- there did not appear to be serious money involved (Michael concluded this from the modest sum Robert requested for the video rights).

I wanted to know who would be able to give a professional opinion, knowing that Michael's organisation often used experts in many fields. He asked if I knew of Hannah Koren, a graphologist who worked for the Israeli Defence Ministry from time to time. She had given evidence in many fraud trials in Europe. She had never been proved wrong. If this was a hoax, Michael assured me, it wouldn't take Hannah long to confirm it. Michael had used her services and had been astounded at the problems she had solved for his employers.

Michael gave me her telephone number in Israel and said I could mention his name as an introduction, adding that under no circumstances should I tell Hannah anything about the document, what was in the document, or who was supposed to have written it. Hannah's reason for examining it should be purely to validate the authenticity of 'some papers'.

So I contacted Hannah Koren. By now it was December 1992 and I had only until the end of the year to conclude the transaction with Robert Smith. That was the timetable Robert had stipulated when we had originally negotiated terms.

When I mentioned Michael Marx to Hannah it was very clear there was tremendous mutual respect. I asked her when she was next in London and my heart sank when she said it would not be until March. What if we picked up the expenses of an unscheduled trip?

She said she could come on 23 December, but would have to return that evening. But what was the urgency? I told her Michael had suggested I tell her nothing.

'Then don't,' she said. 'I'll see you on the twenty-third.'

During the couple of weeks while I was awaiting Hannah's arrival I discussed the subject of handwriting analysis with Michael Marx. I wanted Hannah to know that she had to be absolutely sure with her conclusions. I knew that if I got involved in the project it would only be because it was real and would need a great deal of financial investment. I did not want to make that investment unless I was certain there was something very special about the diary. I was beginning to hope that Hannah would knock this on the head. If she even suggested that the writing was not authentic, I could then get on with the documentary I wanted to make. Hannah's fee would be much smaller than the cost of any further involvement.

Michael continued to fill me in on his experiences of Hannah's work. Eventually I was convinced that, if anyone could prove the diary to be a fake, she could – and would.

Robert Smith brought the diary to my office on 23 December. His author, Shirley Harrison, researcher, Sally Evemy, and Doreen Montgomery, their literary agent, were there also. Michael Marx could not resist coming along too. Keith Skinner arrived towards the end of the meeting.

Hannah was late. The hour's delay seemed like three.

Eventually Hannah arrived – a small, round woman with an endearing smile. Hannah was led to the boardroom where the top of the table was reserved for her use. She was given the diary and asked if she could give us her initial reactions. She asked us to talk among ourselves. We tried to.

Everyone was on edge. Apart from Michael, nobody in the room, to the best of my knowledge, had any experience of graphology. Hannah seemed to flick through the diary quickly and casually. It was clear she was not reading. Occasionally she would stroke the surface of the page with her hand. It was only fifteen minutes or so before Hannah closed the diary. I knew she had not seen the signature on the last page. Surely now this document would be crucified once and for all. Sally Evemy was poised with her pen. Hannah spoke in broken English, with her attractive Israeli accent. The following is precisely what Hannah said, in the sequence that she said it, as taken down by Sally:

- Disturbed, possibly mentally
- Very strong imagination
- Fluctuating self-esteem. Varying from domineering to deprived

- Sexual problems – lack of satisfaction
- Problems with mother image
- Ambivalent feeling about father
- Much aggression – also towards self
- Multiple personality
- Lack of stability
- Changes his mind
- Dramatic sense – me as 'victim'
- Has ideas, is imaginative – but can't always execute
- Likes games – sees people as pawns
- On the outside he can control himself – inside is like a volcano which sometime will burst out
- The crosses – possibly there's a religious link
- No trust for others
- Hypochondria
- Stubborn
- Has had disappointments in the emotional area
- Very strong guilt feelings
- Compulsive thoughts – neuroses – repetitive
- Drugs or alcohol? Something physiological

There was a stunned, almost deathly silence around the room. We had already learnt in the embryonic stages of research that James Maybrick was a hypochondriac. He was a drug addict. Whoever Jack the Ripper was, he was clearly mentally disturbed but would have been able to appear to the outside world as perfectly normal.

As our research continued we would find out just how accurate Hannah's analysis had been.

The silence in the room continued. Indeed it was Hannah who broke the tension. 'What *is* this?' she asked.

Before I told her, I wanted to know the answer everyone was waiting to hear. 'Could this be forged?' I asked. Her response was immediate: '*Impossible!*'

'How do you know?' I think I was shaking at this point. I was certainly in a state of shock.

'Firstly, the handwriting is fluent; it has not been copied. It was written as it was thought. Secondly, it is not a disguised hand. It is completely natural. And finally, the handwriting has so many complications and disturbances that it could only have been written by the individual who felt these emotions. I have studied graphology for twenty years and know what I am looking for. I could not re-create one sentence, let alone all these pages. Whoever wrote this, *felt* what he was writing.'

Michael immediately asked a further question. From the tone of his voice, I think he was expecting a positive response. 'Has the book been written with a lot of energy?'

'Michael, I don't know. This is a very old document and the pressure marks left by a pen are no longer there.'

Was that why she was stroking the pages earlier? I asked.

'Yes.'

To this day, I believe that Shirley, Sally, Doreen and Robert are not convinced that I had not briefed Hannah before she arrived, but probably they have never thought deeply enough about the circumstances surrounding the meeting. I had, after all, wanted the damn thing to go away. Now I knew it would not.

'Hannah,' I said at last, 'I will now tell you what you've been reading. It's supposed to be the diary of Jack the Ripper.' There was obvious excitement in the tone of my voice.

'Who?' Hannah asked. It was clear that she could not instantly recall the Ripper stories until somebody reminded her of the monstrous crimes that took place in Whitechapel just over a century ago. Even then, Hannah would only confirm that she remembered 'something'.

After some refreshments, Hannah left us. The diary now sat in front of Robert. I opened it, more reverently this time. Were these really the murderer's personal thoughts? Or could this document be a forgery after all?

But I couldn't get out of my mind the vehemence with which Hannah had uttered her verdict:

'*Impossible!*'

CHAPTER

2

'DO SOMETHING WITH IT . . .'

I WAS NOW WELL and truly involved with this project. I had to know the background to the diary. With the help of Robert Smith and his author Shirley Harrison, I became familiar with the extraordinary story behind it.

Born and bred a Liverpudlian, Michael Barrett is now unemployed owing to illness. He has been since around 1976. Before he became ill he'd been a merchant seaman, an oil-rig chef and, latterly, a scrap-metal dealer. It's August 1975, and he meets Anne Graham in the Irish Centre, a city club mainly frequented by Catholics. Although they marry within four months, it is six years before their only child, Caroline, is born.

It's Mike Barrett's habit to drink every afternoon in the Saddle, a Victorian pub in Anfield standing halfway between the Everton and Liverpool football grounds. The Saddle is close to Caroline's school, from where he collects her on his way home. It was in the Saddle that he'd first met Tony Devereux, a retired printer. They have since become friends.

It's Christmas 1990, and Tony fractures his hip, so Mike runs small errands for him and does some of his chores. In May 1991 Tony gives him a parcel wrapped in brown paper, tied with string and says, 'That's for you.'

Rather surprised by this, Mike asks, 'What the hell is it?'

'Take it home and do something with it.'

When he arrives home with Caroline, Mike opens the parcel to find an old, good-quality, black and gilt, leather-bound book. The first forty-eight pages have been cut out with a knife and are missing. Knife marks can be seen at the bottom of the first few remaining pages and on the inside bottom edge of the back cover. The remaining pages, sixty-three in all, are covered in untidy hand-writing, chronicling events of the most sensational and lurid nature. Astonishingly, the last entry reads:

I give my name that all know of me, so history do tell, what love can do to a gentle man born.

Yours truly,
Jack the Ripper

Dated this third day of May 1889.

Mike told his story in the pages of Shirley Harrison's *The Diary of Jack the Ripper*. 'It was like a knife going into me,' he said, adding, 'but I didn't believe it. Who's going to believe that in a million years.' He decides to telephone Tony. 'Who are you kidding?' he asks. Then he pesters him, hoping to find out where it has *really* come from.

'I pressurised that man, and I asked him question after question after question, and Tony would never, ever give me an answer,' Mike said eventually.

Mike did what he could to discover who had written the diary. There are no dates in the document except the one at the end where the author signed and dated it. The author's real name is never mentioned. It is a diary in the sense of its being a journal. The two words tend to be interchangeable these days, but 'diary' is what it was dubbed, and that word has stuck. Within its pages were certain clues of a personal nature, including the pet name of the purported author's wife, 'Bunny', and those of his children, 'Gladys' and 'Bobo'. On the second page it said, 'I may return to Battlecrease . . .'

Mike told Shirley Harrison, 'I read a book by Richard Whittington Egan called *Murder, Mayhem and Mystery*. It was about crime in Liverpool, and there was the name Battlecrease House in an account of the Maybrick affair.'

This statement by Mike was crucial. It would later allow us to validate his story.

Unfortunately, Tony Devereux died in August 1991 so Shirley Harrison was unable to obtain confirmation of Mike's account of how he got possession of the diary. The cynics even callously implied that Devereux's death was 'convenient' for Mike Barrett. Martin Fido dismissed the diary instantly. Mike Barrett's story of how he obtained it was, according to him, 'just not good enough'.

Fido was entitled to be sceptical, of course, but he had never even met Mike Barrett. Paul Begg had, and when interviewed in July 1993 for my video, also called *The Diary of Jack the Ripper*, Paul said, 'Those of us who have been a little less critical of Mike Barrett are those who've met him.'

I was astounded, even at this early stage of my involvement, at Martin Fido's totally negative reaction to this document. Mike Barrett's story may well have been a lie, but it could also well have been true. Paul Begg pushed Martin Fido on this point.

'Martin, are you saying that because you think the provenance of the diary is "not good enough", it should be left on the shelf to gather dust? That we should not investigate it?'

Martin surprised Paul. 'Yes, that's what I'm saying.' This was probably the first time I realised how difficult this job was going to be. How were my team going to get answers from experts who just didn't want to know?

Once Mike Barrett had ascertained that James Maybrick was the apparent author of the diary, he took it to Doreen Montgomery, a London literary agent. He had been given her name over the telephone by Pan Books when he had tried to sell them the publishing rights.

This little bit of information just *felt* genuine. It was a naive action on Mike Barrett's part. Anyone wanting to launch a fraud or forgery on to the market would surely have had agents and publishers lined up, and be ready to make a killing from the highest bidder.

Mike told Doreen Montgomery that, since he'd had possession of this document, it had changed his life.

'I haven't had a proper night's sleep from that day to this. I've eaten and drunk the diary. It's virtually destroyed my life and my marriage.'

Indeed, just under two years later, Anne and he would separate.

Shirley Harrison was commissioned to write a book and in June 1992 Robert Smith, of Smith Gryphon, secured the world publication rights.

It would be fair to say that Shirley Harrison was, at this stage, still doubtful about the authenticity of the document. Who wouldn't be?

Shirley went to work quickly. She took the diary to the British Library on 5 June 1992. Robert A.H. Smith (no relation to the publisher), curator of the Department of Manuscripts, said that he 'saw nothing in the diary inconsistent with it being of a late-nineteenth-century date'.

Shirley Harrison and Smith Gryphon set out to establish the age and authenticity of the diary. Shirley Harrison was now ready to undertake, and pay for, scientific tests.

Dr David Baxendale, a former Home Office forensic scientist, who runs Document Evidence Ltd in Birmingham, was the first scientist to get involved with the project. The publishers requested tests on the ink and paper. They wanted to know the age of the ink and, if possible, when the ink was put to paper.

Baxendale's report was disappointing to Robert Smith. He appeared to deal three body blows. First, he said that the ink dissolved quickly, whereas old ink should take several hours. Secondly, he stated that his chromatogram showed patterns characteristic of inks containing a synthetic dye called Nigrosine, which he claimed had only been used in inks after World War I. Thirdly, there was nothing to suggest that the ink contained iron, an ingredient of most Victorian inks.

Robert Smith could well have shelved the project. Instinctively, he felt another opinion was crucial.

Dr Nicholas Eastaugh was contacted. He is a specialist in identifying and dating materials used in manuscripts and old masters. His methods to test the diary were the same as those used to prove the Vinland Map a modern forgery.

He conducted a more exhaustive set of tests at Oxford University, using a nuclear microscope. These included making comparisons with other ink samples taken from a scrapbook. The writing in it dated from 1871 to 1915. Comparisons were also made with the ink on various postcards dated 1907, 1910, 1922, 1937 and 1950. In his report, dated 2 October 1992, he stated:

> The ink analysed does not appear to be substantially synthetic as previously suggested for other samples. Iron is apparent in the ink.
> We may also comment that there is clear evidence that synthetic dyestuffs were being used in ink formation at an early date: the identification of such a compound in a postcard of 1907 demonstrates this. Moreover, the dye Nigrosine mentioned as being present in the ink of the diary was first synthesised prior to the supposed date of the diary.

Shirley Harrison then obtained confirmation from the Patent Office that Nigrosine was patented in 1867 and in general use in ordinary writing inks by the 1870s, eighteen years before the Ripper murders.

Dr Eastaugh also confirmed that the paper in the diary contained no 'nylon fibres or the fluorescent brightening agents that the Hitler Diaries were so quickly faulted on'.[1] Baxendale's conclusions were suspect at the very least.

Dr Eastaugh tested some black powder found between the leaves of the diary and concluded that it was 'possibly bone black', a pigment used in ivory black paint. Bone black was also used as an antidote to strychnine poisoning.

James Maybrick was an arsenic and strychnine addict.

---

[1] Letter to author dated 19 April 1993.

The author of the diary had claimed he had given up 'the dreadful stuff'. If this diary was a fake, the fraudster had certainly demonstrated attention to detail.

Dr Baxendale was made aware of Dr Eastaugh's findings. A written agreement between Smith Gryphon and Dr Baxendale should have resulted in the permanent confidentiality of the report prepared by Dr Baxendale but the following events superceded their agreement.

In April 1993, Robert Smith was hoping to sell serial rights for Shirley Harrison's forthcoming book to the *Sunday Times*. This newspaper had made an embarrassing mistake with buying rights to the infamous 'Hitler Diaries'. I suppose it was not unreasonable for them to think: once bitten, twice shy. After all, it had taken just six weeks to prove that the notorious Hitler Diaries were fakes. In contrast, no one has been able to prove that the diary of Jack the Ripper is a fake, though many have tried during the last four and a half years of intensive study and research.

The *Sunday Times* paid Smith Gryphon a non-returnable advance of £5,000 for serialisation rights, against a final purchase price of £75,000. It may be argued that the advance was all that the *Sunday Times* ever intended to pay. One can imagine that this might have been a low-cost, low-risk way to exposing a 'Ripper diary hoax'.

I invited Maurice Chittenden, the journalist in charge of the project, to view my research material. I was confident that a responsible journalist would see that the evidence we were uncovering merited further serious research. I hoped that the newspaper would recognise that *this* diary was different. During Maurice's visit, however, I began to suspect that the newspaper had already concluded that this remarkable document was a fake. Although I explained to Maurice the four different possibilities that I saw as being relevant to the authenticity of the diary (which he ultimately used in his article), it was clear that, despite his assertion that he still had an open mind, he did not – and the *Sunday Times* did not. Their minds were well and truly shut. As Maurice was about to leave my offices in Baker Street, I encouraged him to contact the 'pro-diarist' camp of experts. Maurice already had the views of Melvin Harris, an author of two books on Jack the Ripper. He said it was a hoax. Why complicate matters?

On 19 September 1993 the *Sunday Times* published the double-page report on the diary. It was written by Maurice Chittenden, the associate news editor, and Christopher Lloyd. Their conclusions were based on the opinions given by the 'experts' they hired to inspect the diary. They made reference to the logical assessment that the diary could be one of four things:

1. A genuine document
2. A modern hoax
3. A fantasy written by James Maybrick
4. A Victorian forgery (perhaps invented in an attempt to secure the release of Florence Maybrick, but never used)

These four possibilities amounted to the only information that I gave Maurice Chittenden that was reproduced.

The newspaper repeated the Baxendale claim that what appeared to be glue on the inside cover of the diary suggested that it had been used to hold a photograph. There was an indentation, which had possibly been caused by one such photograph. A torn corner of a photograph was found lodged in the binding, which seemed to confirm Baxendale's view. The size of the impression, 3½ by 2½ inches was, they claimed, a popular size of photograph used between the two world wars. Therefore, the diary was forged.

Before we obtained further advice, I wondered how these experts could justify using this evidence to dismiss the document's authenticity. After all, any of the diary's owners over the last 103 years (assuming it to be genuine) could have stuck a photograph in it, only to remove it later. Would it not also be possible for the impression only to be of the area that was stuck to the book and not necessarily of the entire photograph? I felt at the time that the failure to identify even these possibilities showed the lack of balance within the article. It was becoming clear that some people were prepared to use any means to prove the diary a fake, without properly verifying their theories or even checking their so-called facts.

A forensic document examiner, Dr Audrey Giles, concluded that ink blots and smudges in the diary were put there to make it look soiled, and therefore older than it actually was. Dr Giles stated, 'I found no evidence that the diary was written by Jack the Ripper.'

I found that last remark astonishing. So much so that I wondered if it was a misquote or had been taken out of context. What evidence had the doctor expected to find? Dr Giles had spent no more than a few minutes examining the document in Robert Smith's offices on 22 June 1993. No support or explanation was given to substantiate the doctor's conclusions. The team of detractors were not prepared to accept the positive reactions of the British Library, Hannah Koren and others, and the *Sunday Times* was not even prepared to print them. Nobody seemed remotely concerned with the truth. This surprised me and bothered me. I was beginning to feel extremely isolated. My resolve to find the truth strengthened.

In that same article, Dr Kate Flint, a lecturer in Victorian and modern literature, picked up on the diarist's use of the term 'one-off'. As Shirley Harrison wrote, 'The earliest date for the expression given in any British dictionary was 1934, in the *Oxford English Dictionary*. In America, *Webster's Dictionary* dates its first written occurrence as 1925.'

I was always prepared to accept that any linguistic anomalies would prove this diary a fake. If a doodle in the same hand as the diarist's were found within its pages saying 'I Love *Coronation Street*', I could hardly argue that it was written in 1888–9. While that, of course, is taking the argument to the extreme, I am simply trying to demonstrate that *if* it could be proved that certain catchphrases or words were not known or in common usage at the time, I would accept the inevitable and go after exposing the forger. But only three phrases from sixty-three pages had been picked up, the other two being 'gathering momentum' and 'top myself'. When I learnt that Dr Kate Flint was not a lecturer in English *language* or linguistics, I suspected an error, again, had been made. I reasoned that, if somebody had taken the trouble to forge sixty-three pages of Victorian language, something as glaring as the term 'one-off' would not have been overlooked.

Shirley Harrison, however, discovered the term in engineers' records belonging to Trayners of Kent and dated 1860 – twenty-four years before the Ripper murders and seventy-four years before it found its way into the *Oxford Dictionary*. Harrison also discovered that 'dictionary research revealed that the expressions "topped" (meaning hanged) and "gathering momentum" were in use before late Victorian times'.

This diary had already proved several experts wrong. The discovery by Shirley of the use of the phrase 'one-off' proved the *Oxford English Dictionary* wrong. Yet still, people did not want to take it seriously. The truth was, as I was beginning to realise, that people were frightened of it. If they supported it, could they be made to look foolish, as had been the case with the Hitler Diaries?

By July 1993 Robert Smith had sold the American publishing rights to Time-Warner Books, but at the end of the month the *Washington Post* ran a story about the diary expressing the writer's doubts about its authenticity. They put pressure on Warner to do their own tests and Warner commissioned an investigation, which Kenneth Rendell, an American antiquarian bookseller, was asked to coordinate. Kenneth Rendell had been involved with the Hitler Diaries exposure. His team of experts on the Ripper investigation included Robert L. Kuranz, a research ink chemist, and Rod McNeil, who apparently had worked for the FBI and the American secret service. Rod McNeil had devised an ion migration test, which he claimed could date when ink was put on paper. On 20 August 1993 Robert

Smith flew to America with the diary and met Rendell's team in Chicago – and we'll be returning to this part of the story later.

If this was a modern forgery as the detractors were shouting from the rooftops, this was the team which would prove it for them. But did they?

3

'I AM JACK'

SHORTLY AFTER THE STORY had broken in the Liverpool *Daily Post* in April 1993 that the diary in the possession of Shirley Harrison was that of James Maybrick, purporting to be Jack the Ripper, Albert Johnson, a man in his late fifties, contacted the *Post*'s Harold Brough. He explained that he believed he owned the watch that once belonged to the Ripper.

On the face of it, a most remarkable coincidence. Or was it?

Harold Brough's colleague, Steve Brauner, was soon to dismiss the watch as a fake, comparing the whole episode to the Shergar scandal.[1] It would be easy to criticise Mr Brauner, but Shirley Harrison, Robert Smith and I were also concerned at the timing of this discovery. None of us, however, had yet seen the watch, nor had we met Albert Johnson.

Our information at that time was that a gentleman owned a watch with the initials of the Whitechapel victims scratched in the back, with the words 'I am Jack' and the name 'J. Maybrick'. The concern was simple: had an old watch been purchased and someone scratched the initials of the Ripper's victims in the back of it? If so, it could possibly undermine the progress of the investigation so far. The cynics jumped the gun once more. Before any evidence

---

[1] Steve Brauner could not recall why he used the comparison. Shergar was a champion racehorse which mysteriously disappeared. There seems to be no logical reason for comparing the two cases.

had been produced they dismissed it as an opportunist cashing in on the publicity surrounding the diary. How could these people consider themselves to be serious historians? Is it not the responsibility of historians to examine *all* the evidence before commenting?

I had many conversations with Harold Brough, and in one of them I learnt about the watch. I immediately phoned Robert Smith to ask what he knew of it. He said he had been contacted by Albert Johnson after the *Daily Post* had run their story but that he did not want to bother me with every 'crank call or letter' that came across his desk. I reminded Robert that our contract stipulated that he had to. He duly gave me Albert's telephone number.

I phoned Albert immediately. He was cold and distant, telling me his brother Robert was handling the matter. If I left my number, he would get his brother to phone me. I was not optimistic, but within twenty-four hours I had my first contact with Robert Johnson. It was the beginning of the strangest relationship of my life.

Robbie (as I later came to call him) phoned and asked if I'd like to see the watch. I don't need to tell you my response. 'We'll come to you,' he said. He did, along with brother Albert and their solicitor, Richard Nicholas. They came to my house in Hertfordshire on 5 July 1993. Albert was in his late fifties, tall with grey, balding hair. His brother was forty-three, only about five foot six with fair hair. They were like chalk and cheese. Richard Nicholas looked his part. Although casual, he had the air of a young successful lawyer.

Keith Skinner and Martin Howells (Martin had recently arrived from New Zealand specifically to write the script for the documentary I proposed to make about the Ripper) were also present. In addition, I asked my mother's second husband, Gerald Freed, to come along, as he was a jeweller of some fifty years' experience.

Before we asked questions we each, one by one, looked at the watch. It was gold, back and front, and 'Verity' was engraved on the movement, together with its unique number. The back of the watch had an ornate design around its perimeter, leaving a circle in the middle, where one would have initials engraved. I was startled: initials had been engraved – 'J.O.' Why 'O'? Was this not the watch of James Maybrick? Albert Johnson shrugged his shoulders. He didn't try to explain. He couldn't. But if this was a forgery would it not have at least carried the initials of the man it was supposed to have belonged to? Try as I might, I could not make out the scratches that were on the inside back of the watch, other than the letter H in the middle and what appeared to be a date of '9/3'.

That impressed me a great deal. My research had already gone far enough to convince me of the strong possibility that the diary was genuine. If it was, then Maybrick had claimed his first victim when he had gone to Manchester when it was 'cold and damp'. The next paragraph in the diary said, 'Summer is near the warm weather will do me good.' The ninth of March was consistent with both statements. But that inscription told us even more.

While the Liverpool *Daily Post* had revealed the identity of the author of the diary, it had not revealed the contents. It couldn't. Harold Brough had never seen it. If this had been an attempt to cash in on the diary, Albert Johnson would not have scratched the letter H. Or '9/3'.

The conclusion was indisputable – the watch and the diary were linked. There could be no doubt. Either they were both genuine or both forged by the same person. As Maybrick's family crest said, *Tempus Omnia Revelat* – Time Reveals All.

Only Time would tell whether it would.

We had dinner at a local pub where Albert told us his story.

He explained that in July 1992 he had purchased a gold Verity watch at Stewart's, a jeweller's shop in Wallasey. He said he had bought it as an investment for his granddaughter, who was two years old at the time. He had put the watch in a drawer and thought no more of it until a few months ago when the subject of watches came up with his workmates. Albert told his colleagues that he owned a Victorian gold watch and shortly afterwards took it into work to show to them.

While they were examining the watch the light from the window seemed to show markings on the inside back. Albert and his colleagues decided to examine the watch further by placing it under a microscope. At this moment in our conversation Albert produced a drawing made by a colleague at the time that detailed what he believed he saw. The drawing is reproduced on page 36 in this chapter.

The examination of the watch had taken place shortly after the revelation in the *Daily Post* about the diary purported to have been written by James Maybrick, identifying him as Jack the Ripper. On seeing the name J. Maybrick in the back of the watch, one of Albert's workmates recalled the article and informed him that he probably had Jack the Ripper's watch.

Albert claimed his knowledge of Jack the Ripper was negligible and that he had always believed that the Ripper was (interestingly) a Liverpudlian who emigrated to Australia and buried his victims under the floorboards. (This, I think, must be Frederick Deeming, one of the many Ripper suspects.) He told us about his approach to Harold Brough and the quick dismissal of the watch's authenticity by the reporter. Brough had, however, given him the name of the publishers of the book, and Albert subsequently wrote to Robert Smith. In that correspondence Albert claimed that the watch contained 'seven sets of initials' and explained its background.

Robert Smith had clearly been impressed. He went up to Liverpool and fully examined the watch under the scrutiny of Albert Johnson. He asked Albert to produce the receipt, which he duly did. The wording was simple: 'One Verity Pocket Watch £225'. It was dated 2 July 1992. Ronald Murphy, the owner of the shop where Albert bought the watch, gave a statement in October 1993 in which he says he sold the watch to Albert Johnson on or about the 14 July 1992 for about £250. He had owned it for a couple of years before selling it. ('It had been given to me by my father-in-law, who had a Jewellers Shop himself in Lancaster.')

He said in his statement that there was nothing unusual about it, other than its hallmark of 1846. At first it didn't work, so he had it repaired.

'Having now seen the watch for the first time since selling it, I am almost certain that the markings were present when the watch was sold but they were not markings that I would have taken notice of,' his statement to us says. 'I have been given the impression by certain people in the press that there were engravings in it, which I had not noticed – but this is not the case.'

He states that the watch was bought around 14 July 1992. I was later satisfied by the explanation given to me by Mr Murphy that he was able to identify the period because of the way he catalogued his receipt books. He did not, at the time, look up the actual copy receipt in order to prepare his statement, hence the discrepancy in dates. (I have reproduced his statement as Appendix 1.)

Robert Smith followed up that trip by making Albert an offer to finance the research that would be required to authenticate the watch in exchange for part ownership of it. Robert also advised Albert to go back to the shop to have the date of the hallmark and the number of the watch added to the receipt. (Each Verity Pocket Watch has a unique number, which is engraved on the movement.[1])

Robert doesn't take time out of the office lightly. Indeed, he is one of the hardest-working men I know. He is also thrifty, and his offer to Albert Johnson had been made with the sort of calculation you would expect of any good businessman. I was beginning to think that Robert's reluctance to tell me about the watch had not been

---

[1] My research team have tried, unsuccessfully, to locate the original books of Verity, Lancaster. A watch with a unique number should be traceable back to its original owner if records still exist. Should any reader have any information about Verity of Lancaster, I would be very grateful if they could contact me.

because he believed Albert to be a crank. Indeed, Robert had excitedly contacted Keith Skinner on 4 June 1993, requesting details of any victims murdered in or around March 1889. Robert was clearly referring to the 'H 9/3' inscription scratched in the centre of the inside back. Unlike all the other markings, it was neat.

After Albert had concluded his story and dinner was finished we returned to my house to wrap up over a brief nightcap. I asked if I could contact them again and was told I would be welcome to do so any time. Albert did confirm, at this time, that he had no intention of accepting Robert's offer. He himself would organise whatever examinations needed to be carried out in order to authenticate the watch.

Albert, Robbie and their solicitor left late that evening. It remained for Keith, Martin and me to reflect on what we had seen and what we had been told.

Gerald Freed, the jeweller, had examined the watch for some time before we'd gone to the pub to eat. He had used his eyeglass in good light by the dining-room patio doors. As he left, he would only say, 'Those markings are very, very old. I'll be astounded if anyone could say different.'

Keith, Martin and I spoke for some time. We were confused. Keith was bothered by Robbie's energetic display of enthusiasm. He also noted that Albert had said that, if it was genuine, he would 'prefer to give it to charity'. I felt that this was nothing more than trying to say, 'Aren't we good?'

I was bothered by why Albert had told Robert Smith there were seven sets of initials when his drawing had only six. Martin Howells was the most perceptive. 'How did Albert know that those scratches were sets of initials? He said he knew nothing about Jack the Ripper.'

Whether Jack the Ripper was a subject you knew well or not, the scratches were difficult to make out. Why assume these wild markings were those of the Ripper's victims and not just letters?

My main concern remained the timing of it all. Could

both artefacts be fakes? I turned over in my mind what my research had already shown. I was convinced that the diary was real. Albert knew of seven victims – so did the author of the diary. How? Was there a relationship between the Barretts and the Johnsons? If there was not, then it would appear just a little fortuitous that Albert would buy Maybrick's watch only nine or ten months before knowledge of his alias was to become public for the first time in 105 years. On balance? Ugh. I didn't like it.

It was the 'H 9/3' in the middle of the watch that haunted me. Over the following months I gave the Johnsons some thought. Had they met Barrett? Did they know what was in the diary? Then again – even if they did know – would they have thought of 'H 9/3'?

If the Johnsons had forged the watch's markings, it would not take long to expose them. Science would see to that.

On the face of it, Albert Johnson's story seemed to pan out.

Firstly, his solicitor, Richard Nicholas, had said in an interview with Martin Howells in Liverpool, on film, in September 1993 that he wouldn't be representing them if he felt in any way that they had manufactured a hoax.

Then, Ronald Murphy, the owner of Stewart's, had confirmed in his statement that the watch had been bought in July 1992. His statement (reproduced in the Appendices) also mentioned that before the watch had been sold to Albert Johnson he had sent it to a Mr Dundas, of West Kirby, to be repaired. In an earlier statement, dated 26 June 1993, given by Mr Murphy's wife, she said the watch has been in their family for the last five years. 'My father has not dealt with jewellery for the last ten years as he retired in 1983, and we were given the watch by him,' her statement reads.

We asked the Murphys if we could see their father. Unfortunately, he was not in good health and was unable to see us. Mrs Murphy did speak to her father to find out how he had come by the watch. She said he recalled a little man coming to the shop he once owned in Lancaster. He had requested a sum of money which her father refused and the man left instantly. Mrs Murphy's father had an instant change of heart and ran outside to recall the man. The transaction was concluded.

Mrs Murphy's statement had proved the provenance of the watch to at least as far back as 1983. This date was too early for the doubters to prove their claim that it was a modern forgery.

If this was a den of fakers and forgers, the 'gang' was growing in numbers so rapidly that it was difficult to see how such a plot could remain a secret.

Try as I might to avoid it, the conclusion was inescapable: both watch and diary were genuine or both were fakes. If the latter, and the forger was Barrett or Johnson – or both – then either or both must have considered the probability that the watch would have had more credibility had it been exposed by Barrett at the same time as the diary.

If both artefacts were genuine, then Albert's purchase would appear to be more than just a little bit fortuitous.

Albert Johnson had not gone along with Robert Smith's offer to finance research. He still had total control of the watch. Both Robert Smith and Shirley Harrison had convinced Albert that, in order for the watch to be included in the book, he would have to get scientific support of its authenticity. I do not think that either Robert or Shirley would condemn me now for suggesting that they did not believe Mr Johnson would comply with this request, let alone pay for the investigation.

It was suggested that Albert Johnson should take the watch to the University of Manchester Institute of Science and Technology (UMIST). He did. Dr Stephen Turgoose MA Ph.D. of the Corrosion and Protection Centre would examine the watch and produce a report on his findings.

The first time Dr Turgoose saw the watch he had problems. He could not remove the back and was therefore unable to take micrograph pictures from particular angles. Robbie Johnson telephoned me to say that Dr Turgoose was convinced the watch was old, but he could not get the back off it. 'We don't know what's scratched at 8 o'clock,' said Robbie. I listened and told him to get me a copy of the report as soon as he could. I put down the phone and reflected on what I had been told. Robbie had lied. Turgoose might not know what was scratched at the position of 8 o'clock in the back of the watch, but Robbie and Albert did.

On the very first day I had met the Johnsons they had brought with them a diagram, which I've reproduced over the page. They had already seen what was scratched in that position and from their diagram Keith Skinner, Robert Smith and I, at the very least, also knew. They did not need Turgoose to tell them.

By this time there was a sort of relationship between Robbie Johnson and me. At the very least he considered me his friend. He would even suggest that we were close. In all honesty I did not know him at all. Robbie Johnson had called me on two occasions, after that first meeting, to ask if he could come down and see me in London. I would not be ungracious and told him he would be most welcome. On each occasion he also brought a man who he said was his cousin Gary. The conversation would start with him suggesting that every decision in respect of the watch was his, and I recalled my first conversation with Albert, who suggested exactly the same. I had, therefore, no reason to doubt what I was being told. On both these visits Robbie, Gary and I would debate the watch and the diary until the early hours of the morning. Robbie seemed convinced that the watch was genuine but the diary was not. I had told him that, while the reverse was remotely possible, his theory could not be. These two articles were undoubtedly linked.

Robbie seemed impressed by my involvement in the film *The Krays*. Perhaps when he first came to see me in London he wanted to meet a real film producer and brag to his friends. Or perhaps I was the person he thought would fork out a large sum of money for the watch.

It was during their second visit, however, that Robbie displayed an emotion that went beyond the project. I think we had been talking about personal aggression when

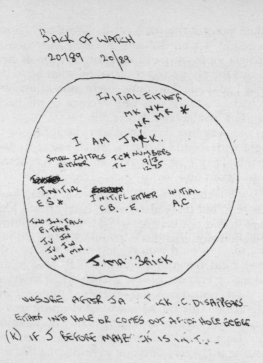

Robbie suddenly shouted, 'Why do you think I walk like this?' I had not noticed that Robbie walked in any way other than normal. He yanked up his shirt, holding it with his left hand around his neck and, with some difficulty, using his right hand to point to a large scar and lump on his back. He did not need to point.

Robbie seemed bitter. He explained that he had loved swimming and particularly diving; he had wanted it to be his life. One day at the local swimming baths he had climbed the steps to the highest springboard and, on reaching it, slipped. He did not land in the water and broke his back. Robbie was only eight years old. His life had hardly begun. He was in hospital for three years. During that time Albert was not just a brother: he was Robbie's best friend. Albert was his saviour.

When I heard this story my immediate reaction was to display sympathy, but I held back. In those few moments I decided that I liked this man, if for no other reason than that he genuinely displayed trust in me. A quality that is sadly lacking in so many people. My response was, for the first time, that of a friend.

I grabbed Robbie by the shoulders and turned him around to face a mirror. I told him he lived because he was supposed to. He could speak, had the use of his hands and legs. I warned him that, if he had told me his story to solicit sympathy, he wasn't getting any, and if it was to gain my friendship he would not have it. I may have been hard on him, but he realised immediately that I liked him as a person and not because of his childhood trauma.

Robert Johnson had just entered my life.

On 17 August 1993, I received by fax the full report prepared by Dr Turgoose dated 10 August. The first page started with a paragraph entitled 'Introduction'. Its first sentence read, 'The aim of the study described below was to attempt to define the age of the engravings in the watch.'

The second paragraph, entitled 'Experimental Studies', began, 'This report is of a scanning electron microscope examination of the inside of the back of the watch.'

The report took us through considerable scientific detail and came to a conclusion:

On the basis of the evidence above, especially the order in which the markings were made, it is clear that the engravings predate the vast majority of superficial surface scratches (all of those examined).

The wear apparent on many of the engravings, evidenced by the rounded edges of the markings and the 'polishing out' in places, would indicate a substantial age for the engravings. The actual age would depend on the cleaning or polishing regime employed, and any definition of number of years has a great degree of uncertainty and to some extent must remain speculation. Given these qualifications I would be of the opinion that the engravings are likely to date back more than tens of years, and possibly much longer.

However, whilst there is no evidence that would indicate a recent (last few years) origin of the engravings, it must be stressed that there are no features observed which conclusively prove the age of the engravings. They could have been produced recently and deliberately artificially aged by polishing, *but this would have been a complex multistage process, using a variety of different tools, with intermediate polishing or artificial wearing stages. Also, many of the observed features are only resolved by the scanning electron microscope, not being readily apparent in optical microscopy, and so if they were of recent origin the engraver would have had to be aware of the potential evidence available from this technique, indicating a considerable skill, and scientific awareness.*

I make no apologies for the italicisation in the above paragraph, which has been done at my insistence.

Shortly after I received this report I telephoned its author. I referred only to its last paragraph: 'If you bought a genuine Victorian watch would you be able to create what you have seen?' The response was firm and clear.

'No'

Although nine months into research and more confident about my own instincts, I was still naive. If he couldn't reproduce it, and from his knowledge and experience the engraving was clearly 'more than tens of years' old, why did he not just say it was genuine? Dr Turgoose responded in a manner that taught me never to ask a question in that way again.

'If I could be absolutely certain that these markings were made in 1888 or 1889, I could not know that they were made by Jack the Ripper.'

Of course he couldn't!

Dr Turgoose had no historical knowledge about Jack the Ripper and was only stating the facts regarding the age of the scratches. I was stunned by the conclusion, but not nearly as much as I believed Shirley Harrison, Robert Smith and the antagonists of the diary were.

So if our watch was a forgery, Albert Johnson, or Mike Barrett, or someone close to them had considerable scientific knowledge. Whoever this person may have been, he or she had clearly gone to incredible lengths to insert a few scratches in the back of a watch. I would have been amazed if any of the individuals I had met were capable of outwitting Dr Turgoose as well as even being aware of the existence of a scanning electron microscope.

It is important at this stage to remember that Robert Smith had made an offer to Albert already. A number of questions crossed my mind.

If Albert had bought the watch from a shop in precisely the manner he had indicated, would he (a) refuse Robert Smith's offer when everyone was crying 'fake'; or (b) invest money (which he could ill afford) in chasing scientific support for an artefact whose authenticity he could not be certain of?

Alternatively, we assume Albert is lying – either by himself or in collusion with Barrett. This suggests forgery with knowledge. Why, then, when it was suggested he go to UMIST, did he? If the engravings were forged, surely now was the time to realise that the game was up.

Now wait a minute, I told myself. Whichever way I worked the fake-watch hypothesis it simply did not make sense. Albert clearly believed the watch was genuine, hence his investment.

And at this point everybody was saying the diary was a fake, yet he was still prepared to spend a significant sum of money on testing the watch to prove far more knowledgeable people wrong. I learnt that Albert liked a little flutter on the horses, but these amounts were much smaller and, in his opinion, spent with some knowledge!

Albert Johnson was not fearful of the scientific outcome of the investigation. Why?

Albert Johnson *knew* that the scientific evidence would

not disprove the authenticity of the watch. He knew far more about the watch than he was prepared to admit.

Now I believed in the watch – after all, Albert Johnson did.

So why the fibs?

4

'AN INITIAL HERE ... AN INITIAL THERE'

I WAS INVOLVED WITH this project because of, I suppose, Paul Begg. Those words 'we simply can't shake it' started my fascination with the document. Over the years the Ripper crimes had been investigated time and time again, yet Paul Begg was adamant: 'There is nothing in this diary that disproves it historically.' Other historians seemed to disagree: they were convinced that the diary contained information about the murders that proved it to be a fake.

It was January 1993. Paul Begg came down from his home in Leeds to stay with me in Hertfordshire. We studied that diary day, night and during the earlier hours of the morning. Voices were raised and my study needed to be disinfected each morning after the chain-smoking of cigarettes by Paul, not to mention the smell of my cigar butts.

We were focusing our attention on the known five victims of Jack the Ripper: Mary Ann Nichols, Annie Chapman, Elizabeth Stride, Catharine[1] Eddowes and Mary Kelly. The diary strongly suggests two other murders – one in Manchester in late February or early March 1888, the other around Christmas 1888 at a venue that is not clear. These murders, although intriguing, were not our prime concern. If the diary was a forgery, then it was probable that its author would have slipped up, somewhere, on some minute detail of the known facts about the 'accepted' victims. Paul Begg and his associates had not discovered any such discrepancy – at least not yet.

---

[1] The unusual spelling of 'Catharine' is taken from her birth certificate.

What of the other two victims? We were to examine these later, but something did stick in my mind all through the investigation. Why would a forger or hoaxer – call him or her what you will – introduce two major events into the life of James Maybrick that might easily be proved wrong? Surely that could only assist in destroying the document's credibility.

Paul Begg taught me a great deal about Whitechapel in 1888, but Melvyn Fairclough summed it all up quite simply as follows:

In 1888 London was the well-oiled hub around which the wheel of the British Empire turned. But still it creaked. It creaked beneath the weight of injustice, poverty and hypocrisy. The teeming masses struggling against these odds lay side by side with wealth and opulence. Nowhere was this more obvious than in the East End, an area to which the most unpleasant industries were banished; unpleasant because of the noise they made or the smells they produced: slaughterhouses, skinners, glue-makers, fish-curers and bell-makers.

Separating the fashionable West End from the East End melting-pot of indigenous Cockneys and immigrants (Chinese, Polish, Hungarians, Russians – you name them, here they were), stood the square mile of the City of London. The Golden Square. The financial centre of the world.

The docks were in the East End, and a bottomless pool of men queued daily for work unloading coal from Newcastle, rosewood from Burma, mahogany from Cuba and Honduras, tobacco and spices from faraway exotic lands – lands they would never see unless they took the King's shilling to fight over a foreign border. Without a safety-net, like modern social security, men were often forced into petty crime to feed their children or drown their sorrows in ale or gin. But it was worse for women. Their men folk, unable to support their families, might turn a blind eye when their wives fell unwillingly into prostitution to earn a crust for a starving child.

The combination of perverse sentimentality and repressed sexuality, coupled with a high incidence of incurable venereal diseases, made virgins highly prized and children could be 'bought' by West End toffs through special agents – the most despicable of pimps. Campaigners (notably Josephine Butler, the women's rights crusader), tried in vain to get an indifferent Government to act against this exploitation. Finally, in 1885, in order to prove to a largely unbelieving public that it was possible to 'buy' children for sex, W.T. Stead, the celebrated editor of the *Pall Mall Gazette*, 'bought' Eliza Armstrong, a twelve-year-old East End girl. Her dissolute mother 'sold' her through an agent for £5. The agent was a reformed prostitute hired by Stead especially for the purpose. Stead, the former prostitute and Bramwell Booth, son of the founder of the Salvation Army, were tried in court and given a nominal prison sentence. Their trial, however, as they intended, was a publicity triumph and led to the age of consent being raised from twelve to fourteen.

According to *The Lancet*, between 60,000 and 80,000 London women had fallen into prostitution. There were 1,200 in Whitechapel alone and one of them was Mary Ann Nichols, whose body suffered the final violation by a man. Today her murder is generally regarded as the first one by Jack the Ripper. Her body was found in Buck's Row, a narrow street running parallel to Whitechapel Road and less than a hundred yards behind Whitechapel Underground Station. Consequently the press initially named the atrocities 'the Whitechapel murders'. Whitechapel was the East End in the East End, so typical was it of that sprawling slum.

Nichols's body was found by Charles Cross, a carter on his way to work, at 3.40 a.m. on 31 August 1888. He alerted another carter, Robert Paul. In the darkness they were not sure whether she was dead or just dead drunk. It took the beam from a policeman's bull's-eye lantern to show that her throat had been cut back to the spine. Her skirt was pulled up, but it was not until later, at the mortuary, that she was found to have abdominal mutilations, exposing the intestines.

A week later, on 8 September, another body was found – that of Annie Chapman – in the yard at the back of 29 Hanbury Street. At 11.30 the night before, Timothy Donovan, deputy of Crossingham's Lodging House, had let her into the communal kitchen. She was still there at 12.12 a.m. and was seen taking a box of pills from her pocket. When the box broke she picked up a torn piece of envelope and put the pills in it. The back of the envelope bore the blue crest of the Sussex Regiment. She then went out, returning around 1.35 a.m. Donovan found her eating a baked potato and asked her for her doss money. 'I haven't got it,' she admitted, adding, 'I am weak and ill and have been in the infirmary.' As she left she said, 'Don't let the bed. I'll be back soon.'

The building at 29 Hanbury Street had two front doors. One led into a shop and the other into the house. The house door, on the left, was usually unlocked. It opened into a hall with a staircase up to the residents' rooms. At the end was the door to a yard where, it was said, prostitutes sometimes took their clients.

At 5.45 a.m., after a restless night and little sleep, John Davis, an elderly carter who lived with his family on the third floor, went to the back yard, where he saw Chapman's body lying parallel to the fence. Her throat was cut, her dress pulled above her striped stockings and her intestines strewn across her left shoulder.

Dr George Bagster Phillips conducted the post-mortem, which disclosed that the uterus with the upper portion of the vagina and two-thirds of her bladder had been removed and were missing. There was also a gaping wound to the throat, of which, according to the *Daily Telegraph* of 10 September 1888, he said, 'There were two distinct clean cuts on the left side of the spine. They were parallel with each other and separated by about half an inch. The muscular structures appeared as though an attempt had been made to separate the bones of the neck.'

When the police arrived they searched the yard and found the piece of torn envelope and two pills in a screw of paper. Dr Bagster Phillips arrived and, after examining the body, discovered that Chapman's pocket had been cut open and its contents were lying in a neat pile: two combs, a piece of coarse muslin and two farthings. The neatness of them strongly suggested that they were put there with deliberate intent. Indeed, Dr Bagster Phillips stated at the inquest – according to the *Daily Telegraph* of 14 September 1888 – that they 'had apparently been placed there in order, that is to say arranged there'.

Newspaper reports had not been consistent about the rings that were on Annie Chapman's fingers. The majority had suggested that there were three; others said two.

I was about to understand just how complex the diary was. Critics were saying it could have been written from existing material. Even at this early stage common sense told me it was not as simple at that. Books were checked for the references to Annie Chapman's rings. Again, there was conflict. If the diary was forged by someone who was not an expert, they had a fifty-fifty choice. Our diarist made his and got it right.

> One ring, two rings,
> a farthing one and two,
> Along with M ha ha
> Will catch clever Jim
> its true
> No pill, left but two

Earlier he had written:

> I have left the stupid fools a clue which I am sure they will not solve. Once again I have been clever, very clever.
> > two farthings,
> > two pills
> > the whores M
> > rings

Although never previously published, a police report signed by Inspector Abberline and countersigned by Chief Inspector Swanson and Superintendent John Shore confirms: 'The deceased was in the habit of wearing two brass rings (a wedding ring and keepers) these were missing when the body was found and the finger bore marks of their having been removed by force.'[1]

The diarist later continued:

Begin with the rings
one ring, two rings,
bitch, it took me a while before I could wrench them off

Whoever had written this diary was either very lucky or had done some serious homework – unless, of course, it was written by the Ripper himself. The right choice had been made about Annie Chapman's rings. The vague reference to the difficulty in removing the rings impressed me also. The unpublished report by Abberline had made specific mention of this.

The Chapman murder needed more work. The critics claimed that the reference to the farthings 'proved' the diary to be a fake. Melvin Harris, author of three Ripper books, claimed the farthings to be a canard. If he was right, then the diary was a fake – even I would not have argued with that. The diarist had made a clear reference to them. So where had Harris obtained this information on which he based his claim?

The source for the argument about the farthings was Richard Whittington-Egan in his book, *A Casebook on Jack the Ripper* (1975).

He claimed, 'There are, *I think*, reasonable grounds for supposing that the story of the rings, pennies and farthings laid at Mrs Chapman's feet has been elaborated . . .' (my italics).

Whittington-Egan goes on to explain that the story had started in 1888 with Oswald Allen, a journalist who covered the crimes and described items that had been

---

[1] Extract of a fifteen-page report dated 19 September 1888, Mepo 3/140/252.

taken from her pockets as 'trumpery articles'. He continues that in 1929, when Leonard Matters wrote 'the first book on the subject', the trumpery articles become 'two or three coppers'. Then, in 1959, Donald McCormick, in his book, *The True Identity of Jack the Ripper*, says Whittington-Egan, adds 'two farthings'. Finally, we are told, Robin Odell adds 'new', between 'two' and 'farthings' – 'and the legend is complete'.

To be fair to Richard Whittington-Egan, he starts his argument with the words 'I think . . .'. He was wrong. The story did not start with Oswald Allen, or Leonard Matters. The farthings were mentioned in the *Daily Telegraph* of 10 September 1888. Furthermore, the theory is disproved by Inspector Edmund John James Reid, head of local CID during the Whitechapel murders. At the inquest on Alice McKenzie[1] he explained that he 'had held a watching brief as coins found under the body were similar to those in Annie Chapman's case'. We should be thankful to Donald McCormick, and I trust that this book sets the record straight. Robin Odell, also, can hold his head up. Major Henry Smith, acting Commissioner of City Police, September 1888, wrote in his memoirs, *From Constable to Commissioner* (1910), of 'a suspected medical student with a reputation for passing off polished farthings . . .'.

Hardly relevant if not connected to the crimes.

Strangely enough, Philip Sugden, in the excellent *The Complete History of Jack the Ripper*, also states: 'Neither rings nor farthings were found at Annie's feet . . .' I say 'strangely enough' because Sugden is clearly aware of the references I mention above. He rests his argument on 'four authentic eyewitness accounts of the appearance of the body in the backyard'. Sugden continues: 'Not one of these accounts mentions any rings or farthings placed by Annie's feet.'

---

[1] Alice McKenzie, known as 'Clay pipe Alice', was found dead on 17 July 1889. The police did not believe her to be a Ripper victim, an opinion shared by most historians today.

The diarist did not say there were rings 'left at the feet'. He simply said that he 'wrenched them off'. Inspector Abberline said that was precisely what happened. Indeed, Abberline's report confirms that Sugden's logic is flawed. The idea that Major Henry Smith and Inspector Reid 'made the farthings up' is simply preposterous.

I was also intrigued by the diarist's reference to 'the whores M'. Every book that I had read had suggested that this letter was compared to signatures of members of the Sussex Regiment. This diary, however, certainly gave the impression that the author disclaimed responsibility. If this was a hoax, would not the diarist have complied with the thinking of all the published authors, who seemed to believe that the scrap of envelope was some kind of clue?

Reports at the time confirmed that on the front of the piece of envelope, found by the side of Chapman, was the postmark 'London 28 August 1888', and the letters 'Sp', thought by the police to be the beginning of the word Spitalfields, and the letter 'M' in what was thought to be a man's handwriting.

In the Scotland Yard files, we discovered a further report that had previously remained unpublished. Why it had not seen the light of day I do not know. It taught me that previous authors either ignored what they read because it did not suit their argument, or they just did not read. Any 'supporter' of the M.J. Druitt theory may have made use of this extract of Inspector Chandler's report:

> Enquiries were made amongst the men [of the Sussex Regiment] but none could be found who corresponded with anyone living at Spitalfields or any person whose address commencing [sic] with 'J'. The pay books were examined and no signature resembled the initials on the envelope.[1]

In a later report Chandler wrote:

[1] Mepo 3/140/16. Report dated 14 September 1888, signed by Inspector Chandler, and countersigned by Acting Superintendent West.

... enquiries were made amongst the men but none could be found who are in the habit of writing to anyone at Spitalfields, or whose signatures corresponded with the letters on the envelope . . .[1]

The envelope contained not just the letter M but also the letter J. The police discounted the first and compared only the letter J, despite the contrary information they had fed to the press. The author of the diary was right, and, if he was a forger, had picked up material missed by every modern author on the subject of Jack the Ripper. The initials, of course, may stand for James Maybrick. Equally, they may refer to the forenames M.J. Druitt. Or James Monro. Or Joseph Merrick. Both of these men have been nominated as Ripper suspects. One thing was sure: our diarist was forcing us to reread source material that was to rewrite history.

Soon after this discovery became known among the inner circle of Ripper authors the argument was put forward that the letter J was in fact a number 2. I could not believe it. The debunkers would, I concluded, argue that black was white if such an argument would prove the diary a forgery. The two reports clearly make reference to letters and initials; at no time is there any mention of a number. I accept the similarity between the inspector's handwriting of a number two and the letter J, but the terminology of the report makes clear what he was referring to.

On 30 September, three weeks after Annie Chapman's murder, two more murders by Jack were committed a few hundred yards apart and within forty-five minutes of each other.

At 11 p.m. on Saturday 29 September, Swedish-born Elizabeth Stride, affectionately known as 'Long Liz', was seen leaving the Bricklayers Arms on the corner of Settles

---

[1] Mepo 3/140/18–20. Further report by Inspector Chandler, dated 15 September 1888, countersigned by Inspector Abberline.

Street and Commercial Road. She was with an Englishman wearing a morning coat and billycock (bowler) hat. According to the *Evening News* of 1 October 1888, they headed in the direction of Berner Street, where they were seen at 11.45 by William Marshall, who, at the inquest, described the man as 'middle-aged'. Ten minutes later Marshall saw them walking down the middle of the road, and they passed by him as he lounged in his doorway at 64 Berner Street.[1] At around midnight they bought grapes from Matthew Packer of 44 Berner Street, a fruit seller in a small way. They were still there at 12.30 a.m. when they were seen by police constable William Smith on the opposite side from Packer's shop. It might have been they who were seen around the corner, talking, in Fairclough Street at 12.45 a.m.[2]

At approximately 1 a.m. Louis Diemschütz, returning on his pony and cart from Upper Norwood, Sydenham, where he'd been peddling cheap jewellery, turned his pony into Dutfield's Yard, off Berner Street. The wooden gates to the yard were open, thrown inward back to the walls. The yard itself was in almost total darkness, the only light being from an upstairs window a few yards from the entrance. The pony shied to the left and hesitated to proceed. In the dim light Diemschütz thought he saw something on his right. Probing with his whip he felt something soft, got down, struck a match and discovered the body of a woman. He thought she was drunk and, possibly, that it might be his wife. He went into the International Workingmen's Educational Club, on the right of the yard, where he was steward, returned with Isaac Kozebrodski and discovered, in the light of a candle,

---

[1] *The Times*, *Daily Telegraph* and *Daily News* (6 October 1888) give slightly different reports of Marshall's 5 October deposition.

[2] Deposition of James Brown, *The Times*, *Daily Telegraph* and *Daily News* (6 October 1888). The woman Brown saw may not have been Stride because he did not notice the flower pinned to Stride's dress, nor did he notice the man's cap. The couple he saw may have been the courting couple reported in the *Evening News* as being in a street that crossed Berner Street, as did Fairclough Street.

blood trickling up the yard. The two men ran off to fetch a policeman. When they did not find one they returned to find a group of club members around the body. It was then, for the first time, that Diemschütz saw the ghastly wound to Stride's throat.

The timing of some of the evening's events given by witnesses were at odds with one another. William Marshall, as noted, stated that he saw Stride with a man in Berner Street at 11.45 and that they passed him ten minutes later. This is at variance with another witness, Israel Schwartz, probably the most important one, although he was never called to the inquest. He volunteered his testimony at Leman Street Police Station later on the day of the murder. The day after the murder, on 1 October 1888, the *Star* published their own version of Schwartz's story:

Information which may be important was given to the Leman Street police late yesterday afternoon by an Hungarian concerning this murder. This foreigner was well dressed, and had the appearance of being in the theatrical line. He could not speak a word of English, but came to the police accompanied by a friend, who acted as an interpreter. He gave his name and address, but the police have not disclosed them. A *Star* man, however, got wind of his call, and ran him to earth in Backchurch Lane. The reporter's Hungarian was quite as imperfect as the foreigner's English, but an interpreter was at hand, and the man's story was retold just as he had given it to the police. It is, in fact, to the effect that he saw the whole thing.

It seems that he had gone out for the day, and his wife had expected to move, during his absence, from their lodgings in Berner Street to others in Backchurch Lane. When he came homewards about a quarter before one he first walked down Berner Street to see if his wife had moved. As he turned from Commercial Road he noticed some distance in front of him a man walking as if partially intoxicated. He walked on behind him, and presently he noticed a woman standing at the entrance to the alley way where the body was afterwards found. The half tipsy man halted and talked to her. The Hungarian saw him put his hand on her shoulder and push her back into the passage, but feeling rather timid of getting mixed up in quarrels, he crossed to the other side of the street. Before he had gone many yards, however, he heard the sound of a quarrel, and turned back to learn what was the matter, but as he stepped from the kerb a second man came out of the doorway of the public house a few doors off, and shouting out some sort of warning to the man who was with the woman, rushed forward as if to attack the intruder. The Hungarian states positively that he saw a knife in this second man's hand, but he waited to see no more. He fled incontinently, to his new lodgings.

He described the man with the woman as about 30 years of age, rather stoutly built, and wearing a brown moustache. He was dressed respectably in dark clothes and felt hat. The man who came at him with a knife he also describes, but not in detail. He says he was taller than the other but not so stout, and that his moustaches were red. Both men seem to belong to the same grade of society. The police have arrested one man answering the description the Hungarian furnishes. This prisoner has not been charged, but is held for enquiries to be made. The truth of the man's statement is not wholly accepted.

Schwartz's original statement to the police has not survived but its substance was preserved by Chief Inspector Swanson on 19 October. It is at variance with the *Star*'s version. Swanson wrote:

12.45 a.m. 30th. Israel Schwartz of 22 Helen Street [i.e. Ellen Street], Backchurch Lane, stated that at that hour on turning into Berner Street from Commercial Road & had got as far as the gateway where the murder was committed he saw a man stop & speak to a woman, who was standing in the gateway. The man tried to pull the woman into the street, but he turned her round & through [sic] her down on the footway & the woman screamed three times, but not very loudly. On crossing to the opposite side of the street, he saw a second man standing lighting his pipe. The man who threw the woman down called out apparently to the man on the opposite side of the road 'Lipski' & then Schwartz walked away, but finding that he was followed by the second man he ran as far as the railway arch but the man did not follow so far.

Schwartz cannot say whether the two men were together or known to each other. Upon being taken to the Mortuary Schwartz identified the body as that of the woman he had seen & describes the first man who threw the woman down – age about 30, height 5ft 5in, complexion fair, hair dark, small brown moustache, full face, broad shouldered; dress, dark jacket & trousers, black cap with peak, had nothing in his hands.

Second man, age 35, height 5ft 11in, complexion fresh, hair light brown, moustache brown; dress, dark overcoat, old black hard felt hat wide brim, had a clay pipe in his hand.[1]

He was taken so seriously by the police that they gave his description of the man who pushed Stride to the ground to the *Police Gazette*, who published it on their front page on 19 October, the same date as Swanson's report.

The differences between these two versions of the same account could be explained by the fact that Schwartz could not speak a word of English.

In his post-mortem report, Dr George Bagster Phillips made reference to cachous found in the left hand of Elizabeth Stride.[2]

---

[1] Report by Chief Inspector Swanson, 19 October 1888, HO 144/221/A49301C/149–151.
[2] Dr Phillips's deposition to the inquest, 3 October 1888, see *Daily Telegraph* and *Daily News*, 4 October 1888. Cachous are tiny sweets for freshening the breath.

Paul Begg and I, in that January of 1993, debated the murder of Elizabeth Stride for hours. It was around this time that modern authors on the subject were wondering whether this victim was one of Jack the Ripper's at all. If she was not, then the diary was a fake. I accept that the information that is available to the public now makes you wonder why she was considered a victim. The weapon that killed her was clearly different from the one that killed the Ripper's other victims and she clearly was not mutilated. The police, at the time however, were in no doubt and they were privy to information we are not. That is the respect that modern historians must pay to the professional investigators involved at the time.

Parts of the diary have attempts at poetry. Some of it is crossed out, rewritten, and crossed out again. Among these ramblings are lists of words. Debunkers asserted that they were 'clues' put there by the forger. They are not. The more Paul and I read and reread, it became clear that they were the words that the author wanted to use in his poetry, and listed them to test them for rhyme.

The diary seemed to unravel Ripper folklore bit by bit. Paul Begg and I seemed to get to grips with Stride's murder *because of the diary*. I discuss this fully later.

The diarist had written of this murder, as follows:

To my astonishment I cannot believe I have not been caught. My heart felt as if it had left my body. Within my fright I imagined my heart bounding along the street with I in desperation following it. I would have dearly loved to have cut the head of the damned horse off and stuff it as far as it would go down the whores throat. I had not time to rip the bitch wide . . .

At the end of this passage he made the following list of words:

Red – head
horse,
cryed
smelt breath

The cynics were soon off their starting blocks: Elizabeth Stride did not have red hair – it was black! But the mention of the colour red was not a reference to Stride's hair. It alluded to blood, and it was a device the diarist did frequently throughout the diary. He refers to it as 'the red stuff'. Every entry containing the word 'red' is a reference to the blood of his victims, other than one, in which he refers to the colour of a cigarette case. The head? Well, the earlier paragraph surely indicates ownership of the head as being that of the horse.

On 30 September, the Ripper killed twice. Stride had escaped mutilation – his next victim would not. Her name was Catharine Eddowes, victim of the only Ripper murder committed in the City of London.

On 27 September she returned to London from Kent, where she and John Kelly, her common-law husband, had been hop-picking. They had earned very little and on 29 September decided to pawn a pair of Kelly's boots. They parted at 2 p.m.

Later that day, at 8.30 p.m. Eddowes was arrested outside 29 Aldgate High Street for causing a drunken disturbance, taken to Bishopsgate Police Station and locked in a cell until she sobered up. By 12.15 the following morning she was singing to herself and at 12.30 asked to be released. She was let out at 1 a.m. – just as Diemschütz's horse shied away from the body of Stride.

At 1.35 a.m. Joseph Lawende, Joseph Hyam and Harry Harris saw Eddowes at the Duke's Place end of Church Passage, a covered entrance to Mitre Square. She was talking to a man, one hand resting on his chest. The couple were not there five minutes later when City Police Constable James Harvey walked up Church Passage. He saw and heard no one in the square, which he did not enter. About five minutes later Eddowes was alone in the darkest corner of the square. She was dead, her throat cut, her body mutilated.

Catharine Eddowes was discovered by City Police Constable Edward Watkins at, by his own estimation, 1.45 a.m. He alerted George Morris, the nightwatchman at Kearley and Tonge's opposite where the body lay. Morris ran off to Aldgate, where he found Constable Holland, who crossed the road to fetch Dr Sequeira from 34 Jewry Street. The doctor stated later that he arrived in Mitre Square at 1.45. This was the time Watkins said he found the body. Clearly, one of them was mistaken, because a couple of minutes must have passed between finding the body and Dr Sequeira's arrival.

The body was removed to Golden Lane mortuary, where Dr Frederick Brown conducted the post-mortem that afternoon. When the clothing was removed a piece of Eddowes's ear dropped from it. According to Brown's extensive report some of Eddowes's intestines were strewn over her right shoulder and two feet of the colon was detached and placed between the body and her left arm. The left kidney and the uterus had been removed and taken away.

The diarist had written of this crime:

> The thrill she gave me was unlike the others, I cut deep deep. Her nose annoyed me so I cut it off, had a go at her eyes, left my mark, could not get the bitches head off. I believe now it is impossible to do so. The whore never screamed. I took all I could away with me.

According to Dr Brown 'the tip of her nose was quite detached'. He continued: 'The face was very much mutilated. There was a cut about a quarter of an inch through the lower left eyelid, dividing the structure completely through . . . The right eyelid was cut into through to about half an inch . . . There was on each side of cheek a cut which peeled up the skin, forming a triangular flap about an inch and a half'.[1]

The police surgeon's diagram of mutilations to Catharine Eddowes face is shown opposite.

Once again the diary pointed us in a particular direction. The two inverted Vs underneath the eyes could certainly be interpreted as a letter M. If so, this could be

---

[1] Dr Brown's post-mortem report, Corporation of London Records Office, Coroner's Papers (London), 1888, No. 135.

what the diarist meant when he wrote 'left my mark'. If the diary was a forgery then again an observation had been made that had never been made before. Once again, supporters of the Druitt theory could have used it, but they did not. If this was a forgery it was written by somebody special, somebody who was far more careful about checking source material than any of the Ripper authors. The author of the diary was always right – much as the cynics did not want to accept it.

Whether the marks on Catherine Eddowes's face really do form an M is open to interpretation, but it is fascinating to note that it was the author of the diary who first drew attention to it.

My investigation had really only just started. Many things impressed me, as they did Paul Begg, but I had learnt enough to know that James Maybrick's life was well documented and if he was not the Ripper it would be easy to prove.

The diarist had written seventeen pages following the murders of Stride and Eddowes. That represented more than twenty-five per cent of the diary as we know it. If our 'forger' was to slip up, we believed we might find some mistake by comparing the events as our diarist saw them to known historical facts.

It should be noted that James Maybrick's younger brother Michael was a noted composer. His *nom de plume* was Stephen Adams. Throughout the diary the author resents the ability of Michael to compose verse.

The diarist made another attempt to outdo his brother:

> One whore no good
> decided Sir Jim strike another.
> I showed no fright and indeed no light,
> damn it, the tin box was empty
>
> Sweet sugar and tea
> could have paid my small fee.
> But instead I did flee
> and by way showed my glee
> By eating cold kidney for supper
>
> Oh Mr Abberline, he is a clever little man
> he keeps back all that he can.
> For do I know better, Indeed I do
> did I not leave him a very good clue.
> Nothing is mentioned, of this I know sure;
> ask clever Abberline, could tell you more
>
> Sir Jim trip over
> fear
> have it near
> redeem it near
> case
> Poste haste

Modern writers have tended to play down the role of Inspector Abberline, yet he is the only policeman on the Ripper case named by the author of the diary.

Though not in charge of the case Abberline coordinated

the ground-level enquiries and was therefore perceived as being in charge. The newspapers most certainly gave him top billing.[1]

The official police listing of her clothes and possessions, taken at the mortuary, was as follows:

- Black Straw Bonnet trimmed with green and black velvet and black beads, black strings . . .
- Black cloth Jacket, imitation fur edging round collar, fur round sleeves . . . 2 outside pockets, trimmed black silk braid and imitation fur
- Chintz Skirt, 3 flounces, brown button on waistband . . .
- Brown Linsey Dress Bodice, black velvet collar, brown metal buttons down front
- Grey Stuff Petticoat, white waist band . . .
- Very Old Green Alpaca Skirt . . .
- Very Old ragged Blue Skirt, red flounce, light twill lining . . .
- White Calico Chemise . . .
- Mans White Vest, button to match down front, 2 outside pockets . . .
- No Drawers or Stays
- Pair of Mens lace up Boots, mohair laces. Right boot has been repaired with red thread . . .
- 1 piece of red gauze Silk . . . found on neck
- 1 large White Handkerchief . . .
- 2 Unbleached Calico Pockets . . .
- 1 Blue Stripe Bed ticking Pocket, waist band, and strings . . .
- 1 White Cotton Pocket Handkerchief, red and white birds eye border

---

[1] Even as early as the murder of Nicholls the *Yorkshire Post* reported Abberline and Sergeants Godley and Enright as 'experts from CID'. More evidence that Abberline was perceived in the press to be the leading police officer was in *The Times* of 12 November 1888: 'Detective Inspectors Reid, Moore and Nairn, and Sgts. Thick, Godley, McCarthy and Pearce have been constantly engaged *under the direction* of Inspector Abberline of Scotland Yard' (my italics). See also *The Times*, 7 December 1888.

- 1 pr. Brown ribbed Stockings, feet mended with white
- 12 pieces of white Rag, some slightly bloodstained
- 1 piece of white Coarse Linen
- 1 piece of Blue and White shirting (3 cornered)
- 2 Small Blue Bed ticking Bags
- 2 Short Clay Pipes (black)
- 1 Tin Box containing Tea
- 1 do do do [ditto] Sugar
- 1 Piece of Flannel and 6 pieces of soap
- 1 Small Tooth Comb
- 1 White Handle Table Knife and 1 metal Tea Spoon
- 1 Red Leather Cigarette Case, white metal fittings
- 1 Tin Match Box, empty
- 1 piece of Red Flannel containing Pins & Needles
- 1 Ball of Hemp
- 1 Piece of old White Apron

Beside the body, Sergeant Jones found three boot buttons, a thimble and a mustard tin containing the pawn tickets for Emily Birrell's[1] man's shirt, and Kelly's boots.

Press reports add part of a pair of spectacles, one mitten, and a printed card for 'Frank Carter, 305 Bethnal Green Road'. They describe the outer chintz dress as having a pattern of chrysanthemums or Michaelmas daisies and lilies. The white apron was so dirty that at first glance it seemed black. However, one thing on the official police list never published was the 'Tin Match Box, empty'.

Our diarist had written, '. . . damn it, the tin box was empty.'

Not only was the complete police list never published at the time, but the existence of this list was not even known about until the original document was rediscovered in 1984. It was not even published until Donald Rumbelow and Martin Fido did so in their books on the subject of Jack the Ripper in 1987.

The fact is that the empty tin matchbox did not appear in any press report at the time. As happens today, police

---

[1] Emily Birrell met Catharine Eddowes in Kent a day or so before the latter was murdered.

held back information from the press that only the murderer would know.

The seven words that our diarist wrote meant that the diary either had to be a modern forgery or we were looking at a document that nobody ever felt would be discovered, the emotions and words written by the perpetrator of the Whitechapel murders.

If the diary was a modern forgery, then once again its author had shown his diligence. He may have read the list of Catharine Eddowes's belongings in the books published in 1987, but could not have known that the 'Tin Match Box, empty' was held back from the media ('Oh Mr Abberline, he is a clever little man/he keeps back all that he can') without checking every newspaper report of the period – something we were forced to do. This is a hugely time-consuming undertaking on which we embarked in order to verify the diary's references to the tin box and Abberline's withholding details. Why would a forger have bothered to check the list of belongings against the newspaper reports? The forger would not have known that Abberline had not released the entire list of belongings to the press. Would he really have done all that research on the off chance that he just *might* find something that *might* give him a couple of throwaway lines in his sixty-three-page masterpiece?

These questions went round and round in my head. If we did not have the diary then we would not have checked the official police list against the contemporary newspaper reports. Donald Rumbelow did not and neither did Martin Fido. Nor did anyone else, until I began investigating this diary.

From the evidence we had it was clear that the police had not informed the press of this particular item only. Why? Why that one? It must have been relevant to the *murderer* and not the victim.

The purported author of the diary was James Maybrick, a self-confessed junkie who bragged at one time of taking 'more than any other man alive'. The anger displayed by the author of the diary when discovering that the tin box was empty fascinated me. Not only had we discovered a new anomaly in Ripperology, but I believe our diarist was suggesting a reason for it. Did Abberline keep the box back because he knew it belonged to the Ripper? Did that box show traces of drugs?

Dr William Sedgwick Saunders, at the inquest of Catharine Eddowes, made it clear that he had examined the victim for drugs. 'I carefully examined the stomach and the contents more particularly for poisons of the narcotic class with negative results[,] there being not the slightest trace of these or any other poison.'[1]

Maybe it was it just coincidence that Maybrick's mother-in-law, Baroness von Roques (her third husband was Baron Adolph von Roques), wrote in a letter to Home Secretary Henry Matthews in August 1892, 'I have an affidavit from one George Bancroft, an intimate friend of James Maybrick, who declares the latter kept a small box in his vest [waistcoat] pocket [containing] small powders which he habitually put into his drinks, and James Maybrick told him arsenic was one of the ingrediants [sic].'[2]

Another significant item on the published list was the 'Red Leather Cigarette Case'. It seems hardly likely that a woman in penury who, that very morning, pawned her boyfriend's boots, would own a leather cigarette case with metal fittings.

Once again, as diligent as ever, our 'forger' had brought our attention to it.

Sir Jim
tin match box empty
~~cigarette case~~
~~make haste~~
~~my shiny knife~~
~~the whores knife~~
first whore no good

---

[1] Corporation of London Records Office, Coroner's Papers (London), No. 135.
[2] HO 144/1640/A5O678D/92. Florence Maybrick file opened to the public in 1985.

According to Mrs Hogg, a Virginia brothel-keeper who testified at Florence Maybrick's trial, James frequented her brothel when he lived in the USA. Mrs Hogg stated that he kept his arsenic 'in a cigarette case'.

In a matter of a few pages in the diary, its author had caused us to debate a red leather cigarette case, an empty tin matchbox and drugs, as well as the marks on Catharine Eddowes's face. None of these topics had ever raised as much as an eyebrow in the world of Ripperology before. What made our diarist so unique? It did not end there.

At 12.45 on the morning after the double event, a policeman on his beat found a knife lying in Mr Christmas's shop doorway in Whitechapel Road, a few hundred yards from Stride's murder. The knife was short – about two inches long according to the *Evening News*, reporting it the following day, 1 October – and at Stride's inquest Dr Bagster Phillips claimed that this knife could have killed Stride. Contemporary records show that prostitutes often carried knives for self-protection, a practice that increased during the time of the Ripper atrocities, and especially in the East End. Significantly, the knife was found in the very same district as the 'Saucy Jacky' postcard was posted. (The Saucy Jacky postcard will be discussed later. For the moment I'll just say that it was a communication to the Central News Agency, and referred to 'Saucy Jackys work'.)

My research on this knife led to corrections made in *The Jack the Ripper A-Z*. The authors had previously reported that this knife was found two days *before* the night of the double event. This confusion, among other doubts, had led modern Ripper commentators to question whether Elizabeth Stride had been a victim of the Whitechapel murderer. As mentioned earlier in this chapter, the police in charge of the investigation at the time seemed to be in no doubt whatsoever. Once again, this extraordinary diary had made us think. The diarist made no attempt to conform with the latest theories. He even made reference to 'the whores knife'. The diarist knew Stride was a Ripper victim. Would a forger have flown in the face of modern thinking, putting his work at risk, by boldly accepting Stride as a victim? I think not.

On 9 November 1888, the birthday of Edward, Prince of Wales, and the day of the Lord Mayor of London's procession through the city, newspaper sellers were once again shouting 'Murder! Horrible murder!'

The killing and mutilation of Mary Jane Kelly, the youngest and prettiest of the Ripper's victims, was the most savage. Joseph Barnett, who had been her lover from Good Friday 1887 until two weeks before her death, said she was twenty-five, just a year younger than James Maybrick's wife Florence.

She told Barnett that her family left Limerick, on the west coast of Ireland, and settled in Wales. She said that at sixteen she married John Davies, a collier who, soon afterwards, died in a mining explosion. Research has shown that no such marriage was ever registered in Britain, and perhaps she invented the story as an excuse for becoming a prostitute, claiming that she did so out of desperation now that the man who supported her was 'dead'. Or she may have lived with Davies unmarried.

The day before her death Kelly spent the afternoon with a friend, Maria Harvey, and the early evening with Lizzie Albrook, to whom she gave the timely advice, 'Whatever you do, don't you do wrong and turn out as I have.' A short time after 7.30 p.m. Barnett called on Kelly at her home, 13 Miller's Court, Dorset Street, a small ground-floor room partitioned off from the rest of the house. He left at 8 p.m. and her movements for the next few hours are uncertain.

At 11.45 p.m. Mary Ann Cox, a prostitute who also lived in Miller's Court, saw Kelly returning home in company of a man. She described him as being in his thirties, stout, shabby, having a blotchy face and a carroty moustache, wearing a billycock hat and carrying a quart can of beer. The pair turned into Miller's Court with Mary Cox behind them. Kelly was very drunk and could barely answer when Cox said goodnight, but managed to tell her she was going to sing. And sing she did, from before midnight to 1 a.m. Her choice was the sentimental ballad, 'Only A Violet I Plucked from My Mother's Grave'. After a few bars of Kelly's refrain Cox went out again, returning just after midnight. She went out once more just after 1 a.m. and when she returned at three the light in Kelly's room was out.[1]

George Hutchinson, a labourer who knew Kelly, told the police that he saw her at 2 a.m. His statement to the police (MEPO 3/140/227-229) read:

About 2 a.m. 9th I was coming by Thrawl Street, Commercial Street, and just before I got to Flower and Dean Street, I met the murdered woman Kelly, and she said to me, Hutchinson will you lend me sixpence. I said I can't I have spent all my money going down to Romford, she said good morning I must go find some money. She went away toward Thrawl Street. A man coming in the opposite direction to Kelly, tapped her on the shoulder and said something to her they both burst out laughing. I heard her say right away alright to him, and the man said you will be alright, for what I have told you: he then placed his right hand around her shoulders. He also had a kind of small parcel in his left hand, with a kind of a strap round it. I stood against the lamp of the Queen's Head Public House, and watched him. They both then came past me and the man hung down his head, with his hat over his eyes. I stooped down and looked him in the face. He looked at me stern. They both went into Dorset Street. I followed them. They stood at the corner of the court for about 3 minutes. He said something to her. She said alright my dear come along you will be comfortable. He then placed his arm on her shoulder and [she] gave him a kiss. She said she had lost her handkerchief. He then pulled his handkerchief a red one and gave it to her. They both went up the Court together. I then went to

---

[1] Greater London Records Office, MJ/SPC/NE 1888, Box 3, Case Paper 19.

the court to see if I could see them but I could not. I stood there for about three quarter of an hour to see if they came out. They did not so I went away.

Circulated to A.S. [All Stations]

Description, age about 34 or 35, height 5ft 6, complexion pale. Dark eyes and eye lashes. Slight moustache curled up each end and dark hair. Very surly looking. Dress, long dark coat, collar and cuffs trimmed astrakhan and a dark jacket under, light waistcoat, dark trousers, dark felt hat turned down in the middle, button boots and gaiters with white buttons, wore a very thick gold chain with linen collar, black tie with horse shoe pin, respectable appearance, walked very sharp, Jewish appearance. Can be Identified.
George Hutchinson.

Although, on the face of it, a prime suspect (George Hutchinson was the last man seen with Mary Kelly before her gruesome death), Hutchinson's (strangely) detailed statement was not only accepted but publicly endorsed by the police as being accurate. We would have to come back to this point later in our quest.

Half an hour after Hutchinson saw Kelly, Sarah Lewis was making her way to 2 Miller's Court to spend the night with a Mrs Keyler. She gave the police a statement in which she said she saw a man standing opposite the court, wearing a wideawake (felt, wide-brimmed) hat. Presumably this was Hutchinson, who at that time said he was still watching out for Kelly and the man with the horseshoe tie-pin. Lewis also saw a woman with a man wearing a round, high hat. She claimed that he was the man who, carrying a black bag, accosted her and a friend in Bethnal Green the previous Wednesday, two nights before the murder.

The *Star* on 10 November reported a Mrs Kennedy's claim that she and her sister were accosted in Bethnal Green on that Wednesday. The man had invited her

to a lonely spot, as he was known here and a policeman

was looking at him. She asserts that no policeman was in sight ... He carried a black bag ... He avoided walking with them and led them into a very dark thoroughfare, inviting them to follow, which they did. He then pushed open a pair of large gates and requested one of them to follow him, remarking 'I only want one of you.' Whereupon the women became suspicious. He acted in a very strange and suspicious manner and refused to leave his bag in the possession of one of the females. Both women became alarmed at his motions and escaped at the same time raising the alarm 'Jack the Ripper'.

She also said that she had seen this same man with a woman in Dorset Street around 3 a.m. on the morning Kelly was killed. This was half an hour after Sarah Lewis's sighting of the man. If Lewis and Kennedy were sisters relating the same incident, why did Kennedy say she was with her 'sister' in Bethnal Green, when Lewis said she had been with her 'friend'? As Paul Begg has suggested, the two stories might have been told by the same person using two different names.

Kelly's landlord was John McCarthy who owned a chandler's shop at the entrance of the arched passage into Miller's Court. At 10.45 a.m. on 9 November he sent his employee, Thomas Bowycr, to collect Kelly's rent, which was six weeks overdue. Bowyer got no reply when he knocked on her door, which he found locked, and went to look through the window. He reached through a broken pane, pulled aside the curtain and a pilot's coat, also hanging over the window, and to his horror saw a sight he would never forget. He returned immediately to McCarthy, who took a look through the window himself. He said later, 'It looked more like the work of a devil than a man.' He sent Bowyer to Commercial Street Police Station, following him a few minutes later, returning to Miller's Court with duty officers.

Kelly's remains were on her bed – except those parts that were on a table at the side. At least she was thought to be Kelly. Her nose and the skin on her face had been removed and Joseph Barnett said, in his deposition to the inquest, that he recognised her by her 'ear and the eyes'.[1] (The ears had been partially severed and Barnett might have been misheard, in which case he could have identified her by the hair and eyes.) Until two weeks before, Barnett had lived with Kelly for eighteen months, had seen her regularly since then, usually to give her some money if he had any, and was clearly still very fond of her.

Kelly's room wasn't broken into immediately because bloodhounds were expected to be brought in. When Superintendent Arnold arrived with news that the dogs were not coming he ordered McCarthy to break in, which he did with a pickaxe at 1.30 p.m.

Two days before her murder, Kelly had bought a candle in McCarthy's chandler's shop. The police found half of it left. One candle in a room provides a very feeble light (about enough to read a book by if the candle is close) and Inspector Abberline speculated – according to *The Times* of 11 November 1888 – that the hat and some clothes, the remains of which were in the grate, had been burnt to provide extra light. Kelly's post-mortem was conducted by Drs Bagster Phillips, Bond and Gordon Brown. Dr Bond's report describes the horrible mutilations.

The body was lying naked in the middle of the bed, the shoulders flat, but the axis of the body inclined to the left ... the head was turned on the left cheek ... The legs were wide apart, the left thigh at right angles to the trunk & the right forming an obtuse angle with the pubes.

The whole of the surface of the abdomen & thighs was removed & the abdominal cavity emptied of its viscera. The breast were [sic] cut off, the arms mutilated by several jagged wounds & the face hacked beyond recognition of the features. The tissues of the neck were severed all round down to the bone.

---

[1] Greater London Records Office, MJ/SPC/NE 1888, Box 3, Case Paper 19.

The viscera were found in various parts viz.: the uterus & Kidneys with one breast under the head, the other breast by the Rt foot, the liver between her feet, the intestines by the right side & the spleen by the left side of the body. The flaps removed from the abdomen and thigh were on a table . . . The face was gashed in all directions the nose, cheeks, eyebrows and ears being partly removed . . . The Pericardium was open below & the heart absent.[1]

What was it about the kidneys? It was probably the removal of these that led to the rumour that the Ripper was a doctor or medical student. They are, after all, 'among the most inaccessible organs'. And I quote those words from *Aid To Bible Understanding* (1975), p991 because – although it seems like a leap in reasoning – an idea came to me and wouldn't go away.

Was it Masonic? Or did it perhaps have a religious significance?

Jehovah [the biblical name of God] knows the makeup of man in the most thorough and intimate manner, therefore He is said to search out and to test out the kidneys, even though his Son also searches the 'inmost thoughts (literally, 'kidneys') and hearts.' [Ps 7:9; Rev. 2:23]. Jehovah can 'refine' the kidneys or 'deepest emotions' of a person . . .[2]

Whether the heart was removed from the body, found by the doctors and put back or removed by the murderer, who took it away with him, was not made clear by Bond, who merely stated that it was absent from the pericardium, the membranous sac that encloses the heart.

Was the heart taken away by the murderer? If it was, then our diary was a fake: 'I took none of it away with me'.

Alternatively, could the diary answer the puzzle that has haunted Ripperologists since the discovery of Dr Bond's report?

---

[1] MEPO 3/3153/15–18.
[2] *Aid To Bible Understanding* (1975), p. 991.

Another conundrum that has led to conflict among historians is the matter of the locked door of Kelly's room. Her lover, Joseph Barnett, told the police that once when Kelly was drunk she broke a window pane (the one through which Thomas Bowyer had first seen Kelly's body). This proved useful, he claimed, because when he lost the only door key they had they were able to secure and unlock the door by reaching through the window for the door bolt.

Why did the police order McCarthy to smash down the door to Kelly's room when they could have unbolted it in the way Kelly and Barnett did, by reaching through the broken window pane? The bolt must have been visible. If McCarthy usually held spare keys to rooms he rented out he may have given Kelly one to her room after her own was lost. Alternatively, she may have found the original lost key. Either way the fact of the matter is perfectly clear: the door had been locked with a key. Indeed, *The Times* of 10 November 1888 said that 'the murderer apparently took the key away with him when he left, as it cannot be found.'

Later, the *Star* on 12 November reported that 'The key of the woman's door has been found . . .'.

The diarist had not made an error here, claiming 'and with the key I did flee', but that did not really surprise me. Barnett's claim that the door was opened from the broken window did, particularly as the police found it necessary to use force to open it. Barnett, like Hutchinson, would have also been a suspect. I would have to look at these two gentleman a little later – and a lot more closely.

The diarist described Kelly as 'young' (she was twenty-five, although some authorities say twenty-four) and says that she 'reminded' him of 'the whore'. It is clear throughout this section that the author is referring to James Maybrick's adulterous wife, Florence (aged twenty-six). He further wrote:

A whores whim
caused Sir Jim,

to cut deeper, deeper and deeper
All did go,
As I did so,
back to the whoring mother.
An initial here and an initial there
will tell of the whoring mother.

A visit to the Black Museum, courtesy of Bill Waddell, then the curator, had resulted in the temporary loan to me of the remaining *original* photographs taken by the police at the time of the Whitechapel murders.

With the diarist's reference to 'an initial here and ... there' in mind, I paid a visit to Direct Communications Design in Chiswick. Their computer technology allowed me to examine the photographs in great detail. It was also the first time anybody outside of Scotland Yard had ever seen the 'other' picture of Mary Kelly, taken from a closer position to the body, but different angle. This picture reveals Mary Kelly's eviscerated abdominal cavity. The light from the gap between the door and door frame can be seen in the background.

It was, however, the published photograph that produced the information we were looking for. After breaking down the photograph into two-inch squares, we would systematically blow each of the squares up. Three-quarters of the way down, to the right of the centre, were marks that stunned us. There was no doubt, the initials 'FM' were clear and precise. The initials of Florence Maybrick, the adulterous wife of James.

Now, hang on a minute. This photograph was not a forgery! It had come from Scotland Yard and had been taken at the time of the murders. If this diary was a modern fake, our mysterious hoaxer had not just been extremely lucky but remarkably observant. Since 1975, when Donald Rumbelow first had the photograph published in his book, *The Complete Jack the Ripper*, nobody had ever noticed these two initials. I was later to learn that Simon Wood had, in 1988, noticed the presence of letters but not the two initials 'FM' together.[1] They would seem to have been marked in blood, but too bold to have been put there by a finger or even a hand. This, of course, assumes that they were put there at the time of the crime, but that would seem a reasonable assumption given the fact that the jury at the inquest on Mary Kelly were taken to the scene of the crime and asked 'to take special notice of the bloodstains on the wall'.

I recalled a sentence written by the diarist: 'I left it there for the fools but they will never find it.' And then another: 'I placed it all over the room.'

What was 'it'?

I was surprised at Philip Sugden's criticism of the diary, referring to this entry. It is, nevertheless, worth examining, to demonstrate how the public can 'misunderstand' information they are given.

Sugden writes, 'We are told that various parts of [Mary Kelly's] body were strewn "all over the room", and that her severed breasts were placed on the bedside table and that the killer took the key of the room away with him. None of these statements are true.'

Really, Mr Sugden? The key and breasts I have already dealt with. The diarist did *not* say that 'various parts of the body were strewn all over the room . . .', did he? The diarist said, 'I placed it all over the room . . . but they will never find it.' Sugden has clearly chosen to interpret the diary in this manner to dismiss it. If the diarist, genuine or hoaxer, wanted his words to reflect Sugden's interpretation, he would hardly have said 'they will never find it'.

Furthermore, Walter Dew, a policeman at the scene of the crime, may have argued with Sugden that parts of the body were all over the room.[2]

Sugden's book is, in my opinion, a most detailed and thorough investigation of the known material that exists of Jack the Ripper. It is spoilt by a weak and unsupported

[1] Paul Begg, Martin Fido and Keith Skinner, *The Jack the Ripper A–Z*, 3rd edition, Headline Books, p. 487.
[2] Walter Dew, *I Caught Crippen* (1938).

attack on the diary, as is demonstrated in a later chapter.

The only organ not accounted for by Dr Bond, in or out of the body, was the heart. It was not the uterus as reported by *The Times* on 10 November 1888.

The bits and pieces of Kelly's body that were all over the floor were swept up and put in a bucket. They were taken, together with the body, to the mortuary.

The *Observer* on 11 November 1888 reported:

> The doctors were engaged some hours yesterday morning at the Mortuary, Shoreditch churchyard, making a post-mortem examination of the body. Every portion of the deceased was fully accounted for, and at the conclusion of the investigation the various pieces were sewn together and placed in the coffin.

The heart was the only organ unaccounted for by Dr Bond. After the media had speculated that one of the organs had been taken away, the majority later disputed the suggestion. On balance, the reports stated as above, 'Every portion of the deceased was fully accounted for.'

The heart may have been in pieces, mixed with the rest of mess. That would explain why Dr Bond did not note it. The heart is symbolic of the human soul, and would be the only organ that the mortician would be justified in 'sewing back together'.

The heart is a very strong organ, as any doctor will tell you, so how could it have been broken into pieces?

Could it be that the diary had given us to a clue to the most rational explanation ever offered for why the media had confirmed that no portion of the body was missing, after Dr Bond had stated 'The heart was absent . . .'?

I wondered. Was the diary genuine? Had James Maybrick used the heart (or 'it') of his victim to scrape on the rough walls of that small room in Miller's Court the initials of his unfaithful wife?

CHAPTER

5

'AND MAY THE LORD HAVE MERCY ON YOUR SOUL'

THE DEATH OF JAMES Maybrick on 11 May 1889 resulted in one of the most famous trials in British history. His young widow, Florence, was the first American-born woman to be charged with murder in this country. Her being found guilty and sentenced to death caused an uproar on both sides of the Atlantic. This trial was, ultimately, partly responsible for the introduction in Britain of the Court of Criminal Appeal.

Could the crimes of Jack the Ripper in that autumn of 1888 in Whitechapel, London, and the 'Maybrick Mystery', as it came to be known, be interwoven? Was it possible that James Maybrick and Jack the Ripper were one and the same?

While I had read a fair bit about the events in the East End of London, I knew little of the Maybrick case.

Florence Elizabeth Maybrick, a pretty southern belle, had descended from a long line of illustrious forebears. She was born in Mobile, Alabama,[1] though Darius Blake Holbrook, her maternal grandfather, was from a Shropshire family. His mother, a Ridgeway, whose family left England for America in 1628, was descended from Richard Ridgeway, brother of Sir Thomas Ridgeway, the first Earl of Londonderry.

---

[1] Florence's date of birth is uncertain. Her 1913 passport application in her own hand gives it as 3 September 1861. Her death certificate gives her birth as 1 September 1862. Her birth certificate was destroyed in the American Civil War.

Florence's father was William G. Chandler, a banker, whose family was among the earliest pioneers in the southern states of America. He died during the American Civil War, after three years of marriage, leaving her mother, Caroline Elizabeth, a nineteen-year-old widow with two children: Florrie and her brother Holbrook St John.

Her paternal grandfather, Daniel Chandler, a lawyer of high standing in Georgia, one-time Assistant Secretary for the Confederacy, and a judge of the Supreme Court of the United States, married Sarah, sister of the Hon. John Campbell, a descendant of the Argyles.[1]

Florrie's maternal great-uncles, the Reverend Joseph Ingraham and his brother John, were known for their religious works and traced their family back to the life of Edward II.

Florrie's widowed mother married her second husband, Captain Franklin du Barry, so that she could nurse him with propriety after his fateful wounding during the bombardment of Charleston during the Civil War. He was the grandson of Benjamin Franklin and the son of Count du Barry, who was known to and admired by Emperor Napoleon III and the Empress Eugenie.[2] To escape the war Caroline du Barry took her children to Europe to be educated.

When Florence met James Maybrick, her mother was married to her third husband, Baron Adolph von Roques, a Prussian cavalry officer in the Eighth Cuirassier Regiment of the German Army, stationed at Cologne.

Before her marriage Florrie was fond of tracing intricate designs and drawing churches and cathedrals. Her real passion, however, was riding.

James Maybrick came from humbler origins. The

---

[1] According to the 1850 Federal Census for Mobile, Daniel Chandler was forty-four in that year.
[2] The family history is taken from Florence's mother's petition to Queen Victoria. HO 144 1639, A50678D/57, and from page 15 of Florence's own story, *My Fifteen Lost Years* (1909).

Maybricks hailed originally from the West Country. One branch of the family, like many country folk during the Industrial Revolution, removed themselves to a large city, in their case London, settling in Whitechapel and Stepney in the heart of the East End. By the late 1760s unemployment forced them to seek work elsewhere and they moved to Liverpool, which was becoming a thriving prosperous port, owing mainly to the import of American cotton for the Lancashire mills.

James, the third of seven children, all boys, was born on 24 October 1838 and christened at St Peter's Parish Church in the heart of Liverpool. The parish clerk there was James's grandfather. He died when James was six and was succeeded as parish clerk by James's father, William, a twin, and a copperplate engraver by trade. Little is known about the Maybricks' parents, William and Susanna, or the boys' upbringing, their schooling or the larger influences that forged their futures. Of James's six brothers, two did not survive to adulthood. One brother, James, was his namesake and died in 1837 at the age of four months. Alfred Maybrick died at the age of four in 1848.

In 1874, at the age of thirty-six, James went to Norfolk, Virginia, where he started the American end of his transatlantic cotton business. In 1877 he contracted malaria and was prescribed quinine, which proved ineffective. A second prescription of arsenic and strychnine was soon dispensed and thereafter he took both regularly.

James Maybrick had become addicted to drugs inadvertently.

Many brokers on the Exchange in Liverpool habitually popped into chemist shops for pick-me-ups containing arsenic as a tonic. When James returned there, from Virginia, his cousin William, who worked for a wholesale chemist, supplied his pernicious need. When William was sacked, James turned to Edwin Heaton, his chemist in Exchange Street, who supplied him over a ten-year period, increasing the doses from four to seven drops. He sometimes went there five times a day, consuming, in liquid form, one-third of a grain in total. One grain is enough to kill. Mindful of his continuous needs, James had Heaton make up large quantities for him to take away on business trips.

James fell in love with Florence Chandler when they met aboard the SS *Baltic*, travelling first class from New York to Liverpool in March 1880. She was eighteen and accompanied by her mother, Baroness von Roques, and her brother Holbrook. James was alone and forty-one.

Perhaps in James she found the father figure she had never known. Whatever the attraction was that the portly middle-aged cotton merchant held for Florence, she had accepted his proposal of marriage by the time their ship docked in Liverpool.

On 4 July 1881 – American Independence Day – James was granted a family crest, and just over three weeks later, on 27 July, he and Florrie were married at St James's Church, Piccadilly. James's address on the marriage certificate reads simply 'St James's', rather than an address in his home town, Liverpool.[1] Clearly he lodged there – probably in a hotel – perhaps in order to ensure that 'St James's' appeared on his marriage certificate. Florrie was given away by her brother Holbrook, who travelled from France, where he was studying medicine.

James's nickname for his bride was 'Bunny'.

On 1 November that year Florrie wrote to F.L. Armstrong, her solicitor in Kentucky, who was dealing with a land claim. She ended the letter: 'The Baroness von Roques trusts to your honour and discretion with regard to any "private matters" she may have confided to you and as my husband is quite ignorant of her personal affairs I must beg of you only to give information in reference to the Virginia claim and on no others.'

Clearly, Florence and/or her mother had skeletons in the cupboard.

Soon after their marriage, James and Florence returned

---

[1] The 1881 census, taken on 3 April, lists Maybrick as a guest at the Adelphi Hotel, the most upmarket and fashionable hotel in Liverpool.

to America, making their home for a short while in Norfolk. For the next two years they spent half their time in Liverpool and half in Virginia.

The Maybricks first child, James Chandler, known affectionately as 'Bobo' and sometimes 'Sonny', was born in Liverpool on 24 March 1882 at 5 Livingstone Avenue. His birth, a difficult one for Florrie, was registered by James, without his forenames. Their second child, Gladys Evelyn, was born on 20 July 1885, at Beechville, a house in Grassendale, which James rented from Mrs Matilda Briggs, the estranged wife of Thomas Briggs and one of three Janion sisters who were family friends.

By 1884 James had an office at 32 Knowsley Buildings, Tithebarn Street, where he employed George Smith as a bookkeeper and Thomas Lowry as a clerk. It was near both the Cotton Exchange and the Stock Exchange.

Late in 1884 Holbrook St John Chandler went down with consumption and he died in Paris the following April. Victorian convention forbade women at funerals, so Florrie did not attend and James travelled to France alone.

In 1887 scarlet fever, called black scarlet fever, raged through Liverpool and Bobo was seized with it. To protect one-year-old Gladys, James took her to Wales for six weeks, accompanied by the children's nurse Emma Parker.[1] They probably stayed at the Hand Hotel, Llangollen, where James and Florrie, along with Gertrude Janion, stayed for a week during the previous April.[2]

In August 1887 Florrie was concerned about the nurse, Emma Parker. In an undated letter to her mother she wrote:

Nurse is quite changed since baby's birth. Poor little mite. It gets neither petting nor coaxing when I am not with it and for every cross word that nurse says to her. I cannot understand why she does not take to the child.

----

[1] Interview with Baroness von Roques, *Liverpool Echo*, 14 August 1889.
[2] This is confirmed by an entry in the Hand Hotel register dated 3–10 April 1886, deposited with the County Record Office, Ruthin, North Wales.

I am afraid she is getting too old for a young baby and has not the forbearance and patience to look after Gladys. When she had Bobo with her it was a labour of love ... with poor Gladys it is a labour of duty only.[1]

Another nurse was sought. She was found in the person of Alice Yapp, who was employed by a family by the name of Gibson in Birkdale, Southport. Convention held that household staff were interviewed and hired by the wife; it was virtually unthinkable that the husband should concern himself with such domestic matters. Also, the prospective employee would be expected to go to the employer's home for the interview, and not the other way round. And yet, despite this, James travelled to Birkdale to engage and hire the twenty-six-year-old nurse.

James's perceived success as a businessman was reflected in his lifestyle: he joined the fashionable Palatine Club, where he often dined with his best friend, George Davidson, and became a Freeman of the City of Liverpool. Florrie and James enjoyed going out together in their horse and carriage, and liked to play whist. Their shared passion, however, was racing and every year they attended the Grand National at Liverpool's Aintree.

In February 1888 the Maybricks moved into a large rented house in Riversdale Road, Aigburth, a suburb south of Liverpool populated by wealthy merchants and shipping owners. Opposite the house is the Liverpool Cricket Club, where James and his younger brother Michael were members. The ground could be seen from the first-floor windows of the house, aptly named Battlecrease.

Battlecrease was surrounded by flower beds and lawns, had stables at the rear and a driveway to the front door that went around a small ornamental pool stocked with fish. It stood about three hundred yards from the Mersey, which could be seen from the front gate. In the corner of

---

[1] Reproduced from *Etched in Arsenic* (1969), by Trevor Christie, p. 46.

the garden was a small gate opening on to the path down which James walked directly to the nearby railway station to catch the train to work. The household staff comprised James Grant, the gardener, who married a former housemaid, Alice Jones; a maid, Mary Cadwallader, known as 'Gentle Mary'; and the children's nurse, Alice Yapp. Later in the year Elizabeth Humphreys joined as cook and Bessie Brierley joined as a housemaid. All the staff wore smart uniforms.

Florrie, however, had discovered that James had a mistress and by July 1888 the Maybricks were sleeping in separate rooms.

In August 1888 James's youngest brother, Edwin, went to Virginia to take care of the American end of Maybrick and Company's cotton business.

The murders in Whitechapel had begun in August 1888.

The Maybricks gave frequent dinner parties and dances, and at an earlier one, in 1887, Florrie had met Alfred Brierley (no relation to the housemaid), a cotton broker and business acquaintance of James's. After a dance in November 1888 Brierley, thirty-six years old, tall and slim, bearded, unmarried and attractive, became more intimate with Florence Maybrick.

On 19 November James went to see Dr Drysdale, complaining of attacks of pain from side to side of his head, a creeping all over his head, preceded by pains on the right side, and a dull headache. He had had these for three months and was never free from pain except in the early morning, and sometimes in the forenoon. He consulted Drysdale again on 22 and 26 November and 5 and 10 December. In December he also consulted the family doctor, Arthur Hopper, who had attended Florrie during her confinements.

The period in which James suffered these pains covered the precise period of the Jack the Ripper crimes in Whitechapel, London.

James's brother Michael, an enormously successful musician who lived in a stuccoed Nash terrace in London's Regent's Park, visited Battlecrease just before Christmas

1888. He suggested to James that he consult his London doctor, Charles Fuller.

James had gone away for Christmas but was back home by the end of the month. According to Florence, in a letter to her mother dated 31 December 1888, 'In his [James's] fury he tore up his will this morning.'[1]

In January 1889 James met Valentine Blake. Knowing that James dealt in cotton, Blake asked his advice on importing ramie, a Chinese and East Indian plant of the nettle family, and the fine fibre made from it. This is a substitute for cotton but four times stronger. Blake happened to mention that arsenic was used in the manufacture of ramie and James obtained Blake's promise that he would get some for him. A few weeks later he gave him about three hundred grains. Blake said later, 'I told him to be careful with it as he had enough to poison a regiment.'

Between 23 and 26 February 1889 James, his friend George Davidson and three other men stayed at the Hand Hotel in Llangollen, North Wales.[2] The following month the two children had whooping cough, a serious and often life-threatening condition before the advent of antibiotics. They were attended by Dr Humphreys and at some point during one of his visits Florrie told him that James was taking a white powder. That same month she wrote to Michael Maybrick telling him the same thing.

On 7 March James consulted Dr Drysdale for the last time. He was still complaining of headaches along with numbness in his hands and legs; and complained that his tongue was a little furred.[3]

On 16 March Florrie telegraphed Flatman's Hotel in London's Cavendish Square and Henrietta Street to reserve a sitting room and bedroom for Thursday the 21st

---

[1] *Etched in Arsenic* (1969), by Trevor Christie, p. 49.
[2] This is confirmed by an entry in the Hand Hotel register dated 3 to 10 April 1886, deposited with the County Record Office, Ruthin, North Wales.
[3] *The Necessity For Criminal Appeal*, J.H. Levy (1899), p. 228.

and Thursday the 28th. She booked them in the name of Mr and Mrs Thomas Maybrick. The following day she wrote to them confirming the reservation and suggesting the kind of dinner they would like. She wrote again the next day saying that Mrs Maybrick would arrive on the 21st and stay for a week. On 19 March both Florrie and James told Dr Hopper that Florrie was going to London to accompany her aunt, Countess de Gabrielle, on a visit to Sir James Paget, the surgeon. The following day a John Baillie Knight received a letter from Florrie asking him to meet her at Flatman's on the 21st. She arrived there at 1 p.m. and Baillie Knight arrived at 6 p.m. She told him James was cruel, had struck her, was keeping a woman in Liverpool and that she was in London to consult a solicitor regarding plans for a separation. They dined at the Grand Hotel before going to the theatre.

When Baillie Knight called upon Florrie the following day he was told that she was out. That evening she dined with Alfred Brierley and later moved into the hotel rooms 8, 16 and 21 in Henrietta Street. They slept in the same bedroom, room 21.

Despite sharing Florrie's bed, Brierley had the poor grace to tell her about his attachment to another woman, which probably accounts for their leaving the hotel abruptly the next morning. Brierley paid the bill: £2 0s 13d (£2.05).

John Baillie Knight later saw her to the home of his aunt, Miss Baillie Knight, where she stayed the night. The next day Miss Baillie Knight took Florrie to see the solicitor, Markby, of Markby Stewart and Company, in Cursitor Street, London.

That evening Michael Maybrick took her to dine at the Café Royal and later they went to the theatre.

Florence returned to Liverpool in time for the Grand National. On that morning, 29 March, James left the house as if going to his office as usual.

Around 9 or 10 a.m. Bessie Brierley saw Florrie leaving the house in a cab, accompanied by her friend, Mrs Holden.

Later, an omnibus waited outside James's office to take a party to the races. The party included James, Florrie, a family friend, Christina Samuelson, and Alfred Brierley.

The Prince of Wales graced Aintree to mark the fiftieth anniversary of the Grand National, and, after the race was won by Frigate, James saw Brierley walking arm in arm with Florrie.

James and Florrie arrived home separately, and James was furious, shouting at her, 'Such a scandal will be all over town tomorrow. I never thought it would come to this.'

A furious row continued in the bedroom and James told the servant, Bessie, to get a cab for Florrie and send her away. Florrie, wearing a fur cape, came down to leave. The buttonholes of her dress had been torn. James refused to let her go in the cape, complaining that he bought it for her to go to London. Bessie pleaded with him, 'Oh master, please don't go on like this. The neighbours will hear you.'

James replied, 'Leave me alone. You don't know anything about it.'

Bessie pleaded, 'Don't send the mistress away tonight. Where can she go? Let her stay until morning.'

James shouted, 'By heavens, Florrie, if you cross this doorstep you shall never enter it again.'

And with that he fell exhausted across the hall settle. The cab was sent away and James spent the night in the dining room.

Next morning Florrie awoke with a black eye. She went to see Matilda Briggs to tell her about the quarrel and seek advice. They went to see Dr Hopper. Florrie confided to him that James had beaten her, that she was up all the previous night, that she could not bear to sleep with James, and that she was off to see a solicitor.

Just before noon Bessie Brierley found fly papers soaking in the bedroom. Florrie was there at the time. After noon Dr Hopper arrived to see the children.

Before 4 o'clock tea Bessie told Alice Yapp about the fly papers. The following day Bessie found bits of fly paper in the wash basin. Later, Dr Hopper called on James and Florrie to discuss Florrie's health and some debts she had incurred, which James promised to honour.

Next day, 1 April, Hopper visited Florrie and found her hysterical in bed. James had been questioning her about her trip to London and they both told him that she went there to visit her aunt, Countess de Gabrielle. By the time he left he believed that the couple had fully reconciled their differences.

Five days later, on Saturday, 6 April, Florrie went to meet Brierley. Some time after the 6th Brierley received two letters from Florrie, which he destroyed.

Some time prior to 13 April, when James visited Michael in London, he had written to him that he could not understand the nature of his illness and that should it prove fatal his body should be subjected to medical examination. The following day Florrie went to Dr Hopper complaining that she was not feeling right internally. He was on his way out and had no time to examine her.

The following day in London James consulted Dr Fuller for his health, and paid off Florrie's creditors, whoever they may have been. While he was in London he received a pleading letter from Florrie. It ended:

> Darling try and be as lenient towards me as you can. For notwithstanding all your generous and tender loving kindness my burden is almost more than I can bear. My remorse and self contempt is eating my heart out and if I did not believe my love for you and my dutifulness may prove some slight atonement for the past I should give up the struggle to keep brave.
> Forgive me dearest, and think less poorly of your own wifesy.
>
> Bunny

And it added a PS: 'I hope you are well. I have been nowhere and seen no one.'

James returned to Liverpool on Monday, 15 April. He

felt much better and was back in his office on Tuesday. Two days later he telegraphed Dr Fuller for an appointment and received confirmation of it.

On Saturday Florrie bought some fly papers and James went to London for a 3 o'clock appointment with Dr Fuller, returning on Monday to Liverpool, where he went to the chemist, Clay and Abraham, to have two of Fuller's prescriptions made up.

The next Thursday, 25 April, James's brother Edwin returned from America. James Maybrick's will was also dated that day.

James's clerk, Thomas Lowry, thought that James seemed in good health. Next day a parcel of medicine arrived from London, which Mary Cadwallader took up to James. Later James met with Edwin at the office. That evening Edwin dined at Battlecrease but, as James was unable to eat solid food, he took his meal separately, in the breakfast room, eating the light food ordered by the doctor.

The next morning, after taking an overdose of medicine containing strychnine, James complained that his stomach was playing havoc with him. His limbs were stiff and he was unable to move properly.

Later, Bessie Brierley saw husband and wife descending the stairs together, James saying that his feet and legs were dead to the knees.

At 10.30 the next morning, 27 April, James was back in his office. Back home, Florrie informed Alice Yapp that James had taken an overdose of medicine and that he was very sick. Between noon and 1 p.m. James went home for his horse, went down to the ferry, crossed over the Mersey and rode over to the Wirral races in a continuous drizzle. He arrived wet and shaking and when he met his friend William Thompson he told him that he had taken a double dose of medicine that morning. Thompson noted that James had difficulty remaining in his saddle. Later, when he met the wife of an old friend from America, Mrs Morden Rigg, he told her he had taken a double dose of strychnine.

Despite being soaked to the skin, he later dined with some other friends, the Hobsons. They noted that he was so ill that he could hardly hold his glass, and he spilt his wine.

He was even worse next morning and both the nurse and the servant could see that he was ill. Florrie gave James a mustard emetic, and Bessie gave him a hot-water bottle. He told Florrie that he felt dizzy after taking the double dose of 'London' medicine.

Dr Humphreys was sent for and James said he became ill after taking a cup of tea at breakfast. When Edwin arrived, James was on the sofa, and he told him how he had become ill the previous day. James went to bed at 8 o'clock and Edwin sat with Florrie in the breakfast room talking for an hour. Around 9 p.m., James complained of numbness in his legs, which Edwin rubbed until Dr Humphreys arrived a second time. He gave James a morphia suppository.

On the evening of 29 April, Edwin escorted Florrie to a private domino ball in Wavertree. He stayed the night at Battlecrease.

On 1 May, James arrived at the office between 10.30 and 11 a.m., and a little later Edwin arrived. James left the office around 5 o'clock and was visited at home by Dr Humphreys at 6.30 p.m.

Edwin dined with them, and Captain Irving of the White Star Line was there too. He remarked to Edwin how ill James looked. Edwin said that it was on account of the strychnine he took.

The next day, 2 May, James was back at the office with some food that was prepared at home. After lunch he felt very ill. He went home between 4 and 5 p.m. Edwin slept at Waterloo, in Liverpool.

On 3 May, Dr Humphreys called again at Battlecrease and James went to the office at 11 a.m. Sometime during the day James went to the Turkish bath. At 4.45 p.m. Dr Humphreys met James at the station. They had both missed their trains. James finally arrived home at 5.30 p.m. feeling ill, and Florrie told Bessie Brierley to prepare a hot-water bottle for him. It was the last day th[...] James Maybrick would go to his office in Tithebarn Stree[...]

It was also the day that the last entry in the purporte[...] diary of Jack the Ripper was signed.

Later, on 3 May, Florrie met Alice Yapp on the stairs and told her that James was ill again and Yapp suggested sending for the doctor. He was called around midnight.

The doctor called again at noon the next day, 4 May, and advised James not to take anything by mouth, as he was unable to retain even water. Later, the chemist's delivery boy arrived with some medicine and the cook Elizabeth Humphreys put it in the master bedroom. When Florrie saw it she became angry with Humphreys, saying that she should not leave any medicine unless she see it first. She told her that if James took that much more of the London medicine he would be a dead man.

Dr Humphreys called next morning, 5 May, and found James feeling better but advised him to take no fluids except, if possible, a little iced water. The doctor told Florrie to obtain a second opinion and, according to Florrie, he told her that James was dangerously ill.

Edwin visited and stayed the night.

The next morning, his clerk Thomas Lowry arrived from the office with some letters and gave them to the cook. She took them and a telegram to James, who told her to send Lowry up to him. He stayed for ten minutes while James signed some papers. Florrie went off to Liverpool.

During the next day, 7 May, Florrie sent Cadwallader to telegraph Edwin, asking him to bring his own doctor. Later that day he telephoned Dr William Carter and arranged for him to consult with Dr Humphreys at 5.30 p.m. Edwin met them at the house.

The family friend, Matilda Briggs, received a telegram from James's brother Michael, informing her that his brother was ill and asking her to call at Battlecrease.

Alice Yapp claims that at 8.30 p.m. she saw Florrie on the landing with two medicine bottles. She was pouring the contents of one into the other.

The following day, 8 May, around noon, Alice Yapp met Mrs Briggs and her sister Mrs Hughes. Alice Yapp said, 'Thank God, Mrs Briggs, you have come, for the mistress is poisoning the master.'

Michael Maybrick received three telegrams: two from Edwin and one from Mrs Briggs.

What happened next is crucial to this account.

At 3 p.m. Alice Yapp was sent to the post office by Florence Maybrick with a letter addressed to Alfred Brierley. The letter was dropped in the mud by the Maybricks' two-year-old daughter, Gladys, who was with Alice Yapp. The nurse opened it, to put it in a clean envelope, and inadvertently read it. She immediately gave it to Edwin Maybrick.

Well, that was her story and she stuck to it, and so did Edwin – almost.

Michael Maybrick, James's younger and more successful brother, arrived from London at around 8.30 p.m. He had been met at the station by Edwin, who had sent him two telegrams.

Michael Maybrick claimed that at 2 p.m. on 10 May he saw Florrie changing labels on the medicine bottles.

James was much worse on 11 May. His children were taken in to see him. Florrie was in her dressing room all day, prostrate.

The same day, Dr Carter told Michael and Dr Humphreys that he found a metallic poison in James's meat juice.

That night James Maybrick died.

Did Jack the Ripper die with him?

The funeral was on Thursday, 16 May 1889.

On 19 May, Florence Maybrick was formally charged in her bedroom and left locked up in it. The charge was murder, and she was taken to Walton Prison.

On 31 July 1889, the trial of Florence Elizabeth Maybrick opened in the court of St George's Hall, Liverpool. The judge was Sir James Fitzjames Stephen. Mrs Maybrick's defence team was lead by Sir Charles Russell.

When Dr Humphreys was called to the stand, he was asked what was, in his opinion, the cause of Mr Maybrick's death.

'Acute congestion of the stomach,' he answered.

With great deliberation, Russell asked Humphreys to mention any post-mortem symptom distinctive of arsenical poisoning but not also distinctive of gastric illness or gastro-enteritis (inflammation of the bowels).

'I cannot. I could not swear to distinguishing between the two,' said the doctor. When asked about the prisoner's treatment of her husband, he replied that she was very attentive, and did everything he had asked her to do.

On the third day of the trial Inspector Baxendale detailed the findings of the poisoned articles and vessels found at Battlecrease.

The evidence of Dr McNamarra, chief consulting physician to Dublin Leek Hospital, agreed with Dr Tidy, a previous witness, that the cause of death was gastro-enteritis. He said, 'I agree with Dr Tidy, but I go beyond him in my belief.'

Dr Frank R. Paul, Professor of Medical Jurisprudence at University College, Liverpool, and examiner in toxicology at Victoria University, said his opinion was that Maybrick died from gastro-enteritis. He based this on his experience of between two and three thousand post-mortems.

Another expert said that arsenic found in the stew pan, and alleged to have been put in the food sent down to her husband by Mrs Maybrick, could have come from the enamel on the pan. The enamel, he said, contained arsenic. Florence added that she was in total ignorance of the charge against her and that 'for the sake of our children . . . a perfect reconciliation had taken place and that the day before he died I made a full and free confession of the fearful wrong I had done.'

On 5 August Mrs Maybrick was allowed to make a statement in which she said that she sometimes used a facial wash for her complexion, and had soaked fly papers to obtain the arsenic that this cosmetic required. She needed the cosmetic for some eruptions on her face that she wanted to remove before a forthcoming ball. She had, unfortunately, lost the prescription that she obtained from New York. (The prescription was found in Florence's Bible after the trial.)

On 7 August the jury returned after an absence of a mere thirty-five minutes. The verdict: guilty.

The judge put on the familiar black cap. 'Prisoner at the bar,' he intoned, 'I am no further able to treat you as being innocent of the dreadful crime laid to your charge. You have been convicted by a jury of this city, after a lengthy and most painful investigation, followed by a defence which was in every respect worthy of the name.' The law, he said, left him no alternative. Florence Maybrick would be taken back to her cell, 'and from there to the place of execution and . . . you [will] be there hanged by the neck until you are dead; and . . . your body [will] be afterwards buried within the precincts of the prison in which you shall have been confined after your conviction. And may the Lord have mercy on your soul.'

At the beginning of the trial public opinion had been against Florence. By the end of it few people considered her guilty. When the verdict became known outside St George's Hall there were load groans and hooting from the crowd, and for a long time afterwards large groups were assembled in Lime Street.

The judge's carriage drew up outside the north entrance to the court and a mob of at least a thousand people ran after it as it drove away up Islington, hooting and jeering at its occupant.

As he was driven away, Florence Maybrick was being led back to her confinement – and my story began.

CHAPTER

6

'SCIENCE DATES THE DOCUMENT TO A HISTORICALLY IMPOSSIBLE PERIOD'
– Martin Fido 1993

AS WE SAW EARLIER, Kenneth Rendell had been involved with the Hitler Diaries exposure. His team of experts on the Ripper diary investigation included Robert L. Kuranz, a research ink chemist, and Rod McNeil who had apparently worked for the FBI and the American secret service. Rod McNeil claimed that his ion migration test could date when ink was put on paper. On 20 August 1993 Robert Smith flew to America with the diary and met Rendell's team in Chicago.

The report that Kenneth Rendell submitted to Time-Warner Books in 1993 concluded that the diary was written in or around 1921. Martin Fido responded: 'Science dates the document to a historically impossible period.'

Another Ripper writer, Colin Wilson, commented on the results: 'That proves the diary is genuine.'

Kenneth Rendell informed Warner's that he believed the diary was a forgery.

Martin Fido and Colin Wilson, although they came to different conclusions, based their analyses on the same premise: that the diary was either a very modern forgery or it was genuine. They had, correctly, taken into account the internal evidence of the document. Rendell had not.

Martin Fido elaborated. Speaking on Radio 4's *Kaleidoscope* programme on 9 September 1993, he said, 'Personally I don't believe that the journal is genuine at all . . . In this case one can say it was certainly not forged in 1921. However, the whole shape of the case is either genuine or derived from post-war books, and, more importantly still, it describes Catherine Eddowes' matchbox among her possessions as being empty and made of tin [see the later chapter, Evidence Has Been Withheld . . .]. This undoubted fact was not in the public domain until 1987 so the journal is either genuine or a very modern forgery.'

Kenneth Rendell's conclusions required further analysis. In his report, he stated:

> We were all very suspicious of the fact that approximately 20 pages at the beginning of the book had been torn out. There are no logical explanations as to why the purported author, Maybrick, a man of means, would have done this. First of all, he would have bought a normal, Victorian diary, but if for some reason he wanted to use a scrapbook he would have bought a new one. He would be unlikely to take one he already had and tear out the contents.

At the front of the diary were several missing pages. They had clearly been deliberately cut out. Rendell's statement is almost mocking, and displays that he was unable to comment without bias.

If the diary was genuine, then we could not know where it had been for over a hundred years. Whoever owned it during that period may have been responsible for cutting out the missing pages. Perhaps with good reason. Rendell's speculation is what Keith Skinner would describe as a 'leap'. Rendell's conclusions that the diary had been used before Maybrick began his journal, and that the missing pages were his handiwork, was completely irrational.

Rendell also commented on the provenance of the diary, stating that 'it took over 100 years to find the diary despite its author stating "I place this now in a place where it shall be found"'.

Astonishing. I accept that the provenance was weak. Mike Barrett's story that he got it from Tony Devereux, however, could have been true. For all Kenneth Rendell knew, Tony or his wife or mother or aunt may have been a descendant of James Maybrick.

If the diary was real, then it had not just 'turned up'.

My research team seriously questioned the apparent superficial thinking behind some of Rendell's observations. Warner Books were having to make a decision on whether they were going to publish the diary based on this report. Rendell continued:

> More startling is the paragraph of Dr Forshaw's report [Dr David Forshaw holds a diploma in the history of medicine from the Society of Apothecaries] . . . 'In view of the detail of the Journal and the insights into the most likely psychopathology of serial killers contained within, it would seem, to me anyway, that the most likely options are that it is either genuine or a modern fake . . .' After I read Dr Forshaw's report, its importance in establishing the diary's authenticity was severely diminished. I decided that having two noted forensic psychiatrists who specialise in serial killers review the text . . . would be unnecessary.

Why was it diminished? Dr Forshaw had not arrived at his conclusion based on the same evidence as had convinced the historians.

Rendell was 'surprised that the diary was written in a scrapbook, not a normal diary book. Scrapbooks, much larger in format and containing very absorbent heavy paper, were used for mounting postcards, photographs, valentines, and other greeting cards, and I had not previously encountered one used as a diary. It was possible but very unlikely.'

Rendell did not explain how he had ascertained that the leather-bound book was a scrapbook. It does not resemble the scrapbook in which Inspector Abberline had kept press cuttings and handwritten notes; nor does it compare to Alexander MacDougall's book of press cuttings with handwritten notes, which as I write is in my possession. (Alexander MacDougall, a barrister, had, in 1891, been the first author to identify the relationship of James Maybrick and a woman called Sarah Ann Robertson. We'll come to her later.)

Rendell said, 'I had not previously encountered one used as a diary.' He failed, however, to give even one example of ever having seen a book similar to the Maybrick diary, and describe what it was used for.

Does Rendell mean, when he says 'a normal diary book', a book with dates? If so, why the surprise? The text does not purport to have been written on a daily basis.

Commending the report on the diary by the ink expert Dr Nicholas Eastaugh, Rendell stated that his tests were 'very competently carried out ... His findings that there are no elements in the ink that are inconsistent with a date of 1888 is correct.'

One claim made by some critics, repeated by Rendell, was that it is 'relatively easy today to obtain or make ink with elements that were used in Victorian England'.

So Mr Kuranz, employed or consulted by Kenneth Rendell, confirmed Nicholas Eastaugh's findings that the ink is of Victorian age. Rendell did not find, as he expected he would, any evidence of a modern ink. He attempts to overcome this with a claim of 'relatively easy'.

Is it?

Nicholas Eastaugh confirmed that you could buy a bottle of unopened Victorian ink, but it would not be usable. Easy to make it? I am sure that everyone reading this book could do it tomorrow, and avoid the detection of scientific analysis. Just look it up in a book, folks? I think not.

Rendell also said in his report that 'what is not reported is that [Eastaugh] stressed as early as October 1992 that other major tests needed to be done as well.'

Rendell does not quote his source. In June 1993, Paul Begg asked Dr Eastaugh whether 'every reasonable test' had been done. The answer was yes. Dr Eastaugh did say that further tests could be done to try to establish when the ink was applied to the paper. He could not, however, guarantee that these tests would give a definitive result. Moreover he could not be sure that they would determine whether or not the ink had been applied since 1987.

Who would want to bother financing expensive

procedures that, even the expert was saying, could never be conclusive?

According to Rendell 'the writing [of the diary] is not consistent with the letter formations of the late 1880s; there is a uniformity of ink and slant of writing . . . that is unnatural and very indicative of a forger writing multiple entries at one time. A lack of variation in layout also leads one to the same conclusion.'

There is no doubt that multiple entries were made at one time. However, a study of the text indicates that those entries display a pattern. The author writes when he purports to be angry with his wife. In these entries he is 'planning' his campaign. The other entries were written after he purported to have committed his crime.

The entries are not willy-nilly.

As for as the writing and its inconsistency with Victorian letter formations, the letter on page 97, sent to Dr Forbes Winslow at the time of the Whitechapel murders, displays exactly the same kind of formations as were used in the diary.

On page 10 of his report, Rendell summarises the result of Rod McNeil's ion migration analysis, which indicated a date of composition of the diary between 1909 and 1933.

My understanding of Rod McNeil's ion migration test was that, by using a scanning auger microscope, he could measure the distance that the iron used in old ink moves along the fibre in the paper upon which the ink has been written. I wondered if the temperature and humidity under which a document had been kept affected the outcome of his tests. Also, could the results be affected if a document had been moved from one environment to another? I decided to telephone Rod McNeil.

One of the phrases he used, as I recall, was 'under normal circumstances'. So I asked him what was normal. Is what's normal for one place, let's say sunny California, the same as what is normal for a damp port like Liverpool? His oral answer was confirmed in a statement he sent me dated 14 October 1993:

Thus far, neither myself or any other member of the forensic community (of whom I'm aware) that has used the technique has discovered any short term environmental variable that might influence the rate of ion migration (effects such as temperature or humidity). As we discussed, it *may* be possible that long term storage of the document · retarded ion movement, thereby creating a later date than the test should otherwise indicate, but I have no experimental evidence to suggest whether this is possible or probable. A control study of this proposed hypothesis would require 20+ years to evaluate.

In other words, as it stands now, no one knows whether the differences in humidity and temperature can affect the dating of a document using an ion migration test. Well, I wasn't going to wait twenty years or more to publish this book.

There was, however, something more telling and important in McNeil's statement: 'It is my strong opinion based on the auger-stms results that the document is not new.'

The scientists whose services Kenneth Rendell had utilised had both, at the very least, concluded that they could not find anything that suggested the diary was modern. Rendell himself believed that the handwriting was of an early-twentieth-century style, not a late-Victorian one. The conclusion of his report was that the diary was an early-twentieth-century forgery.

The Time-Warner Books' response to Rendell's report was to pull out of their intended deal with Smith Gryphon and within days banner-headlines crying 'Fake' appeared around the world.

At some point Melvin Harris, the author of two Ripper books, contacted Rendell to give his opinion on the diary. He believed from the outset that it must be a modern fake, as some of the internal detail in the diary was not known by historians until the late 1980s. Indeed, Harris bellowed this from the rooftops. At the beginning of November

22 Hammersmith Rᵈ
Chelsea.

Oct 29ᵗʰ 88

Sir
        I defy you to find out
who has done the Whitechapel
murder in the summer not
the last one   You had
better look out for yourself
a else Jack the R may
do you. something is your
house to before the end of
this mends now the 5ᵗʰ of Nov there
may be another murder so
look out old siʳ pencil funk funk
tell all London another Jripper ghen
will take place some one told me
about the 8ᵗʰ or 9 of Proximo not in
whitechapel but in London
perhaps in Clapham or the
West End. Write to the Poste
shante Chering X. address
to P S R Lenigi.

        to Oct 19ᵗʰ.

97

1993, Rendell was inferring in a letter that Harris knew who forged the diary and that the bellicose author would announce this in his next Ripper book.[1]

Poor old Rendell was now stuck firmly on the horns of a dilemma, faced, as he was, with two sets of opinions. On the one hand there were historians and authors who, like Harris, believed the diary was a modern fake, and on the other hand was the scientific evidence from his own people saying it was written in 1921 – plus or minus a dozen years. Confronted with the opinions of those who knew more about the Ripper crimes than he did, he was unprepared to debate how the information had come about, and where it had come from. If not one Ripperologist could, then how could he?

Oh dear.

Now, Mr Rendell could accept the reasonable possibility that the unknown conditions that the diary were kept in may have been responsible for the twenty missing years. But by now Warner Books had pulled out of their deal with Smith Gryphon Ltd.

Oh dear.

Imagine our surprise when, on publication of his aptly titled book, *Forging History* (University of Oklahoma Press, 1994) Kenneth Rendell wrote that it 'was written very recently, probably within a year before its announced "discovery" . . .'.

The statement was, like many of Mr Rendell's, unsupported. He makes no attempt to explain how he has discarded the results of the scientists he employed.

Elsewhere in his book, Rendell stated categorically that 'Every area of examination indicated or proved the diary was a hoax.'

What *proved* it, Mr Rendell? If there was just one piece of evidence, why were you changing your mind from a 1921 to a 1991 forgery? Who forged it? When? And, most importantly, how?

---

[1] A letter from Kenneth Rendell to Christopher T. George, dated 4 November 1993.

I requested from Rendell copies of the full reports provided to him by the team he employed. He declined his assistance.

In October 1994, I commissioned Martin Fido to prepare a detailed critical analysis of the Rendell report and Martin subsequently wrote to Kenneth Rendell on 9 November 1994:

> Dear Mr Rendell
>
> Mr Paul Feldman, owner of the film rights to the alleged 'Jack the Ripper Diary', has been continuing research on the subject (making some very interesting discoveries along the way) and has now made arrangements with a publisher to bring out what he believes will be a complete rebuttal of the diary's critics.
>
> He does not, however, wish to launch criticisms of their work without inviting them to respond to his points, and he has ingeniously decided to employ me to approach the critics directly since I was one of the original advisers called in by Robert Smith ... Mr Feldman hopes that his good faith will be recognized in submitting you to interrogation by someone who essentially agrees with you, and I have agreed that my correspondence with the diary's critics may be published, with their answers, to allow readers to judge whether there was any deception or entrapment. In the event that you prefer not to answer any of the attached questions, I should be most grateful if you could briefly let me know why, as Mr Feldman also proposes to publish the fact if his offer of space to support your case is refused, and will obviously be inviting readers to conclude that he or I have raised unanswerable objections.

Rendell declined to comment on any of Martin's points on the grounds that he did not understand the basis of the questions and furthermore:

> Mr Rendell's work and report was for Time-Warner, and if there are questions concerning it, it is

Time-Warner's decision whether to engage Mr Rendell to pursue these issues beyond the scope authorized by him.

(Letter to Martin Fido dated 8 December 1994)

Martin responded on 9 February 1995:

... he [Paul Feldman] is particularly anxious not to misrepresent people (like myself) with whom he disagrees, and would really prefer not to be writing sentences such as, 'Mr Rendell has variously ascribed the composition of the diary to 1921 ±12 years, the last few years, and the twentieth century in general. When asked for clarification, his secretary only responded that his work on the diary was for Time-Warner, who should be contacted.' Mr Feldman will be very surprised if it transpires that the relevant chapter in *Forging History* represents consultative work committed to Time-Warner, and not the opinion of the author offered to the public in general.

This time there was no reply at all!

In or around September 1996, Keith Skinner made an important observation. 'Let us suppose,' he said, 'that when James Maybrick died there were no repercussions. Florence was not arrested, there was no trial and no "Maybrick Mystery". Therefore the name "Maybrick" would have meant nothing to anybody, anywhere. Let us also assume the document still existed. Would there then have been such strong doubts about its authenticity?'

Probably not, Keith, probably not.

Our research team were well focused.

Identify the historical criticisms and examine their credibility. Research the Maybrick family and examine the Home Office documents on the Florence Maybrick trial. Examine all letters sent to the police purporting to be written by Jack the Ripper, paying particular attention to those published in the media. Search for other examples of James Maybrick's handwriting and ...

... investigate the provenance of both the diary and the watch.

CHAPTER

7

'SIR JAMES'

IT WAS THE EARLY summer of 1993. We continued to debate the diary against known Ripper history. The fact was that we could not find anything that positively proved or conclusively disproved the document.

The Jack the Ripper letters were a matter of continuing research, but the fact that the author of the diary claimed ownership of them did *not* prove the diary a fake. Most modern authors did not believe, anyway, that the Whitechapel murderer wrote the letter that gave the name Jack the Ripper to the world. But there were authors who did – Colin Wilson, perhaps the most notable. The diary had to be investigated on the facts, not on authors' beliefs.

I noted the frustration of both Keith Skinner and Paul Begg. They were both responsible historians who were intrigued by the simple fact that they – considered experts in Ripperology – could not state from fact that the diary was a hoax, fake, forgery, call it what you will. They had expected a more rational and reasonable approach from their fellow writers on the subject. There seemed to be little support for a serious and thorough investigation.

'Believing' or 'not believing' the diary was not important to them. If it was genuine, then one of the greatest crime mysteries of all time had been solved. In fact, maybe two had. If it was proved to be a fake, then they would want to know *when* was it faked, *by whom* and *why*.

Paul Begg was the first person, as I recall, to seriously consider the possibility that the diary could be an old forgery, perhaps written to somehow help Florence. But the historical content of the diary would keep pushing the date to modern time.

Keith Skinner started his work on the diary by investigating James Maybrick, not Jack the Ripper. Keith's early observation was that the diary was probably written by Maybrick, but that he was not Jack, and had merely deluded himself. Keith's early research on Maybrick suggested that the author of the diary had excellent knowledge of the life of the cotton broker.

Again, the historical information within the text of the diary would make such a theory very difficult, if not impossible, to check. Where would James Maybrick have got the Ripper detail from? As we have already seen, it was not all in the press.

Paul's and Keith's views were, I repeat, early instincts, and intended only for internal debate. Because these two gentlemen were impartial and serious, they had opted for an 'old' document. They felt that the scientific tests carried out on the diary by that time would, if it had been a modern document, have conclusively proved it so already.

Even Martin Fido, who was certain that the document was a modern fake, would concede, 'More detailed research has been done on this document than has ever been done on any discovery connected with Jack the Ripper.'

On Paul Begg's recommendation, I invited Melvin Harris, now author of three Ripper books, to examine the document. The day he spent with me in the summer of 1993 was of great use. Inadvertently, as it turned out, he was to provide me with information that showed great knowledge by the author of the diary. This is discussed in the chapter, Yours Truly, Jack the Ripper. Melvin Harris took a copy of the diary away with him and it was agreed that he would write to me to give his valued opinion.

Mr Harris's letter was received on 23 July 1993; it read:

Sorry to have to tell you that the account is a hoax and a recent hoax at that. Of this there is no doubt whatsoever. On analysing it one can see that the hoaxer could have created the text using two books only . . .

That was it. No evidence to support it. No facts. Nothing. Because of his reputation, I had expected a detailed analytical report, to 'help' me, as he had said originally. What did he want a copy of the diary for?

Imagine our surprise when Melvin Harris had his third book, *The True Face of Jack the Ripper*, published in 1994. His publisher would advertise it as 'including the chapter that debunks the Jack the Ripper diary'.

Harris had changed his mind, apparently, since he wrote to me. That 'chapter' included the words, 'Finding out about arsenic and strychnine addictions is almost as easy. As for expertise in inks and paper, this is never called for. Stick with an authentic Victorian paper, use a simple ink (plenty of recipes around) and the game's afoot. Just three source books are all you need to provide the crime facts and their backgrounds.'

So now there were three books, not two. We studied a document circulated by Melvin Harris in summer 1993 prior to the publication of *The Diary of Jack the Ripper*.

There was mention of *Clarence* by Michael Harrison, *The Lodger* by Marie Belloc Lowndes, a book by Aleister Crowley, a pamphlet produced by John Morrison on the theory of James Kelly and Peter Underwood's *Jack the Ripper, 100 Years of Mystery*. But the 1987 hardback edition of *The Complete Jack the Ripper* by Donald Rumbelow or the hardback edition of that same year of Martin Fido's book must have been responsible for inclusion in the diary of the *Punch* article or the reference to the empty tin matchbox. It was Martin Fido's 1989 paperback that carried the information about Mary Kelly's heart. Of course, they are before we pick up one book on the Florence Maybrick trial.

What did Melvin Harris tell me after analysing the diary?

'The hoaxer could have created the text using two books only . . .'

I found this amusing, as I did the reference Harris makes to *The Lodger*.

'Look again at the clues: Regent's Park, Liepsic, Chandler, Liverpool, Poisener (sic) Mrs Maybrick. Where do you find them altogether, and in the company of Jack? Answer: *The Lodger*.'

The implication from Harris is clear: the *facts* about James Maybrick have been 'created' on *fiction* written by Marie Belloc Lowndes. I have heard of fiction written around fact but not the other way round.

Two books, three books – or a hundred and three. There is information in this diary that could not be found in *any* book, *anywhere*, but we have a few chapters to go yet.

In October 1994, Martin Fido sent me a detailed analysis of Melvin Harris's debunking of the diary (appendices 7–10 *The True Face of Jack the Ripper*).

Martin's report described Harris's appendices as 'biased, self inflating, inaccurate, and often logically inadequate'. Martin also stated that 'His further assertion that the diary could have been "concocted by drawing on three books at the most" cannot be substantiated. On the telephone to me (15.10.94) he evaded the point by referring to the numerous books and articles on the Maybrick case that exist . . .'.

On the question of other points raised in Harris's chapter, perhaps we'll just have to accept that Melvin Harris is far more an expert in the subject of medicine than Dr David Forshaw, who was extremely impressed by the way the author of the diary had treated James Maybrick's addiction to arsenic and strychnine. As for the ink, I have dealt with this in my earlier chapter, Science Dates the Document . . .

Dr Joe Nickell, a member of Kenneth Rendell's team in America, wrote in *Who was Jack the Ripper?* by Camille Wolff (Grey House Books, 1995), 'Neither James Maybrick nor any other candidate for Ripperhood could have written a diary a century after the events this amateurish fake purports to describe.'

I am not sure I can understand what the sentence means by 'amateurish'. I wonder if Dr Nickell will stand by that after reading this book. At least Dr Nickell was honest enough to say, 'We determined the diary was an obvious forgery, based primarily on conclusive handwriting evidence . . .'

Conclusive? We had asked three different experts to give their opinions, and each of them responded differently. Why did Rendell's team not attempt to contact Hannah Koren to ask for her reasons why she felt it was impossible for the diary to have been forged. And why did they not ask Reed Hayes, who had done forensic handwriting analysis for the FBI, and whom I contacted on Colin Wilson's advice? Was it because he did not agree with this 'conclusive' evidence?

What was interesting is that it was not science that appeared to be a problem, and there is no attempt by Joe Nickell to explain the findings of Rod McNeil. How convenient.

It has been said that Kenneth Rendell had 'concerns' over Rod McNeil's tests. Then why did he employ him? What is conclusive is that there are contradictory statements about the date of the document from people within the Rendell team.

There were other criticisms, and one that some were prepared to accept was conclusive evidence that the diary was a hoax.

In Camille Wolff's *Who was Jack the Ripper?* Roger Wilkes, a BBC producer, had correctly pointed out that the Poste House (mentioned in the diary) was not in Cumberland Street in 1888, as Shirley Harrison said it was.

But Shirley Harrison did not write the diary. The person who did wrote: 'I took refreshment at the Poste House[;] it was there I finally decided London it shall be.'

There is no mention of Cumberland Street, or any mention of Liverpool. Indeed, if the sentence implies anything, the Poste House could well be in London. The letter sent to Dr Forbes Winslow and reproduced in the chapter, Science Dates the Document ..., mentions a Poste Restante[1] at the Charing Cross Hotel.

It may be worth recalling that the police were looking for a man who left a black bag at this hotel and who went by the name of 'Mibrac'. So far I've been unable to find such a name – but switch the A with the I and we have a familiar-sounding surname.

Andrew Perry of the Royal Mail Archives and Records in London has confirmed that any establishment that used to accept post for collection and distribution could have been known as a poste house, even if that was not the name of the establishment.

The spelling of 'poste' or 'post' would differ depending on which part of the country you were in (*poste restante* is French for 'post remaining').

In short, the Poste House could have been anywhere in Liverpool or London or anywhere else. There may not be any record of the establishment, just as there is not today of many restaurants within hotels.

What surprised our team is how easily apparently responsible historians were prepared to accept 'conclusive evidence'. They did not seem to test such evidence when confronted with it.

We were determined, however, to evaluate this document responsibly. Keith was of the opinion that researching James Maybrick would lead us to the truth about the diary.

Shirley Harrison had learnt from Roger Wilkes that private research papers of the Maybrick case could be found at Wyoming University, USA. They had belonged to Trevor L. Christie, who wrote *Etched in Arsenic*, an account of the Florence Maybrick trial. The book was first published in America in 1968, and in Britain a year later. After Christie died, his wife donated all his papers to Wyoming University.

Keith was impressed with the book. The material in it displayed a consistently high level of research. He

---

[1] Dr Forbes Winslow transcribes this as Poste Restante, but close examination shows that it could be 'Poste House'.

recommended that we should obtain a copy of the Christie papers, which the author's widow had deposited there in May 1970.

Keith Skinner visited Wyoming University from 28 to 30 June 1993. He communicated with John Hanks and Rick Ewig, at the American Heritage Center where they were stored, to ascertain that nobody else had spent three days photocopying the entire collection. The possibility of a diary hoax was ever present in Keith's mind, although this would appear to be carrying it to extremes.

When Keith returned to England, he proceeded to review and digest the documents from Wyoming University. A set was photocopied for me and we both studied them continuously for days. The collection included copies of unique correspondence between Trevor Christie and Florence Aunspaugh, which had been written in the early 1940s.

Eight-year-old Florence Aunspaugh had spent the summer of 1888 at Battlecrease House as a guest of James and Florence Maybrick. She was the daughter of John Aunspaugh, a close friend and business associate of her host.

Florence Maybrick later wrote to Ms Aunspaugh from her prison cell; it was August 1897.

> You ask if I remember you? Indeed I do remember the vivacious, pert little miss, with big brown eyes and long brown curls, who kept the entire household in an uproar of laughter.

Keith phoned me one morning to discuss a specific reference he had noted in the Aunspaugh correspondence: 'She [Nurse Alice Yapp] did not see why Sir James (Mr Maybrick) ever brought me there any way.'

The diarist had referred to himself thirty-three times as 'Sir Jim'. Referring to the name 'Jack the Ripper' the author wrote:

> All whores will feel the edge of Sir Jims shining knife. I regret I did not give myself that name, curse it, I prefer it much much more than the one I have given.

The diary was written by someone who also clearly played games with the name Maybrick.

We had already noted that 'JA' from 'James' and 'CK' from 'Maybrick' provided 'JACK'. Fortuitous for a forger. Now he had been lucky again, as we had discovered a reference that proved Maybrick was referred to in his own home as Sir James. But there was more.

The Christie collection led to us finding a further example of James Maybrick's use of his name. A letter to J.S. Potter dated 12 December 1887[1] had been sent from 32 Knowsley Buildings, Tithebarn Street, and the cable address was given as 'BRICKMAY' Liverpool.

In the Home Office Records, deposited at the Public Record Office, we found among the court exhibits a copy of a telegram from Florence Maybrick (undated),[2] which read: 'Recalled owing to May's critical state . . .'

From a letter sent to Alfred Brierley from Florence Maybrick[3] (sent to be posted on 8 May): '. . . M. has been delirious since Sunday . . .'

The author of the diary had used 'May' and 'M' several times. Was Maybrick ever called Jim?

A letter from Florence Maybrick, which was reproduced in *Etched in Arsenic*: '. . . when Jim comes home at night it is with fear and trembling that I look into his face to see if anyone has been to the office about my bills.'

And how about Jack the Ripper? An article in the London evening newspaper, the *Echo* on 1 September 1888, was read with interest

WHO IS JIM?

There is another point of some importance upon which the police rely. It is the statement of John Morgan, a coffee-stall keeper, who says that a woman, whose description answers that given to him of the victim,

---

[1] Records of Richmond City Chancery Court, Virginia State Library and Archives.
[2] HO 144/1638/A50678D/13.
[3] MacDougall, 1891.

called at his stall – three minutes walk from Buck's Row – early yesterday morning. She was accompanied by a man whom she addressed as Jim . . .

But it was the reference that we got from Florence Aunspaugh that interested Keith. 'Sir James' was a name that connected with Maybrick in the privacy of his own home. How could that information have been known or accessed by any hoaxer or forger? The only explanation of why the sobriquet is used in the diary, if the document is not genuine, is that four letter word, 'luck'.

But more was to be revealed in the Christie Collection. Florence Maybrick has been written about extensively. So has her relationship with Alfred Brierley. She was clearly a striking woman, and Ms Aunspaugh describes her as follows:

She was about five feet four or five inches in height, rounded figure, well developed bust and hips, slender waist tapering arms and legs, small wrists and ankles, small feet and hands with rather long tapering fingers. Her figure would be considered a little too plump now for the present day style. Had a fair clear complexion with rosy cheeks . . . the crowning glory of her person was her hair. It was a blonde, but not the dead faded out type of yellow, had just enough tinge of red in it to make a glossy rich deep golden. It was inclined to be curly and always arranged in a very becoming style.

Straight nose, rather high forehead, small mouth, thin lips. Her front teeth seem to have a broader space between them than is ordinarily the case with a persons teeth.

Mrs Maybrick's eyes were the most beautiful blue I have ever seen. They were large round eyes and such a very deep blue that at times they were violet, but the expression was most peculiar. I will quote to you the description I have heard my father make: 'You would focus your eyes on hers with a steady gaze. They would appear to be entirely without life, or expression, as if you were gazing into the eyes of a corpse, literally void of animation or expression. As you continued your gaze her eyes seemed to change and have the look of a frightened animal ... Then again as your gaze continued her eyes seemed to grow larger, more round, with a look of childish wonder, amazement and astonishment. At no time was there any expression of intellectuality either in eyes or face. Yet there was a magnetic charm about her countenance that greatly attracted one and seemed irresistible'. My father said her eyes were a birth mark. 'A pair of birth-marked eyes lead poor James Maybrick to hell' ...

The diary had made a reference to Florence's lover as her 'whore master'. This was early in the document, which we can date at around February or March 1888. The entry after Christmas, however, says, 'The bitch, the whore is not satisfied with one whore master, she now has eyes on another.'

Most literature that existed on the relationship between Alfred Brierley and Florence Maybrick suggested that it had begun around November 1888. Although Alfred Brierley had met Florence Maybrick about a year earlier, it is a private letter from Charles Ratcliffe, a great friend of the Maybricks, to John Aunspaugh that confirms that the affair did not begin until 1888. 'Think Alf is getting the inside track with Mrs M's affections,' it said. It was dated 22 November, 1888.

Now, our diarist is clearly referring to Alfred Brierley when he refers to another whoremaster, not just because of the timing, but because he adds, 'A friend has turned, so be it ...' Alfred Brierley was the friend who turned. Who, then, was the first 'whore master'? Or was the author of the diary just guessing?

Ratcliffe, continued:

Michael, the son-of-a-bitch, should have his throat cut. Mrs Maybrick was sick in bed when James died. He had only been dead a few hours when Michael forced her to get up and go with Tom to Liverpool on a trivial affair which he represented to her as being most important. While she was gone Michael and two policemen searched the house, and in her room they claim to have found quantities of arsenic, thirteen love letters from Edwin, seven from Brierley, and five from Williams.

I always knew the madam was dumb, but I must frankly admit I did not consider her that dumb as to leave her affairs accessible to any who choosed to penetrate.

Two other relationships. One was the younger brother of James Maybrick. Edwin, however, had been in America since the spring of 1888, not returning until 25 April 1889. The diarist was aware of this detail as well, commenting that he had not heard from Edwin since he had left.

The words of the diary clearly suggest that one relationship is leading into another, but was there any evidence to support that claim?

Florence Aunspaugh, in a private letter to Trevor Christie, wrote:

In discussing the tragedy with my father, Brierley most earnestly proclaimed Mrs Maybrick's innocence of the murder of her husband. He said: 'She had no motive in getting rid of him . . . that her amorous feelings for both Edwin Maybrick and Williams was waning, but was very much increasing for him . . .

Although her affair with Edwin Maybrick and Williams was not made public as it was with Brierley; yet there were quite a number who knew it outside the Liverpool cotton brokers.

Mrs Maybrick began her lapses soon after her first child was born. The cotton broker's and their wives knew this . . .

And Charles Ratcliffe's letter to John Aunspaugh (reproduced in full as Appendix 2) tells us why those letters from Williams and Edwin were never produced at the trial.

Edwin is in bed with 'nervous prostration'. Tom and Michael are seeing to it that he leaves England, and Michael says Edwin's letters will never be produced in court. Brierley immediately evaporated from England when it was made public of Mrs Maybrick's arrest. Williams says his letters to Mrs Maybrick will never be brought into court.

Incidentally, Brierley's sworn statement claimed that he wrote to Florence only once.

The diary clearly suggests that the motive for James's Whitechapel crimes is revenge. He wants to kill 'the whore master', but concludes it will lead to his being caught. As the diary progresses, it becomes clear that James adores Florence, wanting only her, and, when their relationship would appear to be patched up, he would throw his knife in the river and end his campaign.

It should be noted that James Maybrick lived in Riversdale Road. The River Mersey is just a hundred yards or so from Battlecrease House.

What of the motive? Realistic? Do 'Rippers' kill for revenge against their loved ones?

I was interested to note the motive of Peter Sutcliffe, the Yorkshire Ripper, in *Voices From An Evil God*, written by Barbara Jones.[1]

Sonia, by now Sutcliffe's regular Saturday night date and his serious girlfriend, had been spotted by Mick in the passenger seat of a red sports car driven by a flashy-looking Italian boy who was a local ice-cream salesman. Sutcliffe was utterly devastated. Even now, he remembers the pain and feeling of betrayal that overtook him when he learned that Sonia had rejected him and was seeing someone else.

'I decided what to do. The next day I left my work at the Water Board a couple of hours before going-home time. I just walked out at about 4.30 p.m. I hung around outside the tech college in Bradford

---

[1] Blake Hardbacks Ltd, 1992.

where Sonia was studying for her A-levels. I saw her walking down the road . . . she suddenly spotted me waiting for her . . .

'I asked her, about a million times, if it was true, she was seeing someone else . . .

'She wouldn't answer my questions. I knew it was true anyway, I just wanted her to say something to me, either to reassure me or tell me it was over between us. I went away feeling worse than ever. When Sonia doesn't want to talk about something, there is nothing anyone can do to persuade her.'

That night, the 'voices' talked to him instead. 'They were stronger and louder than ever, drumming inside my head. They reasoned with me – "you must take this out on someone. You must get your own back. Don't take it out on Sonia. You could lose her. Take it out on someone else." '

Driven by manic revenge, Sutcliffe toured the streets . . .

The claims that this diary was 'created' by using two or three books and Joe Nickell's unsupported charge of 'amateurish fake' sounded more and more ludicrous as our investigation continued. If it was not genuine, then somebody had gone to great lengths to obtain detail.

Florence Maybrick's relationship with Alfred Brierley had progressed. On 21 and 22 March 1889, they arranged to meet at Flatman's Hotel, London. That meeting would yield unexpected results.

Dr Hopper made sworn statements on 3, 4 and 5 July 1889.[1]

I did not see her again until after Mr Maybrick's death. On the 12th May I was sent for to see Mrs Maybrick. I found that she was suffering from a sanguinias [sic] discharge which might have been a threatened miscarriage and she told me that she had not had her

[1] HO 144/1639.

monthly periods since the 7th March. I was unable then to tell whether she was pregnant or not but I think it could be ascertained now by examination.

I am not a doctor, but I am the father of three children. Florence Maybrick was in the middle of her cycle when she met Alfred Brierley in London, and now she was pregnant by him.

Now, with no wish to offend, if a woman thought herself pregnant by a man other than her husband, and indeed had not been sleeping with her husband, what would *most* women do?

Within ten days of her meeting at the Flatman's Hotel in London with Alfred Brierley, Florence was to effect a 'full reconciliation' with James Maybrick. And how the mood of the diary changed, from referring to his wife as 'The bitch, the bitch, the bitch', we are suddenly confronted with, 'my dear Bunny'.

Could our 'hoaxer' have really known so much?

In Christie's notes, handwritten on yellow foolscap paper, is a sheet headed RUSSELL'S BRIEF. Sir Charles Russell was Florence's defence counsel at her trial. Those notes revealed that Florence had not slept with her husband since July 1888, just a month before those horrendous murders in Whitechapel, London.

Florence Maybrick was pregnant at the time of her arrest, and the media knew.

On 26 May 1889, the Liverpool *Echo* reported that Florence Maybrick had been remanded for seven days after a certificate had been signed by Dr Beamish: 'This is to certify that in my opinion Florence E. Maybrick in her present condition cannot be removed from here and undergo the strain of an inquiry without incurring grave risk of serious consequences on medical grounds.'

On 28 May 1889, the day the inquest opened into her husband's death, the same newspaper reported:

Florence Maybrick is not present and Dr Beamish is in court to read his certificate. The coroner asks Dr Beamish:

C.	Do you think it would be dangerous to have her here?
Dr B.	I think it would be dangerous to have her here.
C.	When do you think she will be able to attend in court?
Dr B.	I should think in the course of a week
C.	At present you see nothing to prevent her attendance this week? We only want her here in order to be identified by a witness and after that is done if necessary she can retire to another room.
Dr B.	That would minimise the risk unquestionably. The more rest she has at present the better from a medical point of view.
C.	She will have to attend sooner or later.
Dr B.	The later the better.
C.	Do you think a week is late enough?
Dr B.	I am inclined to think in the course of a week she will be able to attend with comparative impunity.

But on 2 August 1889 the *New York World* stated: 'It is beginning to leak out that no baby will be born, after all, her hopes in that direction having been destroyed by the illness from which she suffered during her incarceration in Walton Prison.'

It seemed as if a miscarriage was likely, but nine days later a *Weekly Times and Echo* headline spoke of:

A STARTLING RUMOUR

Though there is no reference at all in the Liverpool papers to the following suggestion, it may be said that it is mentioned in several provincial journals that it is understood that another important question arises in the case, and one which a jury of matrons will be empanelled to try. Of course in the event of that jury finding the fact to be as it is alleged, the execution would necessarily be postponed, and probably would not take place at all. It is believed that there has been no instance of the execution of a woman who, at the time of her trial, was in Mrs Maybrick's supposed condition, since the execution of Margaret Waters nineteen years ago.

By this time Florence would have been five months pregnant, but there was nothing in her medical records at the prison to indicate a birth or miscarriage. This suggests that, if anything, a birth was the most likely outcome.

If the child was born, it was not registered to Florence Maybrick or Florence Chandler.

Intriguingly, buried away in the Home Office files, Keith discovered a small newspaper article, which stated that Mrs Maybrick had given birth to a child in prison. The story had been picked up and printed in the *Daily Mail*, 18 May 1896, causing Florence's mother, Baroness von Roques, to write an indignant letter from Paris to the Home Secretary. This had sparked off an internal inquiry which ultimately identified the originator of the report as an unnamed Member of Parliament. The source of the story, however, or what it had been based on, was never conclusively established.[1] But we were to come back to the rumour of an illegitimate child in a way that nobody ever expected, a way that dramatically changed the whole focus of our investigation.

Our research into the Maybrick story had only just begun, but we were discovering information that had never previously been published. We certainly had not proved or disproved the authenticity of the diary.

But it was early days yet . . .

---

[1] HO 144/1640/A50678D/301–305.

CHAPTER

8

'TO MY DARLING PIGGY . . .'

KEITH SKINNER FOCUSED HIS research on a lady by the name of Sarah Ann Robertson.

Sarah had been James Maybrick's lover while he was working in London when he was in his mid to late twenties. Various reports and books suggested that the relationship continued for at least twenty years.

Alexander MacDougall, in 1891, was the first author to identify the relationship between James and Sarah. He had clearly not obtained his information from research as we know it today, so one must pay respect to the information we gain from him. The details of Sarah Ann Robertson's whereabouts at the time of the trial, and her address in London, could have been obtained from only one person. Florence Maybrick.

When Keith Skinner went to Wyoming University to view the Christie Collection, he discovered a scruffy, handwritten note by Trevor Christie. It read as follows:

RUSSELL'S BRIEF:

At the age of 20 he went into Shipbrokers office in London and met Sarah Robertson, 18, an assistant in a jewellers shop, she lived with him on and off for 20 years as his wife. Her relatives thought she was married and she passed as Mrs. M. with them. They have five children all now dead.

He returned to Liverpool a few years later and they lived in Chester for 3 or 4 years and at Manchester and Liv[erpool] . . .

He supplied Robertson with money from time to time until 1880. In 1881 he suddenly informed her he was married and she would get £100 annually. This allowance paid irregularly. R. living in Sunderland in 1889.

Nigel Morland had written of five illegitimate children also:

It was inclined to stand as a footnote to something which many people learned, that James Maybrick's mistress in England had borne him three children, and two after his marriage – when earlier intimacy was resumed. It was also realised that Florence had found this out, and such was her revulsion against him that for two years before his death they had not lived as man and wife. It excused, in some minds, the London visit with Brierley.[1]

Trevor Christie's source is not clear; Nigel Morland deliberately withheld his. 'Russell' is of course Sir Charles Russell, leading counsel for Florence Maybrick at her trial. We do not know where Russell got his information from either.

The illegitimate children referred to by Russell and Morland are a mystery. If Morland is right (three before, two after), then Russell cannot be. His 'brief' indicates that James Maybrick's relationship with Sarah ended prior to his marriage with Florence.

Had all five children died? Certainly, there were no death certificates under the name of Maybrick or Robertson that could be associated with either James or Sarah for the period 1865–1889. We could not find, despite Sir Charles Russell's brief, any confirmation that there had been any births either.

Modern research has proved MacDougall's references with regards to Sarah Ann Robertson to be accurate. Therefore, an attempt to discredit him, such as some Ripper authors have made, is illogical and irresponsible. It

[1] Nigel Morland, *This Friendless Lady*, Frederick Muller Ltd, 1957.

118

is far more reasonable to pay attention to the detail we get from MacDougall about the relationship between James Maybrick and Sarah Ann Robertson.

According to Alexander MacDougall, Florence confronted James Maybrick with the knowledge of his lover and his illegitimate children. According to legitimate records, these children were not born, were not married and did not die. Not any one of the five of them.

Bobo and Gladys, born to James and Florence Maybrick, had no known offspring while married.

James Maybrick and Sarah Ann Robertson had children. Did they live?

Keith Skinner knew that, if any children from this relationship did survive, their descendants might well hold the answer to the Maybrick/Ripper puzzle.

Keith went back to source material and provided me with his findings.

In 1851 Sarah Ann Robertson is shown on the census return as aged thirteen and living with her aunt Christiana and her aunt's husband Charles J. Case at 1 Postern Way, Tower Hill. Ten years later Christiana and Charles had moved to 36 Jamaica Street, Mile End, but Sarah is no longer with them.

Christiana's husband died in 1863 at 3 Jamaica Street (just down the road). She was remarried three years later, to Thomas David Conconi. Their address is given as 43 Bancroft Road, Stepney. Thomas Conconi was also listed in *Kelly's Street Directory* at 55 Bromley Street, Commercial Road, Stepney.

As our research on Sarah unfolded, a number of curious facts emerged. In 1868, Thomas Conconi drew up his will and included the following text:

> ... my dear friends Sarah Ann Maybrick the wife of James Maybrick of Old Hall Street Liverpool now residing at No 55 Bromley Street Commercial Road London ...

Since the publication of Shirley Harrison's book, the marriage records have been checked for Scotland, the Isle of Wight and the Isle of Man, as well as England. There is no record that such a marriage ever took place. It is, of course, remotely possible that they were married and divorced outside this country. However, Keith uncovered the marriage licence that was taken out when James was to marry Florence. It is clearly stated that he is a bachelor, not a divorcee.

In the 1871 census Sarah Ann Maybrick is listed at 55 Bromley Street as a 'merchants Clerk wife' (sic).

In 1891 the census for 265 Queens Road, New Cross, lists:

Sarah Robertson, single, 44,
Christiana Conconi, Head widow, 69, own means
Gertrude –, Daughter, single, 18

More anomalies. Sarah's age is ten years less than it should be; Christiana's is four years out. Sarah's birth was never registered in Sunderland, County Durham, which each census return had given as her place of birth. Of course, she could have been registered elsewhere, but there was no registration of any Sarah Ann Robertson anywhere in the country, with a place of birth as Sunderland, County Durham. Accordingly, we do not know who her parents are, although the most likely answer, given that she lived with Christiana from the age of thirteen, is that she is really her illegitimate daughter.

Gertrude is also a bit of a mystery. As Christiana was really seventy-four years old in 1891 and not sixty-nine, as the census states, it would mean that she would have given birth at the age of fifty-six. Not impossible, but I wondered whether we had discovered an illegitimate James and Sarah offspring, born in 1873. Gertrude certainly was not registered at birth as a Conconi, as the census return of 1891 suggests she should have been. When she married in 1895, she gave her name as Gertrude Blackiston 'otherwise Conconi'. Sarah 'Maybrick' was a witness at the marriage, and Gertrude's address is given as 265 Queens Road. This was Sarah's permanent address in 1889, according to Alexander MacDougall. Needless to say, there is no record of the birth of a Gertrude Blackiston either.

Sarah's aunt, Christiana, died at 265 Queens Road in 1895. The informant of Christiana's death was Sarah Maybrick, who stated that her aunt was seventy-two at death. However, Christiana was born in November 1817, and was seventy-eight years old.

Sarah Ann Maybrick 'otherwise' Robertson, died at Tooting Bec Hospital in 1927. She was reported to be aged seventy-two, of 24 Cottisbrook Street, New Cross, a spinster of independent means. The informant was one Alice Bills, of the same address. Sarah, however, must have been eighty-nine when she died, and not seventy-two.

Alice Bills was the last known link to Sarah Ann Robertson. Keith Skinner continued his research.

How Melvyn Fairclough spent the hours that he did in St Catherine's House I will never know. The Maybrick family, their offspring, the Barretts, the Grahams, the Johnsons, etc. We followed every lead that we could in order to find people alive today to whom we could speak.

I joined Melvyn on occasions. Unfortunately, I chose a burning hot day in the summer of 1994 for my 'baptism'. The air conditioning, if it does exist, did not work. The stench of sweaty armpits was overpowering.

Sally Evemy, while working with Shirley Harrison, produced a list of known Maybrick relations, together with the relevant reference code for each certificate. Keith Skinner recommended that we track every Maybrick, and order every relevant certificate.

Melvyn started with 1837, the year that certificates were first used. Systematically, decade by decade, he ordered each birth, marriage and death certificate of anyone with the name of Maybrick.

Melvyn would later follow the family lines of every female Maybrick who had married, and was closely associated with James.

As Melvyn collated the certificates, a pattern evolved. Or non-pattern. I am not sure which. A series of births, marriages and deaths of Maybricks who we could not link to anyone else who was carrying or had carried that name began to appear. Curiously, the majority of these originated in Huntingdon, a part of the country that was not associated with the Maybrick dynasty.

Whittlesey, in the Fens, lies about four miles outside Peterborough. Peterborough is in Northamptonshire, while Whittlesey is in Cambridgeshire.

Travelling less than twenty miles by road, south from Whittlesey, the traveller arrives at Huntingdon. Across the River Ouse is Godmanchester, an inland port linking itself to the Wash and the North Sea, through Kings Lynn in Norfolk.

James Maybrick's business interests could well have made Godmanchester a relevant place to visit.

Godmanchester lends its name to the Duke of Manchester, who has held lands in Huntingdon.

I was intrigued by the connection to Godmanchester. Our diarist had referred to two visits to a 'Manchester'. The wording of those entries had given me the distinct impression that the place referred to was not in Lancashire. I had considered Manchester, New Hampshire, USA, which was considered at the time to be the cotton industry's world capital, but could not find any evidence of James Maybrick's having travelled there.

The author of the diary had claimed his first victim had been killed in 'Manchester' and wrote, after describing the murder, 'Manchester was cold and damp very much like this hell hole.'

The text gives the impression that the entry is made in late February or early March. The weather in Huntingdon would certainly fit such a description.[1]

When Melvyn had completed his work on the 1920s, we reviewed the certificates that were causing us problems.

---

[1] The *Hunts County News*, 10 March 1888.

EARITH

The Weather – Last week we had skating most mornings on the Old West River, but the ice got very treacherous towards noon, and several skaters measured the depth of the water. On Friday, some found that it reached up to their waist, and in one case much higher even than that.

All these certificates were registered in Whittlesey, Cambridgeshire.

Melvyn discovered three marriages where the girls married with the maiden name of Maybrick. Elizabeth Susannah, Emily Minetta and Annie had two things in common. They had not been born in this country with the name of Maybrick, but all married with it.

Strangely enough, we discovered a birth of a Maybrick in Whittlesey that we were not able to fit into the family tree. Ruth Mary Maybrick had been registered, without a father, by a Margaret Minetta Maybrick in 1912.

We could not identify the background to a Margaret Maybrick at all.

The marriage certificates identified a Mark Maybrick as father to all the girls, including Ruth Mary, apart from Emily Minetta. We had not come across Mark Maybrick's name either.

There were also deaths registered, again in Whittlesey, again to individuals carrying the name Maybrick, where there was no record of the deceased having ever been born.[1]

ELTON

Heavy Snow Drifts – The high east winds which prevailed during the recent severe weather carried a large amount of snow from the adjoining fields into the road leading from Elton to Haddon, and completely blocked it. Men were set to dig out the road, but the authorities soon stopped them as the cutting almost immediately drifted full again. On Friday and Saturday eighteen men were employed to clear the road, which was blocked for nearly three-quarters of a mile, the snow lying from two to five feet deep as it drifted.

FARCET

Open Coursing Meeting – The recent day's coursing in this neighbourhood having been so successful, the committee determined to have a repetition of the sport. Tuesday last was the date fixed, but the alternating frosts and thaws made it a matter of speculation as to whether a postponement would not be necessary.

[1] 1911: Death, Naomi Maybrick, age eight months. The informant was Margaret Minetta Maybrick, mother. The death was registered in Whittlesey in the County of Cambridge. *There was no record of a Naomi Maybrick having been born eight months earlier.*

1912: Birth, Ruth Mary. The address was Eastrea Field, Whittlesey, the same address where Naomi had died. No father was named. The Informant, once again was Margaret Minetta Maybrick. We were to

We contacted Brian Maybrick, the grandson of James Maybrick's first cousin, John. Other than Brian's son, David, he was the only living Maybrick, at the time. We had learnt from Shirley Harrison that Brian had extensive knowledge of the family. Brian had conducted his research, in the main, from the IGI,[1] which does not cover the twentieth century. Brian's information about recent Maybrick history had come from within the family. He had never heard of any Maybricks who lived in Whittlesey. He was baffled, as he felt he was aware of the whole Maybrick family.

We realised that the only way to identify who these people were was to track their descendants. The first marriage we looked at, Elizabeth's, produced no children. The next was Emily's. Her marriage did. Her son George (Porter) was born to her on 14 June 1935. We were also successful in finding births to Annie. We were hopeful that the fact that they were born in the 1930s would mean that they were still alive. Melvyn paid a visit to British Telecom Records and Archives and looked at the directories for the Huntingdon area. There was a George Porter listed, but was it our George?

Melvyn telephoned Mr Porter. We had the right one. Mr Porter was helpful, but seemed to know little. He told Melvyn that the family 'historians' were Jeanette Grady and Janice Roughton. Mr Porter said he would call them and, if it was OK, he would give Melvyn their telephone numbers. In the meantime, he was able to confirm that Elizabeth, Emily, Ruth Mary and Annie were all sisters. Annie, he said, was still alive and well. Her daughter was Janice Roughton. There had been another sister, Rose Ellen, who was born between Elizabeth and Emily. Rose's daughter was still alive, and was the Jeanette Grady referred to above.

---

learn from this certificate that she was a housekeeper by occupation.
1923: Death, Jack, aged eight years, of Basing House, Whittlesey. Jack was the son of Margaret Maybrick. *There was no record of a Jack Maybrick having been born eight years earlier.*
[1] International Genealogical Index. A register of baptisms, marriages and deaths compiled by the Mormons from church records.

It was not long before we got the green light. George told us the ladies' telephone numbers, and that they were expecting us to ring.

Janice's voice was strong, but friendly. 'I wondered how long it would take you to find us . . . I phoned the studio, you know, when Shirley Harrison was on television promoting her book. She couldn't have got the message . . . Of course you can come and see us.'

Of course, we brought up the problems of the certificates there and then, and Janice helped us, instantly.

'Mark Maybrick's real name was Mark Woolstone. In fact, there are several different spellings of his surname. It was Grandma who was the Maybrick. My mum was brought up as a Maybrick like all the girls, but it is a long story and I will tell you it all when I see you. I have been researching this for years.'

As things turned out, it was Melvyn who went to see Janice first. I was to visit the Gradys. In the meantime, armed with information from Janice Roughton, we went to seek out our missing certificates.

It was then that Keith Skinner, genealogist extraordinaire, finally accepted that birth, marriage and death certificates do lie.

The relevant birth certificates of Margaret Maybrick's children were obtained. The ambiguities were astonishing.[1]

Furthermore, it was clear that the two registrars,

---

[1] 1905: Elizabeth Susannah. Father: Mark Woolerson. Mother: Margaret Manetta Woolerson formerly Edgis.
1907: Rose Ellen. Father: Mark Woolston. Mother: Margaret Woolston formerly Maybrick.
1909: Emily Menetta. Father: Mark Woolstone. Mother: Margaret Woolstone formerly Edgis.
1910: Naomi. Father: Mark Woolston. Mother: Margaret Woolston formerly Egges.
1913: Sheppard Shalgrave. Father: Mark Woolstone. Mother: Margaret Woolstone formerly Maybrick.
1915: Ann. Father: Mark Woolston. Mother: Ann Woolston formerly Shelgrave.
The spelling differences are as they appear on the certificates.

brothers John and George Lefevre, had not been, shall we say, 'responsible'.

In 1995, after we had a full set of this family's certificates, we wrote to the Office of Population Censuses and Surveys (OPCS) for their comments; they duly responded on 14 July 1995.

Dear Mr Fairclough

I have been asked by Mrs J Elliott, Superintendent Registrar, to reply to your letter about the registration of events relating to the Maybrick family.

I have looked at the copies of the register entries you have forwarded for our scrutiny. I would not wish to speculate on the discrepancies you have highlighted and can only advise you on the requirements for registration.

The registrar is required to record the particulars given by a qualified informant. If there is any doubt about the spelling of a name, and if the informant cannot read or write, the registrar should try to find out the ordinary spelling, however, if the informant insists on some other form, it must be used.

It is essential that the registrar takes the details from the person who has the best knowledge of the event. In most instances a relative, who also has a duty placed on them to register, will give information. The onus, however, is on the informant to give details of the event to the best of his/her knowledge and belief.

The registrar will strongly advise any person who knowingly and wilfully gives false information or makes a false declaration that he/she is liable to prosecution for perjury. The act of perjury must be

---

The registrar for both Sheppard and Ann was George Lefevre. The registrar for the other births was John Lefevre, his brother.

There was no marriage between a Mark Woolston and an Ann Woolston.

Every birth had been informed by Mark, except for the birth of Sheppard, when Margaret was the informant.

Naomi Maybrick, who died aged eight months, was born Naomi Woolston. The registrar in both instances was one John Lefevre.

proved and the registrar cannot rely on local knowledge or rumour.

The registrars, Messrs Lefevres, were required to follow these regulations and requirements of the relevant registration Acts.

I am sorry that I cannot be of more help in providing an explanation for the difference in spelling or surnames and other details in these register entries.

Yours sincerely

Mrs V. Boyd

Marriages & General

Janis Roughton would later tell me, 'I think one of the strangest things during my research of birth certificates was that the registrars were two brothers who must have known the family very well. They registered all the girls and Jack. When Naomi was born she was registered as Naomi Woolston. When she died eight months later she was registered as Naomi Maybrick. Both certificates were registered by the same registrar.'

We continued to talk on the telephone with Mr and Mrs Grady and Janice Roughton prior to meeting them. That is when we learnt that Margaret Minetta Maybrick had yet another name. She was also known as Elizabeth, although she answered to Margaret as well.

During one conversation, Janice surprised me when she told me that Grandma Elizabeth, together with the five girls and Jack, entered the Whittlesey Workhouse in 1913. Janice had copies of the workhouse records, which, in themselves, she thought strange. I knew I would be travelling to Peterborough frequently over the next few months.

I met Jeanette and Jim Grady for the first time on 19 August 1994. I was accompanied by my assistant, Martine Rooney. I was struck by how tidy the house was, full of interesting old English furniture and with a cosy feel about it. Mr and Mrs Grady were very hospitable and tea or coffee was soon offered. It had been a long time since I had drunk coffee out of a china cup.

During the telephone conversations with Mr and Mrs

Grady they had told me some fascinating stories and I was anxious to get them on tape. I reproduce a transcript here.

PHF   Mrs Grady, your maiden name is?

JG   My maiden name is Cooper. I am the daughter of Rose Ellen Maybrick.

PHF   Did you find it strange that your family birth and marriage certificates seem to be somewhat contradictory in terms of birth and marriage names?

JG   No, because there was always a secret with my grandmother.

PHF   Can you tell me more of what you know about that secret?

JG   The family have never known where she came from and what her real name was. My mother was the second eldest daughter. The eldest daughter was my Aunt Elizabeth Susannah Maybrick, and she told my mother and my mother's sister, the youngest daughter Ann, that when they queried as to things about Grandma and things about the birth certificates they were told by Elizabeth that 'It's a secret and it's a terrible secret and I would never tell you and if you ever got to know you would wish that you hadn't'.

PHF   Did you ever wonder what the secret was?

JG   Yes, I did, and there has always been a connection with the Florence Maybrick poison case. And I thought she was something to do with that – a relative – because she used the name Maybrick.

PHF   Am I right in saying that the belief in the family was that it was your grandmother that was a descendant of Maybrick, rather than Mark Woolston?

JG   That is correct – Mark Woolston never came into it. There was nothing ever said about Mark Woolston.

PHF   Can you offer an explanation as to why your grandma used the name Elizabeth Maybrick and yet on every certificate she is known as Margaret?

JG   Why she used the name Elizabeth? No, I do not know – full stop – though I feel that there is a connection somewhere because she called her eldest daughter Elizabeth.

PHF   I understand there is another story in the family when they actually buried her [your grandma].

JG   My parents came back home [after her funeral] and my father, who had known her when he was a little boy – he lived next door to her – he said to my mother, 'Well, she has gone now. She is buried and she took her secrets to the grave.' . . . My father he used to call her Flo as a nickname because of the Florence Maybrick connection – she didn't seem to mind that.

PHF   She didn't seem to mind it?

JG   No, and he would also say to my mother, 'My tea tastes a bit bitter,' which was a family joke – it has always been in the family.

PHF   And have the recent revelations come as a shock to you?

JG   No. It doesn't bother me at all. I am very, very interested. I just wish my mother – Rose Ellen Maybrick – was still alive to hear it, because she'd love it. She tried to trace Grandma and never could – it all came to a dead end.

PHF   Elizabeth/Margaret, when she was in the workhouse with the kids, I understand something strange used to happen?

JG   Yes, my mother told me that you would get chauffeurs with the big cars, which were then used in those days – would draw up and in would come parcels. There would be a [not audible] for Grandma, and chocolates which would be shared out amongst the kiddies . . . My Aunt Ann, who is the youngest daughter, says that one time she remembers in the workhouse this car coming and this man coming in and trying to get my grandma to go off with him but she refused.

Jim   The person who came used to wear a top hat and

	they thought he was the station master at King's Cross Station.
JG	Yes.
Jim	Because at that time they did wear big top hats.
PHF	Can you tell me about the connection to Liverpool?
JG	Yes, my father used to talk to Grandma a lot and then I think she died [not audible]. He said she talked about Liverpool – she knew Liverpool and she also talked about America . . . She used to tell me tales about the devil – she said she could communicate with the devil – so much so that my father had to tell her to stop telling me all these tales. He said he used to sit on the end of her bed and she would tell him things . . .
PHF	Do you know what she was trained for – what did Grandma do?
JG	She was very well educated. To me she came over as an educated Victorian lady and a bit of a prude. Which is why I cannot understand the certificates. She never swore, she could play the piano and she didn't like dirty jokes. Proper Victorian lady . . .

We continued to chat, comparing certificates and research, but it was time to get back.

Melvyn had not had much luck with Janice Roughton. I had built a little rapport with her on the telephone, and we thought it would be a good idea for me to pay her a visit. I called Janice, the next day, and arranged to go up within the following week.

I seemed to immediately connect with Janice and Paul Roughton. Janice was eager to share her knowledge, and Paul was quietly intrigued. They made me feel as if I was a welcome friend, and my relationship with them developed quickly.

I visited Paul and Janice Roughton regularly. I was to meet and have several chats with Janice's mother, Annie Maybrick. Annie was almost eighty years old, but a wonderful character, and most certainly still 'all there'.

The 'mystery' was not solved, but the key issues were identified.

Sheppard Shalgrave Woolstone/Maybrick seemed to have vanished into thin air. He is born in October 1913. Margaret was admitted with the five girls and Jack to the Whittlesey Workhouse in December 1915. Mark Woolstone is not listed as being with them. Margaret gave her name as Elizabeth Maybrick and her religion as Roman Catholic.

Sheppard would have been two years and two months old on entering the workhouse. Jack's age is given as one year old. Although no birth certificate could be found for Jack, the age entered at the workhouse is supported by his death certificate which, in 1923, gave his age as eight.

Mark Woolstone died, aged forty-seven, in December 1916, at the County Lunatic Asylum. The family knew very little about him other than that 'he taught Latin'. Mark's birth certificate could not be found.

On 15 November 1917, again as Elizabeth Maybrick, Margaret took the five sisters with Jack to Saint Mary's in Whittlesey. They were all baptised. Each child's first name was given, with the middle name Woolston and the surname Maybrick.

Annie Maybrick has never believed she was the daughter of Margaret. Even today, she is angry that she has never known who her parents are. There is no doubt that she descends from the Maybricks, as she says:

'Now that I have met Brian Maybrick, he is the image of one of my sons. I showed his picture to my neighbour, who thought it was Tony, and my granddaughter said, "This is uncle Tony." After meeting Brian I think my three boys are very like him – they look like brothers.'

Annie always had a smile. Her childhood memories were not happy. Annie did grin, however, when she told me, 'I remember catching cockles by the seaside . . .'

Elizabeth Susannah, the eldest of the five girls, died as recently as 1992. She spent the last period of her life being looked after by Paul and Janice Roughton.

Janice was always convinced that 'Lizzie' had all the answers:

'Elizabeth was very different from the rest of the family.

She married Leonard Ward, a gentleman's gentleman. They had no children and their family was made up of cats. Leonard died very suddenly, without warning, and my mother went to stay with Lizzie to sort things out. Eventually Lizzie came to stay with me, for two weeks, but stayed until she died. After a couple of months I thought it would be a good opportunity to find out about the family history. Auntie Lizzie was very secretive. Although ninety years old, she did the *Telegraph* crossword every day and dealt with all her own affairs. She never told her husband about her family history, or that she was illegitimate. On her marriage certificate she put her father's name as Mark Maybrick – not Woolston.

'Lizzie would not tell me anything. One day I asked her if she wanted to read a book I had on the Maybrick case. She became very defensive, would not discuss it, and said it was all nonsense. "If you are beginning to investigate this story, leave it alone, Janice. It will do you no good whatsoever. It does not need to be revived." All she would say was "Leave it alone". She did not want to discuss with me what had happened in her past life or her mother's past life. I am absolutely convinced that she knew something she was keeping to herself and was not going to reveal it to anyone.

'After about two years, Lizzie had a stroke and for about one week appeared to be living in the past. I told Mother that, if she wanted to ask her any questions, maybe this was the time. Mother came over and she said to Lizzie, "Where did I come from?" Lizzie's reaction was immediate and angry: she went for Mother, tried to hit her, threw her handbag at her. Even the doctor said that if it was not sad it would be funny to see this lady's reaction, after just having a stroke, when we started to talk about the Maybricks. Lizzie thought she was back in the workhouse, talking and imagining people. I believe she knew everything we wanted to know – everything there is to know about the Maybrick family.

'Lizzie did tell me that the family had a book, with family names and information about their family and past family. One day, she said, someone came to the house and the book disappeared. There was also a sea trunk, supposedly belonging to Margaret, that disappeared when they went to the workhouse.'

Peter Jepson, one of Annie's sons, often stayed with his Aunt Lizzie. He recollected:

'It would be Christmas 1948 and she took me to London and the zoo and before we went to the zoo we went all around a place in Whitechapel and we went all the way round. She said to me these places would become significant to me in later life. We spent a couple of hours there . . .

'Grandmother Margaret? I spent my summer holidays with her in the war. Very, very positive woman. Spoke with a cockney accent. She wore typical old long clothes like a nun. You could not speak to her about the family. She had always known she originated from Whitechapel. It was impossible to question Grandmother about the past because you would get nothing. The only background material I ever received was from Lizzie when she took me to Whitechapel.

'We *knew* we were connected – everyone in the family knew we were connected – to the Maybricks and the Liverpool events. I believe the diary . . .'

Janice did not seem to disagree with her brother:

'When I first heard that James Maybrick could have been Jack the Ripper, I was not that surprised. I had always known that there was something sinister in this family that I have been researching. I could not find the key to it, the missing link . . . I have done a lot of research and it has always led me back to James and Florence Maybrick. I was not surprised at all because in all the time researching there always seemed to be something secretive along the line.'

Secretive? That was the understatement of our investigation.

During this investigation we would examine the background of over a hundred families. I never saw a series of certificates where the information was so corrupt.

Keith Skinner and Melvyn Fairclough were far more familiar with family trees than I, but the Whittlesey collection was unique, even to them. Even the OPCS seemed surprised.

If James Maybrick was not Jack the Ripper, then the past events in this family seem all the more peculiar. The 'illegitimacy' was not a secret, so what was? The Florence Maybrick trial was public knowledge, as was James's drug addiction and womanising. So what did Grandma mean when she said 'It's a secret and it's a terrible secret and I would never tell you and if you ever got to know you would wish that you hadn't'?

What struck me was that this family folklore was extremely fortunate if, as some critics were saying, the diary was a modern forgery. Of course, you could say, 'You are reading what you want into it.' Maybe. But a hoaxer could not have hoped in his wildest dreams that a Maybrick family would be able to tell of such a strange background. In some cases, these 'ordinary' people would find their lives affected by very influential people . . .

Janis explains:

'I work in the nursing profession and at one point decided that I would like to work for the prison service. I applied for a job in a high-security prison and was short listed twice – after which I was turned down. I thought the interviews had gone very well and decided to ask why I had been turned down. They said it was a "Home Office directive", that there had been documents in the Home Office that I was not a suitable candidate for the job I had applied for.'

We knew we had identified a family of illegitimate Maybricks. The family folklore strongly suggested they were connected to James. There was not any proof that James had anything to do with Jack the Ripper, just curious stories. Janice continued to assist, as did the rest of the family.

The home of Janice and Paul Roughton was where Lizzie died in 1992 and where her personal bits and pieces remained. There was not much. A small pocket diary, a book of poems that Lizzie had written herself and hundreds of photographs. Many of those pictures were of Lizzie herself. Some had names written on the back but many could not be identified by Janice.

What had been just names on certificates were now faces: Margaret, the five sisters and Jack. If Mark Woolstone was there, it was not evident. There were several of an 'Auntie Wadham'. She looked between twenty and thirty years older than Lizzie. Janice had not met her and neither had her mother. Annie was certain that 'Auntie' was family and not just a close friend. A reasonable assumption would have been that she was Margaret's sister and, if so, another Maybrick. Auntie Wadham was important. More certificates required.[1]

One picture of Lizzie showed her drinking from a china cup, while talking to a very old woman in what seemed to be a back garden. I thought that Lizzie looked in her late teens or early twenties, which would date the picture at around 1921–1926. Annie felt that it might have been a 'Mrs Read', whom, she remembered, Lizzie had often gone to visit. It was Sarah Ann Robertson's death in 1927, when she was eighty-nine, that was playing on my mind. Maybe it was wishful thinking.

Who was Margaret Maybrick? The information she volunteered about herself would seem to conflict with every document she was associated with.[2]

---

[1] Auntie Wadham was traced. She died, aged ninety-five, in 1968. She had married in 1896 as Elizabeth Knight. Not surprisingly, her birth certificate could not be traced and the man named as 'father' on her wedding certificate did not seem to exist. Elizabeth Knight married Albert John Wadham, whose family originated from Wimborne, Dorset.
 Elizabeth Wadham, Margaret Minnetta Maybrick and Sheppard Shalgrave would continue to be researched.

[2] We learnt that Margaret had married Charles Mattin. After Charles died, she married Edward Coney, to whom she had been housekeeper. The year was 1942, and Margaret gave her age as sixty-four.
 For some reason, Margaret had made herself three years older than she was. When she was admitted to the workhouse in 1915, her age is given as forty-one, suggesting a year of birth as 1874. Who was Margaret or Elizabeth? Melvyn had a difficult task. He had a list of the maiden names she had given on various documents, the 'father's' name

We had gone as far as we could. Margaret Minetta Maybrick's connection to James was clearly not going to be found through certificates, wills, electoral registers or street directories. I was not despondent for too long: Keith phoned with some good news.

Keith Skinner had been to see Barbara Parkinson, the daughter of Alice Bills. Alice had been living at the same address as Sarah (Maybrick), James's lover, at the time of her death. Barbara had in her possession a Bible. It was a very special Bible. As you opened it, on the first right-hand page, was a handwritten inscription:

To my darling Piggy. From her affectionate Husband JM
On her Birthday August 2 1865

We had finally discovered handwriting of James Maybrick that was not in the public domain. The writing bore little resemblance to either his will or the diary. The initials, however, were similar to those of the signature on his wedding certificate.

---

of James Edges, as well as 1871, 1874 and 1881 as possible dates for her birth.

Edges was an unusual surname. It did not take long to order every certificate of that name, covering almost a century. A Margaret Jane was born to a Jacob James Edges and Elizabeth King on 19 June 1881. Jacob and Elizabeth had several children, but it would appear that none kept in contact with our Margaret from Whittlesey. There was no marriage registered between Jacob and Elizabeth King. When Margaret's brother James was born in 1885, Elizabeth gave her maiden name as King-Underwood.

By ordering all the certificates, we discovered that Elizabeth Susannah was not the first child born to Margaret. She had given birth in 1902 to a Winifred May, who died aged five months. Margaret had registered the birth as a single parent and had given her occupation as a domestic servant, confirming the knowledge that the Whittlesey family had of her background.

This collection of Edges certificates revealed Jacob James's parents. On paper, Margaret's grandmother was Jane Margaret Sumner. After Jane's husband died, she married again, in 1880, this time to a Francis John Maybury.

Brian Maybrick had told us that the Maybury name was a derivative

The term of endearment that James used for Sarah, 'Piggy', was interesting due to the fact that later he was to call his wife 'Bunny'.[1]

The inscription also indicated that James and Sarah played the charade of marriage even with each other.

Sarah Ann Robertson was known by Barbara Parkinson as 'Old Auntie'. Alice Bills was very close to a Nellie Hartnett. It had been Nellie's mother, Hannah, who had originally taken Sarah in as a lodger. Keith Skinner interviewed Barbara for a video in April 1995.

KS   Do tell me the story of Old Aunt, how she came to be in your family and your life?

BP   Old Aunt joined the Hartnett family, to the best of my knowledge, after the death of Mr Hartnett – she went to live with Hannah Hartnett. Hannah, after her husband's death, started work and Old Aunt helped to look after Hannah's three children when she was not there. When Hannah married again, Old Aunt stayed with the family but the oldest daughter, Nellie, moved out and went to work. When Hannah died, Nellie came back to stay with her younger

---

of Maybrick but did not know how the change had come about. Indeed, Michael Maybrick, James's brother, had been listed in the 1881 census as Michael Maybury.

We felt compelled to follow the Maybury line, and discovered that the family had owned original shares in the Anglo Condensed Milk Company, now known of course as Nestle.

[1] Pamela West, who wrote a novel entitled *Yours Truly, Jack the Ripper*, had examined the letters in the Public Record Office that had been 'signed' by the Whitechapel murderer. One read, 'Dear Copper, I am the master of the art. I am going to be heavy on the guilded whores. Oh, we are masters. No animal like a nice woman, the fat are the best. My mouth waters when I think of the next nice fat partridge. They'll find nice little partridge breasts some day in their cupboards. Jack the Ripper.' Pamela lived in America but paid me a visit in early 1996. On seeing some of my research material, she immediately recalled this letter. We have since tried to locate the letter, but without success. The reference to a woman as an animal is interesting in that it is a habit shared by both Maybrick and the author of the diary. It might also be noted that the reference to 'guilded whores' should read 'gilded whores'.

brother and sister. The family did not get on very well with Hannah's second husband – he was not very nice and Nellie decided to move to other accommodation with William, Elsie and Old Aunt. Although William and Elsie married, Nellie stayed single and looked after Old Aunt. It was just before the First World War when Old Aunt became ill and Nellie went into the missions, where she met my mother. Nellie tried to put Old Aunt into a mental hospital and it was my mother, Alice Bills, who looked after her. Old Aunt was, I was always told and understood to be, the mistress of Maybrick – James Maybrick. That was the only connection she had with the Bills family. It was circumstances. That was the only connection with the Hartnett family – she lived with them for many years.

KS Could you tell me how much you know about Old Aunt. You said you were told that she was Maybrick's mistress – what else did they tell you about her?

BP I understood her name was Sarah – but she was never referred to as Sarah, only Old Aunt, and Maybrick himself was never mentioned as a man. The impression I got was that he was not around at the time she lived with the Hartnett family. He was never mentioned directly, only as 'she was a mistress to James Maybrick who was poisoned by his wife'. That is the only connection I can tell you. I do not think he was there at the time – he did not visit at the time – and that the lady who became my stepmother, Nellie Hartnett, ever met him. I think she knew what she knew from her mother.

KS Did they tell you the name of Maybrick – did they say James?

BP No, I don't think they did – she was Maybrick's mistress.

KS How much did they let you know about the crime?

BP Very little – only that she was the mistress of the man who was poisoned by his wife. Most of what I know is from family conversations and when I spoke about Old Aunt to my stepmother, Nellie Hartnett. She was quite a lady in her own way. We went to Cottisbrook Street after Auntie died. My mother, Alice Bills, became ill, and Nellie moved to Welling so that she could nurse my mother for the last two years of her life. All I was told was that the Bible was given to Alice Bills during these last two years when she became rather religious. After my mother died, my stepmother Nellie gave the Bible to me but, to be quite honest, I did not look inside it – I just put it on the shelf. It was not until my stepmother died that I looked at it properly. It came down to me but its origins I could not say.

KS How did Old Aunt come to live with the Hartnett family?

BP I think after the death of her [Hannah's] husband she was possibly looking to rent rooms and Old Aunt was looking for somewhere to live. I do not remember any reference to Old Aunt when William Hartnett was alive.

KS What sort of person was Old Aunt?

BP Until she became ill I was always told that she was quite a lady and behaved in a ladylike manner. She was extremely good with children. She didn't have any relations to the best of my knowledge. When she died Alice Bills, my mother, registered her death. She was a very dear, sweet old lady until she became ill.

KS How did Nellie feel about putting her in a mental home?

BP Very, very disturbed. I think Old Aunt set fire to the house and, as Nellie was working long hours, she felt she had no other option. It was not until she visited her at the mental home that she realised just how horrendous it was and she was so upset about it that my mother, Alice Bills, said that Old Aunt should come and live with us.

KS She became part of the family?

BP She did.

KS   How did the family feel about her?

BP   My father used to go to her in the evenings. They had a great respect for her. There was no relation – it was just a courtesy title.

KS   Did your family ever talk about what her background might have been?

BP   Not really – if there was talk I cannot remember – apart from the fact that she had been quite a lady in her time, when she had been with Maybrick. They did not speculate on her life with Maybrick; nothing was really known about him other than he had money. We never speculated on the murder.

KS   In 1927 your mother registered her death – did your mother have knowledge of Old Aunt's background?

BP   No – but then again I could be quite wrong.

KS   Where did she live in Cottisbrook Street in relation to the rest of the family?

BP   This is pure conjecture but I thought she had rooms upstairs. It was not a very big house. I was only two when I lived there but I thought Nellie spent her time upstairs with the old lady when she was not at work.

KS   Did your father go up and see her?

BP   Oh yes, in the evenings, to keep an eye on her. She used to call my father the butler. She thought he was the butler. She called him 'Bills' – she was obviously harking back to the past.

Hannah Hartnett's maiden name was Reed. Upon learning this, I asked Keith to send Barbara a copy of the photograph of Elizabeth Susannah Maybrick drinking tea with the old lady.

Sarah Ann Robertson had attended the wedding of Hannah's son, William Hartnett, and Ethel in September 1923. Ethel, when shown the photo by Barbara in 1995, had no doubt that the old lady in the picture was definitely Sarah Ann Maybrick. Even the location of the photograph was recognised. It was 24 Cottisbrook Street.

The connection to the Whittlesey Maybricks was now firmly established.

James Maybrick's and Sarah Ann Robertson's illegitimate children had not all 'died', as Sir Charles Russell had been told. We may even have discovered living descendants of the notorious Whitechapel murderer.

CHAPTER

9

'I FIRST SAW THE DIARY IN 1968 OR 1969'

I FIRST MET ANNE Barrett in February 1993. It was also the first time I had met her then husband Michael and their only child, Caroline, then aged eleven.

I made the trip to Liverpool with Paul Begg and Martin Howells. None of us knew what to expect. What we found was a terraced house in Goldie Street, not more than half a mile from Liverpool Football Club.

Mike Barrett appeared strange to me even then, but I put it down to my own inability to understand those males born and bred in Liverpool. My experiences over the next two years, however, would soon improve that fault in my education.

'Promise me that my family won't be involved in this,' Mike said almost as soon as I had got out of my car. First, I could not promise him anything and, secondly, Anne and Caroline were already there. I certainly had not insisted on their presence.

The house was modest, but it was very much a home. As we entered I remember thinking about the Hitler Diaries, Konrad Kujau's lifestyle and his Nazi memorabilia. Although this diary had been compared to the work of Mr Kujau, it clearly was not the same kettle of fish.

We sat in the front room and my eyes wandered to the bookshelf. The only Jack the Ripper book on view was Colin Wilson's and Robin Odell's. Paul, Martin and I had long since concluded that, *if* it had been forged, this diary had involved extensive research.

As we all continued to talk, I noticed a distance between

Mike and Anne but put it down to eighteen years of marriage. (I was not far wrong, but hadn't the foggiest idea then what I would find out about their relationship eighteen months later.)

Mike told us his story about how he obtained the diary from Tony Devereux. He said he did not know where Tony got it and would show concern at this point as to whether the diary could be 'taken away' from him. Anne and Caroline did not say anything but Anne's eyes were knowing. One thing I was sure of: Anne knew something that we weren't being told. It certainly did not occur to me that Mike didn't.

We had promised to take the Barretts to lunch. A cab was ordered for them as we could not all fit into my car. Caroline asked if she could travel with us. I said it was OK, but Caroline sought confirmation, 'Is that OK, Mum?' There was no attempt to discourage her. Paul Begg and Martin were relentless. The poor kid had barely sat down in the car when they started a cross-examination. 'Do you remember when your dad came home with the diary? Do you remember whether your dad phoned Tony and asked him where he got the diary from? Do you remember the row when your dad told your mum he was going to get it published?'

I wished I had trusted my initial instinct. Caroline remembered clearly the day that would change the Barretts' lives for ever. She remembered the day her dad came home with the diary. She remembered her dad pestering Tony, and she could not forget the row between her mother and father. Caroline told the truth; that is all a kid of eleven can do. Caroline then added a detail that her parents would later confirm: her mum had wanted to burn it after one horrible row when her dad said he was going to get 'the diary' published.

After a quick tour around the centre of Liverpool, which included a trip to the Cavern, Tithebarn Street and Whitechapel, we settled at the Moat House for a Carvery lunch. I sat at the head of the table with Mike and Martin to my right, Caroline and Anne to my left, and Paul Begg opposite. My only clear memory of that lunch was when Martin was questioning Mike.

'We believe that you got the diary from Tony, but there must be more.'

Mike replied, 'Would you split on a mate?'

Anne's ears seemed to act like a radar. 'What was that?' she asked, as she turned her head away from Paul, to whom she had been speaking, and towards me, who had not said a word. I explained to Anne that we accepted the story of Tony Devereux but felt that if Mike knew that Tony had perhaps bought something that was not quite kosher he would not be able to say so. Anne's response was, 'Did you nick it, Mike?'

What on earth was that all about? Did this mean that Anne did not believe what Mike had told her? If that was the case then Caroline was lying, but I didn't think so. Anne's comment bothered me, but it was going to be a little while yet before I would understand it.

We returned to Goldie Street. My questions were directed at Anne. 'What was your maiden name?' 'Graham.' 'What do you do for a living?' 'I'm a personal assistant to a stockbroker.' Mike was yapping to the two authors, but the wry smile of this intriguing woman said far more than I could understand – then.

Paul Begg, in a letter to Keith Skinner dated 24 July 1994 recalled his memories of that first meeting.

Regarding why Mike Barrett didn't go to the library for Maybrick books. I am not sure to what extent Barrett actually researched either the Ripper or Maybrick. His knowledge of both the Ripper and Maybrick has always struck me as negligible and to the best of my knowledge he has never attempted to show off his learning, volunteer information, or otherwise attempt to influence the research. Further, when I visited him with Paul Feldman and Martin Howells, he claimed never to have heard of *The Uncensored Facts* until he got it from the library on hearing that I was going to be paying a visit. I think he was also completely ignorant of *The Ripper Legacy*. Without seeming to be big-headed, such ignorance of leading Ripper titles suggests to me that he had not done research. Finally, neither he nor his wife displayed any emotion except amazement when Paul Feldman showed them how JUWES could become JAMES. I think I'd have laughed out loud at that if I had forged the Journal. My overall feeling was that he'd done very little and probably no research and that his statement to have undertaken a lot of work on the Journal was largely to secure for himself a claim to having identified Jack the Ripper as James Maybrick and thus more than mere ownership of the Journal.

Over the next couple of months, when I found myself unable to communicate with Mike, I would ask if I could speak to Anne. I am not sure why – other than that I seemed to be able to get her to listen to me while Mike seemed at times to be almost incoherent. He appeared to be drinking more each time I spoke to him.

During the next conversation I had with Mike when he was sober he muttered, 'I always talk to Anne's dad about this. He said I should have gone with you.'

I did not understand what Mike meant and told him so. He simply explained that he discussed the diary with his father-in-law when drinking at the Legion, but it sounded as if Anne's father had pretty definite opinions about the thing.

'I'm just repeating what he said,' Mike explained. 'I don't know why he said it.'

None of us had taped any of the general chatter on that first day. I was later to regret it. There were many occasions, a year or two later, when I would desperately try to recall my conversation with Anne. She had mentioned the name Jones, and a birthday at Christmas.

'My first son was due to be born on Christmas Day and my wife was born on December the twenty-first,' I told

Anne. I think we were discussing astrology at the time. However, it was an envelope I had noticed on that first visit to their home that was playing on my mind. It had been addressed to 'Ms Susan Barrett'. Not Mike, not Anne nor Caroline. Susan. Why?

After coffee at the Barretts', Mike offered to show us the grave of Maybrick and Battlecrease House. The grave made me shiver. The photograph I had seen in a book written in the 1970s had a cross above the headstone. It was no longer there. It had not fallen off: someone in the last twenty years or so had clearly vandalised the headstone. There had been no similar attack on any other grave in Anfield Cemetery.

Let me make myself clear on one point: while I am a believer in God, I have always found it difficult to accept that there is life after death. There have been times when I'd have liked to, but I've always thought that life after death is the human way of facing the inevitable end. During this investigation, however, I began to wonder. On the back of the gravestone was a water stain that had manifested itself over time. To me it looked exactly like a man holding a knife.

On to Battlecrease House, still semidetached and, apart from the gardens, looking almost identical to the photographs of 105 years ago. As we drove up, I recognised the house on the left of the semi as the one I had seen in *Murder Casebook*, but Mike insisted it was the one on the right. Out of respect we followed Mike's lead. The owner was mowing his lawn and came to see what we wanted. Was this once Battlecrease House? we asked. No, that was next door.

Paul Dodd, owner and occupier, answered the door. He was unable to invite us in as he had guests at the time but was very amenable and offered to answer some questions.

'Have you sold any furniture recently?'
'No.'
'Have you had a robbery in the last few years?'
'No.'
'Has there been any work done recently?'

Paul Dodd had heard – from Shirley Harrison, on the telephone – that Maybrick's diary had recently been discovered. He went on to explain that new storage radiators had been installed in 1988 or 1989. I was standing at the top of the small flight of stairs that led from the garden to the back door. As the house had been converted into separate flats, this was Mr Dodd's 'front' door. To my right at the bottom of the stairs stood Paul, Martin and Mike. Mike's reaction to Mr Dodd's statement played on our minds for months. He visibly staggered backwards. Had something connected? Mr Dodd gave me his telephone number and said I could phone any time and arrange to come and see him.

I was to discover on my return to Battlecrease that the work that had been done was in the very room in which James Maybrick had slept. Had the diary been found in the house by an electrician? Was it stolen? Had Tony Devereux bought it 'off the back of a lorry'?

I was already a firm believer in the authenticity of this document for reasons I have explained. I was beginning to wonder if the diary had been found in the house and subsequently sold to Devereux; Mike's reaction to Mr Dodd's comments made me feel that, at that moment, Mike had suddenly come to a similar conclusion. It was time to speak to the electrical contractors hired to do the job.

Paul Dodd told me they were called Portus and Rhodes, and he gave me their phone number.

I contacted the company's owner, Mr Rhodes. He said that he had never heard any whispers from his staff about anything unusual happening while they were working on the premises. He went as far as to say that one electrician had found a Victorian newspaper and asked if he could keep it. Paul had said he could. Although I had got Paul Dodd's mind wondering, he and Mr Rhodes said that they would be very surprised if anything had been taken. I, however, remained suspicious.

Mike Barrett had taken the diary to the literary agent Doreen Montgomery in April 1992. Three years before, in

1989 – for the first time since Maybrick's death on 11 May 1889 – the floorboards in what was his bedroom had been removed. I was finding it difficult to accept that there was not a connection between the two events.

Mike Barrett did not change his story. He continued to insist that the diary had been given to him by Tony Devereux but knew nothing else. Mike and Tony became friends after regular meetings in a pub called the Saddle.

I obtained the telephone numbers of the electricians involved with the job. My questions were the same whomever I spoke to: Can you remember anything being found? Do you know the Saddle in Anfield (the pub Mike and Tony used to drink in together)? Do you know of the names Devereux and Barrett? In each case the answers were negative. Was I barking up the wrong tree? I had already come to know some Liverpudlians as braggers as well as blaggers. Surely someone must know something.

One evening as I returned home from my office in Baker Street, together with Martin Howells, my wife informed me that a man with a Liverpool accent had telephoned wanting to speak to me.

He had not left a name or phone number, and would ring back later. Martin and I had dinner together, as my family had eaten earlier. Who had made the phone call? I was excited and on edge.

It was not long before I got my answer. It was one of the electricians who had worked at Mr Dodd's house. The chap will remain nameless: I have no wish to embarrass him.

He informed me that he overheard two of his colleagues, during a tea break while working at the house, mentioning 'something to do with Battlecrease'. Number 7 Riversdale Road had not been known as Battlecrease since Mr Fletcher Rodgers took over the property after James Maybrick's death.

If my contact was telling me the truth then the diary had been removed from the house. Somehow and at some time Tony Devereux, with or without his drinking companion Mike Barrett, must have purchased the diary.

So my instincts were correct, were they? Was he confirming that I had not been wasting my time? Yes, he said, he could confirm that, provided I agreed not to mention his name to the other electricians. I duly agreed.

Our conversation continued. He had been in a car with the colleagues he had mentioned. He said he had noticed a parcel wrapped in brown paper under the front passenger seat. The journey took them to Liverpool University. His colleagues were attempting to 'authenticate' whatever was in that parcel. He was to wait in the car.

(Mike Barrett had always said that Tony Devereux had given him the diary wrapped in brown paper with string tied around it.)

My contact went on: 'I remember something being thrown out of the window of the room where we were working at Mr Dodd's house. It was put into the skip. With everything that I've since heard about the diary and considering the trip to Liverpool University, I think I've solved your problem.'

We contacted Liverpool University. They recalled the visit of these two gentlemen. They could not confirm that what they had seen was a diary, journal or anything similar. Unfortunately, they could not, or would not, tell me what they did examine.

I had to contact the two electricians identified by their colleague. The first denied all knowledge of anything, but informed me that his associate (the second electrician) did indeed drink at the Saddle. He lived around the corner. As I mentioned earlier, Mike Barrett's first concern was that he might lose ownership of the diary. It was around the time that I was speaking to the electricians that I recalled this concern. Did Mike know the diary had been stolen – from Battlecrease? If so, did he think that if this was discovered he would lose ownership?

I spoke to the landlord of the Saddle. He remembered Tony Devereux, Mike Barrett and occasionally Mike's father coming in for lunchtime drinks. He could not remember ever having heard about the diary until long after the news had broken in the *Liverpool Post* and Mike Barrett had come in with a cheque in his hand claiming 'he had the diary of Jack the Ripper'.

I was almost certain that the diary was stolen. The electrician who had telephoned my home said he would go on video and state that it had been removed from Paul Dodd's house, provided he was not identified.

He then seemed totally focused on what money he would receive for his appearance. For the first time his story bothered me. I am only being honest when I say that I pushed this thought to the back of my mind – of course he was telling the truth. It *had* to be the solution. The diary had been stolen. Mike Barrett was concerned that when this came out he would have to return the diary to Paul Dodd. I wanted these to be the answers – but were they?

Why did I feel so uncomfortable with these thoughts, despite their logic?

I tried to telephone the electrician who lived near the Saddle – one of the two who had been identified to me by the man who had telephoned. His girlfriend answered. He was not there. I left my name and number and described myself as a film producer (in the past this always ensured a return call). He did not call back. I felt more confident. Maybe he did have something to hide.

I left it a few weeks before phoning him again. This time I was lucky: he answered. I accused him of theft. He would neither admit nor deny that he had removed the diary from the house. He continued, 'What is my confession worth?'

I contacted Mr Dodd and asked him if he would fight for repossession of the diary if it was ascertained that it had been removed from his property. Mr Dodd assured me he did not expect its complete return. 'Possession is nine-tenths of the law, but I don't want to see someone else become extremely wealthy upon my misfortune.' Paul Dodd is the headmaster of a local school, honourable and honest. He gave me permission to approach Mike Barrett with a commercial deal.

'Mike, an electrician's prepared to confirm that he took the diary from Battlecrease in 1989. I've spoken to Paul Dodd and he's requested five per cent of whatever you receive in order not to contest ownership of the document. Can I tell him he has a deal?'

Mike's reply was, 'Tell him to fuck off. The diary never came from the house.'

Within twenty-four hours Mike Barrett had knocked on the door of the said electrician; he accused him of lying and told him he would never do a deal.

My worst fear had been realised. My contact and his fellow electrician would lie for the right price. It seemed as though I was no nearer the truth. I had been convinced that the diary was stolen. I had been wrong. The diary had not been stolen and Mike Barrett knew it. If he was telling the truth about Devereux being vague about where the diary had come from, then Barrett would never have missed this opportunity to settle with Paul Dodd. Barrett knew the diary had not been stolen. More importantly, if the diary was forged by Mike Barrett, or anyone associated with him, here was an opportunity to 'create provenance'. For five per cent, Mike now had the chance to 'prove' where the diary had come from, and associate the thing directly with James Maybrick. He refused. One thing was certain: Mike did not forge it. His immediate response to my question also confirmed that there was no Mr (or Ms) Big in the background. There was no need for him to discuss the proposed deal with anyone else.

From this I concluded that Mike Barrett knew the diary's provenance. I believed that he knew its entire history. I was mistaken, but was not to realise this until six months later. The same mistake was also made by Scotland Yard, understandable at the time, given the evidence and circumstances.

All went quiet until January 1994, when I learnt that Anne had left Mike and taken Caroline with her. This marked the beginning of a series of extraordinary phone calls that would start at any time of the day, or night, from a man who was broken, hurt and angry about his wife's departure. Was I about to get to the truth at long last?

When Mike Barrett made his first call to me, after Anne had left, he claimed he wanted to help. He gave the impression that, while in the past he had never said anything to anyone, he now wanted me to discover the truth so that the diary would gain its rightful place and be recognised as genuine. Mike would not 'split on a mate' but would give me 'clues', knowing that I would follow them up.

The first clue?

Early in 1994, Mike Barrett ended a conversation with the words, 'When you know the name of my solicitor then you will really know the truth.' What did this mean? I sent Melvyn Fairclough to the Law Society to find out what he could about Barrett's solicitors, Morecroft, Dawson and Garnett. The answer must be here. Mike Barrett's phone call suggested he was pointing me in the direction of the truth.

Melvyn returned that day dumbstruck. One of the practising partners of this firm had the name George R. Davidson. George Davidson was the name of James Maybrick's best friend, in whose arms he had died. Was there a family connection?

Maybrick's friend had died in mysterious circumstances leaving a gold watch under his pillow, which was discovered after his death. Subsequent visits to St Catherine's House enabled us to track down the lineage of Mr Davidson the solicitor. There was no connection whatsoever to Maybrick's friend. Follow-up calls to Barrett were met with nothing further to add to what he had already told me. He did not even comment on whether George R. Davidson was the person he was referring to. More work was carried out on the company.

The solicitor representing Mike Barrett was a Mr Bark-Jones. We discovered that Mr Bark-Jones had worked at Bell Lamb & Joynson in Liverpool. So had Albert Johnson's solicitor, Richard Nicholas. Barrett had the diary. Albert Johnson had the watch. Was there a connection?

Melvyn was dispatched back to the Law Society.

An hour later he telephoned me, excited. Very. 'You'll never guess the history of Bell Lamb & Joynson.' He continued: 'They used to be known as Raynor and Wade inc. Cleaver and Cleaver. It's the same firm that Florence Maybrick used to represent her at her trial in 1889.'

Another coincidence, or was it? Yes, unfortunately. We contacted Mr Byron of Bell Lamb & Joynson. He wrote to me on 11 April 1994:

> So far as Richard Nicholas is concerned he was employed as an Assistant Solicitor with Raynor & Wade between 17th September 1979 and 28th November 1980. As I recall he joined us after completing his Articles following his first qualifying as a solicitor. Richard Jones was articled to Raynor & Wade from 1978 and following his becoming qualified remained with the firm, firstly as an Assistant Solicitor and subsequently as a Junior Partner. He left in December 1985. Because of my prior association with the firm before either of these persons joined it, it would come as a very great surprise to me if they had found anything relating to the Maybrick case . . .
>
> The only Maybrick document which is held is an original Will made by Florence Maybrick dated the 8th March 1890, made presumably after her death sentence had been commuted to life imprisonment. So far as disclosure of this document is concerned however I take the view that it in fact belongs to Florence Maybrick's descendants, whoever they may be, and without their authority I am unable to disclose it to anyone.

The connection between Richard Nicholas and Mr Bark-Jones was a mere coincidence. Nothing more.

The work on the firm of solicitors had been time-consuming and expensive, but, having got so far and been unable to extract any further information from Mike Barrett, we had to continue with our enquiries. We followed up on the name Garnett. The full name of Florence Maybrick's solicitors at the time of her trial was Cleaver, Holden, Garnett and Cleaver.

Another red herring?

More birth certificates, more marriage certificates, more death certificates (St Catherine's House never gave us a discount!). There was no connection with the Garnett who was a partner at the firm who represented Florence at the time of her trial and the Garnett at the firm who now represented Mike Barrett.

I was devastated. High hopes and much hard work had led only to a brick wall, a wall that was so high I was beginning to feel that I would never reach the top. I had to believe I would – I had to continue. The cynics had got to me. Each of them had his own suspect, and his pride would not allow him to even *consider* Maybrick, whatever the evidence.

I knew that the diary was not a forgery and, therefore, there had to be an answer. I could only pray that the answer had not died with Tony Devereux.

Our investigation into Tony's background was detailed and thorough. Despite my belief about the authenticity of the diary, I had to eliminate the possibility that he had forged it.

His daughter, Mrs Nancy Steele, a charming woman, was to provide the answers. She knew nothing of the diary. 'If my dad had owned it, he wouldn't have left it to Mike Barrett. They were friends, yes, but he had others who were much closer. His grandchildren, who he adored, were most important of all. I don't believe this was left to Mike by my father, and I resent the implication.'

Nancy Steele later confirmed that the handwriting in the diary was not her father's. Tony's will supported that. The witnesses to his will were also investigated. The Ripper author and diary detractor Melvin Harris also investigated the will. He concluded that Mr Cain, one of the witnesses, was the forger. According to Mr Harris, Mr Cain's handwriting matched that in the diary and he had mysteriously 'disappeared around the time that the diary became public'.

On hearing this I contacted Nancy Steele once more. Harris should have done the same thing. Mr Cain had not disappeared. The poor man suffered from a severe illness, which left him unable to go up and down stairs. He had moved to a bungalow. No mystery, Mr Harris. It would not be the only time Harris could consider himself fortunate not to be sued.

A later conversation with Mrs Steele did, however, give us an intriguing clue.

She recalled, 'I do remember my sister asking my dad whether she could borrow a book that was on his table. It was called *Murder, Mayhem & Mystery*, by Richard Whittington-Egan. My father told my sister, "OK, but let me have it back on the weekend; it belongs to Bongo."' That was Tony's nickname for Mike.

This was the very book that Barrett said had led him to deduce that the diary had been written by James Maybrick. (That book, with Mike Barrett's name in it, was eventually handed over to New Scotland Yard.)

Another piece of the jigsaw. This time supporting Mike's story. Devereux, at the very least, was aware of the diary's existence. He was part of the story.

March 1994. Another day, another phone call from Mike, another clue. This time I learnt that Anne was employed by a firm of stockbrokers called Rensburg. Their office address was Silk House Court, Tithebarn Street. My memory recalled the address of Maybricks offices, Knowsley Buildings . . . Tithebarn Street. Investigations continued. Silk House Court had been built on the very site where Maybrick had worked. Had Anne discovered the diary here? Had she removed it without permission? Was this why Mike was frightened of losing ownership and why he did not want his family to be involved? Rensburg were later to move to 100 Old Hall Street, Liverpool. Old Hall Street? In 1868, Thomas Conconi had referred to James Maybrick in his will as '. . . of Old Hall Street Liverpool . . . now residing at No 55 Bromley Street, off Commercial Road London'.

Silk House Court was built in the late 1960s. Anne did not work there until the 1980s. Unless old furniture was the answer, this might prove to be another red herring. A visit to Rensburg and conversations with directors of the company convinced me a herring it was. The firm had inherited no old furniture with the premises.

Once again, it seemed, Mike *could* have created provenance. History would have supported him. The main criticism of the diary, when Shirley Harrison's book was published in 1993, was its provenance. Its history was not known. There had now been two opportunities for Mike Barrett to be dishonest. Either the electrician's story or some story about Silk House Court would probably have convinced the world of the diary's authenticity and, thereby, increased his royalty cheque.

It was becoming apparent to me that Mike Barrett was looking for the answer himself, searching to find the connection. His clues were pointing the finger at Anne. Why? Two clues, and both had led to nothing. Mike's suggestions indicated that he knew that the diary had come from Anne, but I now realised he did not know how, or why. Mike was guessing.

Mike contacted me again and this time talked about the Maybrick 'illegitimates'. He said there were four, not five, as had been reported by MacDougall and every subsequent writer. Their names? Matthew, Mark, Luke and John. Was the Mark anything to do with the Mark Maybrick I had discovered in Peterborough? Mike Barrett seemed unable, or unwilling, to explain where he got these names from.

Then Mike came up with another gem – another 'story': 'Anne's grandfather had been a prison warder. Why don't you look into that?'

As with all the little clues Mike gave me, I repeated it to my researcher Keith Skinner. He was circumspect. We had discovered a report that in 1895, six years into her prison sentence, Florence Maybrick had had a child in prison and that the father was a prison warder. Further work was carried out but nothing could be found that would connect the warder to Anne's family.

The next time Mike and I spoke, he ended the conversation by screaming, 'Find Anne and ask her to swear on Caroline's life that she is not a Maybrick.'

I was intrigued. The diary was in Mike's possession and recently he had suggested that there could be a connection to Anne through James Maybrick, or through Florence and a prison warder, and he had even implied theft via Silk House Court. Subtlety no longer played a part in Mike's hints. Was Anne now an illegitimate Maybrick?

Anne and Mike had been together when the diary had come into Mike's possession. If Anne had given it to him, surely Mike would have asked her where she had got it. It was clear, however, that he did not know. I could only conclude, therefore, that Anne had not given Mike the diary. So why was Mike connecting his wife to it?

By now I was sure that the diary had come from Anne. If I was right then she was hiding its origin, even from her husband. James Maybrick's five illegitimate children were not registered with his surname, but they did exist and the probability was that they had had children who had also had children. If Anne had descended from this line, what we knew would start to make sense. The diary would have come through the family and her silence was to protect her eleven-year-old daughter. If Jack the Ripper was her ancestor, maybe Anne had decided that the secret should die with her. Would any mother want to pass that burden on to her child?

I could not dismiss Mike, though, but as yet had not found a Maybrick connection in either Mike's or Anne's direct lineage (although Mike Barrett's great-grandmother was called Mary Kelly).

I was confused. Were we being side-tracked deliberately? Did Mike know the answer and were his clues simply a device to throw me off the scent? I remembered the envelope. Damn it! Who was Susan Barrett? Was Anne really Susan? I expressed my concern to Keith Skinner. He was sure that Mike and Anne were who they said they were. To confirm this Keith checked local Liverpool newspapers for any report of their marriage. His objective was to match an address with one that we could connect to Anne or Mike.

While researching, Keith came across something which I did not expect.

He had discovered a report in a newspaper of a Michael Barrett who had had a 'confrontation' with the police in 1974 in respect of a violent incident. Details are not necessary for this story.

I was astounded at this report. This could not be the Mike Barrett I knew, surely. He may have been canny. But violent? No.

We managed to obtain a description of the man: it could have been Mike but there were discrepancies. However, the detailed description of a scar on the man's leg would be conclusive. I telephoned Mike and asked him if he had a scar. I described it in detail and described where it was. He denied it.

I had asked my researchers to check every Michael Barrett and Michael John Barrett who had been married in Liverpool circa 1975. John had been the middle name given to Mike when he was confirmed. Were this couple who they had said they were? I had always believed that the Ripper was known to the Establishment. If he was, would the government have protected his descendants or deliberately confused their records?

Carol Emmas obtained a copy of a marriage certificate of a Michael John Barrett married to a Susan Claire Jones. I looked at the signature: it was Mike's. What on earth was this about? Who was Susan Claire Jones?

There was only one way to resolve all of these questions. At the beginning of July 1994 I arranged to see Mike in Liverpool. I needed to know whether he had a scar on his leg. I needed to know about Susan Claire Jones.

And there had been another development. Mike had just told the Liverpool *Post* that he had forged the diary.

On Tuesday morning, 5 July 1994, at 11 a.m., Robert Johnson, Carol Emmas and I drove to Goldie Street. I knocked on the door; there was no answer. I knocked louder. Still no answer. I tried to look through the net curtains but could not see anything. However, there was a gap at the edge of the window. The room was no longer like the one I recalled on my first visit to the Barretts. The furniture had gone, the warmth had gone, it was no longer a home. My eyes focused on the farthest point of what was the lounge/dining room, but it was not until they reached the nearest point to the window that I saw a pair of legs crossed and stretched outright. Barrett was asleep. I now banged on the window. He woke and came at once to the front door and greeted me like a long-lost friend. He invited all three of us in. He slumped immediately back into his chair and lit a cigarette. He stank – the whole place stank – and his trousers were wet. On the floor next to him was an empty whisky bottle and an ashtray full of cigarette stubs. Robbie asked him when he had last eaten, but he could not remember.

Robbie went to the kitchen and found some soup and proceeded to heat it. Mike had been sitting on a letter written to him by Anne. What had broken them up at this point I did not know and did not understand. I did know that whatever it was, he couldn't live with it and my heart went out to him despite my anger with him for consistently lying to me.

I asked him to roll up his trouser leg. There was no preamble: I was direct. He did so. The scar was there. He had previously denied in telephone conversations that the man referred to was him. He had denied any knowledge of what I was talking about and had denied having a scar on his leg. Once again, he had lied. When challenged, he simply said, 'Shall we play cards?'

I asked Mike why he had claimed to have forged the diary. Mike's response was 'I can prove it.' I told him to prove it. Mike said, 'Ha, ha, ha, underline, ha, ha!' It was pitiful. I looked at Mike, remembering the photograph he had arranged to have taken by the Liverpool *Post* the previous week, standing by Maybrick's grave.

It was almost as if Mike Barrett was attempting to re-create the author of the diary in his own image without, fortunately, also re-creating the Whitechapel murders. He was even beginning to look like Maybrick, cutting his moustache the same way. You could hear the words of the diary '. . . 'tis love that she spurned, 'tis love that will finish me'.

Mike Barrett adored both his wife and daughter, but I had a job to do and I knew that now was the time to strike. He was weak, but, while my heart went out to him, I knew that Barrett would have done the same had the tables been turned. I took out the marriage certificate, switched on the tape recorder in front of him, and showed him the signature – but only the signature. 'Did you sign this, Mike?' I asked.

'Yes, I can't deny that,' he replied.

'Then, Mike, who the fuck is Susan Claire Jones?' I said.

The whole certificate was then given to Mike. His response was honest, but intriguing. 'What the fuck is my signature doing on this? I married Anne.' Mike was clearly as confused as I was. He was also still trying to understand Anne's connection with the diary. He got his address book out and gave me the telephone numbers of all the people he believed had a close connection to Anne. 'Take them, I've had enough,' he said. 'Find out.' I was not going to stay long – there was nothing more to be gained.

As we were about to leave the telephone rang, and I answered it. That phone call, that moment, was to lead to the truth – finally. Had I not been there, had I not answered the phone on that day at that moment, perhaps we would not know the truth today.

The voice on the other end of the telephone was that of Mike's sister Lynne. She had been concerned. I told her of the condition I had found Mike in and that he had now been fed. She said Mike had been staying with her and that his habits were similar in her home and that was why he had gone back to Goldie Street. She had her family to consider. Lynne thanked me for what I had done, asked me not to contact her parents, and was clearly very resentful of what the diary had done to the family.

I was on a roll here as well. I asked Lynne if I could contact her at home at a later date, and she gave me her telephone number.

Robbie, Carol and I returned to Robbie's house. What was going on? Was Barrett a bigamist, or was Anne Graham really Susan Jones? That would certainly explain the envelope that I recalled seeing when I first saw Mike. It would also explain why I recalled that Jones was a name in Anne's past. But then again, Susan and Jones are very common names.

I had tracked down where Anne was now living. I could not, however, discover her telephone number. As I was about to leave Liverpool to return to London I asked Carol Emmas to go to the address where Anne lived and put a note through her letterbox to ask her to call me. It was time to go home.

Back in London I showed the marriage certificate to Keith Skinner and Melvyn Fairclough. They both felt it was Barrett's signature. I faxed it to Martin Fido, one of the diary's major detractors. He too believed it was Mike Barrett's signature (I had several examples of Mike's handwriting and signature: he had signed many documents for me for New Line Cinema, who had acquired the film rights to *The Diary of Jack the Ripper*).

Melvyn Fairclough was dispatched on another trip to St Catherine's House, this time in order to obtain the background to Susan Claire Jones and Michael John Barrett. Within forty-eight hours we had discovered that the Michael John Barrett who had married Susan Claire Jones had been born at the top of the road where Michael Barrett, the owner of the diary, had been brought up.

However often Mike had lied to me, I know he was no Laurence Olivier. He had admitted his signature at the bottom of the certificate but could not accept why it was on a certificate of marriage to someone he was not married to. It had been a genuine reaction. If he had anything to hide he would not have agreed that the signature was his. It's more likely that his comment would have been 'Prove it.' That would have been Mike. What was this all about?

Needless to say the note through Anne's letterbox had no effect. A week went past, then two. I was toying with the idea of ringing Lynne, but what would I say?

I took the plunge, and called her. My concerns about our conversation were unwarranted. She did the talking.

'When are you going to leave us alone? When will this stop?'

'It won't,' I said. 'Not until I know the truth. I've invested too much time and money to let it go away.

'If it is a fake, then I want to know who faked it. It means I've been conned and have wasted a big chunk of my life. If it's genuine then it's not by accident that it's in the hands of your brother. Until I know the truth you will have to put up with it.' Lynne was in tears and very upset. I felt rotten.

She put the telephone down on me. Who could blame her?

On July 20 1994 my brother-in-law Jon paid me a visit. I was updating him on our latest discoveries and investigations into Maybrick when the telephone rang. Jon answered and said it was someone called Anne.

'Who?' As I had not spoken to Mrs Barrett for six to eight months it did not cross my mind that this had anything to do with the diary.

She bellowed in my ear, 'Paul?'

Then she told me I had no right to upset her friends, and should 'back off'. Who did I think I was?

I told her I'd bought the film rights to *The Diary of Jack the Ripper*. I had paid for that and spent almost two years of my life employing people to ascertain the truth behind the diary. I was not going to let go now.

'I believe that you are connected to this diary,' I told her. 'I believe this has come from your family and I want to know the truth.'

What else was said I am not sure. I know we spoke for nearly four hours. At some point during the conversation Anne reminded me she was paying for the call and asked if I would phone her back. I immediately did. Not out of sympathy for her finances, but because she would have to give me her telephone number.

'If I agree to meet you, will you back off from the Barretts?' she asked.

'Why should I?'

'Because it has nothing to do with them.'

We arranged that I would see her at her home, and she repeated her request that I leave the Barretts alone.

'I promise, I won't contact anybody until we meet,' I said.

This was at the end of the four hours. I already sensed in her some new respect for me – but I sensed guilt, too.

Asking family to keep a secret is one thing; when the secret strays outside the family it is another. The diary and its origins were beginning to impact on people's lives. Anne had realised that my perseverance and her concealing the true story would only drag more innocent people into the affair.

Anne's upbringing made her feel guilty about that. Someone had telephoned her, clearly upset. I concluded that it must have been Lynne Barrett because of recent events, and later discovered that I had been right. But I remember thinking at the time: why has Lynne contacted Anne if the diary belongs to Mike? I was just a few days away from finding out more than I had hoped.

Shortly before these conversations took place I had asked Keith Skinner to check on one or two references that I recalled having read, but could not remember from which book. On 17 May 1994 Keith sent me a fax with other information he had found. He described this information as an 'observation', identifying a sentence on page 228 of the hardback edition (1957) of *This Friendless Lady*, by Nigel Morland: 'In January of that year she was moved from Aylesbury Prison to the house of the Epiphany, on the banks of the Fal in Cornwall, where, as Mrs Graham, she was to try to regain some of her former health and strength.'

Florence had called herself Mrs Graham, the same maiden name as that of Mike's wife, Anne Barrett. What was the connection? If Anne was connected to this diary then surely she was a Maybrick and had to be connected to the Whittlesey family.

If Anne had been connected to Florence, what was there to hide?

Although Florence Maybrick had been imprisoned for the wilful murder of her husband, it was later admitted by the Home Secretary that her conviction was unsafe and that she had not murdered James. Every book that has been written about her over the past century has been in total sympathy with her plight. But surely Anne must be a Maybrick, descended from one of the five illegitimate children identified by MacDougall in 1889.

I suspected that Florence Maybrick may have used the name Graham to give the whole world a clue about her husband's illegitimate children. That would be consistent with my thoughts about the letter she had written to her mother from Walton Prison on 21 July 1889.[1]

Keith's fax also pointed out page 229 of Nigel Morland's book:

> In July Florence Maybrick left the Home of the Epiphany, vanishing from the sight of the encamped reporters with a deft piece of official magic which somehow laid a false trail and got Florence into a train, unseen by anyone.
>
> But there was one lady in the carriage next to Florence who had been acquainted with her in Liverpool* and spent the journey with her.

The asterisk led to a footnote: 'Who generously gave me these details and a number of intimacies of Florence Maybrick which I cannot reveal.'

On Friday 22 July 1994 I drove to Liverpool. I had arranged to meet Anne at 1 p.m. the next day and Robbie Johnson had said I could stay with him on the Friday night. I did not arrive in Birkenhead until about 11.30 p.m. The traffic had been horrendous and on top of it all I had been stopped for speeding on one of the few occasions that the traffic cleared. Fortunately, I was only cautioned. After I had been asked where I lived, I was then

---

[1] The letter is fully transcribed and discussed in Chapter 15, Time Reveals All.

asked where I was going and why. It was as a result of this lengthy discussion that the kind officers (you have to say that) were so lenient.

As always, I got a warm welcome from Robbie. But I knew I was in for a night of Ripper chat. When I told him I had come up to see Anne he could not believe it. It had been only a week or two earlier that Carol Emmas had posted the note to Anne and the last time he had spoken to me at length on the phone. She had not then responded.

Robbie and I argued and drank, drank and argued. He *almost* convinced me he knew everything.

My investigations into the diary were now focused on Anne; my investigations into the watch were focused on Albert's wife, Valerie. 'It has nothing to do with either Valerie or Anne,' Robbie told me. 'Look at me, look at my brother, look at Mike Barrett.' Fortunately, by this time, Robbie had contradicted himself enough times that I knew I should not read too much into this statement. I suspected that he wanted me to believe he knew more than he really did. I think we dropped into our respective beds at around 6 a.m.

I recall a strong sunlight shining through the windows. The telephone woke me up; it was nearly 12.30 p.m. I panicked. I called Anne immediately and made some excuse as to why I would be late.

Robbie could still not believe I had an appointment with Anne. He drove in front of me in order to show me the way. On the way we picked up some flowers for Anne and a Disney video for Caroline.

As I got out of the car and walked the steps to Anne's flat in a semidetached house in Toxteth Park, Robbie drove off. I rang the bell and to my surprise Anne answered the door with her coat on (she had clearly changed her mind about inviting me in). My gifts were something of a surprise and she seemed a little perplexed about what to do given that she had a coat on and did not want to invite me in. She opened the door enough to take the flowers and video from me but made it clear that I should wait on the doorstep. I waited. It was not more than thirty seconds before she returned, and during that time I was trying to think where we could go to talk.

I recalled the Moat House, the place where I had taken the Barretts on my first visit, and asked Anne if she knew the way. She said she did, and although we got there eventually I learnt then, and have been reminded frequently since, that Anne's sense of direction leaves a lot to be desired.

When we finally arrived the public bar was closed, and so was the restaurant, but fortunately they allowed us to sit in the bar area and served us with drinks. After the conversation we had had earlier in the week, Anne had come fully prepared.

She was aware that I was not convinced she was who she said she was and had brought with her documents and photographs to prove me wrong. 'This is Mike and Caroline when she was four. This is me in Australia when I was a nurse.' Anne did admit to me that my reasons for thinking that she may have been Susan Claire Jones (I had told her this on the telephone) were valid.

'Since I spoke to you I obtained a copy of the wedding certificate myself,' she said. 'I was so convinced that it was Mike's signature that I wondered whether Mike had committed bigamy.' The marriage certificate for Michael John Barrett and Susan Claire Jones was a complete red herring. The similarity between the signatures of the two Michael Barretts was sheer coincidence. They were two totally different people. The time spent researching and puzzling over the marriage certificate had been completely wasted, although Anne did compliment me on my memory for recalling her 'Jones' connection.

'My grandfather married twice; his first wife's surname was Jones.'

What about the envelope? Anne explained: 'Mike has three sisters, one called Susan . . .' The Christmas birth? 'Susan was born on December the twenty-fourth.'

I went on to tell Anne my suspicions that the diary had come through the family. I then showed her the page in

Morland's book where he referred to Florence calling herself Mrs Graham. I also showed her a report that I had asked a private investigator to prepare about her background. This report and the page from Nigel Morland's book played on Anne's mind, but I was not aware of this at the time. I am not at liberty to reveal the details of the report.

That day was the twenty-fifth anniversary of my mother's second marriage, and I was due back in London between 7.30 and 8 p.m., but I had to phone home to say I was not going to make it.

Anne and I had been talking for three to four hours. I felt I had been a fool and my only consolation was that my convictions would lead me to the truth anyway.

It was becoming clear that no genealogist or historian would find the truth through pieces of paper and bureaucratic bullshit. This was later conceded by more than one of the historians working with me. On publication of this book, historians will try to hide behind pieces of paper. They will attempt to disprove what I have discovered by waving around official documents. While they may be able to use such 'evidence' to find fault with what I have discovered, I can assure you that these historians have never spent time with the actual people involved in the diary affair. Official documents can also, as we have discovered, tell lies.

Those who would dismiss the diary, of course, have still, after nearly five years, to prove how or why it was forged, who could have forged it, and when. No historian, genealogist, journalist or Ripperologist (there are a few exceptions, but they know who they are) has tried to get to know the people, talk to them, live in their environment. I did. It cost me dear. That is another story and maybe another book!

I am sure I don't have to emphasise further that these people are real. They go to the bathroom in the morning, they eat meals and they have emotions and, yes, they told fibs. But it was not to extract money from members of the public. They told lies to protect their families. Wouldn't you?

On that day, at the Moat House, I played police officer; I pressured Anne and I made accusations with the ultimate aim of finding the truth.

I accused Anne of not telling the truth in order to protect her daughter.

No, she said, I was wrong.

Mike?

Nope.

'Then who?' I asked.

'Not until my father is buried will I tell you what I know, but I can assure you it has nothing to do with the Barrett family. Please let them be.' There was an honesty in her voice. I did not know Anne, was not even sure that I could trust her, but I knew this was not a West End show staged by her and Mike for my benefit.

'Anne, a couple of questions. I assume that the Devereux story was rubbish?' Anne looked embarrassed. 'No, it was not. I gave it to Tony. I've always wanted to apologise to the Devereux family.'

'Why did you not give it to Mike direct?'

'Maybe I will tell you that story when I know you a little better.'

I asked my second question: 'What did you have to do with Mike's solicitors?'

'Not a lot. I just told Mike that they were a very respected firm with a first-class reputation. I knew of them during my time at Rensburg.'

Now I knew what had given Mike the idea about the solicitors.

I drove Anne home from the Moat House and little was said. In fact I think I played Anne a cassette of songs that my fifteen-year-old son had written and performed, so that she would realise that I was human too, that I also had emotions and I understood that family were more important than anything else. I was feeling confused and despondent because inside I knew that Anne was the person she said she was. Despondent because I had not uncovered a government protection scheme, despondent because Anne Barrett was Anne Graham. She was not Susan Claire Jones. The diary had nothing to do with Mike. I felt for her. She was suffering. She was not doing this for selfish reasons and she was not trying to increase her bank balance. She could have done that any time in the previous five years, as I was later to discover.

As I drove home from Liverpool my mind was racing. OK, Feldman, what *is* the answer? You wanted there to be a deep mystery behind the identities of Anne and Mike. There isn't one. Don't feel ashamed, though. You *were* right: Anne *was* the key, always had been. You had known from the start.

With a little positive thinking, I began to believe in what I had achieved. What more was to come?

On the very next day, Anne telephoned me. 'We need to talk,' she said abruptly. 'Are you coming to Liverpool this weekend?' I had in fact planned to, but as she had requested the meeting I saw an opportunity. 'No, I can't. I've spent too much time away recently. You come here. Come during the week. I'm sure Caroline will get on with my daughter and you can get away for a couple of days yourself.'

'Are you sure? Should you ask Carol first?' Of course, she was right: only women think of things like that. So I made the request of my wife there and then. Confirmation was given to Anne. Anne said she would come down by train.

A day, or two, later I received another call. There was a rail strike. I was not going to miss the opportunity to get to know Anne better. I was not going to give her time to change her mind. I arranged for her to be driven from Liverpool. Anne and Caroline arrived as planned. We ate and talked about everything but the diary. When the washing-up was completed and the sun had gone down, I suggested to Anne that we go into my study for a chat. She insisted on going into the garden. She admitted her fear, there and then, that I had bugged my study. To make her feel at ease I did not argue and complied with her request.

We walked the thirty yards to the end of the top lawn, where steps led us down on to the lower lawn. We sat on those steps. She said her father had encouraged her to come down to talk to me. She had also been concerned by the report that I had shown her at the Moat House, although, at the time, she had expressed nonchalance. Anne 'created' a story about why the confidential report's strange information existed. It sounded like bullshit to me. Anne knew I thought that.

'Do you believe what I've told you?' she asked.

'Not a bloody word,' I responded. 'I didn't think you would,' she said, unable to keep a straight face. The ice was broken.

Unfortunately, I cannot reveal the contents of the private investigator's report. I can only say that it confirmed that I was talking to the right person.

Whether it was the way I listened, or because of my honest response, Anne displayed trust for the first time. She agreed to come to my study – after I assured her it was not bugged. Anne sat on the opposite side of the desk to me.

I played her a tape, a conversation I had had with Annie Jepson (formally Maybrick). Annie recalled 'catching crabs by the seaside'. I then told Anne about my investigations into the Maybricks in Whittlesey. Sheppard Shalgrave Maybrick had a brother called Jack. Sheppard had disappeared before he was one year old; Jack died when he was seven. I suggested to Anne that Sheppard may have been her father. Anne had listened to me without comment. Then, quite unexpectedly, she said, 'You just might have something here, Paul. Believe it or not, I know very little about the diary. I first saw it in 1968 or 1969 when Dad was about to move house. I was packing up a lot of things and saw it in a black trunk with white writing on it. In the trunk was some tropical gear and a crucifix. All I have ever really known is that Dad was given it on Christmas Day 1950, by his stepmother Edith. She told him that his granny had left it to him.'

I was riveted. I asked what she thought when she first saw it.

'Not a lot really, Paul. Jack the Ripper was to me a bogeyman of my youth. I'm not sure that I even knew he was real. I briefly looked at it, but left it to read at another time. I was busy at the time, packing. When I eventually did ask my dad about it he was doing his [football] pools and just ushered me away. You didn't ask twice. I don't know when, but I also picked up that Edith's mother, Elizabeth, was a good friend of Alice Yapp. According to my father, his step-granny, of whom he was very fond, accompanied Yapp to the trial of Florence Maybrick.'

Anne's whole character seemed to change before my eyes. It was only a week or so ago that we had had that four-hour phone call. At best, when we finished, she did not hate me. When I took her to the Moat House, there was still anger. Earlier in the evening, I had felt there was still deep suspicion. It now appeared I had her complete trust. Or was it Anne's guilt surfacing once more? Now she had seen first-hand the amount of work that I had done and the money that had been lost due to her silence, maybe she felt bad. Still, I could not blame her. She was trying to protect her family.

Anne continued, her voice was almost apologetic. 'After my dad's second wife died, in 1989, he decided to move into sheltered accommodation and gave me a lot of his books and belongings. He had to make space. He gave me the diary with the words "You may as well have this too." I didn't tell Mike about it. I'm not sure why. Perhaps we just weren't sharing things at the time.'

Now Anne seemed sad. I kept her talking. 'How did it get to Tony Devereux? Why?'

'Mike had lost his self-esteem. He was drinking a lot, and I blamed myself for the problems we were having. He wasn't working: I was, and I enjoyed it. Mike was keen on writing, so, one day, on the spur of the moment, I decided to give him the diary. I thought he would try to write a novel around it. I never thought he would try and get it published. I gave it to Tony for two reasons, though. I didn't want Mike to know I was helping him. If he was going to be successful, I thought it best to distance myself.

I suppose the most important reason, though, was that I didn't want Mike to know it had come from my family. Mike would have pestered my father to the extreme.'

'Anne . . . why Devereux?' I tried again.

'I wanted Mike to make a success of himself. Perhaps my respect for the man I loved and married would return. It was not money, just the self-confidence. It did work for a while as he threw himself into research. Tony? He was close to Mike at the time, and I happened to know where he lived. I wrapped the diary in brown paper, and tied it with a bit of string, I think. I took it around to Tony and rang the bell. He took a long time to open the door. I nearly went back . . . I wish I had.' Anne giggled. 'I don't know what Tony must have thought. I just told him to give it to Mike and to tell him to do something with it. According to Mike, he faithfully did that. I don't know whether he ever told Mike or not.'

I was convinced from what Anne had told me that Mike had been told by Tony. Now I knew why Mike was continually implying his wife's involvement.

I spent very little time with Anne during the rest of the time she was with us. She chatted with my wife, and Naomi and Caroline, as I had predicted, got on well. Little was I to know that Anne's mind was working overtime. Her father had told her that he thought he was a twin. Her father had also told her that he believed the twin had died when he was seven years old. The crabs at the seaside? Anne's father had the same memory! She must have been thinking very hard. Twenty-four hours after she arrived, Anne departed with a promise: 'I will ask my father if he will see you.' Once again, I thanked her.

Anne phoned the next day. The tone of her voice was one of surprise. 'Dad said that he would talk to you. Can you come up on Saturday?'

I did not need to be asked twice.

10

'HOW I FAKED RIPPER DIARY'[1]

I HAVE ALREADY MENTIONED that Mike told the *Post* that he forged the diary. We need to go back a few weeks to look at this in more detail.

On Saturday, 25 June 1994, I was awoken by Robbie Johnson. I was staying at his cottage in Birkenhead. 'The diary, the watch. It's all a load of bollocks,' Robbie was saying. He was angry. A newspaper landed on my face.

'What the fuck are you talking about now?'

I had responded with 'now' because Robbie (God bless him) often had outbursts and, more often than not, had no reason to.

'Look at that,' he wailed, pointing to the newspaper lying next to me. 'Front page.'

The pages were upside down or back to front. I located the article Robbie requested: FRESH MYSTERY IN JACK THE RIPPER 'DIARY' SAGA.

It went on: 'The man who claimed to have been given the diary of Jack the Ripper last night claimed that the affair had been a hoax.'

I smiled. Mike Barrett had said that he wrote the diary. I knew he had not. Now I had the opportunity to prove it!

'What are you smiling at?' Robbie screamed. 'You should see your face . . .' I pointed to Barrett's statement. '*This* is a load of bollocks,' I said.

My frame of mind at the time was very positive. Mike had been threatening to make this statement for a month

---

[1] Liverpool *Daily Post*, 27 June 1994.

or two. Mike made then, and continued to make, many threats. Their content was always manufactured. I admit, however, that I did not expect to read this.

Robbie asked whether this bothered me. No, I said. I would now knock this on the head once and for all. There was information in the diary whose truth had been established through obscure references. In order to have written this document Mike would have had to know of these. I told Robbie I'd challenge Mike through the media, if need be, to prove his claim.

Robbie calmed down but appeared puzzled. 'So why has he said it? Won't it hurt the book and his income?' I shrugged my shoulders. At this point, while I knew Mike had not forged the diary, I could not even begin to comprehend his motive for maintaining that he did.

Two days later, Mike Barrett's estranged wife of some six months appeared to be fairly sure of his objective . . .

The *Post* of the following Monday, 27 June 1994, had a follow-up under the headline, HOW I FAKED RIPPER DIARY. To the right of the article was a picture of Mike Barrett standing over the grave of James Maybrick. Above the headline and photograph, in smaller print were the words, SELF CONFESSED HOAXER DECLARES: NOW I FEEL AT PEACE WITH MYSELF. Mike was quoted as saying, 'Yes, I am a forger. The greatest in history.'

Harold Brough, who was responsible for this 'exclusive', went on to write, 'Mr Barrett, who is seriously ill, says that he has decided to confess to his actions, after being told by his doctor that he has only days to live.' (I am writing this chapter on 30 September 1996, and I am delighted to say that Mike Barrett is alive and well and living in Southport.)

At the time, the cynics should have taken note. They should have been as cautious with Mike's confession as they had been with the diary. They were not. What did you expect? One expert who had originally claimed that the diary had been written 'by someone most likely to have been schooled in the 1930s' was now happy to accept it was written by someone not born until 1950!

174

Albert Johnson,
owner of the
Maybrick watch

Sister Mary Joachim, born
Ursula Maybrick

Albert Johnson's grandmother,
Elizabeth Crawley

Margaret Minetta Maybrick,
mother of the Whittlesey sisters

Are the facial similarities of the owners of the watch (*left*) with the known
Maybricks (*right*) really just a coincidence?

Above left Florence Maybrick, 77

Above right William Graham

Left Mary Graham

Again the strong facial resemblances in these photographs suggest close family ties

Above Billy Graham, William Graham's son and father of Anne

Right Anne Graham, who was inadvertently responsible for The Diary of Jack the Ripper being published (*Carol Emmas*)

Above A wood engraving of James Maybrick made from an 1887 photograph

Right Florence Maybrick as a young woman

The five Maybrick sisters. Left to right: Anne, Ruth, Emily, Rose (*standing*) and Elizabeth Susannah

Auntie Wadham — daughter of Jack the Ripper?

Jack Maybrick (died aged eight), brother of the five Whittlesey sisters

Elizabeth Susannah Maybrick and Sarah Robertson, photographed in the garden at 24 Cottisbrook Street, New Cross, South London in or around 1925

Alice Yapp (*right*) (*Jo Brooks*)

Aigburth Drive in Liverpool as it was when Maybrick lived nearby in Battlecrease House. The diary's author wrote 'Strolled by the drive. . .'

Above James Maybrick photographed around 1887

Right Daily Telegraph picture of Jack the Ripper suspect published 6 October 1888

To be fair, Harold Brough had no alternative but to print what Mike Barrett had told him. Did Harold believe, however, what he had been told? Perhaps everyone should have read and absorbed the last two paragraphs of that Saturday article.

Harold described the moment that Mike had poured himself a whisky and said, 'I did it because I could not pay the mortgage. So I thought "What can I do?" and the only thing I am good at – apart from being a scrap metal merchant – is writing. So I thought I would write the biggest story in history.'

You could almost see his smirk when Harold finished that article by writing, 'But he [Mike] was unable to explain how he managed to write a book which fooled experts or answer basic questions about how he found the old paper of the diary or old ink.' Of course, later, Mike Barrett would attempt to manufacture answers to these points. I paused and thought. This statement made by Mike was even more positive than I had originally thought. I knew I could prove that Mike could not have written the diary and now I knew that the 'Mr Big' hypothesis could not be true either. Had anybody financed a hoax or forgery they would hardly have allowed Mike Barrett to go public and state it was a fake. Barrett was in control of the diary; he reported to no one. He made the decisions.

In Liverpool, cash has a language of its own. Forget cheques or credit cards. The first time I met Mike I had expressed my desire to own half the diary. In order to tempt Mike, who I knew had financial problems, I let him know that I was carrying a substantial sum of cash in my case. Mike wanted to draw up a contract and sell me his share of the diary there and then. Some knowledge of the law persuaded me that, even if he signed a contract that was not independently witnessed, it might not stand up in a court of law. I had told Mike to think about it overnight, to get independent legal advice and after that, if he still wished to sell to me, I would be delighted. (The offer is still open, Mike. In fact you may even be able to talk me up on price.)

A couple of days later Mike confirmed that he wanted to conclude the deal. Indeed, he called me in London, from Liverpool's Lime Street Station, to tell me he was on his way. He did not arrive. He told me there had been a bomb scare. I checked – there had not. Mike, for whatever reason, chickened out.

From the first time I met the Barretts, I knew that, if this detailed and complex document had been faked, then their only involvement would have been as a front. This had been insinuated by the cynics and at this early stage of my research I had to consider every scenario. A hoax by the Barretts? A hoax by a mysterious 'Mr Big', with the Barretts being used as a front? Or did the diary have a provenance? Mike would have done the deal had I not told him to contact a solicitor. It seems highly unlikely, then, that anyone else could have been involved, outside his immediate family. There was no 'Mr Big'.

I kept my promise to Robbie. On 28 June 1994, Harold Brough published my response to the Mike Barrett article. It was headed RIPPER DIARY FORGERY CLAIM 'IS TOTAL RUBBISH'. I had phoned Harold on the Monday. I told him to ask Mike five questions. If he could answer them then I would go public and admit that he forged the diary. If he could not answer, then he was not a forger. Harold thought I was brave, but our research had reached the point where I knew that this was a far better bet than crossing the road! The questions I wanted asking were these:

- 1. How did he know that James Maybrick was indeed away from home at Christmas 1888?
- 2. How did he know that there were two, not three, brass rings missing from the body of the Ripper victim Annie Chapman?
- 3. How did he know that the Ripper victim Elizabeth Stride had red hair?[1]

---

[1] The colour of Elizabeth Stride's hair was not claimed to be red by the author of the diary, although we had misinterpreted it at the time. The references 'head . . . red' and 'A rose to match the red' were for the sake of rhyme, which Maybrick used so often in the diary, and as a reference

- 4. How did he know that James Maybrick struck his wife Florence several times before the Grand National in 1889?
- 5. How did he know that the daughter of James Maybrick, Gladys, was consistently an ill child?

Each of these questions was based on information gleaned from the diary that Mike Barrett said he had written. He could not answer any of them.

Harold Brough, in the same article, asked Paul McCue, owner of the Bluecoat Art Shop, how Mike Barrett could have written the diary. He said, 'Mr Barrett would probably have bought manuscript ink, supplied by Diamine, of Bank Hall, Liverpool.' Shortly after this article, guess what? Mike Barrett said he wrote the diary with Diamine ink – and the cynics believed him!

The most important clue to the origin of the diary was indeed in the article of Monday 27 June 1994. My colleagues and researchers were surprised to hear the delight in my voice when I asked them if they had seen the *Post* of that date. They expected me to be despondent. They had not focused. Barrett's confession is all they appeared to have paid attention to. I pointed to Anne's statement.

Harold Brough had contacted Anne Barrett after speaking to Mike. 'He told me that he got the diary from Tony Devereux and that is all that I know. He is now trying to get back at me because I have left him. The whole thing is an absolute nightmare.' Anne continued, 'But I will fight like a tiger to protect myself and my family against anything he says.'

It was at that moment that I knew my instinct about Anne was right. Was it not Mike Barrett who confessed to a forgery? Why had Anne assumed Mike was getting back at her? What did it have to do with her family? If the damned thing was forged, then Mike had taken the rap.

to blood. At the time Paul Begg had thought he had found a reference that Stride's hair was indeed red (*Evening News*, 1 October). The article was in reference to Eddowes, not Stride.

Inadvertently, Anne had deflected the attention from Mike to herself.

On Thursday, 30 June 1994, Richard Bark-Jones made a statement to Harold Brough. A few words said a lot. This was Mike Barrett's solicitor telling the world that the diary had origins of which he was aware. The trouble was, nobody wanted to listen – except me. The article carried the headline RIPPER FORGER CLAIM DENIED. After a brief explanation of the events earlier in the week the writer of the article continued:

> Last night the following statement was issued by [Mike Barrett's] solicitor, Richard Bark-Jones: 'With regard to the statement (confession) made by Michael Barrett that he himself had written the diary of Jack the Ripper, I am in a position to say that my client was not in full control of his faculties when he made that statement which was totally incorrect and without foundation. Michael Barrett is now in the Windsor Unit of Fazakely Hospital.'

The Windsor Unit is for alcoholics. This statement from the solicitor was hugely significant. I was astonished when I read it. There was no preface to the statement using words such as 'on my client's instructions I have been asked . . .'. I telephoned Harold Brough. 'Is this the full statement?' Harold assured me it was. He promised to fax what he had received from Mr Bark-Jones, and did so. Word for word, the *Daily Post* had reported accurately. To me this strongly implied that the firm of solicitors, and particularly Mr Bark-Jones, had information in their possession that meant they could speak freely and openly without their client's consent. The statement delighted me. It said all there was to say. No reputable firm would make a statement like that without being absolutely certain that they were right.

By 1 July 1994, Cynics Incorporated were gloating, 'Oh, it was Barrett . . .' I could not believe how intelligent and supposedly responsible historians were prepared to accept anything negative in respect of this diary. When Barrett said he had forged it nobody even tried to compare his handwriting to that in the diary. An example of Mike Barrett's handwriting is shown in the illustration section.

One such historian was Martin Fido. Barrett's 'confession' justified (in his mind, I think) why he had not spent much time investigating the internal evidence of the diary. He seemed mightily relieved when he spoke to me on, or shortly after, 1 July. I begged him: 'Martin, have you not seen the statement that Richard Bark-Jones made on the thirtieth of June? Please don't fall in the same trap as others.' I faxed Martin the statement made by Mr Bark-Jones, not the one in the newspaper, but the one sent to Harold Brough. He responded with a telephone call.

'Remarkable.'

Morecroft, Dawson & Garnett are one of the most reputable legal firms in Liverpool. In representing them, Richard Bark-Jones had made a pronouncement categorically stating that his client had lied and that he was in a position to make that statement.

If anybody claims after this that Mike Barrett forged the diary then they are also claiming that this firm of solicitors were lying as well. They will have to answer that criticism, not to me but to Morecroft, Dawson & Garnett.

The *Sunday Times* had published Barrett's 'confession'. They did not contact Mr Bark-Jones after this statement was published. They never published Mr Bark-Jones's retraction of Mike Barrett's confession.

I telephoned Mr Bark-Jones, and put it to him that his statement suggested he had information that proved that the diary was not forged by Michael Barrett and that had not needed Mike's permission to say so. 'You're the only one that spotted it,' he said.

'Are you telling me that nobody's called you and questioned you about this statement?'

'No, you are the first.'

As I understand it, I was also the last.

I had felt, over the previous couple of months, that Mr Bark-Jones knew more than he had let on. In May 1994 I had arranged a meeting with Mr Bark-Jones. I told him I had important information to discuss with him regarding Michael Barrett and the diary of Jack the Ripper. He welcomed my approach and agreed to see me. There was no mention of fees. I took along my personal assistant Martine Rooney as a witness to the conversation. The meeting took place during the time that Keith Skinner and Melvyn Fairclough were following up and testing the 'leads' that Mike Barrett was giving us. I drove to Birkenhead in the early morning, stopping at Robbie's house for a coffee (actually, I had no idea how to find the solicitors in Liverpool and wanted to follow him there). Robbie could never say no to a friend. It was hot, it was sunny and I am not sure that Robbie even believed I had an appointment with Mike Barrett's solicitor. I think he stood outside 1 Dale Street for the duration of our visit. The building was large and the firm's offices were on the second floor.

The objective of the meeting was to determine whether I was on the right track. I make no apologies: the information that I would feed Mr Bark-Jones at that time was nothing more than calculated conjecture.

I started by asking him whether he represented both Michael Barrett and Anne Barrett. Like a true solicitor (and/or a politician), he responded by saying, 'I represent Michael, but am not sure of the situation since he and Anne have separated.' I did not push him on his point but was later to learn that I should have done. He did not represent Anne and never had. He never said he did. He sold me a dummy, and I bought it!

Hesitantly, I started my story. Why was I hesitant? I was pretty sure of what I was about to say to him, but I had little hard evidence to back it up. For all I knew at that point, he could have known everything. I had to choose my words carefully. As the conversation went on I became more confident. If this man knew I was talking complete bullshit he would have kicked me out. If he knew the truth then what I was saying must have struck a chord. If he knew nothing at all, then at the very least, he was interested. I told Mr Bark-Jones that I had evidence that Anne was related to Maybrick (I had nothing of the sort). He was not shocked by what I had said. I asked him whether he knew the name of Maybrick's best friend. He did not. I told him, 'George R. Davidson. Does the name ring a bell?' Mr Bark-Jones's complexion appeared to turn a little paler. He understood the implication. 'Do you know why Mike contacted this company in the first place?' He did not comment, but his face clearly told me that he did not know. His mind was now working overtime.

I went on to suggest to him that if he would try to persuade Mike and Anne to face the press and tell the truth about the diary then I would protect them in whatever way he felt was best. He responded, 'Send me the evidence. I will send it on accordingly and tell them what you have said and if I believe that it is in the best interests of everybody concerned I will inform my client accordingly.'

After ninety-three minutes I knew I had not wasted my time, and Mr Bark-Jones clearly felt he had not wasted his. This man did not know everything but knew enough to think that, possibly, *I* did!

Mr Bark-Jones's statement of 30 June 1994 confirmed what I had felt as I left his office on that hot day in May. Little did we both know that I was only a month away from knowing the truth. Little did Barrett know that if it was not for his 'confession' we might never have known it.

11

'LOOK OUT ... JACK THE RIPPER'S ABOUT'

ON FRIDAY, 29 JULY 1994, at around 6.30 p.m., I started on a journey to Liverpool. I was to stay with Robbie Johnson that night and see Anne's father around noon the next day.

I recall the weather that Saturday as being beautiful. The sun was shining and it was very hot. I was sweating. It was not the weather, just knowing that I was shortly to learn the truth about this remarkable document. Why was I so sure?

Because Billy Graham, an eighty-year-old man who I knew was dying of cancer, had granted me an interview. He had a reason. I surmised that while Anne had suggested the meeting to her dad, he had welcomed the opportunity.

The positive response seemed too immediate. Had Anne told her father of my conversation with her at my house? I assumed so. I must be right. Billy was about to tell me of his connection to Sheppard Shalgrave Maybrick, the missing illegitimate descendant of James Maybrick and Sarah Robertson.

Robbie drove me to Anne's home that Saturday morning. A feeling of guilt suddenly came over me. Anne's dad was dying. He was about to see me. Was it because Anne was frightened? I tried to justify my reasons for being so callous. I'd paid for the visual rights to that diary, I reminded myself. Research was costing the business more than I could justify. I was entitled to the truth. Then ... that horrible feeling of paranoia. Supposing it *was* a forgery.

Was Billy Graham about to confide in me to protect his

daughter? Logic overcame fear. Florence Maybrick used the name Graham when she was released from prison in 1904. Now I was about to find out why.

During the journey across the Mersey, my guilt resurfaced. Robbie filled up with petrol while I bought goods for my hosts. Flowers for Anne and another Disney video for Caroline. Across the road I spotted an off-licence. A bottle of Scotch, then, for my interviewee.

Robbie took me to Anne's front door. He agreed to pick me up ninety minutes later. I was aware of a time limit. Billy wanted to go to the British Legion for an afternoon drink with his friends. He wasn't too concerned that I had travelled all the way from London to see him – but, then, who could blame him?

I felt in control. I knocked loudly on the door. In one hand a leather case filled with research material and photograph albums, in the other, gifts. Anne seemed extremely pleased when she answered the door: 'You needn't have . . .' Round One to me.

I followed Anne up the stairs to a door that led straight into a living room. She introduced me to her dad. He was sitting in an armchair close to a window. The television was in front of him and he looked up at me as I entered the room. His eyes were a penetrating deep blue.

Billy wasted no time (after all, the British Legion was beckoning): 'What I'm about to tell you, I don't want anything for . . .' I was no longer in control. Anne put the kettle on as I sat down on the settee next to Billy's armchair. I asked if it would be OK if I taped our conversation. Billy said yes, and, as I rummaged through my bag for my tape recorder, I asked Billy to sit next to me. I was concerned that my machine would not pick up his voice from a distance. I had never conducted an interview of this nature before, and, while I had asked Anne if Keith Skinner could accompany me, Anne had responded, 'Not this time.'

From my bag I produced a photo album containing the pictures I had been given by Janice Roughton. I asked Billy if he could tell me whether he recognised any of the people in them. He could not. I moved on to Jack Maybrick, the boy who had died aged seven. Billy had always believed that he had a twin brother, Harry. Harry had died when he was eight. Anne wondered whether Harry and Jack were one and the same person. I told Billy that Harry, although his brother, was not his twin according to their birth certificates. Billy seemed surprised and disappointed. The conversation continued:

AEG Do you remember when Harry died?

BG   Yes. I remember him getting buried. I could take you to the grave.

PHF Do you remember where the grave is?

BG   Yes. It's at the – you'd have a job to find it now probably – you know the Liverpool Cathedral, the Protestant one?

PHF Yes.

BG   Well at the back there is a cemetery called St James's.

PHF All right.

BG   St James's Cemetery. Now they've got a lot of vaults in there, but where he got buried is just at the back. And next to him, a mason on the top – doing all the stone work – he fell off . . .

PHF Yes.

BG   And he dropped right by my brother and they buried him next to my brother. Where he dropped he got buried.

AEG Which one did you say it was, Dad?

BG   St James's Cemetery.

AEG Behind the Anglican Cathedral?

BG   Yes.

Clearly there was no connection between Jack Maybrick in Whittlesey and Harry Graham in Liverpool. By now my mind was in a whirl. I was completely confused. I started talking to Billy about his parents. He could not tell me anything about his mother. Billy's father, William Graham, married for the first time on 27 July 1911 to a Rebecca Jones, a widow. Rebecca already had six children. She was to have three more with William – Mary, Billy and Harry – before she died on 9 October 1918 in the great flu epidemic.

I went to my bag once again and reached for my copy of *This Friendless Lady* by Nigel Morland. At the bottom of page 228, the last paragraph read: 'In January of that year [Florence] was moved from Aylesbury Prison to the House of the Epiphany, on the banks of the Fal in Cornwall, where, as Mrs Graham, she was to try to regain some of her former health and strength.'

I started to read to Billy, pointing to the words as you would to a child.

I hoped that Billy would at least tell me why Florence used the name Graham. On seeing the name, Billy slumped back in the settee and muttered, 'If my dad could see . . .' It then sounded as though he continued with the words 'the old girl down there'. And then he read aloud, '. . . she was to try . . .'

I emphasised the point.

PHF When Florence came out of prison, Billy, she called herself Mrs Graham.

BG Did she? She must have had a crush on the old fellow, eh? [laughs] I don't mind you saying that it is . . . about him, you know – eh?

PHF She called herself Mrs Graham . . .

BG Yes. Dirty old git . . .

PHF What?

BG But that wouldn't be my father though!

PHF I don't know what she –

BG Well if she called herself Mrs Graham . . .

PHF Well she's not related, what she is doing is – erm – I'm not quite sure what she's doing. I can only speculate . . .

At this point my inexperience as an interviewer showed itself. I took Billy off the subject and pursued other lines of enquiry. However, Billy stayed with the subject and, all the time I was speculating on other areas, Billy was thinking about that 'Mrs Graham' reference.

BG	Well I was working out with my father – being her son.
PHF	Say that again!
BG	It's possible – being her son – my father – being Maybrick's son. Because at the time he'd be – I can't work it out – you could. He'd be . . . er – she was fifteen when she had him. Well that's possible . . . [next inaudible].
AEG	Who was fifteen?
PHF	You're saying Billy's mum?
BG	No – my father.
PHF	Yes.
BG	Right – now – she – if she was to have – if she'd had him she would have been fifteen. With me?
PHF	I'm with you.

I wasn't, but something was happening. I knew that James Maybrick had at least five illegitimate children . . . Was I right after all?

BG	And it's possible that he could be if, er . . . because she was only fifteen wasn't she?
AEG	Who?
PHF	Who – what – Billy . . . er – Billy Graham's father was – erm . . .
BG	No.
PHF	Your dad's mother was only fifteen . . .?
BG	No. No. My dad – if she's trying to . . . She was trying to claim . . . that my dad was her son?
PHF	Right.
BG	Right, now at the time she was in America, wasn't she?
PHF	Oh, you're talking about Florence . . .?
BG	Yes, yes. She was in America when she was only fifteen . . . Right. Well she could have – she had a child didn't she – before?
PHF	Before she married James?
BG	No. You know – she had . . . the Maybrick one had a child before she married him.

PHF   Did she?
AEG Who told you that?

The penny had finally dropped. Billy's father was Florence's son. Nobody had ever suggested in the last 106 years that James's wife had given birth prior to her marriage.

I recalled Florence Aunspaugh's description of Florence Maybrick's eyes: 'Mrs Maybrick's eyes were the most beautiful blue I have ever seen. They were large, round eyes and such very deep blue that at times they were violet.' Just like Billy's.

Something else hit home – hard. Anne had also heard this for the first time. She was angry. Billy knew it.

AEG Who told you that?
BG   Somebody told me that, didn't they?
AEG I don't think anybody's ever told you that, Dad.
BG   I'm sure they have.
PHF   And what?
BG   She had an illegitimate child ... [looking at the Morland book ... puzzled] Where did she get Graham from?

During all the conversations with Billy, he would never refer to Florence Maybrick by name. 'The Maybrick one', 'she', 'git' and 'dirty old cow' were just a few of the derisory ways in which he would refer to her. I thought this significant.

PHF   So why do you think you would have – OK – so Edith [Edith Formby – BG's stepmother] never told you where this [the diary] came from when she gave it to you?
BG   No. No. No.
PHF   There was no letter or anything like that?
BG   No. Oh, she mentioned something about me ganny. I remember she said ... er ... Ganny said, 'Here y'are – that's yours.'
PHF   That's yours?
BG   Yes, and I didn't take no notice of it, because she

was good to me, my ganny. She was all right. The only one that ever did [what] no one else did.

PHF   She does [pointing to Anne].

BG   Yes, but at the time I needed someone.

PHF   I know.

BG   I was only a kid, like, you know, and I needed someone. I'd lost my brother and I was, er, upset. I was a rebel after [that]. I never done anything really bad, like, you know . . .

PHF   She said that was yours.

BG   Eh?

PHF   Did she tell you what to do with it?

BG   No, no. My ganny couldn't read or write. I used to draw her pension for her and she used to put a cross [not audible] she couldn't write. She went – Eadie [Edith Formby] went to, er, St Paul's School. Now St Paul's School is just around Belvedere Road here and that's where they all went.

PHF   If Florence would have had an illegitimate child when she was fifteen years old –

BG   Yes . . .

PHF   – then that child would have been born in 1878 or 1879.

BG   Yes.

PHF   That was when Billy's father was born.

BG   Yes.

PHF   Do you think all this happened in Hartlepool? Do you think your dad was born in Hartlepool?

BG   Yes. I think so – yes, yes that's where . . . He was a Geordie, because they used to talk about him where he worked.

PHF   He was definitely a Geordie?

BG   He was a bad-tempered old git, because they used to say 'bad-tempered old Geordie.'

The doorbell rang. As Anne went to answer it, I attempted to validate her story.

PHF   Did you give him the diary – did you give Mike the diary?

BG   No – I never give it to him . . . I wouldn't give him
      nothing – I wouldn't even give him a bleeding kind
      word. Bad news that lad . . .

Anne returned with Caroline. Caroline was now twelve.
Her manners were impeccable. She kissed Billy. It was time
to switch off the tape recorder. Caroline told us that there
was a man outside sunbathing on top of a car and I guessed
it was Robbie. The bell went again. I assumed it was
Robbie and told Anne. Robbie had made contact with
Anne once before, uninvited. He had been trying to find
out about the watch that his brother owned. Anne and
Robbie had not got on well that day. Robbie had
'demanded' information. Anne had not given it. I did not
want to spoil what was turning out to be a very special day.
   To my surprise, Anne sent Caroline down to let Robbie
in. Anne's manners had taken priority over her emotions.
I updated Robbie on what had happened, with the
permission of my host and hostess. Just before we left, I
asked Billy whether he thought anyone else in Liverpool
had known who Jack the Ripper was?
   Billy believed many did and went on to recite a
wonderful story.
   'We used to go down there [Riversdale Road] and nick
apples. We would run past his [Maybrick's] house towards
the river pretending we were Fred Archer, the jockey . . . I
think it was Fred Archer . . . you know, the American who
brought the "crouch" over to this country. Jockeys used
to sit up straight, you know. Anyway, we would smack
our backsides [Billy imitated at this point] and shout
"Look out, look out, Jack the Ripper's about."'
   That was about as much as I was going to get that day.
Billy was like a cat on a hot tin roof. Precious time at the
Legion was being lost. Billy agreed to see me again with
Keith Skinner the following week and I said my farewells
to Anne and Caroline. I think I was still in a sort of shock
when Caroline said, 'We're not related to *him*, are we,
Mum?' Anne laughed. 'No. His wife, it would seem.'

                        *   *   *

After picking up my car from Robbie's cottage, I started the tortuous journey back to London. For the first time that day, I was able to think clearly.

Billy knew he was dying. Anne and Caroline were his whole life. Mike Barrett's 'confession' meant that Billy *had* to tell the truth. Billy had chosen that moment, not just to tell me, but his daughter as well. I considered how the diary's critics would view today's events. Could Billy be lying in order to protect his daughter – or himself – from prosecution for forgery and fraud? I was sure he was not. Florence Maybrick was thought to have come to England in 1880, when she had met James on the boat from New York. Billy had said his father was born in Hartlepool in 1879. If Billy was telling the truth, then Florence must have been in England in 1879. Could we prove it? I was sure we would. If Billy had lied to me he would be hurting the people he loved most – and I could not accept that he would do that. I had not just witnessed some kind of performance staged for my benefit: I had seen real people, and real emotions. I wondered how Anne was feeling.

I phoned her from the car and asked if she was all right.

'I'm still in a state of shock,' she said. 'I always thought the thing [diary] had been nicked from the [Maybrick] house, although when I had heard about the Maybrick illegitimate children, I had wondered. I certainly didn't expect this.'

I told Anne that I was to meet Robert Smith on the following Monday. I asked whether I could tell him what had happened.

'Oh . . . he will be furious . . . Doreen as well . . . and Shirley.'

I tried to make Anne feel better: 'Anne, you didn't know?'

Anne was not, as I was soon to realise, someone who shirked responsibility. 'No . . . but I didn't tell them what I did know.' She paused. 'Do you think I should prepare a statement for you to show them?' I said I thought that would be a good idea. Anne was about to get to work. 'I'll call you tomorrow,' she said, 'and read it to you. You can let me know what you think.'

I sensed that Anne was almost relieved. No more hiding. No more lying. Everyone would soon know all that she did. I decided to phone both Paul Begg and Keith Skinner. Paul agreed that, if the story was a lie, it would hurt only Anne. He started to analyse the scenario immediately. Keith? I was to learn much later that he was very 'excited' and was delighted to know that Billy had agreed to see him. He understood that it was vital that he should focus his research on whether or not Florence was in England in 1879, the year of William Graham's (Billy's father's) birth.

The next 150 miles or so did not seem as long as usual. I felt good. I wondered: who was the real father of William Graham? Florence was the mother, but it takes two to tango – or make babies! What else were we going to learn?

Over the next few days, Melvyn Fairclough, Keith Skinner and I reread all the press cuttings we had on Florence Maybrick. Was there anything that could support the idea of her being in England in 1879? We found the following article in the Home Office files. It had appeared in the *Sunday News*, 1 May 1927:

A MOTHER'S ANGUISH

Woman Who Was Central
Figure in Great Poison
Drama of the Nineties

CAME FOR RECONCILIATION, BUT –

Unknown to anyone save her solicitor and a few personal friends, Mrs Maybrick, the central figure in one of the most sensational poison dramas of the last decade of last century, has just concluded a brief visit to England, and the only interview she gave during her stay is published exclusively below:-

Sad-faced, gentle-voiced, with hair turned to silver, the Mrs Maybrick of to-day is but a shadow of the striking looking woman who made a lasting impression on those who saw her in the dock at Liverpool, 37 years ago, fighting for her life against the mass of circumstantial evidence linking her with the murder by arsenical poisoning of her husband, a wealthy Liverpool stockbroker.

'I feel death's shadow over me, and I have come back with one object only, to effect a reconciliation with members of my family, if that be possible. To that end I am trying to clear myself of the charge of murder of which I was convicted and sentenced to death.'

This statement was made to me at my first meeting with the once notorious woman. Later, when she had made overtures through friends, she confessed sadly that her hopes of reconciliation were dead. 'It is bitterness worse than death,' she said.

'All the years that have passed since that terrible day when I heard the verdict of guilty I have longed for my children, who were but babes at the time, and the mother hunger in my heart was so strong that I felt I must make this journey now in the hope of seeing them.'

When the Liverpool *Post and Mercury* picked up the story on 2 May, 1927, they included in their headline the words 'secret visit to Liverpool'.

On the face of it, this whole interview did not make sense. There can be no doubt that Florence Maybrick was talking of 'my children' and not 'my child'. However, the first child born to Florence in her marriage to James was a son called James (Bobo), who had died in April 1911. Gladys was now living in Wales, so who were the children Florence was referring to, and who was she seeing in Liverpool? Moreover, Florence Maybrick, by all accounts, was poverty-stricken. Where did the money come from to pay for this journey?

We considered the possibility that Florence Maybrick was not aware of Bobo's death. We examined all the newspapers following her son's fatal accident in April 1911. The Chicago *Daily Tribune* carried an exclusive interview with Florence Maybrick, on 10 May 1911: ' "The past is dead," his mother said as she passed a hand slightly over her forehead. "This boy has been dead to me for more than twenty years . . ." '

During this period Keith Skinner reminded me of the reference we had discovered in the Christie collection he had brought back from Wyoming. The very short list of Florence Maybrick's belongings when she died was reported by Samuel A. Woodward as including 'a faded black address book, with all the G's torn out'. All The Gs? All the Grahams?

Coincidence? Possibly, but too much was beginning to fit together. Further research showed that the black address book was also mentioned by Bernard Ryan when he wrote about the Maybrick trial. Bernard Ryan also reproduced photographs that once were the property of South Kent School. When we contacted the school to see if they still had the address book and they said no, I was pretty sure I would know where it would be found. Bernard Ryan still has that address book. We had hoped that there would be an imprint on the next page that might help to identify the missing Gs, but this was not to be the case. We did, however, manage to correct one piece of history.

A picture, reproduced in Bernard Ryan's book, was said to be that of Gladys, James's and Florence's youngest child. I was doubtful, as she was so unlike the woman identified by Trevor Christie as Gladys. Bernard confirmed to me that he must have guessed, as the original picture, which he still had, gave no means of identifying the girl. Florence Maybrick had written to Florence Aunspaugh from Aylesbury Prison on 10 August 1897. She commented: 'Indeed I do remember the vivacious, pert little miss, with big brown eyes and long brown curls, who kept the entire household in an uproar of laughter.'

Bernard Ryan's photograph had been identified.

I travelled up to Liverpool on Friday, 12 August 1994, spending that evening with Robbie Johnson. Keith had decided to travel up by train on the Saturday morning. We were to meet up that morning at Anne's house and she would take us to see Billy, who had moved to sheltered accommodation. I had never had a reason to visit sheltered accommodation before and did not know what to expect. For some reason I believed this was where old people were *put*, but did not *choose* to go, although Anne had given me the impression that it had been her father's choice.

Shortly after we arrived we were shown into a room that could only be described as an extremely large reception area. Elderly men were playing chess and cards while enjoying a pint of beer. It was far more like a holiday camp than the depressing picture I had conjured up in my mind. Anne spoke to someone who gave us the OK to go up and see Billy. As we entered I remembered Anne telling me how she had been given most of Billy's belongings. I was not surprised. The room was small and cramped, it was a living room/bedroom with a small kitchen just off it. Billy had no room for the things he had given to Anne.

Billy sat in front of a wardrobe, facing the TV, with a small table in front of him. Keith and I positioned ourselves opposite. Anne put the kettle on and started to potter around the room tidying up for her dad.

Anne had made it clear that this was not to be 'an interrogation'. Her dad was very ill and we should respect that. Keith promised just to chat and try to develop a relationship that we could build upon. He had picked up a few things from the earlier transcript I had made of my interview with Billy and wanted to clarify them. In particular he was interested in Billy's response when shown the Nigel Morland reference to Mrs Graham.

KS   And when Paul showed that to you I wonder whether you can remember what you said. How you referred to her – to Florence Maybrick. What you called her?

BG   I don't know.

KS   Well what you said was you called her 'a dirty old cow'.

BG   Oh . . . I . . . yeah – I recognise that . . .

KS   Why, why did you call her that, Billy?

BG   Why – well she must have been if she had an illegitimate child – didn't she?

KS   Was that something that you heard during your childhood?

BG   Yes, yes – that she had an illegitimate child.

Although Billy said 'yes, yes' he said it without conviction. He wanted to move away from the subject. We were not going to push any point and allowed Billy to dictate the conversation. At a convenient point Keith asked Billy what he knew about the Maybrick Case.

BG   Well they talked about it for years – they all talked about when she come to Liverpool and my grandmother went with the skivvy. She was the one who opened the letter and she went to the Assizes. That's what they tell me, like.

KS   Who was it that told you that your grandmother – that must be Granny Formby – went with the skivvy and that that was the skivvy who opened the letter?

BG   It could have been my sister, or my granny could have told me – everyone talked about it. They talked about – you know when a murder came up – big licks it was – everyone was dashing up to buy a paper and half of them couldn't read or write. My grandmother couldn't read or write – and I used to have to read it out to her.

KS   And was it this skivvy that used to visit your grandmother?

BG   As far as I know it was – her name was mentioned a lot and she said she was from [not audible] and there was some talk about her coming down looking for a job and they were trying to get her a job with a big shipping firm.

Keith went on to ask Billy if he could remember how old this woman was?

BG   Well I reckon when she used to be coming to us she was about fifty-odd or something like that . . .

KS   How old would you have been?

BG How old was I? I was about, er – I must have been eight, nine or ten – I must have been thirteen when the strike was on – 1926 . . .

Billy Graham was born in 1913. The period to which he was referring would, therefore, be between 1921 and 1923. Through detailed research we established that Alice Yapp was twenty-six years old at the time of the trial (1889). The event Billy is talking about took place between thirty-two and thirty-four years later when Alice Yapp would have been in her late fifties.

Billy Graham's recollections were open and honest. I was confused, however, as there appeared to be two connections. Billy's father William was apparently the illegitimate son of Florence; William Graham married twice, his second wife being Edith Formby. Edith's mother, Elizabeth, would appear to have accompanied Alice Yapp to the trial of Florence Maybrick. Was this merely a coincidence?

Anne had got the impression that Elizabeth Formby was the 'local fence'. Billy had explained to Keith and me that Elizabeth Formby had run a laundry at 10 Peel Street. Battlecrease House used this establishment and when the servants wanted to steal items from the premises in which they worked they would wrap them up in the laundry. Billy recalled tales of legs of lamb being removed. A man by the name of Jack Tyrer had some involvement, although it was not clear what. At the very least I understood why Anne believed the diary had been stolen from the house.

Billy Graham joined the army in 1933. During the war he fought in Sudan, Egypt, Malta, South Africa and NW Europe. Before the war he was stationed in Malta and India. For his services to the country Billy was awarded the following medals; 1939–45 Star, Africa Star with 8th Army Clasp, France and Germany Star, Defence Medal, War Medal 1939–45.[1]

---

[1] Information obtained from Ministry of Defence in a letter from Mrs K. Welbourne (for Departmental Record Officer) dated 20 April 1993.

Billy Graham fought in hand-to-hand combat and in 1992 was awarded the Maltese Cross. I was, therefore, surprised that he left the army at the same rank he went in as: number 4123032 Private William Graham, Cheshire Regiment. Anne was later to explain that Billy was a bit of a rebel and a story about his throwing soup over an officer was not the only account of such transgressions. He was promoted and demoted frequently.

Billy went on to show us the medal he got in 1992. He took a key out of his pocket and stood up to unlock the wardrobe behind him. He seemed careful not to open the doors but slid his hand in, took out the medal, and immediately relocked the wardrobe door. I commented, 'I'd love to know what's in there.' Billy responded, 'She'll [Anne] know soon enough.'

In 1946 Billy married Anne's mother Irene Bromilow and before Anne was born, in 1950, they had two sons. Unfortunately, neither lived for more than a month. Irene's father and uncle were also heroes, albeit for a different reason. They played football for Liverpool and Everton respectively and the latter also played for England.

Irene died in 1965 when Anne was just fourteen, leaving Billy to bring her up during those difficult teenage years. Anne left England in 1970 to nurse at a hospital in Australia.

Keith tried to verify when Billy first became aware of the diary.

KS   Do you remember your Granny Formby?
BG   Yes.
KS   Were you close to her?
BG   Oh aye, yes. I used to draw her pension for her and she couldn't read or write, so she used to put a cross on her pension book. It was only ten bob then, about fifty pence. She was active as an old woman and liked to do a little bit of shopping and she wouldn't have anyone with her, and I used to have to sneak behind her to see that she was all

right crossing the road and all that. Oh, we were very close, oh, aye, yes, and she trusted me. When I got a little bit older I used to – she'd get a letter and I used to read her letters for her. She had two sisters, or stepsisters – I don't know who they were – and they belonged to shipping owners, the Flinns, because she was related to them, but she seemed to be the poorest of the lot. Now they used to come down [to visit] – they lived over in Birkenhead in a place called the Woodlands. I never seen them over there and they had their own carriages – horse and carriage, you know – and they used to come over in that – down the street and the street used to be out then. So when they come they used to leave her a few shillings before they left and now and again they would write to her and I'd read the letters and sometimes there would be a pound in there. She wouldn't let no one else read her letters, only me, like, and she trusted me. I used to do that for her.

KS   The journal that's come down to – well to Anne – which was, I believe, given to you – is that correct, the diary?

BG   The diary?

KS   Yes.

BG   Well what happened was this. I never looked – I never bothered about it – at the time. I left [to go in the army] and my granny died. Now I came home in 1943 – that's right – been ten years abroad without coming to England – now it wasn't [not audible] and her when I got home [not audible] a tin box upstairs and I never bothered about it. But I seen this book and I just seen very small print and I just put it down – didn't want to know. So, any rate, it was Christmas Day, 1950 – just after she was born in the October – and Christmas Day my mother sent it across and she had this book, my birth certificate, my father's death certificate and all that, you know – a lot of things she had – and she

	said, 'Here y'are.' And she gave it to me – so she just said, 'Your granny left you that.'
KS	Granny Formby?
BG	Yes, so I just threw it in the . . .
PHF	Did she name Granny Formby?
BG	Yes, yes.
PHF	But you said it was there in 1943 . . .
BG	I came home in 1943.
PHF	Did you see the diary then, or you only saw it in 1950?
BG	Well that's right yes – I took no notice of it – it was in a tin box in my room.
PHF	So it was there in 1943. You just hadn't taken any notice of it?
BG	My father was alive then and my Uncle Billy and they were living with my mother. I wrote to her – that's right – then, when I came home, she lived in Woodland Road, Clubmoor, and I went there and I stayed there. [Not audible] box upstairs, a tin box. So when I come back after the war she shifted and was in Norris Green and the tin box was still up there.
KS	I wonder why Granny Formby wanted you to have it.
BG	Well I don't know. I said to the old lady, 'This is not mine,' and she said, 'Your granny left it to you.'

Billy Graham had recollected how the diary had come into his possession on three occasions. He always said the same thing: that Edith said '*your* granny . . .' (my emphasis). It is possible, of course, that this was a manner of speech. The phrase, however, seems to distance Edith from Billy's granny. If it had been Granny Formby, she was referring to her own mother. Had Billy assumed, incorrectly for all these years, that the diary had come from Granny Formby and not his other grandmother? Florence Maybrick died on 23 October 1941. Billy first saw the diary in 1943, in a black tin box. Anne had expanded upon her original description of the box, saying it was a black metal box, under knee high, with three or four letters stencilled in white paint on it.

The black metal box was, unfortunately, discarded by Billy when he married Maggie Grimes in January 1970.

As the conversation developed it became clear to both Keith and me that Billy had not taken any notice of this 'book' all the time it was in his possession. As Anne went into the kitchen to make more tea and coffee, Billy said, 'I didn't know what it was worth. I'd have cashed it years ago. Blimey, I wouldn't have been slaving in Dunlop's – twelve-hour shifts – on dirty big tyres if I'd have known . . . I'm not short – and it's not worrying me now because it's no bloody good to me now; years ago it would have done. I could have been lying on the beach now with a couple of strippers all over me! Tickling me with a feather!'

(Keith later told me that this 'throwaway remark' by Billy 'just resonated with truth'.)

Billy had not realised that Anne was standing by the door while he had said the above and on seeing her bellowed, 'I didn't know you were there!' Anne's reply was, 'No you didn't, did you?'

The 'legitimate' parents of Billy's father William, named on his birth certificate, were Adam Graham and Alice (née Spence). Billy confirmed that he had never heard of either of them and then went on to give us further information about Florence Maybrick.

BG   Yes, well, they used to talk about her in the shops and all that; she had a kid before she was married and all this. It was a terrible thing in them days – you had to turn your face to the wall if that happened to you. You were condemned right away – you were an outcast after that.

PHF   So you would suspect that we would be able to find Florence in Hartlepool in 1879?

BG   I wouldn't doubt it – yes.

Keith enquired about the watch. Billy thought it was a load of 'bollocks'. This was the word Robbie Johnson had used to describe the diary. These individuals had been described by some of the diary's detractors as 'co-fraudsters'. They were, however, hardly trying to support the authenticity of each other's belongings. I might add that Robbie's view of the diary was not held by his brother, Albert.

There was still one question I wanted to ask Billy before we left: 'Billy, what was your reaction to the experts who said it had been written in the last seven years?'

Billy's voice was firm. 'A load of rubbish that. They want to get their name in the paper – rubbish, that's all it is.'

We had also talked about playing cards, football, horse racing and boxing to name just a little. Although Billy seemed to enjoy the chat, he appeared to be getting tired and it was time for both Keith and me to go. Billy told us that we could come and see him at any time and, indeed, agreed to go on camera to relay his story. He had no family pictures and no letters (unless they were locked away in the wardrobe).

Although we knew that Billy was ill, we did not realise when we left that day that we would never see him again.

12

'SHE'D BEEN TO OUR HOUSE; SHE SPOKE TO MAMA'

ANNE SEEMED TO FIND a new lease of life. She no longer seemed as despondent as the day I took her to the Moat House. Frankly, Anne was hooked. She wanted to know everything there was to know about Florence Maybrick and was reading voraciously.

She went to Liverpool Library continuously reading press reports of the trial and after. I introduced her to Carol Emmas who was researching for me in Liverpool. Anne wanted to help.

In the couple of weeks following our visit to Billy, Anne told me that Mary, her father's sister, and Alice Dean (née Jones) were still alive. Mary lived in Chester and Alice in Harrogate. Anne had not seen either for many years but I asked her whether she would contact them, with a view to meeting. In the meantime I had my press cuttings copied and sent to Anne. It was Anne who found the first positive report that Florence had lived in England prior to her marriage to James. The three books[1] that had previously attempted to tell her life story had only picked up on rumours that she was 'educated in England and Europe'. The article from the Liverpool *Echo* dated August 9 1889 is reproduced below:

MRS MAYBRICK'S CHILDHOOD

Residents at Kempsey, near Worcester, recollect that twenty years ago Mrs Maybrick, then a little girl, lived

---

[1] Nigel Morland, *This Friendless Lady*; Trevor Christie, *Etched in Arsenic*; and Bernard Ryan, *The Poisoned Life of Mrs Maybrick*.

at 'The Vineyards' there, with her sister and mother, Madam Du Barry. A German governess educated the children. The mother is described as a fine, handsome woman, and good company. The house was nearly always full of visitors. After a residence of about two years, the family suddenly left. Local friends have since visited Madam under her more recent title of Baroness von Roques.

Curious. To the best of our knowledge, Florence never had a sister. She did, however, have a brother. It may have been due to their youth that the writer of this article assumed both children were girls. Nevertheless, we had now established that Florence certainly had roots in England ten years before she met James. Could we now find the evidence that she was in England in 1879?

In the meantime, Anne tracked down 'Auntie Mary'. She was thrilled to hear from her niece, whom she had not seen for about eighteen years. Mary was delighted to hear that Anne would be coming to see her. I was excited: after all, what Billy did *not* know, Mary might. In all probability, Mary was the granddaughter of Florence Elizabeth Maybrick, the wife of Jack the Ripper.

On 19 August 1994 another trip to Liverpool. I arrived early at Anne's. Coffee and breakfast awaited when I arrived at about 10. Scrambled eggs, I seem to remember. Caroline was still remotely interested. 'What's happening today, Mam?' I had left Potters Bar in Hertfordshire around 6 a.m. Anne and I had talked on the phone almost every day since Keith and I had seen Billy. While we were not quite friends, Anne appreciated the work I had done and was keen to get to know more about her ancestry.

The trip to see Mary in Chester was full of expectation. Once more, special old people's accommodation impressed me. Mary greeted us at the back door, which was also the entrance to her living room. She was eighty-three and puffing away on a cigarette. There was something about Mary, something familiar: I felt I had seen her face before.

I felt something of an intruder into an emotional family reunion. It certainly was not the time or occasion to switch on a tape recorder. While Anne and her aunt talked about the family, I just kept staring at Mary's face. I started to browse through the books in my bag. The photograph albums first. I turned to the Whittlesey Maybricks. Nothing. Where had I seen that face?

Anne touched on the diary with Mary for the first time. 'You better ask your dad about that, Anne' was all that Mary would say. Anne would go around in a circle, arrive back at the point she started, and end up with the same response: 'Ask your dad.'

I did not want to push it this time. Mary left us an open invitation to visit her whenever we wanted.

Keith Skinner was busy. Very busy. He was more focused than ever. Melvyn Fairclough was on his way to Hartlepool. Did anything connect Florence Maybrick in 1879 to this north-east port?

When Florence Maybrick had visited England in 1927, she had travelled under the pseudonym of 'Elizabeth Ingraham'.[1] In 1904, when Florence Maybrick left England to return to America, she used the name 'Rose Ingraham'. Ingraham was a family name, being the maiden name of her mother. The Baroness had written on 23 May 1890 to Queen Victoria, saying, 'Allow me to appeal to your Majesty's consideration as being as a stranger, English though, born in America. My mother's brothers the Reverend Joseph and John Ingraham, may both be known to your Majesty, by their religious works, they trace their family back to the time of Edward 2nd of England.'

Keith saw the criticisms coming. He anticipated them. When the news broke of the Graham connection, Keith was proved right. The cynics immediately screamed, 'misprint'. However, on 21 and 25 June 1994, Keith had visited the Newspaper Library in Colindale, following up

---

[1] Passenger lists BT27/1155.

on the reference he had earlier found in Nigel Morland's book. The *Daily Illustrated Mirror*, which had first traced Florence to Truro, did *not* use the name Graham. It wrote in February 1904: '... the Epiphany Sisters and the servants of the Truro Sisterhood have no idea that Mrs G ... is really Mrs Maybrick. (We refrain from mentioning the name under which Mrs Maybrick conceals her identity ...)'

Later, newspapers were not so diplomatic. The *Cornwall Gazette* of 21 July 1904 reported: 'The Home is a building in the Tudor style, situate in large and beautifully kept grounds, and a laundry and Rescue Home for fallen girls are adjacent to the main building, in which Mrs Maybrick has lived under the assumed name of Mrs Graham.'

Alex Chisholm, a critic who tried to debunk this book before he had even seen it (and before I had even completed it), would only say in respect of Florence's pseudonym, 'Ah, but how many people are called Graham?' I replied, 'How many people are not?' The critics just appeared to go from the sublime to the ridiculous.

There was no doubt that Florence Maybrick called herself Graham, the maiden name of Anne Barrett. Now could we establish whether Florence Maybrick was in England in 1879, as the testimony of Billy Graham would indicate? The Home Office files gave us our first clue. An affidavit of John Baillie Knight dated 17 August 1889 stated: 'I first met the Prisoner about two years previous to her marriage in or about the year 1879 at the house of my Aunts the Misses Baillie ...'[1]

John Baillie Knight's aunts lived in London. Further support came from Trevor Christie's private notes, which we had obtained from Wyoming University. He wrote: 'The Baroness and her children came to the US in 1879 to settle the Chandler estate.'

Trevor Christie's source was the *New York Times* dated

---

[1] HO 144/1638/A50678D/24.

8 August 1889. The family had indeed arrived from Liverpool that month.

Christie also produced a timetable of Florence's movements. That showed that Florence was living in England in April 1879. This would appear to be confirmed by Bernard Ryan who, in his book *The Poisoned Life of Mrs Maybrick*, wrote, 'She had attended the Grand National at Aintree last year.' Bernard Ryan was referring to a conversation that Florence had had with James on the boat coming to Liverpool in 1880.

Anne had tracked down her long-lost family and discovered that Alice Dean, her father's stepsister, was still alive and living in Harrogate in sheltered accommodation. Alice was almost ninety. She did not remember the Maybrick trial, nor did she recognise the name. My last resort was to ask her to go through my three photo albums to see if she could recognise anybody. I have literally hundreds of pictures.

The newspaper photograph of Florence Maybrick when she left prison stopped Alice in her tracks. She banged her finger on the woman's face. 'She'd been to our house; she spoke to Mama.'

Alice had remembered the event as the woman had ridden up in a carriage and was very smartly dressed. Alice thought she had been 'a little girl, no older than five or six' at the time. Alice was born in 1906 and yet the only two years that we know Florence came to England are 1906 (the year Alice was born) and 1927 (when Alice would have been twenty-one). Neither year made any sense of Alice's statement, but she was adamant that she remembered the occasion. We had more homework to do.

The trip was extremely valuable because Alice had a picture of Anne's grandparents, William Graham and Rebecca Jones. We had also learnt that it was around 1909 that William met Rebecca and was indeed living with her. Rebecca was the woman whom Alice claimed Florence had come to see. One look at William, and his face, too, seemed familiar. Again, I went through my photograph albums; again I could not find the face that resembled the one I was looking at.

Extraordinarily, it was research material that we were collating on Mary Kelly that gave us supporting evidence for Alice's story.

In Melvyn Fairclough's book, *The Ripper and the Royals*, Joseph Sickert claimed that Mary Kelly did not die and that the woman who was killed in that room was a friend. He claimed that Mary Kelly's aunt had sent Inspector Abberline a postcard from 'Roofer Castle'. There is no such place as Roofer Castle. Paul Begg wondered whether the castle referred to may have been 'Ruthin'.

Our work was thorough and detailed and led us to a book written by a Helen Spinola,[1] entitled *Nothing But the Truth*.[2] Helen recalled an evening reception at the Duchess of Sutherland's in London in the year 1909:

> 'That's Lady Marjorie Manners,' Stella told me. 'Come – I'll introduce you . . . No – wait! You'll have more to talk about with that pale lady in the corner – the one sitting alone. Such a dear creature! She's Mrs Maybrick, the murderess. She was released from prison only last week [sic].[3] It's her first big London party, so she feels shy, too.'

Florence Maybrick had made a trip to England other than the ones in 1906 and 1927. There has not been any reference to this in the books written about her trial. Alice Dean had recalled an exceptional visit from an exceptional woman. Was it *another* lucky guess (as Cynics Inc. would

---

[1] Helen Spinola was the daughter-in-law of Mrs Patrick Campbell, whose second marriage was to George Cornwallis-West, whose family home was Ruthin Castle. Ripper enthusiasts will be fascinated to know that Mrs Patrick Campbell was a known lover of Edward VII. George Cornwallis-West's first marriage was to Lord Randolph Churchill's widow, Jennie.

[2] Published Gollancz, London, 1961.

[3] As Florence Maybrick was released from prison in 1904, we tested Helen Spinola's recollection of this event as having taken place in 1909. However, the year of 1909 was the year of Helen Spinola's (née Bull) marriage to Lieutenant Patrick Campbell as confirmed by *The Times*, 1 May 1909. Perhaps Florence had been *in London* for only one week.

have us believe)? Or are these recollections simply the truth that nobody wants to accept?

On 11 November 1994, I arranged a conference. Albert and Robbie Johnson, the Maybrick descendants from Whittlesey, Brian Maybrick and Anne Graham were invited for an informal chat at the Post House in Peterborough. Paula Adamick, a freelance journalist commissioned by London's *Evening Standard*, was also there, following up on an earlier story she had written: WHY I BELIEVE EVIL DIARY OF THE JACK THE RIPPER IS NOT A HOAX. Memories were exchanged and family memorabilia was there for all to see.

A messenger was sent to the room in which we had congregated. There was a phone call for Anne. Urgent. Having nursed and cared for her father almost day and night for the last three months, Anne was devastated to hear he was dying and might not be alive by the time she got home. Anne left immediately. I had met Billy only twice, but he was a special man, a real character. When he had seen me on 30 July 1994, I guessed that he knew that this day was not far away.

I went to Liverpool on 18 November for Billy's cremation. It was highly emotional. As the doors to the furnace area opened and the coffin disappeared inside, the loudspeakers rang out with the song 'Beaches'. Caroline held her mum close.

As Billy would have wanted it, the congregation were invited back to the British Legion for a drink and lunch. Keith Skinner was there as well. We talked to Billy's close friends. They remembered him with only love and affection. Billy Graham was a respected man.

Before I returned to London, Anne asked me if I would go back with her to her dad's room at the sheltered accommodation. She had to take whatever was left – and open that wardrobe. The room was almost bare. Most of Billy's belongings had been transferred to Anne's place in the last three months while she had been nursing him. My heart pounded as Anne put the key into the ornate lock. The doors opened to reveal just the inside of a wooden shell. Nothing. Not even dust. The medal that had been in there had already been given to Anne. Anne was as perplexed as I. We still are.

It was about a week after the cremation that I asked Anne if there was anything else she could remember, anything at all, to do with family. She recalled that her father frequently took her to a tiny graveyard in Croxteth. She could not remember the name of the deceased person, but remembered her father saying, 'He's family, Anne, he's family.' Anne said she would go back to the gravestone and take a photograph of it. She knew exactly where it was.

Anne wasted no time. Within three days I had received the Polaroid in the post. The gravestone was that of Henry Stanley Flinn, who had died on 7 March 1927. He was born 18 March 1858. Who was he and what was his connection to the Graham family? It did not take long to work out that if this was a family connection then it must have been an illegitimate one. Billy had suggested that his father was illegitimate by Florence. Could this be Billy's real grandfather?

Henry Stanley Flinn was not an ordinary man. That was evident from his headstone alone. Henry was a very important man. Indeed, he owned the Dominion Line of Liverpool. He was a wealthy ship owner.

Melvyn Fairclough went to trace the descendants of this family immediately. Flinn married in 1890, the year after Florence Maybrick's trial. We followed the birth lines of his brothers and sisters as well as those of Henry himself. There were no living descendants. The bloodline had died out and this was probably due to the high rate of syphilis that ran through the family. Henry never had children, but we managed to track down the sister of the woman who married his nephew. Muriel Cheeseman, aged ninety-two, confirmed that, to her knowledge, there were no Flinns alive.

Brian Maybrick, whose grandfather, John, was first cousin to James Maybrick, knew of the Dominion Line. His grandfather was a senior pilot employed by them.

Henry Stanley Flinn paid John Maybrick's wages. Quite apart from the diary, 'family' of Anne Graham now seemed to be directly linked to the Maybricks. Coincidence? Again?

Was Henry Stanley Flinn the father of Florence's child, born to her in 1879? Was his death in 1927 the reason that Florence came to England? His family could most certainly have afforded to pay for the cabin that Florence occupied on her trip. Could Florence have used her influence with Henry to get James's cousin, John, a job? In 1879, Henry would have been twenty-one, Florence just sixteen. Indeed, Florence would have been just fifteen at the time of conception. Florence was the daughter of a baroness and in the hypocritical Victorian era she could not have registered an illegitimate child in her own name. She would have brought shame to the family and ostracised herself from society.

We may never know for sure the answers to the questions I've been posing. We did try to ascertain, however, whether there was any other evidence that would connect Florence to Henry. While we could not find anything concrete, we did find two rather curious references.

In 1889, a pamphlet was published and entitled 'Florence Maybrick – A Thrilling Romance'.[1] The details of the trial are clearly fact, but the characters' names and roles are changed (probably for legal reasons). In this tale, Florence has an affair with a cotton broker called James Douglass but marries a shipowner named Jasper Loftus:

> 'He's very rich, I've heard since, is this Mr Jasper Loftus,' said the Amazon-like beauty, with strangely flashing eyes. 'Owns over a hundred ships and employs nearly a thousand hands.'

Florence Maybrick was being romantically linked with a ship owner in 1889. It may of course be a coincidence – another one, or was the author in the know?

In 1897, Mary H. Krout, a reporter for the Chicago

---

[1] Published in London: G. Purkess, 286, Strand (author unknown).

Inter Ocean, visited Aylesbury Prison for an exclusive interview with Florence Maybrick. Florence made the following statement: 'I have seen the children's pictures and Henry has grown so tall . . .'[1]

It was common at that time to name your first son after his father (as James and Florence later did), but the home that William Graham was brought up in already had a child by the name of Henry living there. Does a mother normally forget the name of her child? Why the slip of the tongue? Another coincidence – or her other son?

Henry Stanley Flinn and James Maybrick certainly had friends in common. A Mr T.A. Hamer attended the funerals of both.

It was vital during our research to continually reread material we had collated. A name may have meant nothing six months ago, but would become significant later. The book by Nigel Morland, *This Friendless Lady*, which had revealed that Florence used the surname Graham, would have been one of the first to be read. By the time we were researching the family tree of Mike and Anne Barrett, the reference might have been forgotten. After all, it did not appear significant at the time. It was on reading the book again in May 1994 that Keith Skinner homed in on it. I browsed through the book by Bernard Ryan. I flicked through the pictures – and looked again. A shiver, and then a smile. An old lady, sitting on a lawn in South Kent, Connecticut. Florence Maybrick, aged seventy-seven. That was the face. The likeness to William Graham and his daughter, Mary, was astounding.

If the cynics were right in their assumption that the diary was a modern forgery, then our forgers were lucky in the extreme. No, this was all becoming too much. Billy had told us his story, Alice Dean hers. The information we had obtained could be supported by remote references. This was not a conspiracy as some had cried. The idea is

---

[1] Trevor Christie wrote this statement in his book, *Etched in Arsenic*, with 'Bobo' replacing 'Henry'. His source, the *Inter Ocean*, Chicago, October 1897 reads 'Henry'.

preposterous. Florence Maybrick must be related to the Grahams. That is why she used the name and why her son and granddaughter shared her looks. Simple.

It was time to see Mary again. Carol Emmas, our Liverpool researcher, and Martine Rooney, my assistant, joined Anne and me this time. It was now 31 August 1995 and I wanted to tie up any loose ends I could before starting to write this book. My objective was to establish whether Mary had any knowledge of the Flinns and whether we could obtain further information about Mary's father and Anne's grandfather, William Graham.

According to Mary, William was told to leave 'home' and make his own way in life at the age of eleven or twelve. He was told that the money had run out. He left Hartlepool for Ireland looking for work. He returned a few years later to work at the shipbuilders Cammel Laird and Harland and Wolfe in Liverpool. He became educated, although Mary did not know how he had done so by reading law and becoming 'important' to the trade unions. Mary was surprised that his birth certificate stated that he was born in Hartlepool, as he had always said he was born in Cumberland. Like Billy, Mary had not heard of Adam Graham or Alice Spence, the 'parents' on the certificate of her father, William.

When Rebecca, William's wife, died he moved back to Hartlepool for a short while with the children. Even then, the family never met Adam or Alice Graham. Mary attempted to explain. 'He would never talk about his family. If we asked him anything about his family – if he had a grandma or anything like that. You know, when you're kids you want to know this, that and the other. He always told you to shut up and mind your own business.'

William had been told to leave home in or around 1890. This was shortly after the trial of Florence Maybrick. Was this why the money had run out? After going to Ireland, William came to Liverpool, but why? It could have been for work, or did he discover his family, his real father, Henry Stanley Flinn? Someone paid for his education.

Could Billy Graham's visit to the ship owner's grave be out of respect and love?

Mary confirmed that she knew of the Flinns. She was unsure of where they fitted in the family tree and, unlike Anne, she had never been taken to the grave of Henry Stanley Flinn. Mary, in fact, worked for 'one of the Flinn sisters, Mrs Elizabeth Borrows', she said. Mrs Borrows owned a tobacconist's. She knew a fair bit about the family. Mary knew of the 'legitimate' Flinns who lived in Birkenhead and of the Flinns who owned auction rooms in Rock Ferry. Elizabeth Borrows was an illegitimate. When she died, William Graham was the informant on her death certificate – as 'cousin'.

To dispute that the true provenance of the diary is through Anne's family is to dispute the word not only of Anne, but her father, his sister and stepsister. They would have had to create this entire story and collude in order to sustain it! Not only that, but dates and events in history just happened to pan out in their favour. Billy could not make Florence be in England when his father was born – but she was. He could not 'make' his father look like Florence – but he does. Mary looks like her, too. How did they know of the Flinns and the intimate family details? By this stage of our investigation it was abundantly clear that the true provenance of the diary was beyond doubt. In all probability we had also discovered the true parentage of William Graham.

I would like to believe that Florence's use of the name Graham was to acknowledge the son she had abandoned. I would like to believe that Henry Stanley Flinn took responsibility for William after Florence was imprisoned and educated him. When Billy saw that Florence 'Graham' reference, he said, 'If only my father . . .' and then stopped. Did he know what that would have meant to his dad? Billy's obvious hatred of Florence would be understandable if he was aware that she had abandoned his father at birth. His respect for Henry would make sense if the ship owner finally came to terms with his responsibilities.

Henry Stanley Flinn may have been Florence Maybrick's first lover, but he was not to be her last.

CHAPTER

13

'I DID IT FOR LOVE . . .'

SO WHY DID MIKE Barrett 'confess' to forging a diary if he had not? Would any forger make such a statement, taking the chance of being criminally prosecuted for obtaining money by deception or being sued by publishers even if he or she had? Michael Barrett did not receive any money from the Liverpool *Daily Post* for the interview he had granted them and therefore the whole episode did not seem to make any sense at all.

To the publishers of *The Diary of Jack the Ripper* and me, it was an irritation. The outside world did not know Mike Barrett and had no reason to disbelieve him. The Ripper experts amongst the detractors should have known better – but they didn't want to. They were happy to accept the confession as an answer to the conundrum.

If Mike Barrett had forged the diary, or indeed had anything to do with forging it, he would have been able to tell the world how, when, with whom and where various references were obtained. As reported by Harold Brough, he couldn't answer those questions then, and he still can't. Remember the words of Harold Brough: 'But he [Mike] was unable to explain how he managed to write a book which fooled experts or answer basic questions about how he found the old paper of the diary or old ink.'

To understand why Mike made this statement is to know Mike. I learnt a lot about him – and continue to learn. My suspicions about his reasons were eventually confirmed by Mike himself in an exclusive interview with Keith Skinner and Martin Howells on 20 July 1995. When asked why he had confessed to something he did not do he responded, 'I did it for love – for love.'

When Mike Barrett married Anne Graham in December 1975, he was full of ambition. In essence, he was a good man and hoped to be a good provider. While he was trading as a scrap-metal merchant, he one day collapsed from haemorrhaging which ultimately led to his role as househusband. He did not like the role, nor did he want it. Mike tried to rid himself of it but luck always seemed against him.

He had always liked a drink but, in or around 1988, the drinking became excessive. The anger he had towards himself he would take out on others, although he was always repentant afterwards. He began to live in a Walter Mitty world, telling tall tales to acquaintances, who soon began to reject anything he said. The members of the British Legion, where he often went with his father-in-law, Billy Graham, took little notice of his stories surrounding the diary.

Tony Devereux *had* given Mike the diary. When Anne left Mike in January 1994, and he started to make those telephone calls to me, I guessed that Tony had also told Mike where he had obtained the diary. In the interview with Keith Skinner and Martin Howells, Mike said that after Tony had given him the diary he had pestered him day and night to tell him where he had got it from. Eventually, Tony told him, 'Look to your own family . . .'

Mike then told us that he first asked his father whether he had given Tony a diary. That made sense, and for once we felt that Mike was being honest. (This version was the first to have independent corroboration. Caroline, on the day that she met Paul Begg and Martin Howells, told them of 'the phone calls to Tony Devereux after he got the diary'.) Mike's approach to his dad was logical. After all, he had also drunk with Mike and Tony at the Saddle. Mr Barrett Snr. knew nothing about it, and neither did Mike's sisters or his mother. Mike went back to Tony. He queried Tony's information.

Tony responded, 'Look on your own doorstep . . .'

It finally clicked that Tony meant Anne. Mike was hurt. It probably would hurt any man. Mike had been married for fifteen years, and, for whatever reason, his wife had not trusted him enough to explain the origins of the document. It must have been difficult for him not to bring it up in discussion with Anne but, knowing Mike, I reckon he would want to find the answer before confronting her.

Judging by those phone calls Mike made to me after his separation from Anne, I think his first reaction was to assume that Anne was an illegitimate Maybrick, from James's side of the family. After all, James was known to have had at least five illegitimate children. Unable to prove that, he moved to the possibility that it had been found where Anne worked. Finally, it would seem that he was reconciled to the probability that Anne had forged it and was attempting to distance herself from it by passing the book on to him via a third party.

Between January and June 1994, there was little or no communication between the separated couple. Anne hid. Caroline was free to see her dad whenever she wanted but chose not to. I have certain knowledge of what went on behind closed doors, but it is not important to elaborate here. Suffice it to say that the domestic situation of this couple was uncomfortable and when I later heard of Caroline's choice I was not surprised. Mike had been devastated at the break-up of his home. He had many faults, but he did seem to love his family.

I would like to think that, when the article appeared in the Liverpool press telling how Mike was supposed to have forged the diary, it was a method that he had devised of communicating with his estranged wife, that it was a message of his devoted love to Anne. It seemed to be saying, 'I am prepared to take the rap for you, darling.' Mike was even prepared to go to prison should that be the ultimate punishment for this 'fraud'. Anne, however, did not forge the diary and consequently this message was lost on her.

Mike followed his solicitor by retracting his statement and even told many that 'Harold Brough misinterpreted what I had said, I was merely telling him that I helped write *the book* with Shirley Harrison.'

For a couple of weeks, there was peace. The people who were seriously interested in the statement had accepted it as the farce it really was. The *Sunday Times* did not publish the end result but only the original confession. We were, however, becoming used to this sort of media coverage of the diary saga.

The matter did not die. Unfortunately. It was my fault as well. At least that's what Mike Barrett felt. It was just over a month after his article appeared that I had my interview with Billy Graham. Mike had considered Billy to be his friend as well as his father-in-law. Billy did not repay the compliment. Then again, Anne was his daughter. Thereby lay the sentiment!

At this time I understood how Mike must have felt. He had been married for fifteen years and, for the last three, this book, this 'Diary of Jack the Ripper', had been dominant in his and his family's lives. Neither Anne nor Billy had confided in him about its origins – indeed Billy was the primary reason Anne had not talked to Mike. Such was the indignation of Billy towards Mike that Anne did not even tell her dad that she had given the diary to Mike (via Tony) until she was in fear of its being published. Anne was fearful of the retribution – she was right to be.

On 30 July 1994, I was told the truth. I was trusted. Both Billy and Anne told me what they could. That would have hurt Mike. I understood. I was not surprised. I imagined there would be a reaction from Mike. There was.

I did not want to write this next passage, I really didn't. Unfortunately, there are still people who want to believe Mike wrote the diary. He did not and they have to understand the man.

In June 1994, when Mike first claimed he had written the diary, I asked him to prove it. He responded by saying, 'Ha, ha, ha, underline, ha, ha!'

Incredibly, he seemed to think that quoting a few words

from the diary (which often appeared underlined) was enough to prove to us that he had forged it.

A year later, in July 1995, Mike came to my office to prove that he and Anne forged the diary together. In a taped interview, with Keith Skinner and Martin Howells present, I asked him to re-create the handwriting of the diary.

MB   I don't suppose you've got a little pen, with a little gold nib, have you? Just for the record . . .

PHF A little gold nib?

MB   Yes.

PHF I'll go and buy one.

MB   I don't suppose you've got one?

PHF Yes, I have.

MH   We could go and get one.

PHF I've got one next door. I'll go and get one for you. All right?

MB   And blot [sic] paper. Blotting paper.

PHF Blotting paper.

MB   Right. Blotting paper.

PHF What is it you actually want?

MH   Blotting paper.

MB   Blotting paper and a proper nib with an ink please.

PHF Right.
     [PHF leaves the room – returning after five minutes]

PHF Which one actually wrote it? Whose handwriting is it – yours or Anne's?

MB   Anne's.

PHF Oh, it's Anne's writing? Why do you want a fountain pen here?
     [pause]

MB   Right – right.

PHF What's the point of getting a fountain pen –

MB   Hang on, hang on, hang on, hang on –

PHF – if she wrote the diary?

MB   Hang on – bear with me – just bear with me. Just bear with me – please, Paul – I ask you to bear with me.

218

When Mike found out that both Anne and Billy had confided in me, the shit hit the fan – big time. With his string of lies and fanciful stories exposed, Mike went downhill quickly.

He started to drink more than ever, at least that was the impression he gave. He would try to see Billy at his sheltered accommodation. When Billy refused, he would shout abuse about his ex-wife for the entire establishment to hear. He even caused similar scenes at his daughter's school. Finally, he obtained Anne's new address, arrived uninvited, and subsequently smashed her windows when she would not open the door.

Mike then retracted his retraction of his original confession. Now he was going to *prove* he wrote the diary.

After his first confession, Mike Barrett swore to Shirley Harrison – 'on Caroline's life' – that he did not write the diary.

Mike was soon to swear a fourth affidavit, this time stating that Caroline was the one person who could say he did forge it.

To me, that says it all. Mike Barrett is prepared to use his daughter's name to add weight and veracity to whatever he says – whether it's the truth or not.

The tape on the answerphone at my office was often filled up with the voice of Mike at his worst. Drunk, angry and full of abuse. When Billy Graham died on 12 November 1994 I was informed that if I attended the funeral I should know that there was a rifle pointing at my head! Hearing this, Keith Skinner remarked that he didn't intend to stand next to me!

Anne was terrified that Mike would turn up at the funeral, drunk, and turn the day into a farce. She decided to meet him to beg him not to come. How difficult was it for Anne to do that? I will tell you.

From the early days of our investigation, I was aware of an envelope in the possession of Mike Barrett's original solicitor, Richard Bark-Jones. This contained the true story of how the diary came into the home of the Barretts. (I say original solicitor because, at the time of writing, Mike Barrett is on either his third or fourth.)

The contents of this envelope, I deduced, was what enabled Mr Bark-Jones to state publicly that Mike Barrett had lied when confessing in the first place. I have always wondered whether the envelope contains correspondence from Tony Devereux.

When Mike was interviewed at my offices by Keith and Martin, he was asked why they should believe that the story he was telling that day was the truth. He immediately phoned Mr Bark-Jones, who unfortunately was not there.

The next day, I phoned Bark-Jones. He confirmed that an envelope did exist but he could open it only with the permission of his client. Actually, on reflection, I realise that Richard Bark-Jones may have been a little more circumspect – perhaps using a phrase such as 'should an envelope exist . . .'. I phoned Mike to ask him if he would so instruct Bark-Jones. His response was predictable: 'Only if Anne meets me at the solicitors – you tell her that.'

Anne would not. Even if this document could prove her story, she would not spend another minute with her ex-husband.

Despite the threats, I did attend the funeral of Billy Graham. I was not surprised to find local police guarding the entrances to the church and the crematorium. Mike Barrett's promises to wreck Billy's farewell were well known in Liverpool and had not been taken lightly.

There were times when Mike realised that his behaviour did not get him anywhere, and he would do a U-turn. Such as the time he gave Keith and Martin their interview. It seemed to happen when he met someone who cared for him. First a Jenny and then a Jackie phoned me. 'Please talk to Mike. He's changed.' I had not taken calls from Mike ever since he became abusive. Both these women seemed warm and caring. I told them that, if he was the same in two weeks, I would consider talking to him. Alas . . .

There were other questions. Other reasons why this chapter had to be written. Andy Aliffe, a competent researcher, had put forward his reasons for not believing the diary to be genuine. Andy's Casebook Interview appeared on the Internet on 3 January 1997 and included the following question:

'Why are there claims that the whole of the diary text were found on Barrett's computer disc?'

I have always failed to see why that gave anyone a problem.

When Mike Barrett decided to take the diary to Doreen Montgomery, he decided to transcribe it on to the word processor, so that a printed version of the text of the diary was available. It would be easier for Doreen or anyone else to read.

He tried to type the transcript himself. The end result was dreadful, and he asked Anne to correct it. Anne told him it would be easier to do it from scratch – and she typed while Mike dictated.

That document was presented to Doreen Montgomery on day one, and is clearly the work of a competent secretary, which Anne was.

That transcript is proof in itself that Mike and Anne Barrett had nothing to do with forging the diary because the typed version was transcribed incorrectly.

Andy Aliffe also asks, 'Why would a wealthy cotton merchant such as James Maybrick resort to cutting the pages from a Victorian photographic album?'

This was the only time Andy disappointed me. I had never known him to ask a question that did not merit some attention. Most of his queries, in fact, we had already raised ourselves. The question of the missing pages, however, has always had an obvious answer.

Andy, who *said* James Maybrick cut the pages? The author of the diary certainly didn't. Read the rest of the book, Andy!

Andy Aliffe was the first researcher/Ripperologist, to the best of my knowledge, to accept the possibility that this was *not* a modern forgery and nominate a potential 'contemporary hoaxer'. His informed suggestion was Dr Forbes Winslow, who had taken an interest in both the

Jack the Ripper and Maybrick events. If Andy was right, why would a wealthy doctor like Forbes Winslow have needed to cut the pages any more than James Maybrick?

Michael Barrett swore another affidavit. This time he said he did forge the diary. He had not wanted to admit this, 'out of fear for my life'. *From me*. I had 'warned' him. He seemed to have forgotten that I did not meet him until two years after the diary was in his possession.

The affidavit this time was far more convincing. But it came as no surprise when it included all the suggestions the critics had made about which books he had used, how he bought this diary and how he considered the Victorian ink, et cetera, et cetera.

Mike does not tell us how he tracked down all the obscure references, or how he learnt how to beat the ion migration test. He does not tell us, either, when and how he studied the science of metallurgy. And so on.

We must all wait, patiently, for his next affidavit. After this book is published, he may 'remember' how he obtained the references about which I challenged him at the time of his first confession.

Shirley Harrison also commented in the same Internet Casebook Interview:

> Stewart Evans and Paul Gainey in their book *Jack the Ripper, the First American Serial Killer* say that Michael Barrett has made a 'sworn affidavit' that he wrote the diary. This, they imply, is the final proof that the diary is indeed a forgery ... What was Michael Barrett's state of health at the time and what was the emotional pressure he was under? His 'confession' was immediately rebutted by his lawyer on the grounds that 'he was not in full possession of his faculties.' These authors have not met Mr Barrett, nor, like most of our critics, have they seen the diary.

I could add to that only by asking why the critics, who called Michael Barrett a liar when he said he got the diary from Tony Devereux, suddenly accepted that he was now an honest man; and why the contracts and affidavits he signed when Anne was with him were wrong but he has now somehow regained his integrity.

Mike has also written to me on numerous occasions and is recorded on tape swearing 'on my daughter's life' that he did *not* write the diary and that it was given to him by Tony Devereux. He has, at other times claimed that his former wife Anne wrote it.

Melvin Harris had apparently been so impressed by Mike Barrett's claim that he had written the diary with Diamine ink that he attempted to prove it. Since 1974, Diamine ink has contained the preservative 'chloroacetamide'. Mr Harris obtained 'six very small ink/paper spots' taken from the diary's pages when Kenneth Rendell's team carried out their investigation. They were sent to a laboratory for analysis. The results read as follows:

ANALYSIS FOR INDUSTRY   19 October 1994
Independent Consultants
Clacton-on-Sea
REPORT ON ANALYSIS NO: 409011

Client:	Mr Melvin Harris
Description of samples:	1) Monochloroacetamide (chloroacetamide)
	2) 1 oz black manuscript ink
	3) Six very small ink/paper spots
	Required to investigate the possibility of the ink spots containing chloroacetamide

CONCLUSIONS:
When the six black ink dots were extracted with acetone and analysed using gas-liquid chromatography procedures chloroacetamide was indicated to be present in the ink used.

D. Simpson
Principal Consultant

The amount of chloroacetemide actually detected by Dr Simpson's tests has never been made public. On 18

November 1994 Shirley Harrison took the diary to Wolfson Laboratory in Leeds, who re-did the tests extracting the ink from the diary itself. They could find no chloroacetamide. Melvin Harris responded by criticising the Wolfson Laboratory.

On 16 January 1995, Mr A. Kazlauciunas answered Mr Harris's allegations:

POINT 1
To use the term 'fatally flawed' in connection with all four Leeds University reports seems to me to be somewhat impetuous.

POINT 2
It is true that Mr G D Edmondson detected chloroacetamide in his GC analysis of the inked diary paper (date 23/11/94). However, when I spoke to him on completion of the analysis work he expressed his concern regarding the results, due to the possibility of contamination of the column from the previously run standard (short cuts in column cleaning had been undertaken due to time shortage)...

POINT 3
I find it quite amusing that the gentleman champions Dr Simpson's equipment in respect of its ability to detect 'ultra-tiny amounts of chloroacetamide as 1.45 nanograms'. Does he not realise that the levels claimed to be detected are in laymans terms 0.00000000145 of a gram! I feel that any so called 'proven anti-contamination procedure' may just leave this 'ultra-tiny' amount of chloroacetamide attached to the column. Therefore I ask the serious question is it beyond belief that despite the use of a so called 'proven anti-contamination procedure' that 0.00000000145 grams of the chloroacetamide standard, might not just have been retained on the column? I think Dr Simpson and her husband as highly qualified and *alert* analysts will readily accept the point I'm putting across.

POINT 4

The gentleman then goes on to scribe some inept ramblings about a link between the Simpsons checking of Vollers chloroacetamide sample to ensure the contents were as stated, and the Leeds University analysis of an 'unanalysed sample of a Diamine Ink'! Well for the muddled gentleman's benefit the history of this particular ink was never a consideration for us. The brief from The Word Team was quite simply ANALYSE THE DIAMINE INK supplied alongside the INK PRESENT ON THE DIARY – then compare. Simple really.

He then states that inept conclusions were drawn from the results. Well, I refute this allegation most strongly. In terms of the brief outline to the Department, the results obtained for both the diary ink and the Diamine ink were compared. We stand by the technique used, the comparisons made and the final conclusion that the Diamine Ink is not the same ink that has been used on the diaries.

POINT 5

There was no gap in our knowledge about iron content – it would appear that the levels present were too low to be detected . . .

POINT 6

Presence of Nigrosine – back to the Ultra Spectrometer at Zeneca. Here's the perfect opportunity to put your money where your [Mr Harris's] mouth is!

In October 1995, Alec Voller, Head Chemist of Diamine Ltd, visited the offices of Smith Gryphon Ltd. He concluded that the ink in the diary was not Diamine manuscript. He also commented on the appearance of the ink in the diary, 'The fading that occurs is quite characteristic of permanent manuscripts inks that are of some considerable age – one does get this effect – they don't fade evenly. You can get two consecutive lines of writing, one of which remains quite legible and the other fades quite badly.'

Unfortunately, so many people have now handled the document, it is possible that particles from their hands and nails might be detected, creating the ludicrous situation where scientists could detect in the diary ingredients for a McDonald's hamburger! One has to apply common sense to the results of any test, unless that is if you do not want to be fair or impartial.

It was Harold Brough who gave Michael Barrett the idea of Diamine ink in the first place, albeit unwittingly.

Earlier, I described Michael Barrett as a sort of Walter Mitty? Perhaps Shirley Harrison summed it up perfectly in that 3 January 1997 Internet Casebook Interview:

> Since the publication of the paperback edition of my book Mr Barrett has 'confessed' among other things: that he is a member of MI5 (Author's Note: This was in a court room, under oath, and in front of a Judge); has single handedly foiled the IRA; would be dead from cancer within 24 hours (three years ago); was re-married in Southport in 1996 and going to live in Russia (the same day he 'proposed' to another lady in Liverpool); that he has had a colostomy (denied by his doctor) is on dialysis (denied by the hospital) and, most recently, is due to be a father in seven months time.

And 'serious' crime historians took this man's word without any cross-examination . . .

CHAPTER

14

'WE CANNOT REALLY DENY IT . . .'

I FIRST SAW BRIAN Maybrick in October 1993 at the launch of Shirley Harrison's book, *The Diary of Jack the Ripper*. I was immediately struck by the similarity of Brian to James Maybrick. It was not really a surprise as Brian's great-grandfather and James's father were twin brothers.

I started to communicate with Brian frequently from early in 1994. I had been told by Shirley Harrison that he had drawn up a family tree of the Maybricks and I hoped that we could trade information, given that Melvyn had been obtaining as many of the Maybrick certificates as we could find. Brian was delighted to help, and began to meet with me and members of my research team on a regular basis. Brian had compiled his family tree mainly from information he had obtained through the years via family. Brian thought he knew of all the living Maybrick descendants, but was fascinated to learn of relatives we had discovered whom he knew nothing of.

We had discovered a birth of a Leonard William David Maybrick in November 1902, in Walsall, West Midlands. The father was named as David William Maybrick. We could not find either a birth or a death for David William. Brian did not know what branch of the family he had descended from, and we still have not found out. David lived in Park Hall Road and was a farmer. Although we were to trace the last living descendant of this line, Janet Wilson, she was unaware of any of the family background.

Another family we had discovered were, the 'Maybrick Maybrooks', most of whom lived in London and Kent.

Brian was once more surprised. He had not heard of them – but relations they most certainly were.

A will dated 1874 of William Maybrick Maybrook was witnessed by Edward Alfred Price of 3 Jamaica Street, the very address where Sarah Ann Robertson, James Maybrick's 'wife', had once lived.

Brian's grandfather, John Maybrick, was James's first cousin and was a chief mourner at James's funeral. That was not the case of all the first cousins. John was clearly close to James. He was a pilot for the Dominion Line, a shipping company in Liverpool, owned by Henry Flinn, whose son, Henry Stanley, is the suspected father of Florence Maybrick's illegitimate son, William Graham.

John Maybrick married twice. His first wife, Elizabeth MacDougal, died in 1888. His second marriage, in 1893, was to Elizabeth Ellison. We had traced the Ellison line as well. The Maybrick connection to the Ellisons would, however, appear to be long before John and Elizabeth married. Elizabeth's older sister by two years, Martha, carried the middle name of Maybrick. She was born in 1855, around the time that James met Sarah Ann Robertson. Elizabeth's first-born brother, Richard, carried the same middle name.

Brian Maybrick introduced us to Alan Bond, whose great-grandfather, Richard Ellison, was Elizabeth Ellison's father.

The introduction to Alan was fortunate, as his knowledge of the Maybrick Ellisons would lead us to an important breakthrough in our investigation.

Meanwhile, Brian Maybrick joined me in Peterborough in April 1995 to be interviewed for a new video I was producing.

'My grandfather, John,' he said in the interview, 'was first cousin to James Maybrick – so I suppose that makes me his first cousin, twice removed. We've always known of the controversy that surrounded his death and the trial of his widow – Florence – but we had no idea about the possible connection with Jack the Ripper, which has recently come to light since the diary was found and brought to the attention of Shirley Harrison . . .

'In the family there has, perhaps, been a difference of opinion about whether or not Florence was innocent or guilty. My father, who was born in 1893, had an open mind on the subject and spoke about it very little, but his sisters, who never married and lived with their mother until she died in 1939, were convinced that Florence was guilty.'

I asked about whether there were reputations to protect in the family.

'Yes, we do know that some people within the family or connected with it are resentful of the enquiries between James and Jack . . . It's well known that he had numerous illegitimate children and possibly some of the people alive today are descended from that line, but wish to retain a certain amount of discretion and don't wish to be involved in discussion about it in public.'

I then asked how he felt about the diary when it was first discovered. Had that changed him? And how did he feel about it now?

'At the beginning I was fairly sceptical about it because it seemed to me that had that been the case – Jack the Ripper being James Maybrick – surely someone in the family would have mentioned it to us via family folklore.

'However, the more I've learnt about it from the research teams, it seems more and more likely now that there was a considerable family cover-up at the time. One of the first questions that Shirley asked was whether there were any family letters from James's side of the family? Now I didn't think it strange at the time and I said, "No, there were none." Though we were related, it was another branch of the family and I would have expected anything of that sort to be claimed by that side of the family, but seemingly there are none. And it therefore seems quite likely to me from what I've read and learnt that after James's death, for one reason or another, and with the suggestion of a connection with Jack the Ripper . . . to protect the family reputation, which was very important to them at the time – especially to Michael Maybrick, who was a very powerful man – it was essential to maintain solidarity. Therefore, they closed ranks and decided to destroy anything that could have sullied the name of the family at that time. It seems Florence was made a scapegoat and was conveniently accused of James's murder to throw a smokescreen around history which might otherwise be attached to James himself.'

I asked whether Brian felt that the diary could be a modern forgery.

'There has been some suggestion in the press and among Ripperologists (which is a breed of person I don't pretend to understand) that this is a modern forgery and indeed at one stage Mike Barrett said that he produced it in eight days on a word-processor! This seems ludicrous because, very nice chap though he is, I think he would be quite incapable of producing a document with such detail and with such knowledge of the family and their life at Battlecrease House – even I could not produce that – and perhaps I know more about the family than he does now. So the suggestion that this is a modern forgery seems to me quite ridiculous.

'From the research I have recently learnt about, all the evidence seems to suggest that it does date from the time towards the end of James's life, and various other artefacts have come to light to support that. Therefore, as time has gone on, my scepticism has reduced and I'm confident in the belief that it's both James's and Jack the Ripper's diary. I have very little doubt of that – unfortunately, from the family point of view. When the book [*The Diary of Jack the Ripper*] was launched in 1993 someone from the media asked me how I felt about it and I said to him and I say again now: It's not a connection that any family would reasonably look for, but if it happens to be true what's the point in making a song and dance and trying to deny it? We can't really deny it because all the evidence seems to point the other way.'

Brian Maybrick's opinion was of value. Being the first

cousin, twice removed, of Jack the Ripper was not something he desired. Brian had studied the evidence himself, and reached his own conclusion. Other little things he remembered seem to start to make sense, and he was fairly sure that at least one living member of the family was aware of the Maybrick–Ripper connection. Brian attempted to communicate with them, but that person wanted nothing more to do with it.

Brian's unmarried aunts, to whom he refers, were not too happy when Trevor Christie released his book. Joe Gaute, from the publisher's, George G. Harrup & Co. Ltd, felt it necessary to put Mr Christie's mind at rest on 6 September 1968.

> Dear Trevor,
> ... I shall hope to see you in October and I shall certainly hope and take every step necessary to see that the Maybricks do not have any possible excuse to seek a court injunction which, of course, they could only do if a living member of the family was libelled. Incidentally, legal action is not an occupational risk of any publisher and he spends quite considerable amounts with his legal advisers to avoid giving offence to anyone which might lead to legal action and indeed if we had thought ETCHED IN ARSENIC was in any sense libellous, I assure you we would have turned it down without any hesitation ...

What were Brian's aunts concerned about? Wasn't James Maybrick just an innocent victim of an adulterous wife? Why should they have been worried over what Trevor Christie had written about?

Brian continued to assist us. He allowed us access to two Victorian photograph albums that had belonged to Elizabeth Ellison, all of the postcards that his aunts had in their possession, and a considerable batch of family correspondence. The postcards were in their hundreds, and from just about every member of the family, but there was not one from the descendants of James or any of his brothers. Brian could not tell us of any family feud that could account for the lack of communication. A family tree, carefully compiled by his aunts, was stolen, some time in the late 1970s.

Alan would recite the family gossip. He told us that Florence Ridehalgh Ellison, another of Elizabeth's sisters, had an illegitimate son, Arthur Burgess. The father was Cecil Pratt, brother of William Henry Pratt, who later became world famous as Boris Karloff.

While all this was fascinating, it was Alan Bond's knowledge of descendants of Richard Maybrick Ellison that was to prove fruitful. Of his children, Vincent Maybrick was still alive and Alan knew of an Irene Riley, Richard's adopted great-granddaughter.

Irene had been adopted by Olga Maybrick Ellison, Richard's daughter. She lived near Birkenhead so I sent Carol Emmas along to see her in June 1995.

Carol was shown a large collection of photographs of Maybricks. Many she had recognised from Brian Maybrick's albums but some she had never seen before.

Irene did tell Carol that her grandmother, Olga, always said that she was the daughter of Michael Maybrick, James's brother. Other than that, Carol believed there was little to learn. Nevertheless, I decided to visit Irene with Carol on my next trip to Liverpool.

Irene was more than prepared to accommodate me, and since Carol's last visit had rummaged through her grandmother's belongings: birth certificates, the Ellison cemetery records, a daily diary and a birthday book were available to me to peruse, as well as the photographs.

An entry in Olga Maybrick Ellison's birthday book caught my eye:

- Mrs Johnson
- 160 Goodwin Avenue
- Bidston

I passed it to Carol, who stared back at me, and said, almost in disbelief, 'I'm sure Robbie told me that they once lived in Goodwin Avenue . . .'

Could this entry refer to Albert and Robbie Johnson's mother? Carol and I went to see Robbie at his bungalow. The family had lived in Goodwin Avenue – in the 1960s.

Keith Skinner arranged a trip to Vincent Maybrick Ellison as soon as he could. It was 17 July 1995 when Keith visited Vincent in Cornwall. The trip was not too successful. Vincent either did not know the family background or was not talking about it. When Keith asked him whether he knew a Mrs Johnson, Vincent suggested we speak to his niece, Norma Meagher. Norma was very close to Olga and also an Ellison by birth.

I contacted Carol Emmas immediately, who in turn phoned Norma, who also lived in Birkenhead. Carol then wrote to me on the same day:

> I have contacted Norma, as you requested, and am due to visit on Friday afternoon, she does not recall much about the Maybrick's, knew nothing about a family of Johnson's, but did actually mention one interesting fact; being that Olga would mention about James May-brick's watch, I asked her how long ago she mentioned it, and she said it could have been any time between the end of the war up until she died [1989], I shall get this information on tape and forward it to you promptly.

On July 22 1995, Carol Emmas interviewed Norma:

CE If you would like to tell me how you are related to the Ellisons and the Maybricks . . .

NM My father was Norman Ellison, one of quite a large family. His mother was Ada Ellison, née Daniels, and she married Richard Ellison, whose parents – great-grandfather was Richard and I think it was Jane – yes – Jane who was the great grandmother – who was my father's grandmother and they were related to the Maybricks. The Maybricks lived in Aigburth. At one time the Ellisons did too, but they moved to Queens Gardens into a square . . . My great-grandmother was related in some way to the Maybricks and I remember Auntie Olga telling me

233

that she was Jane Maybrick – or something like that. But when I asked Uncle Vin and he's ninety-one – I suppose when I reach that age I won't be too good at remembering . . . But I asked him yesterday on the phone he said, 'Oh I don't know – I've forgotten.' I said, 'Wasn't her name Jane?' and he said, 'I think it was – I can't remember.' I said, 'Well they were cousins – wasn't she a Maybrick?' He thought so but wasn't sure. And the Ellisons were seamen and accountants and teachers and the Maybricks were cotton merchants and corn merchants. Apparently from what Auntie Olga told me, in those days it was quite a common thing for people – I mean those with money – higher-up people with money and good positions to take up arsenic. And so from what the story goes within the family, that the arsenic was around the house and Florence Maybrick was blamed for the murder and put in prison. Within the family itself there was always that doubt whether she did it or not. I think they are inclined to think she didn't . . . I've lived with the name Maybrick all my life because my grandmother, every time she had a child . . . the first name and the centre name – the middle name – was always Maybrick. And at one time I said to Dad, 'Well, why have you all got the middle name of Maybrick?' And he said, 'Well it was because your grandmother thought that if we had Maybrick and there was any money due from the Maybricks, that er – we – could you know – sort of . . .' I said, 'Is there any money?' and he said 'I don't think so. It was just your grandma's idea' . . .

CE   Do you know much about Michael Maybrick – Stephen Adams – was that ever mentioned?

NM I don't know the name of Adams but I've heard of Michael Maybrick.

CE   He was a famous musician.

NM Ah well, as I say, the link there was with my grandfather, who was an excellent musician and also used to write his own music too. So it must be in the family somewhere. Not in me [laughs]. Michael Maybrick – I have a feeling in that box of photographs there could have been a Michael Maybrick . . . Auntie Flo – you see – Ellison brought all those with her when she went to live with Auntie Olga. Auntie Flo was my father's and all his brothers' and sisters' aunt. Sister of my grandfather, Richard Ellison. Then Flo had Arthur – you know the story of Arthur? I believe his father was the brother of Boris Karloff – which everyone in the family was hysterical about . . .

CE Did you know about James's lovers?

NM Oh, well, that was one of the things Auntie Olga said. She didn't necessarily name him, but she said about them in those days 'they were always off with different women'. And that was when she said, 'I don't blame her for poisoning him. There must have been some story there.' But most of the family didn't really think she'd done it because the arsenic was already lying around. And I think there's been a build-up of arsenic that's gradually come up on him and poisoned him. But that was what she did say so the story must have been going around then. And Grandma herself, she didn't very much like the Ellisons or the Maybricks because they were too snooty. And – er – just so – Grandma didn't see that she was also a bit on the ladylike side, but she didn't like them, you know. But they were worth quite a lot of money, the Ellisons and the Maybricks, and – I don't know – they must have gone through it all, and spent it all. Then of course the Ellison Shipping Line went to the wall and the cotton merchandising – I think that went too.

CE You mentioned something about an Ellison Shipping Line?

NM Yes, that's right . . . Auntie Olga told me about the shipping line, so when I came home – my husband works on the docks up there – and I told him and he said, 'Oh yes. It's still up, the sign, THE ELLISON

SHIPPING LINE.' I said, 'Really?' He said 'Yes. I often see it when I go up there.' I'll tell you what might help: if you could trace grandma Ellison – her marriage – who she was before she was married, you'd come back to the Maybricks there somewhere.

Great-grandma Jane was Jane Whalley. That was not the connection to the Maybricks. Norma continued . . .

NM Then again about the watch. Can't tell you a lot about the watch because Auntie Olga only mentioned it in passing. I do remember we were talking about it and she said, 'There's a watch that James Maybrick had – and someone in Goodwin Avenue has got it.' I don't remember her saying Johnson but she did say Goodwin Avenue. I presume they must be the same people. Auntie Olga died in 1989 and it was well before that that she told me . . . She brought this big box of photographs down, old ones, and she was talking about it then and telling me things . . . So it was about that time that she was showing me all those photographs that it came up.

CE You said [on the telephone] that she knew that he had his name in the watch. Do you know how?

NM No, she didn't say it had his name in the watch. I presumed that, because she said '. . . has got James Maybrick's watch', and I just presumed that because I thought that, well, she wouldn't have known otherwise, would she? And I don't even know how she got to know it. If she told me I've forgotten.

CE Did she describe what the watch looked like?

NM No, she didn't – not that I recall. Now I don't know whether she told me or not or whether I'm imagining it – but I thought it was a gold watch. And . . . on a gold chain, as I recall.

CE She didn't say why or how it turned up in Goodwin Avenue. Or in what context?

NM No she didn't – well if she did I've forgotten.

The conversation with Norma had provided us with an

important fact. James Maybrick's watch *had* been discussed in the family. Long before 1989. But why, unless there was something important about it?

We were never able to establish a connection between the Johnson in Olga Maybrick Ellison's birthday book and Albert and Robbie Johnson, but investigating this co-incidence *had* at least given us another important lead on James Maybrick's watch.

Quite suddenly, in spring 1996, Brian Maybrick was taken into hospital. At the last meeting he had with us, we had enquired of his health as he had looked very flushed. Brian never returned from hospital and died on 9 April that year.

I attended the funeral a few days later with Anne Graham, Carol Emmas and Martine Rooney, all of whom had come to know, like and respect Brian over the year or so he had assisted us. Shirley Harrison and Sally Evemy also came to show their respect.

'The Holy City', written by another first cousin (twice removed) – Michael Maybrick, alias Stephen Adams – was the hymn chosen for him. The priest spoke of his value to the community and keen interest in his family background.

The congregation were invited into an adjoining hall for tea and coffee while the close family went to Brian's grave.

It was there that I was introduced to Sister Mary Joachim. Sister Mary was Brian's cousin, born Ursula Grace, her father being William Maybrick and, like Brian's father, a son of John (the shipping-line pilot). Having previously seen a photograph of Sister Mary, I had noted the strong resemblance she bore to Albert Johnson.

As Sister Mary and I spoke, members of the family asked about my 'belief' in the authenticity of the diary. I did not sense any resistance when I responded. I then spoke to Ursula of my suspicions that Albert Johnson was a Maybrick.

I will always respect Sister Mary's honest response: 'I knew he was a Maybrick the moment I set eyes on him . . .'

CHAPTER

15

'TIME REVEALS ALL'

RICHARD BARK-JONES, ONE-TIME SOLICITOR for Michael Barrett, had publicly destroyed his client's claim that he had forged the diary. He had also implied that the diary's origins were known to him.

Richard Nicholas, another prominent solicitor in Liverpool, representing Albert Johnson, also supported his client. In an interview with Martin Howells in September 1993, he said:

> ... We made several enquiries among the laboratories in the country ... eventually we contacted an expert in corrosion, Dr Stephen Turgoose ... He looked at it through an electron microscope and he provided some reports for us and it was very very interesting indeed. The conclusions of that report are in it, but basically saying that it would seem that the scratching's go back tens of years although it is impossible to date it exactly ...
>
> All sorts of thoughts went through my mind at first. But after the weeks and the months passed, after we got it examined ... all scepticism that I initially had has evaporated and I – it seems to me to be a very interesting piece of history ...
>
> They have no need to prove the genuineness or otherwise of the watch. They've had their own tests carried out on it, out of their own interest really. Having done that and spent quite a lot of money on doing that, anybody else who wants to check it out is free to do so. In fact if anybody is prepared to pay for

an expert of equivalent status that we've instructed then we would be happy for them to take the watch, under supervision, to be so and to pay for it to be tested . . .

I feel no onus on my clients to have to prove anything. They are not making any statement about it. It's up to the public at large now to take it on board and, if necessary, have it checked themselves . . .

Martin Howells covered himself by asking if Mr Nicholas's clients were actually denying that they had perpetrated a hoax. Mr Nicholas's reply was unequivocal:

Absolutely. I wouldn't be representing them if I felt in any way that they had manufactured a hoax.

'Absolutely'? A strong word for a solicitor. Solicitors, like accountants, are cautious. Yet, unless we had found another member of a conspiracy, here was further support from an intelligent, responsible person who did not believe that the watch was a hoax. Whether his belief had been born from his own intuition, or whether it was from private information supplied by his client, remains open to speculation.

What we must now ask ourselves is, if you were a prominent solicitor in Liverpool, would you publicly put your reputation on the line for no more than a hunch?

At the time I had a hunch, as I did with the diary, that the watch was inherited. I did not know whether it had passed through Albert or Valerie's family.

Although I had met Albert Johnson in July 1993, my first meeting with Albert together with his wife, Valerie, was in the summer of 1994.

Robbie had already told me he believed the watch was associated to his family and not Valerie's. The meeting seemed to confirm Robbie's views. Albert suggested that maybe his grandmother on his mother's side, Elizabeth Crawley, could hold a clue. I did not interrogate Albert further, as I believed he had agreed to the meeting out of respect of his brother's relationship with me. But his comment indicated that, if there was a connection to his grandmother, then his story of buying the watch from the shop did not add up.

I later repeated my suspicion to Robbie with regards to Albert's purchase of the watch. Robbie responded, 'If you don't believe my brother, why don't you speak to the shop who sold him the watch, Stewarts the Jewellers, and to the man who cleaned the watch, Mr Timothy Dundas.'

I did.

I asked Mr Dundas (TD) about a Lancaster Verity watch during a telephone conversation in 1994:

TD   From what I can remember the name was actually on the dial – on the dial as you opened it – on the face.

PHF   On the face of the watch you think . . .?

TD   Verity – yes.

PHF   Just the name Verity?

TD   Yes, that's right – yes.

PHF   You can't remember Lancaster?

TD   Lancaster Verity. No. I remember Verity because that's the actual make of the watch. Probably Lancaster would have been stamped on the mechanism – that's more likely.

PHF   You remember Verity being on the face of the watch.

TD   Oh, yes.

PHF   Right, do you remember any engravings on the back of the watch at all?

TD   No, no I've been asked this and apart from the usual repair numbers which all old watches have . . . repairers and pawn numbers this sort of thing, there was nothing that I noticed out of the ordinary like a persons name or anything like that.

PHF   You didn't notice any engraved initials at all at the back of the watch?

TD   No.

PHF   I am not talking about the inside back, I mean the actual back.

TD   The actual back – no I didn't see any. No.

I was trying to ascertain whether Mr Dundas could recall the 'J.O.' that was engraved on the back, as opposed to scratchings that were made on the inside back of the watch. His response made me wonder whether we were discussing the same watch. I asked him in what colour the word 'Verity' appeared on the face of the watch, black or gold:

TD   Black. In black, same colour as the numbers. They used to just print the numbers and the name on and then just glaze over the top so it wouldn't rub off.

PHF   And the numbers were in black?

TD   Oh yes, yes.

PHF   OK.

TD   On the porcelain dial.

PHF   Did you know what the date of the watch was?

TD   Oh, that's a hard one that. I would have thought just before the turn of the century, around about there, from the style of it.

PHF   Would you say 1846?

TD   No. I wouldn't have put it as early as that myself. I wouldn't have put it as early as that.

I then asked Mr Dundas if he had any paperwork relating to the watch and he told me he did not. He was, however, confident he would know the watch again.

PHF   If you saw it again would you recognise it?

TD   Oh, yes, I would know it if I saw it. Yes, because there are not many Veritys about. It is quite an unusual make, so there are not many about. In fact I haven't had any in since of that particular make, that shows how rare they are because I deal with about, I don't know, a hundred odd watches a week and I haven't had a Verity in since, so there are not many.

The watch in the possession of Albert Johnson does not have a porcelain face, does not have Verity written in black, or any other colour, on the face, and the numerals are not in black. Albert's watch is gold. The face, the numbers, the front, the back and the inside. The back is engraved with the letters 'J.O.'. The numbers on the face are gold, on gold. The name 'Verity' does not appear on the face, but 'Lancaster Verity' is engraved on the workings of the watch. The marking 'No.1286', which identifies it from any other, is also engraved on the workings.

Inexplicably, almost two years later on 3 July 1996, Timothy Dundas swore an affidavit that the watch pictured in the Liverpool *Daily Post* with Albert Johnson in September 1993, was the watch that he 'repaired'. The affidavit that Mr Dundas swore was as a result of an investigation by Mr Alan Gray, a private investigator in Liverpool, working with the full knowledge of a certain Mr Melvin Harris. The photograph referred to, in all fairness to Mr Dundas, was printed in black and white and did not show the back. It was clear, however, that the watch did not have the name 'Verity' on the face.

The affidavit made by Mr Dundas stated:

> . . . Marks on this watch relating to 'Jack the Ripper' have been made on the watch since I examined and repaired it in 1992, the whole suggestion that this watch belonged to 'Jack the Ripper' is completely false . . .

The scratchings, purportedly made by James Maybrick, are barely visible to the human eye. Mr Dundas swears that neither these scratchings, nor any engravings, were there when he repaired the watch.

To which watch is Mr Dundas referring? A porcelain-faced watch, with black numerals and the name 'Verity' written in black on the front? Or a gold watch with gold numerals with the engraving 'J.O.' on the outside back?

I then called Mr Murphy, owner of the shop where Albert Johnson bought the watch. Mr Murphy confirmed that the watch was white faced, with black numbers and 'Verity' engraved in black on the face. I also asked Mr Murphy whether any letters were engraved on the back, as opposed to scratched on the inside back. Mr Murphy categorically stated that there were not and could not have been, as the ornate design left no room for anything else. Mr Murphy had also told Harold Brough, the reporter from the Liverpool *Daily Post*, that while he could remember 'scratches' he could categorically state that there were no engravings.

On 13 February 1997, Keith Skinner, Shirley Harrison and Sally Evemy met Albert Johnson and Richard Nicholas at Stewarts the Jewellers, in Wallasey. Mr and Mrs Murphy were both present. Albert showed Mr Murphy the gold watch which Mr Murphy confirmed had been purchased from his shop. Keith discussed the anomaly of the white-faced, black-numbered watch and informed me by fax on 18 February 1997:

> Mr Murphy confirms that he remembers having a watch by that description. He possessed quite a few of them in his time and that Mr Dundas would probably have been sent them to overhaul.

At that meeting in February, Mr Murphy also implied it was the first time he had seen the watch since he sold it to Albert. This creates further confusion surrounding this watch as Albert had taken the watch back to the shop after he bought it.

When Albert Johnson originally took the watch to Robert Smith, he also took the original receipt. The words 'one Verity pocket watch £225' were all that appeared. Robert Smith recommended to Albert that the watch's date and serial number be added to the receipt by the shop. Albert took the watch back to Mr Murphy, where the shop owner confirmed the year the watch was made by its hallmark. He duly added this date and the serial number to the receipt in his own handwriting.

On 13 August 1995, I was to meet Tracey Johnson, Albert's daughter. Tracey, a nurse by profession, was warm, hospitable and lively. After a couple of hours I felt I had known her for months. Tracey was sure that she had seen, in her parents' home, a white-faced watch with black numbers . . .

It is obvious that two watches must exist and that their existence has caused great confusion, not least for Mr Murphy and Mr Dundas, two entirely respectable gentlemen neither of whom, in my opinion, have made any deliberate attempts to deceive anyone.

In the meantime, Albert had been encouraged to seek a second scientific opinion. He contacted the scientist recommended. On 31 January 1994 R.K. Wild of the Interface Analysis Centre, Bristol University, produced a report. It contained the following:

> The spectra from the gold surface and the engraved surface appear to indicate that the surface composition does indeed vary with depth ... If this enrichment of silver occurs over a long period of time then this result would indicate that the engraving is of an age comparable with that of the watch ...
>
> The particles embedded in the base of the engraving are brass from the engraving tool. The particle investigated is very heavily contaminated and appears to have been considerably corroded ... This suggests that the particle has been embedded in the surface for some considerable time ...
>
> ... in my opinion it is unlikely that anyone would have sufficient expertise to implant aged brass particles in the base of the engraving ...
>
> From the limited amount of evidence that has been acquired it would appear that the engraving on the back of the watch has not been done recently and is probably greater than several tens of years old but it is not possible to be more accurate without considerably more work.

Of course, the cynics criticised Albert for not granting R.K. Wild unlimited access to the watch. They ignore the cost of such an exercise.

I could not believe that the scratchings could be anything other than old, in which case the 'modern forgery' theory could be dismissed. It was then that our research produced information that really intrigued us.

On 21 July 1889, Florence Maybrick was to write to her mother[1] from Walton Prison:

My dear Mother.
I cannot find the letter of Nurse Yapp addressed to Mr Cleaver but she said in it the children had been very ill with bad cold which following after a severe attack of 'hooping cough' naturally makes me anxious & think it might run into congestion of the lungs. I gather from Mrs Woolley's letter that the children return to L.pool on Tuesday. I think that during those day that Nurse Yapp has to attend Court, Edwin Maybrick had better arrange with their old Nurse/now married/Mrs John Over. 47 Timperon Street Smithdown Road 'Edge Hill' to take charge of them during the day as neither Mrs Holdon or her servants can be expected to devote themselves entirely to them for 3 or 4 days at the least ...

By 21 July 1889, Florence Maybrick had absolutely no say whatsoever in where her children should go or who should take responsibility for them. So what was this letter about? If it was for the purpose her sentiments appear to express, would it not be reasonable to assume that Edwin Maybrick, Nurse Yapp or her mother would know exactly where to find Mrs John Over? Or was Florence telling her mother something else?

Mrs John Over was the nurse who brought up Bobo as a child, but whom Florence believed 'was too old' by the time Gladys was born. Her maiden name was Emma Parker. Alice Yapp was to replace her in 1887.

After the trial ended, the media would insinuate a relationship between Alice Yapp and James Maybrick. But they described a nurse who frequently crossed the Ocean with James and Florence. It could not have been Alice Yapp, as Florence did not leave England after Miss Yapp's employment commenced.

Could 'John Over' have anything to do with the initials engraved on the back of the watch?

---

[1] Macdougall, 1891.

Melvyn Fairclough went to St Catherines House to follow John Over's descendants. Bessie Jane Over, his daughter, married in January 1896. One of the witnesses to the marriage was William McKay. We had already ascertained that Albert Johnson's grandmother, Elizabeth Crawley, married her first husband in 1888. One of the witnesses? William McKay. We ordered the originals of both wedding certificates. The signatures were too similar to be from different people. Here was a link between Albert Johnson's family and the Maybricks.

It was all becoming too much. A direct link between Albert Johnson and the Maybrick household, found as a result of a mysterious letter Florence had written to her mother. The reference to Goodwin Avenue, from an interview with another Maybrick descendant. The remarkable similarity between Albert Johnson and Sister Mary Joachim, born Ursula Maybrick.

If Albert Johnson was a Maybrick then I could not believe that by some fluke he had bought this watch from Stewarts the Jewellers.

I reviewed all the paperwork we had in relation to the watch and re-read Albert's interview with Martin Howells, conducted in September 1993. We had all missed crucial words said by Albert himself.

MH And you're convinced it's genuine?
AJ Well I'm convinced whoever Maybrick was it was his watch – but whether it's genuine or not really I leave it to the experts for that.
MH You're not saying if it's Jack the Ripper?
AJ No, no.
MH It's genuinely Maybrick's?
AJ Yeah, yeah. I think it's genuinely Maybrick's watch. Whether he was Jack the Ripper or not I wouldn't know about that. I have to leave that to the experts.

The conversation clearly implies knowledge of the watch's origins. Albert had no more reason to be convinced that this was Maybrick's watch than he did that

246

it was Jack the Ripper's or anyone else's unless he had prior knowledge of the watch's provenance.

In the spring of 1995, I was to learn of an offer made by a businessman from Texas USA, to purchase the watch. The amount was $40,000. Albert refused it.

Both Albert and his wife were reaching retirement age. They were both having to work very hard just to make ends meet. Albert refused $40,000, for a watch he apparently paid £225 for and a watch that the world is crying out 'fake'. It did not make sense, unless Albert had knowledge of the watch's true provenance.

It was not until August 1995 that my relationship with Albert developed. Until then he was Robbie's brother and I was to him 'a nosy Southerner'. Unfortunately, it was tragedy that caused this change. Robbie Johnson went on holiday with his girlfriend to Spain. On leaving a night-club in the early hours of the morning he was hit by a speeding motor bike as he ran across a road. He died instantly.

When Robbie's body was flown back to England, amongst his belongings were his mother's ashes which, for some reason, he had taken with him. At Robbie's funeral Albert addressed the congregation and recited a poem[1] he had written for his brother. More than a hundred people were in stunned silence as Albert revealed his literary ability.

I had been devastated by the news of Robbie's death. I made no attempt to disguise my feelings at his funeral. It was then that Albert realised my relationship with his brother had been one of true friendship. Albert and I began to communicate frequently.

Albert is a devout Catholic and he and Valerie are genuine, hard-working people who adore their only daughter and granddaughter. Albert and Valerie have always been happy and despite their struggles they have maintained solidarity. According to their daughter, Tracey, 'they always discuss everything and there are no secrets'.

---

[1] Reproduced as Appendix 6.

I became convinced that Albert had not told the world everything he knew. And the reason for it was personal and private. The only time I ever knew him to 'fib' was to protect family and close friends of the family. Robbie had told Tracey of my suspicions which I later confirmed to her. She then discussed these with her parents. A little later, she would tell me that she had said to her dad, 'I would rather have learnt that I was descended from royalty!'

The more I got to know the Johnsons, the more angry I became at the ignorant claims of forgery. Insinuations were being made that Albert had scratched the initials and words on the inside back of the watch he had acquired. I presume Albert popped into his local corner shop, picked up the latest scanning electron microscope for a cool £100,000, and then did a crash course on metallurgy. He was then able to identify a brass particle that had corroded for a hundred years and successfully implant it into a scratch that was barely visible to the naked eye!

I suppose our top scientists at UMIST and Bristol University should feel even more angry. With their state of the art 'scanning electron microscope' they were unable to detect an amateur forgery, created by a layman in Liverpool. That is what the cynics want us to believe.

Of all those who have criticised the diary and the watch, not one has got off his backside and attempted to meet and speak to the individuals involved. They were frightened to and still are. Frightened of no longer being able to say 'liars and forgers'. Frightened at having to recognise honest, hard-working people, who love and care for their families. And frightened most of all, of having to accept that the theory of 'a conspiracy of forgers' is pure and utter nonsense.

My feeling at the end of 1995 was that Albert had inherited the watch from his family. In order to leave the watch to his family, he acquired the 'white faced' Verity watch with 'black numbers' from Stewarts the Jewellers. This gave him a receipt, which could then be associated with the watch he already owned. He would not then need to pass on to his own descendants the burden of being branded illegitimate descendants of the Maybricks. There was no intention on Albert's part to inform the world about his possession, until the news broke in Liverpool of the discovery of the diary.

But that was just my theory.

During one telephone conversation with Albert, I asked him why he did not tell the world the truth? I told him that, if he could prove the provenance of the watch, the world would accept it was Jack the Ripper's and he could sell it for a lot of money. Should he be worried about local gossip, he could just sell-up, move away and live the rest of his life in luxury. Albert's only response was to tell me he was 'too old to get up and go'.

In the autumn of 1995, Albert and Valerie Johnson would join the noted criminologist Colin Wilson, his wife Joyce, Anne Graham, Carol Emmas and myself on a visit to Battlecrease House. Paul Dodd was good enough, once again, to display his hospitality.

We all sat in what was James Maybrick's bedroom. All but Albert faced Paul Dodd in a semi-circle of armchairs and settees. Paul explained the structure of the house and how it had changed, answering any questions put to him. Albert, who sat just behind us in a corner of the room, would ask only one, 'Where did the servants sleep?'

On 11 November 1994, I had arranged a 'get together' of a number of the people I had interviewed during my investigation. Among them were Brian Maybrick, the 'Whittlesey' Maybricks, Anne Graham and Albert, Robbie and Valerie Johnson. Paula Adamick, a journalist, would cover the occasion. An article in the London *Evening Standard* three days later carried the headline WHY I BELIEVE EVIL DIARY OF JACK THE RIPPER IS NOT A HOAX.

I requested my guests to bring with them artefacts and any material they had associated with James Maybrick. I did not know if Albert would come, but he did and brought not only the watch but a photograph of his grandmother, Elizabeth Crawley.

Elizabeth Crawley married twice. Her first marriage to

Charles Taylor, on 12 March 1888, ended with his tragic death at the age of twenty-three. They were to have one child, William. In 1899, Elizabeth Taylor (née Crawley) was to marry Patrick Somers. They had two daughters, Mary and Dora. The latter was Albert's mother.

Dora died in September 1992, just three months after Albert had seemingly acquired the watch. His Auntie 'May', with whom he had a special relationship, had died some twenty years earlier. Although born Mary Somers, the name 'May' was shown as her middle name when she married.

We also successfully tracked down the descendants of William Taylor. I was requested not to mention their names. I will not. Their emotions were mixed. They had no knowledge of their family connections to the Maybricks, but were clearly not happy with the association. One of them did remember Dora well and he commented that he would have been surprised if Dora would have held on to a watch for any given period of time. She would have more than likely pawned it.

Carol Emmas told me a curious story that Dora had once told her 'of meeting the devil, who wore a top hat and a cloak and who disappeared down a gutter as she got closer to him'.

In the period between autumn 1995 and the spring of 1996, I disclosed all my research to Albert Johnson. He no longer denied he was a 'Maybrick', but would not alter his story of how he came by the watch. I suggested to him that I must be missing something obvious, but he would only say 'maybe it will come to you'. I will not push Albert; there is no point. Something far more important than money prevents Albert from telling everything he knows and, I am sure, always will. An oath, perhaps? Had he been sworn to secrecy about the watch, I know Albert would never break that promise.

By now, everything seemed to be starting to make sense. The debate about the true provenance of the watch and diary had been answered. Both artefacts had been passed down through the 'family'. The truth had to be simple; it is. There are, however, questions that remain open.

Had Albert bought a gold watch from the jewellery shop, or a white one with black numbers? Perhaps he bought both, knowing that the gold one had been sold to the shop by his mother?

Is the 'J.O.', engraved on the back of the watch, any connection to 'John Over', brought to our attention by Florence Maybrick's extraordinary letter to her mother?

Was Emma Parker, nurse to James and Florence's children and later to become Mrs John Over, lover to the master of the house and did she bear him any children?

We may never know the answers to these questions, but perhaps as James Maybrick's family motto states:

Tempus Omnia Revelat
Time Reveals All

CHAPTER

16

'IMPOSSIBLE . . .'

'IMPOSSIBLE'. THAT WAS THE only word that Hannah Koren said to me when I asked her whether the diary could be forged. This was not, you will remember, what I wanted to hear. It would have been far easier if I could have exposed the diary as a fake in the video I was planning to make.

Hannah explained that the handwriting in the diary was very complex. The lower zones (the so-called sexual ones), were something she had never seen before. Hannah went on to explain that the characteristics displayed by the author could not be forged. Even by her – 'and I know what to look for'.

Hannah Koren is not just a graphologist, as the detractors would like you to believe. She is a 'Forensic Document Examiner for the Israeli Ministry of Justice and the Israeli Social Security Services'. A full breakdown of Hannah's education and experience is detailed in Appendix 3.

As stated in an earlier chapter, Hannah was convinced that the handwriting in the diary displayed a 'multiple personality'. Whoever Jack the Ripper was, as with every serial killer, he most probably possessed this characteristic. Without it, a serial killer would be unlikely to hide his or her alter ego for long.

The diary reflected this: 'I am tired of keeping up this pretence of respectability. I am finding it increasingly difficult to do so . . .'

Sue Iremonger, the document examiner cited by

Kenneth Rendell for her expert opinion, admitted that she had not studied the effects on handwriting of 'multiple personality disorder'. Sue was honest enough to state that she had requested from the institute of which she was a member that an effort should be made in order to accommodate this area of study.

As far as I was concerned, this meant that Sue was not qualified to comment on whether the diary was genuine.

On page 255 is an example of the handwriting of one person who suffers with 'multiple personality disorder'. When Hannah showed me this, I understood that with complex people comes complex handwriting.

The handwriting in the diary, *prima facie*, was a problem.

A will of James Maybrick, held at Somerset House, seemed to bear little resemblance to the handwriting of the diary. The two signatures on the will appeared to be in the same hand as the rest of the text. The signatures were also similar to that of James Maybrick on his wedding certificate. Up to October 1993, when Shirley Harrison's book, *The Diary of Jack the Ripper*, was released, the wedding certificate and the will were the only known examples of James Maybrick's handwriting.

I will reiterate that it was because the handwriting in the diary was, on the face of it, so completely different from the handwriting of the will that both Paul Begg and I were so intrigued. Also, the author of the diary clearly implied that he had written the letter to the police dated 25 September 1888, the letter that had started with the words 'Dear Boss' and ended with 'Yours truly, Jack the Ripper'. The handwriting of the diary bore no visible resemblance to the handwriting of this letter either.

It will be seen later in this chapter that whoever wrote the diary had considerable knowledge of James Maybrick's will. They were well aware of the 'Dear Boss' letter as well. We have already established that a 'forger' would have had to have considerable knowledge of various sciences, Victorian language, Victorian medicines and the psychopathology of a serial killer, and would need to have discovered previously unidentified material in regard to both James Maybrick and Jack the Ripper.

Yet our 'forger' makes no attempt to copy the handwriting, or even a signature that appears on the will of James Maybrick or the 'Dear Boss' letter.

A modern-day forger would know that the handwriting would be the first thing to be compared. It just did not make sense.

I asked Hannah to compare the diary to the 'Dear Boss' letter. This was her faxed response of 11 September 1993:

Dear Paul

Unfortunately I have not managed to reach unequivocal conclusions with regard to the comparison of the letter 'Dear Boss', the letter of the 6th of October, the will of James Maybrick and the diaries [sic] signed by 'Jack the Ripper'. I have invested many many hours into examining these writings during the 9 months that have elapsed since I first saw the Diary in December 1992, and examined [the 'Dear Boss' letter] at the Public Record House.

Here are the causes:

1. The letter 'Dear Boss' which I examined was a photocopy, and therefore I was unable to tell the pressure of writing.

2. This letter was written very slowly. The writing is not spontaneous nor natural, but very artificial.

3. The letter was written in a 'facade' writing, meant to disguise the personality of the real writer, and hence it is very difficult to compare it to a spontaneous writing (the diary signed by 'Jack the Ripper').

4. The will was written with a very thick nib pen, and this rendered it very difficult to compare it with the rest of the documents.

5. The handwriting in the diary seems to have gradually faded with the years, and the writing pressure can no longer be discerned. This also renders the examination very difficult.

6. The writer of the diary was probably schizo-

Above Home Secretary Sir Henry Matthews considering a pardon for Florence Maybrick. This illustration comes from *St Stephen's Review* and was unearthed by Stuart Evans

Left Florence Maybrick's trial as depicted on the front page of Stuart Cumberland's *The Mirror*

Right Florence leaving prison, an illustration used in the Liverpool *Daily Post* on Wednesday 17 August 1904. This is the illustration from which Alice Dean identified Florence as a visitor to her home

Left The Maybrick Watch bearing the initial J O. Was this the watch once in the possession of John Over? (*Albert Johnson*)

Below Brian Maybrick, whose grandfather was James' first cousin, with Peter Jepson, a descendant from the relationship between James Maybrick and Sarah Robertson

THE DECLARATION

OF A

Free Burgess of the Town of Liverpool.

James Maybrick

I DO solemnly and sincerely declare:

That I will be a true and faithful Subject to our Sovereign Lady Queen VICTORIA, her Heirs and Successors, and no Treason do, procure, or commit, or cause to be done, procured, or committed, within this Town, or the Liberties thereof:

That I will also, from time to time, as occasion shall require, aid, assist, and obey, as well the Mayor of this Town as also all other Her Majesty's Officers within the same under the said Mayor, in the due and lawful execution of their several offices, and especially concerning the Preservation of Her Majesty's Peace, the Observation of Good Order, and the ancient and landable Privileges, Franchises, Liberties, and Customs of the Town; which said Liberties and Customs I will further and increase to my knowledge and best endeavour:

That I will likewise by no Covin, Colour, or Deceit, free any Foreigner, or the Goods, Chattels, or Merchandise of any Foreigner, or other Person whomsoever, not Free within this Town, in the name of my own proper Goods, Chattels, or Merchandise, whereby the Customs of this Town may be impaired, hindered, impeached, delayed, or embezzled:

That if I shall know or hear of any unlawful Congregations, Conventicles, Riots, Routs, or unlawful Assemblies, or other disorderly Tumults, to be had or made, or likely to be had, made, or procured by Day, or by Night, within this Town or the Liberties of the same, to the Disturbance of the Peace of our Sovereign Lady the Queen, her Heirs or Successors, I will give Warning and Notice thereof to the Mayor, or his Deputy, with all speed:

And that all and every other Thing or Things which shall either touch or concern the Advancement or Preferment of the Commonwealth and State of this Town, or shall appertain and belong to be done by good and honest Burgesses, Freemen, or Inhabitants of the same, I will for my part do, accomplish, perform, and observe, to the best of my Ability, Power, Knowledge, and Wit.

Declared at Liverpool aforesaid,

this 27th day of *July* 1876

Before me

The signature on this document from 1876, when James Maybrick was made a Freeman of Liverpool, displays a distinctive flourish which was also characteristic of the handwriting of the diarist shown below. (*page from the Diary of Jack the Ripper courtesy Smith Gryphon Publishers*)

Index of Scotland Yard Ripper files (HO144/220/A49301). Why have so many of the files been destroyed?

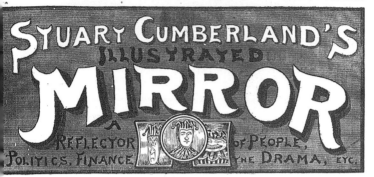

STUART CUMBERLAND'S ILLUSTRATED MIRROR

A REFLECTOR OF PEOPLE, POLITICS, FINANCE, THE DRAMA, ETC.

No. 15.—One Penny.   LONDON, MONDAY, SEPTEMBER 23, 1889.   [Registered at G.P.O. as a Newspaper.

THE GREAT WHITECHAPEL PUZZLE.

Find "Jack the Ripper" and his Knife.

Stuart Cumberland's fascination with the Ripper is displayed here in this rarely seen cover of his *Ilustrated Mirror*

Left 17 September letter
(HO 144/221/A49301C)

Below The Jack the Ripper signature is held in the Metropolitan Police files (MEPO 3/142/40) and displays strong similarities to Maybrick's signature on the company memo discovered in Richmond Chancery Court, Virginia

Facsimile held in Metropolitan Police files of the 25 September Dear Boss letter with its envelope and both sides of the Saucy Jacky postcard reproduced along the bottom

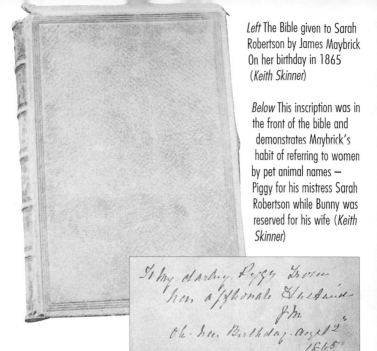

Left The Bible given to Sarah Robertson by James Maybrick On her birthday in 1865 (*Keith Skinner*)

Below This inscription was in the front of the bible and demonstrates Maybrick's habit of referring to women by pet animal names — Piggy for his mistress Sarah Robertson while Bunny was reserved for his wife (*Keith Skinner*)

BATTLECREASE.
THE SCENE OF THE TRAGEDY
NOW CALLED INGLETON.

Battlecrease House — was this the home of Jack the Ripper? (*Stewart Evans*)

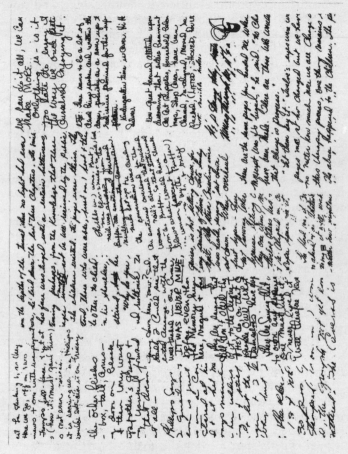

(Handwriting sample courtesy of Hannah Koren)

255

phrenic. Inside the diary itself I found a variety of letter formations and features indicating multiple personalities.

It is known that writers who suffer from this kind of disturbance 'produce' different handwritings, and this rendered it very difficult to come to an unequivocal conclusion when comparing such handwritings.

Thus, I have found both similarities and contradictions in the documents and it is impossible for me to reach a verdict.

Sincerely,
Anna Koren[1]

Now Hannah had produced an honest report. Her opinion that the diary could not have been forged has never wavered and she was filmed saying so. She knew, because I had told her, that the 'Dear Boss' letter should have been written by the same person. Despite that, she wrote the above letter.

Nick Warren, editor of *Ripperana*, chose to represent Hannah's opinions to his readers in the January 1994 edition (issue number 7) as follows:

(1) DR ANNA KOREN, Handwriting analyst.

She first saw the material in December 1992. On 11 September 1993 she issued a fax stating that she could no longer 'validate' the handwriting as being the Ripper's. The writing appeared to her to be 'artificial'.

That is the sort of selective review of evidence that the detractors of the diary have felt necessary to employ in order to 'prove' that the diary is a fake. Surely if it is, such 'editing' would not be necessary. It was at that time that I realised that the detractors were running scared. I also remembered the words of Dr David Forshaw: 'When the Ripper experts start moving the goalposts, then you know you have something real.'

It should be noted that not everybody disbelieved the

---

[1] Hannah is known as 'Anna' professionally.

diary. Indeed, the more you moved away from Ripperology, the more sensible the input from experts became.

Judge Richard Hamilton, who has presided over many cases over many years in Liverpool, spent an evening with me offering his valued opinion. Judge Hamilton had, in 1989, been primarily responsible for reconstructing 'The Trial of Florence Maybrick', at St George's Hall, Liverpool.[1]

The judge assured me that he had tried cases of fraud and forgery. He made a few interesting points.

- A confession of Jack the Ripper would not require more than a few lines; sixty-three pages would seem excessive. The more a forger writes, the more likely he is to be found out.
- Even if one had decided to write extensively, pages of rambling 'poetry' with words crossed out would simply be gross stupidity.
- The entry in the diary concerning Catharine Eddowes's kidney – 'Perhaps I will send Abberline and Warren a sample or two, it goes down well with an after dinner port . . .' – was something that the judge did not believe any modern-day forger would even think about.
- And the diarist's comment, 'Encountered an old friend on the Exchange floor', 'displayed knowledge', according to Hamilton. The word 'Exchange' in reference to the Cotton Exchange was correct usage, but not something easily known by any modern-day forger.

If this diary was a fake, then it had not been created by an amateur. That is why this book is being written nearly four years after the diary was first made public.

I was also pleasantly surprised to read in *Justice of the Peace & Local Government Law*, 22 January 1994, an article by John Hostettler, JP, BA, LLB (Hons.), LLM, Ph.D. (London).[2]

It said:

---

[1] St George's Hall was where the trial took place a hundred years earlier.
[2] Dr Hostettler is a Solicitor of the Supreme Court.

As for the diary itself, it reveals a mind tormented by vile and consuming hatred, an inhuman urge to feed on the bodies of proxies for the 'whore' wife, extending grotesquely, as with other serial killers, even to eating their organs. His appetite was insatiable until death from his own poisons and torments approached.

Having reviewed the evidence for himself, Dr Hostettler concluded:

All these factors point towards the authenticity of the diary. But, although the diarist wrote that he wanted the document to be found, it has not been established how or where it saw the light of day.

I found it somewhat comforting that people who hold elevated positions within our legal system and who are therefore expected to be completely impartial had concluded that the diary was more likely than not to be genuine. In both cases the mystery surrounding the Maybrick affair began to unravel.

Hannah Koren was convinced that the diary could not be forged. Sue Iremonger was convinced that the will and the marriage certificate were written by the same person and that that person did not write the diary. Not surprisingly, Hannah Koren's opinion was ignored by the detractors. Colin Wilson suggested I call Reed Hayes, a graphologist and a forensic document examiner for the FBI.

Reed Hayes's graphological analysis was almost a mirror image of that supplied by Hannah Koren. Reed did not see Hannah's report until after he had completed his own. If the diary had been faked then its author knew what these experts would look for and, therefore, understood graphology as well as they did.

Reed compared the 'James Maybrick' signatures on the will to the James Maybrick signature on his wedding certificate. He gave me his conclusion in a letter:

You have provided the following documents for the purpose of handwriting identification.

Document 1 is a two page will dated 25th April 1889, bearing two signatures which are under question as to identity.

a) Signature number one, appearing on page one of said will, hereinafter referred to as 'Q1', the purported signature of James Maybrick.

b) Signature number two, appearing on page two of said will, hereinafter referred to as 'Q2', also James Maybrick.

Document 2 is a marriage certificate dated July 27, 1881, bearing the known signature of James Maybrick, hereinafter referred to as the 'known signature'.

You have also provided a photocopy signature of Edwin Maybrick, date of the document unknown.

You have asked that I compare the questioned signatures – Q1 and Q2 with the known signature of James Maybrick. My examination reveals that there are 11 similarities between Q1 and the known signature and seven similarities between Q2 and the known signature. Additionally, there are 14 dissimilarities between Q1 and known signature and 12 dissimilarities between Q2 and known signature . . .

FINDINGS FROM EXAMINATION:

In my opinion, based on the documents provided, it is highly probable that Q1 and Q2 were not written by the same hand that wrote the known signature of James Maybrick.

It is also to be noted that nearly eight years have passed between the signing of the marriage certificate and the signatures appearing on the Will. This may account for some of the differences of the signatures.

It should also be noted that the writing and signatures appearing on the will have a *distinctly contrived look*. In my opinion there is an effort to disguise the author's handwriting.

Regarding the signature of Edwin Maybrick I have noted that there are similarities between Edwin Maybrick's signature and the handwriting that appears on the will. However, I do not have enough conclusive evidence to say that he is, or is not, the writer of the will or the writer of the signatures appearing on the will.

So, Hannah Koren cannot be conclusive; Sue Iremonger believes the will and wedding certificate were written by the same person. Reed Hayes believes they were not. I could only conclude that handwriting analysis was still more of an art than a science.

Reed Hayes did point out that the M of 'Maybrick' on the will had been made up of *four* different strokes. Of the fifteen or so other examples of James Maybrick's signature that we eventually tracked down, all of the Ms were of one continuous stroke, as was the M on the wedding certificate.

When Hannah first saw the will, she did not dismiss it as *not* being written by the author of the diary. Indeed, she pointed out the long 'T-bars' that are common to both. Hannah could not prove, however, that they were written by the same hand.

If Reed Hayes was correct, and the will had been written to *look* like James Maybrick's handwriting, it may account for the similarity that Hannah picked up.

When we discovered the handwriting of James Maybrick in the Bible he gave to Sarah Ann Robertson in 1865, it only seemed to confuse. Both Hannah Koren and Reed Hayes confirmed that the author of the inscription, 'To my darling Piggy', was *not* the author of the will. Sue Iremonger was inconclusive this time. Although the provenance of the Bible was impeccable, we seemed to be going nowhere fast.

As far as the style of the writing is concerned, according to Rendell, 'the writing [of the diary] is not consistent with the [handwriting] formations of the late 1880s'.

However, Brian Lake, of Jarndyce Antiquarian Booksellers of London, said, 'From a limited look at the volume, there is nothing to indicate that the Jack the Ripper diary is not of the 1880s and in my view the writing is of the same period.'

What was it that Rendell's team member Dr Joe Nickell said?

'We determined the diary was an obvious forgery, based primarily on conclusive handwriting evidence . . .'

The only conclusive thing about the handwriting evidence was that it was *in*conclusive!

Back to the will.

My study of the Maybrick case led me to the inescapable conclusion that there were extraordinary circumstances surrounding the will. The detractors, and Melvin Harris in particular, seemed to think that my reason for stating my 'doubt' that the will was written and signed by James Maybrick was that the handwriting 'did not match' that of the diary. That was not the reason. I had always expected the formal hand of James Maybrick to be at least similar to that in the will because even Reed Hayes, who concluded that the will was forged, expected that.

Let me make it perfectly clear: I do not dispute that the will currently held at Somerset House is the will that was 'proved' to be that of James Maybrick. Nor do I deny that the words contained within that will were once written by James Maybrick.

Let me explain in a little more detail.

There are two, and arguably three, versions of the will.

First, there is the 'proved' version that currently is at Somerset House.[1] It is purported to have been written and signed on 25 April 1889.

Secondly, there is a version transcribed by A.W. MacDougall in 1891,[2] and said to be written 'in a large and shaky hand and written on blue paper'. MacDougall makes it clear that he made a special journey to the Liverpool District Probate Office in order to see the will.

The description, 'large and shaky', may be accurate in describing pages of the diary, but most certainly does not describe the will at Somerset House. Neither does

---

[1] See Appendix 4a.
[2] See Appendix 4b.

MacDougall's description of 'blue paper'. I visited Somerset House on 19 September 1995, to see the will for myself. The most accurate description is 'grey'. It could be white that has discoloured with age.

Five years later, in 1896, in an update of his book, MacDougall altered his description of the will to 'large and sprawling', which could be a fair description of the will that now exists.

MacDougall had seen the will with his own eyes. Why had he used the adjective 'shaky' if the handwriting was 'sprawling'?

MacDougall makes no attempt to explain the change of description. Nor does he need to. Handwriting that he saw at some time or another was 'shaky', of that there can be no doubt. MacDougall did not know a diary would turn up purporting to be written by both James Maybrick and Jack the Ripper with 'shaky' handwriting.

So what is the relevance of all this?

The will of James Maybrick has not suddenly become a mystery for the convenience of the believers in the diary, as the cynics would have you believe. The will was a question of debate in 1891 when MacDougall published:

Now that document, which is described as a will, purporting to have been signed by James Maybrick in the presence of Geo. R. Davidson and Geo. Smith on the 25th of April, 1889, is a very 'suspicious circumstance'.

A reference to the preceding diary of facts, which transpired during the proceedings, shows that the only thing disclosed during these proceedings of what occurred on 25 April was:

Edwin Maybrick returned to Liverpool, having been on a business visit to America since August 1888.

And the first question that must occur to every mind is why James Maybrick should on that day have drawn up that document. Was there any connection between that document and the business visit to America, from which Edwin Maybrick returned on that day?

The Geo. R. Davidson, who was one of the witnesses of the signature, is the George R. Davidson to whom I have referred as a great friend of James Maybrick, and one of the few who were constant visitors to Battlecrease, and one who was present at the house every day during James Maybrick's last illness. But his name, for reasons that I am unable to understand, was not mentioned during the whole of the proceedings.

The Geo. Smith was James Maybrick's clerk at the office, who was called at the trial as one of the witnesses for the prosecution to prove that James Maybrick's 'health was generally good. He sometimes complained of his liver. He had discussed the question of homeopathy, but not with me.' He also said that, on 27 April, 'the day of the Wirral Races, deceased came to the office at about half past ten in the morning. He was not looking well, and went away between twelve and one.'

Not one word was asked of this witness about the will, nor about the state of James Maybrick's health on the 25 April, nor was the subject of the will referred to at the trial.

I must refer here again to the circumstance I have referred to in a previous note, of Edwin Maybrick's having come out of James Maybrick's bedroom, on Friday night, 10 May, the eve of his death, with some document which he had taken in for James Maybrick to sign, and which Alice Yapp, who is described as 'knowing and hearing everything,' said was the will. It will be remembered that on the occasion of Edwin's taking that document, whatever it was, to be signed, James Maybrick shouted out in a loud voice, which was heard down in the kitchen, 'Oh Lord, if I am to die, why am I to be worried like this? Let me die properly.'

If Edwin Maybrick did succeed in getting a signature to any document on that occasion, what was it? Was it a will? If so, what will? But whatever it was, evidence ought to have been given at the trial about this occurrence, and it was not given.

You will remember the 'search on the premises' (while Mrs Maybrick was lying in a speechless swoon), which Michael, Edwin, Mrs Briggs, and Mrs Hughes made on Sunday morning, 12 May, for the keys of the safe, when they wanted to find the will, and looked under the paper lining of the dressing-table drawer for it and found the letter from Brierley instead. And when they looked in some of James Maybrick's bandboxes and hatboxes and found some bottles with 'black solution' and 'white solution' instead. No mention was made of the actual finding of the 'keys of the safe' or 'the will', nor does it appear when or where this will was found. Probate was not granted until 29 July, the day after the Grand Jury found a true bill against Mrs Maybrick. The document itself is written in a large shaky hand upon blue paper, and had evidently not been prepared in a lawyer's office. The only evidence given concerning it is Michael Maybrick's evidence at the coroner's inquest, on 28 May.

Q. Did your brother make a will?
A. Yes
Q. Can you tell me, sir, are you one of the executors?
A. There are no executors, but two trustees.

Michael's solicitor, Mr Steel, intervened at this point, saying that Mr Maybrick would rather not have the will read 'unless it is material to the case'. The questioning continued:

Q. Mrs Maybrick would have no knowledge of the contents?
A. No; I don't think she even knew of it.

I do not know why, if this will was signed by James Maybrick on 25 April, Michael Maybrick was in a position to know he should have made that statement and repeated it, or why Steel should have supported the statement. But two things are absolutely clear from a perusal of this document. One is that no husband or father could have been in his sober senses when he signed it, and the other is that no wife or mother could have wished her husband to die leaving such a will behind him.

The facts are clear:

- although the will was dated 25 April, there was another, which James's brothers were trying to get him to sign on 10 May;
- the will left little or nothing for Florence, even though they were said to have had a 'complete reconciliation'; in fact, does not the will reflect what Florence wrote to her mother about on 31 December 1888?

On 31 December, Florence wrote to her mother: 'In his fury, he tore up his will this morning, as he had made me sole legatee and trustee for the children in it. Now, he proposes to settle everything he can on the children alone, allowing me only the one-third by law! I am sure it matters little to me, as long as the children are provided for. My own income will do for me alone. A pleasant way of commencing the New Year!'

Our diarist had written: 'I have showered my fury on the bitch. I struck and struck. I do not know how I stopped. I have left her penniless, I have no regrets . . .'

It was not just MacDougall who queried this will. In New York on 2 August 1889, it was reported, 'It is rumoured also that Sir Charles Russell will score a strong point on the curious will which Mr Maybrick made only a few days before his death . . .'

If the will dated 25 April 1889 was the only will written and signed by James Maybrick, then what were the brothers attempting to get James Maybrick to sign on 10 May? Moreover, what was the will that Mrs Briggs was searching for on 12 May, the day after James Maybrick died?

. . . the following curious remark made by Alice Yapp, on Sunday morning, to Elizabeth Humphreys, is significant:

'I will tell all I know, if only to prevent Mrs Maybrick having the children'.

This is a remark that suggests to me the possibility that Alice Yapp knew something about the provisions of this will, and was not quite sure that such a settlement for the children as was made in this will would hold good in law. Then, again, on this Sunday morning, the 12th, and before Mrs Briggs went on the search for the 'keys of the safe' – to find the will – Mrs Briggs took it upon herself (Mrs Maybrick lying in her speechless swoon) to say to the servants, 'Mrs Maybrick is no longer mistress here.' This raises the presumption that Mrs Briggs also knew the provisions of this extraordinary will, before the keys of the safe had been found . . .[1]

Subsequently, on Saturday, 18 May (the day when Mrs Maybrick was removed to Walton Gaol), Thomas Maybrick told Elizabeth Humphreys and Mary Cadwallader to be ready to leave on Monday, 'as the will had been left very awkward'.

Very awkward? Strange. According to Somerset House today, there was nothing awkward about the will at all. MacDougall's version, however, would have been.

On close examination of the two versions, I noticed several differences (see Appendices 4a and 4b for details). On the face of it, the strangest appeared to be the misspelling of James's daughter Gladys Evelyn on the 'proved' version.

More curious, however, was MacDougall's claim that an 'Affidavit of Due Execution' was filed on 29 July 1889. Such an affidavit is required when a will is rejected by probate. All the newspapers on 30 July confirmed that such an affidavit had been filed the previous day. The will currently at Somerset House bears no mention of such an affidavit and, when I queried it, Mr C.W. Fox, the District Probate Registrar, wrote to me on 24 February 1994:

I agree it is strange that the copy will reproduced in the Liverpool *Echo* refers to an affidavit of due execution, whereas the copies from the Principal Registry do not.

[1] MacDougall 1891.

Of course, we only had to ask Melvin Harris for the answer.

He first claimed that there was no evidence that MacDougall ever saw the will (despite MacDougall's telling us that he made a special trip to the probate office in Liverpool, and his description of the writing and colour of the paper). Harris then goes on to explain that MacDougall transcribed the will incorrectly from the newspapers, which had also got the information wrong (but MacDougall's version differs from those of the newspapers).

Harris adds that MacDougall tells us that he got this information from the newspaper cuttings he collected concerning the trial. Although MacDougall does credit newspaper sources and did compile a scrapbook of press cuttings covering the trial I do not believe for one moment that he relied solely upon newspaper sources.

I own MacDougall's scrapbook. I purchased it from Nigel Morland's son, Terry.

The scrapbook does not include a newspaper cutting of a report about the will from 30 July. Had MacDougall been using only newspaper sources for his research it is inconceivable, given the number of other relevant cuttings he saved, that he would not have kept a cutting about the will. So why didn't he? Simple – he went to see the will for himself.[1]

Most revealing in MacDougall's version is the wording of the attestation clause:

Signed by the testator in the presence of us, who, at his request and in the presence of each other, have hereunto affixed our names as witnesses, Geo. R. Davidson, Geo. Smith.

The words 'in his presence' should follow 'request'. They do not. Such a mistake would cause probate to be rejected. Such a mistake would cause an 'affidavit of due execution' to be filed. There was no mistake by the newspapers or MacDougall.

---

[1] HO 144/1640/A50678D/279.

How can we then make sense of the fact that a 'different' will now exists? Clive Dyal, Record Keeper at Somerset House, offered a possible explanation in a letter to me on 17 August 1993:

- A will was rejected by probate and the trustees were informed that, unless another will was found, the testator (James Maybrick) would have died intestate. (Author's note: in such an event, everything would have automatically gone to Florence.)
- Another will was 'found', and together with an 'affidavit of due execution' was filed with the 'rejected' version at the Liverpool District Probate Register Office.
- After fifty years, only the 'proved' will would have been sent to Somerset House, all other documents being destroyed.

We were to find further strong evidence to suggest that James Maybrick did not hand write that will on *25 April 1889*.

The *Pall Mall Gazette* of 3 June 1889 published the following:

THE MERSEY MYSTERY

... Mr Maybrick was insured for £5,000 in the Mutual Reserve Fund Life Association of New York, one of the policies being for £3,000 and the other for £2,000 the latter being in favour of his wife. One policy was taken out in October last and the other in January of the present year, and in both cases it is understood that a strict medical examination was made, and that the deceased was found to be quite healthy.

The policy for £2,000 is mentioned in the will at Somerset House. The policy for £3,000 is not. The largest policy of all would *not* have been overlooked by James Maybrick.

We can now start to understand the sequence of events:

- The will seen by MacDougall was drafted by James Maybrick on, or shortly after, 31 December 1888.

- Maybrick took out a new insurance policy in January 1889.
- After the reconciliation with his wife, in April, James Maybrick wrote another will, redressing the balance.
- The brothers realise the estate will be left to Florence and get James to sign the one he drafted in December.
- The will is entered for probate and rejected. They had overlooked the error made by James Maybrick in his drafting of the attestation clause.
- The brothers 'find' another version of the same will. It is proved.

The final objection to the extant will comes from Florence Maybrick. While in prison, Florence petitioned the authorities (HO 144/1640/A50678D/331) expressing her concerns about the welfare of her children and also stated in reference to the will that '. . . I should have contested on the ground, "That unlawful pressure and influence had been brought to bear on the testator" . . .'.

Florence clearly believed that she could prove that James (the testator) had been forced to sign a will with which he did not agree. Alice Yapp confirmed this happened on 10 May.

As far as the handwriting is concerned, Hannah Koren explained to me that when James Maybrick played the role of a businessman he would write like one. When he was 'drugged up', those characteristics would be displayed in his handwriting. Have you ever tried writing after you have had a few too many? Would it resemble a letter you might write to your bank manager when you were sober?

I held on to something Hannah told me. It was at a time when I could not understand why the diary could not be proved or disproved to have been written by the same author as the 'Dear Boss' letter. Hannah said, 'The more handwriting you find written by Jack the Ripper, and the more you find by James Maybrick, the more likely you will be to find two documents that are very similar.'

The will of James Maybrick has been fundamental to the detractors in 'proving' that Maybrick could not have been the Ripper. The detractors were in for a shock.

17

'YOURS TRULY, JACK THE RIPPER'

IT WAS THE CORRESPONDENCE sent to the police in 1888, signed 'Jack the Ripper', that was probably the most important area of our investigation. The diary's authenticity suffered some of its early venomous attacks because its author claimed that he had given himself the chilling *nom de guerre* 'Jack the Ripper'. He boasted: 'Before I am finished all England will know the name *I have given myself*. Indeed it is a name to remember' (my italics).

Further on in the document he congratulated himself for being the one who had 'the name all England was talking about . . .'.

Finally, of course, the last thing the diarist wrote was a signature: 'Jack the Ripper'.

Letters signed with this now notorious sobriquet were sent to the police at the time of the murders. From then on it was the name by which the Whitechapel murderer became known to posterity.

There could be no denying that the author of the diary was claiming that he had sent these letters to the police. With the exceptions of perhaps Colin Wilson and Bruce Paley, modern authors had long since concluded that these letters were not written by the Whitechapel murderer. If the letters were a hoax then the diary must be a hoax as well.

Simple – the accuracy of our investigation was crucial.

When our work on the letters began I knew enough about the Ripper to understand that at the time of the murders the police were convinced that a letter dated 25

September 1888 and a postcard dated 1 October 1888 were genuine, so convinced in fact that they made colour facsimiles of both and posted placard copies outside every police station. Beneath the facsimile, the poster said in bold black letters:

Any person recognising the handwriting
is requested to communicate with the nearest
Police Station.

Why did the majority of Ripper authors assume that their knowledge of the crimes was superior to that of the police in charge of the investigation?

What puzzled me was that, although the diary showed full knowledge of the letter and postcard, there had not even been the slightest attempt by the diarist to imitate the handwriting on them.

Questions sprang to mind, none of which the diary's detractors seemed to even want to consider:

- Is it not the purpose of a forgery to convince everyone of its authenticity?
- Why, therefore, if the authors of Jack the Ripper books were right – that this diary *was* a forgery – would the forger make reference to the letters, knowing that they would dismiss it immediately?
- Why had the police believed the letters to be genuine?
- Why had the authors arrived at the conclusion that the police were wrong?

One thing soon became clear to me: it was vital for a comprehensive re-evaluation of the facts surrounding the events.

On 27 September just before the 'double event', the 25 September 1888 letter outlining the intentions of the Whitechapel murderer at his next killing was received by the Central News Agency. Written in red ink to imitate blood, and with some words underlined, it read:

271

25 Sept 1888
Dear Boss

I keep on hearing the police have caught me but they wont fix me just yet. I have laughed when they look so clever and talk about being on the *right* track. That joke about Leather Apron gave me real fits. I am down on whores and I shant quite ripping them till I do get buckled. Grand work the last job was. I gave the lady no time to squeal. How can they catch me now. I love my work and want to start again. You can soon here of me with my funny little games. I saved some of the proper *red* stuff in a ginger beer bottle over the last job to write with but it went thick like glue and I cant use it. Red ink is fit enough I hope *ha ha*. The next job I do I shall clip the ladys ears off and send to the police officers just for jolly wouldn't you. Keep this letter back till I do a bit more work, then give it out straight. My knife's so nice and sharp I want to get to work right away if I get a chance. Good luck.

Yours truly

Jack the Ripper.

Dont mind giving the trade name.

Running down the side of the page was this postscript:

'wasnt good to post this before I got all the red ink off my hands curse it. No luck yet. They say I'm a doctor now *ha ha*'[1]

This missive, today known as the 'Dear Boss' letter (but from here on called the letter of 25 September for reasons that will become clear later), was passed to Scotland Yard on 29 September, the day before the Stride and Eddowes murders. The day after this 'double event', 1 October, the Central News Agency received another communication, a postcard that read:

I was not codding dear old Boss when I gave you the tip, you'll hear about Saucy Jackys work tomorrow

---

[1] Mepo 3/3153/1–4.

double event this time number one squealed a bit couldnt finish straight off. had not time to get ears for police thanks for keeping last letter back till I got to work again.

Jack the Ripper[1]

This 25 September letter was the first one made public signed 'Jack the Ripper'. But was it the first letter signed with that *nom de plume*? Most authors have assumed that to be the case.

After reading the diary for the first time, the author Melvin Harris – who has been writing books on the Ripper for years – concluded that the diary must be a forgery because he maintained that its writer had made the same mistake as many authors. In the summer of 1993 Harris told me that the first time the name was used was on a postcard sent soon after the murder of Annie Chapman. He was correct. He told me I would find confirmation in a book by a former policeman, Edwin T. Woodhall, who described the communication. He wrote: '... one particular postcard, written in red ink and received by some press head office ... soon after September the ninth ... these crimes came to be known as the work of one named "Jack the Ripper" ...'[2]

Woodhall quoted what was written. It was this ditty:

I'm not an alien maniac
Nor yet a foreign tripper
I'm just your jolly, lively friend,
Yours truly – Jack the Ripper.

P.S. Look out next time. I'm doing the job more perfect.

There is now some confusion as to whether Mr Harris was, in fact, pointing out the Woodhall poem in order to warn me *against* setting too much store by it. Mr Harris dismisses all of Woodhall's work as 'ludicrous and

---

[1] Mepo 3/142/2–3.
[2] Edwin T. Woodhall, *Jack the Ripper; Or When London Walked in Terror* (1937), p. 25.

nonsensical' and attributes the first use of the name 'Jack
the Ripper' as follows:

> An enterprising journalist had decided that the killer
> needed a memorable name, so hit on Jack the Ripper
> and used it first in a letter then on a postcard. He sent
> off his hoaxing letter on 27 September.[1]

Nevertheless, Melvin Harris had sparked off an interest
for me in Ripper ryhmes and, oddly enough, there is a
different version of the ditty quoted in the memoirs of the
retired Scotland Yard Assistant Commissioner, Sir Melville
Macnaghten. He joined the Yard in June 1889 and perused
all the letters from what he said was a 'bulging post-bag'
filled with 'hundreds of anonymous communications'. He
printed this version at the top of his fourth chapter:

> I'm not a butcher, I'm not a Yid,
> Nor yet a foreign Skipper,
> But I'm your own light-hearted friend, in
> Yours truly, Jack the Ripper.[2]

Why were there two versions? Furthermore, did Mr
Harris's theory prove the diary a fake? Had the author of
the diary singled out the 25 September letter as the first
communication signed Jack the Ripper? Was the postcard
reproduced by Woodhall the one piece of evidence that
proved the diary a forgery?

Mr Harris may have been too swift to disregard
completely the postcard quoted by Woodhall, and Mr
Harris may also have overlooked an important claim made
in the diary where the author wrote: 'Michael would be
proud of my funny little rhyme . . .'

This was written just after the diarist's recollection of
the Annie Chapman murder, precisely where Woodhall's
reference suggested one would find it! So, our diarist was
aware of the earlier communication and Harris's initial
reason for thinking the diary was a forgery was wrong.

---

[1] Melvin Harris, *The True Face of Jack the Ripper* (1994), p. 10.
[2] Melville Macnaghten, *Days of My Years* (1914), p. 54.

Written at the same time as he was penning his recollections of the double event, the diarist decided to 'include my funny little rhyme that will convince them that it is the truth I tell'.

This was the second reference the author of the diary had made to the 'funny little rhyme'. This was extraordinary. In 108 years of Ripper books, not one author had ever commented on the fact that there were two versions of this poem, let alone attempted to explain why. Only the diary told us. Only the diary gave the answer. Not only were two versions of the rhyme sent, but the entries in the diary were precisely where the obscure historical evidence indicated that they should be.

Shortly after the murder of Annie Chapman there was a commonly held belief that the murderer was an overseas sailor; a belief reflected in the first version of the ditty. By the time of the double event, the media had switched their suspicions to Jacob Isenschmid, a butcher, and John Pizer, a Jew. This is reflected in the second version. If the diary was a forgery, the forger must have discovered the verse quoted by Woodhall. This is just one example that shows what considerable lengths he went to in his research. Again, this is contrary to what Harris claimed when he wrote: 'In fact it's quite easy to demonstrate that the diary could have been concocted by drawing on three books at the most.'[1]

In a letter to me, dated 23 July 1993, Harris wrote that a forger of the diary 'could have created the text using two books only'. Later, when Martin Fido asked him to nominate them, Harris couldn't but accepted Martin's suggestion that 'three books must refer to the Ripper part of the case alone'.

The goalposts just kept on moving . . .

Were the Ripperologists right? Were the 25 September letter and the 'Saucy Jacky' postcard both hoaxes? What were their reasons?

The 'Saucy Jacky' postcard would seem to be the focus

---

[1] Melvin Harris, *The True Face of Jack the Ripper* (1994), p. 194.

of attack because it confirmed knowledge of information in the 25 September letter and detailed knowledge of the double event, which took place only twenty-four hours earlier.

Some authors have suggested that because the 'Saucy Jacky' postcard was posted on the same day as the 25 September letter was published (1 October 1888), anyone could have sent it, having simply copied the style and content of the letter. This idea is summed up neatly in *The Jack the Ripper A–Z*, with the following statement:

> Since the text of the 'Dear Boss' letter was published in the morning paper, *Daily News*, 1 October 1888, the 'Saucy Jacky' postcard, printed in the *Star* the same day, might have been an imitative hoax.[1]

This could not have been an imitative hoax. Why? The text of the letter was certainly published in the *Daily News* on 1 October, but a facsimile of the handwriting was not published until 3 October, yet the handwriting of the postcard matched that of the letter. Also, the letter's postscript was written with a different tool from the rest of the letter but the same tool as was used for the postcard.[2]

Despite all the above we are being asked to believe that an imitator not only copied the handwriting of a letter he had never seen, but even knew what writing tool was used.

When we discovered that this oversight had been made by more than one Ripper author, it encouraged us greatly. Ripper authors were not infallible!

The writer of the 25 September letter told the police to: 'Keep this letter back till I do a bit more work, then give it straight out.'

---

[1] Paul Begg, Martin Fido and Keith Skinner, *The Jack the Ripper A–Z* (1994) p. 211.

[2] Missing Suspects File (Mepo 3/141 32–135). The Assistant Commissioner of Rotherham CID, L.S. Bush, in a letter to Robert Anderson, dated 24 October 1888, said that the 25 September letter was written with a steel pen, but that the 'Saucy Jacky' postcard was written with a quill.

The police received the letter from Central News on 29 September. They did keep it back. It was not published until 1 October. They had considered its importance. On receipt of the postcard they *knew* its importance.

Despite previous authors' arguments to the contrary, the 'Saucy Jacky' postcard must have been received prior to the publication of the letter, irrespective of whether the date of 1 October 'proves' it may have been written afterwards. Why? Because of one simple, obvious piece of logic that nobody else has noted: if the postcard had been received after the letter was published surely the police would have taken no notice of it!

In his book on the Ripper, Philip Sugden argues the internal evidence of the 'Saucy Jacky' postcard, where it claimed 'number one squealed a bit . . .'.

Elizabeth Stride did squeal. In a report recorded on file by Chief Inspector Swanson, a witness, Israel Schwartz, claimed that he saw 'The man . . . turned her round and threw her down on the footway and the woman screamed three times, but not very loudly.'[1]

Sugden suggested: 'It is the kind of detail a hoaxer could easily have invented and stood a good chance of getting right.'[2]

Alternatively, he argues:

It might also have been possible for the postcard writer, if he was a pressman, to have learned the detail [Stride's squealing] from Schwartz. We know for certain that one journalist successfully tracked him down to his lodgings in Backchurch Lane, either on Sunday evening or Monday morning, and procured an interview from him.[3]

An interview was procured. It appeared in the *Star* on 1 October and was the only detailed account of Schwartz's

[1] HO 144/221/A49301C/150.
[2] Philip Sugden, *The Complete History of Jack the Ripper* (1994), p. 270.
[3] Ibid.

story. But the police had clearly taken great care in ensuring that the media were not aware of Stride's 'scream', because no mention of it appeared in this or any other press report.

The author of the 'Saucy Jacky' postcard boasted: '. . . had not time to get ears for police.'

Sugden claimed that the Ripper did have time.[1] But he missed the point! How did the writer of the 'Saucy Jacky' postcard know that the ears had *not* been cut off?

So, by now, the 'Saucy Jacky' author (who we have already established is the same author as that of the 'Dear Boss' letter) guessed correctly about Stride, guessed correctly about Eddowes and, furthermore, guessed correctly about Annie Chapman. I hear my contemporaries saying, 'Annie Chapman?' The letter of 25 September claimed: 'Grand work the last job was. I gave the lady no time to squeal.' So following Sugden's arguments he must have guessed right again!

The fact is, to the best of my knowledge, no author has ever focused on this previously.

Let us recap . . .

- Annie Chapman did not make any noise – squeal, scream, shout or whatever. The police knew it – the author of the letter did too.
- Stride did scream – the police knew it, Schwartz knew it and the author of the letter knew it.
- The police were told that the next victim's ears would be cut off. The police knew they were not. The coroner (and probably the mortician) knew also. So did the author of the letter.

There is no doubt that the police took this letter seriously – that is established by their distribution of the facsimile.

A recent author, Bruce Paley, correctly summed up these points when he wrote:

---

[1] Ibid, p. 269.

These letters are too smug, too self-assured and too accurate in their predictions not to have been written by the killer. To have been penned by anyone else would have entailed the most extraordinary series of coincidences and the most audacious luck.[1]

Unlike Sugden and others before him, the police investigating the crimes at the time believed that the information contained in the correspondence could not have been written by anyone other than the perpetrator of the crimes.

While the police, in 1888, did not have the forensic or technological capabilities available to police today, they were not stupid: they would have examined all angles. I believe that no author has put forward an argument, against the letters, that the police did not consider at the time.

There are several references in the police files to comparisons of handwriting, showing just how important they thought some of the Ripper letters were. We discovered, for example, that Chief Inspector Donald Swanson initialled over thirty of the hundreds of letters sent. Beneath his initials in the top left corner of one, he added: 'Put with others.' On another, dated 11 November 1888, just two days after Kelly's murder, he wrote: 'Received from Press officer.' On yet another, received 5 October 1888, he wrote: 'Say he is the murderer.' On a letter received three days later on 8 October, where the writer threatens murder in Blackfriars, Swanson has written: 'Murderer. Telegram to L Divs.' (L Division covered the Blackfriars area.)

Chief Inspector Donald Swanson's initials and comments on the letters clearly show that the Metropolitan Police were taking the letters seriously.

Yet another example of the police comparing handwriting came to light just recently. The authors Stewart Evans and Paul Gainey, quoting from an American newspaper, wrote:

---

[1] Bruce Paley, *Jack the Ripper: The Simple Truth* (1995), p. 101.

The London Chief of Police telegraphed to San Francisco requesting that specimens of Twomblety's [sic] handwriting in possession of the Hibernia Bank there to be forwarded to him. When these are compared with the chirography of 'Jack the Ripper' another chapter may be added to the life of this man of mystery.[1]

Tumblety was a Ripper suspect. But why were the police interested in his handwriting except to compare it to something important?

In 1896 a letter was received signed 'Jack the Ripper'. What did the police do with it? Did they dismiss it because it was eight years since a Ripper murder? Did they dismiss it on the grounds that the letters signed 'Jack the Ripper' were hoaxes? No! They compared it to the 25 September letter. Chief Inspector Henry Moore reported on 18 October:

> I beg to report having carefully perused all the old 'Jack the Ripper' letters, and fail to find any similarity of handwriting in any of them, with the exception of the two well-remembered communications that were sent to the 'Central News' office; one a letter, dated 25th Sept./88 and the other a postcard, bearing the postmark 1st Oct/88., Side copies herewith.
>
> On *comparing the handwriting* of the present letter with hand-writing of that document . . .
>
> A. In conclusion I beg to observe that I do not attach any importance to this communication.

The italics are mine.

At the end of his report Swanson (by now a Superintendent), added:

> In my opinion the handwritings are not the same. I agree as to A. I beg that the letter may be put with the similar letters. Its circulation is to be regretted.[2]

---

[1] Stewart Evans and Paul Gainey, *The Lodger: The Arrest & Escape of Jack the Ripper* (1995), p. 215.
[2] Mepo 3/142/157–9.

Swanson's postscript tells us two things: first, that the letter was circulated, which shows how important they considered the identification of handwriting; and second, the expression 'similar letters' suggests that there were probably two letter files – one for the hundreds of unimportant letters (like this one of 1896), and another one for the letters they considered genuine.

Although this report of Inspector Moore's had been published previously, little or no attention had been paid to it by other authors. I can only conclude that they did not like it, since it seemed to contradict their belief that the letter of 25 September 1888 was written by a hoaxer. A pattern was developing and one I was understanding quickly. When some authors could not deal with a problem, they did not acknowledge its existence.

The hoax theory seemed to hang on the following statement by the Assistant Commissioner of CID, Robert Anderson, expressed in 1910, twenty-two years after the murders:

'. . . he and his people were low class Jews' and 'that class in the East-End will not give up one of their number to Gentile justice'. I will only add here that the 'Jack the Ripper' letter which is preserved in the Police Museum at New Scotland Yard is the creation of an enterprising journalist.[1]

In the same year, 1910, Sir Henry Smith, retired Commissioner of the City of London Police, wrote his memoirs. In his chapter on the Ripper he said:

Since this chapter was written my attention has been drawn to an article in *Blackwood's Magazine*, of March this year – the sixth of a series by Sir Robert Anderson.[2]

---

[1] Robert Anderson, 'The Lighter Side of My Official Life' (*Blackwood's Edinburgh Magazine*, March 1910), p. 358.
[2] Sir Henry Smith, *From Constable to Commissioner* (1910), p. 159.

He then launched a scathing attack on Anderson. He said Anderson's remarks about Jews and the Ripper being a Jew were a 'reckless accusation . . .'[1] and added that '[the Ripper] completely beat me and every police officer in London'.[2]

Smith's inference is that since the Ripper beat every police officer no one, including Anderson, could say who or what the murderer was: Jew or Gentile.

When Anderson said the letter was written by a journalist, was he referring to the one of 25 September? Apparently so. However, Bill Waddell, the former Black Museum curator, told me that to the best of his knowledge the 25 September letter was never in the Black Museum. Even the facsimile was, according to Waddell, not put there until 1921, when the museum was refurbished, which explains why no police journal reported its being there until the beginning of the following year.[3]

The 25 September letter and 'Saucy Jacky' postcard sent to the Central News may have, over the years, become confused with another letter paired with another postcard. George Lusk was the elected president of the newly created Vigilance Committee, formed to succeed where they believed the police had so far failed – in capturing the Ripper. On 16 October 1888 he received a shocking communication in his post: a cardboard box containing what proved to be a portion of human kidney preserved in spirit of wine, and the following letter which accompanied it:

---

[1] Ibid, footnote, p. 160.
[2] Ibid, p. 147.
[3] *Police Review and Parade Gossip*, 27 January 1922: 'The most gruesome relic is the photographic reproduction of the letter written in red ink and sent to a news agency over the signature of "Jack the Ripper", announcing that he should cut off the ears of his next victim to send to the Police. Accompanying it is the later postcard marked with blood stained fingers, regretting that owing to lack of time he was unable to carry out his ghoulish promise.'

From Hell
Mr Lusk
Sor
I send you half the kidne I took out from one woman
prasarved it for you tother piece I fried and ate it was
very nice I may send you the bloody knif that took it
out if you only wate a whil longer.
   signed Catch me when
you can
Mishter Lusk.[1]

This, now known as the 'Lusk letter', is the one Smith
was defending. His attack on Anderson centred around his
belief that this letter was genuine, not a hoax. He wrote:

A facsimile of the writing of the purloiner of the kidney
. . . had appeared in an evening paper . . . and I instantly
laid the letter before [Sir James Fraser].[2]

It is obvious that Smith (despite his arrogant claim that
he knew more about the Ripper than any man living),[3]
writing twenty-two years after the murders, relying on
memory alone, mistakenly lumped together the 'purloiner'
of the 'Lusk' kidney and the facsimile of the letter and
postcard sent to Central News. He must have been
confusing the 'Lusk letter' with that of the 25 September,
since the 'Lusk letter' was never published in facsimile
form. Nevertheless, it is clear that Smith believed the
kidney, and therefore the 'Lusk letter', were sent by the
Ripper.

After Smith published his book Anderson revised his
Blackwood's Magazine articles, re-published them in book
form and defended himself against Smith's attack. He
refuted Smith's contention that the 'letter' was not a hoax.
Since Smith argued for the 'Lusk letter' it must have been

---

[1] The original is lost but a photograph of it is in the Royal London
Hospital Archives.
[2] Sir Henry Smith, From Constable to Commissioner (1910), p. 156.
[3] Ibid, p. 147.

the 'Lusk letter' Anderson argued against, and not the 25 September letter.

If Anderson had been referring to the 25 September letter when stating it was the work of a journalist, he would have been, in effect, criticising his own officers for having the facsimiles made and circulated. Yet, even Smith said that was something Anderson would not have done.[1]

Could it be the 'Lusk letter' that was in Scotland Yard's Black Museum? Donald Rumbelow, a former City of London Police sergeant and curator of the police museum in Wood Street Station believes that the original and a photograph of it were on display at Bishopsgate Police Station in the 1950s. Early in my research, Donald told me that, since the Mitre Square murder was within City boundaries the 'Lusk letter' would have been kept by the City Police and would never have been at Scotland Yard.

Where was it before 1950? The answer is supplied in a report from October 1888 by Inspector James McWilliam, discovered in Home Office files in 1993 by Stewart Evans:

> The kidney was forwarded to this office and the letter to Scotland Yard. Chief Inspector Swanson having lent me the letter on the 20th inst. I had it photographed and returned it to him on the 24th.

So Donald Rumbelow was wrong: the 'Lusk letter' was at Scotland Yard.

In case the answer had been in the media all the time we decided to do a complete sweep of all the contemporary newspapers. A fuller reading of the *Star* of 19 October 1888 revealed, in an article about the 'Lusk letter', a quite sensational statement. It read, in part:

> The handwriting of the letter differs altogether from that of 'Jack the Ripper', specimens of which were recently published. The writing is of an inferior character, evidently disguised, where the spelling, as

---

[1] Sir Henry Smith, *From Constable to Commissioner* (1910), p. 161. 'It would ill become him to violate the unwritten rule of the service.'

will be seen, is indifferent. A few days before he received the parcel Mr Lusk received a postcard supposed to come from the same source . . . The whole thing may possibly turn out to be a medical student's gruesome joke.

So there was a 'Lusk letter' and a 'Lusk postcard'!
The *Star* added:

The Metropolitan Police last night handed the piece of kidney over to the City Police on the assumption that if the whole thing is not, as is most likely, the disgusting trick of some practical joker, it relates to the Mitre Square murder.

These words echo the phrases used by Sir Robert Anderson in 1910, but with regard to the 'Lusk letter', not the 25 September letter!

The implication by Smith of the 'Lusk letter' and kidney is that the kidney was the one removed from the previous victim, Catharine Eddowes. But she was murdered over two weeks earlier. Why would the murderer wait so long before sending them? Could it be that a hoaxer took rather a long time procuring a suitable kidney? It would seem so.

So unimportant did the police consider the 'Lusk letter' that, although they photographed it, they did not publish a facsimile of it as they had of the letter of 25 September.

In his memoirs, Walter Dew, a former Detective Constable in H Division who worked on the Ripper case, reproduced the text of the 25 September letter in his chapter on the Ripper. He then, curiously, claimed: 'The man who wrote that letter was illiterate.'[1]

This must have been very confusing for his readers, since they could see from the text that it was not 'illiterate', that it was written in a neat hand and employed reasonably good grammar. We might expect an illiterate to misspell words like 'write' and 'right', 'squeal', 'enough', 'laughed' and 'caught'. But no, there was *not*

---

[1] Walter Dew, *I Caught Crippen* (1938), p. 127.

one spelling mistake. Was Walter Dew confused? Clearly this letter was not that of an illiterate. The 'Lusk letter' certainly was. Had Dew's publisher made the error of publishing the letter that was in the Black Museum then (1939)?

Conan Doyle also appears to have got his facts confused.[1] He wrote:

> Holmes's plan would have been to reproduce the letters in facsimile and on each plate indicate briefly the peculiarities of the handwriting. Then publish these facsimiles in the leading newspapers of Great Britain and America, and in connection with them offer a reward to anyone who could show a letter or any specimen of the same handwriting. Such a course would have enlisted millions of people as detectives in the case.

What Conan Doyle said should have happened is precisely what did. Further confusion! Sir Melville Macnaghten described the 25 September letter as 'gruesome', the very word used by the media to describe the Lusk letter.

It was clear that there was confusion among people involved with the crime and, therefore, authors writing a hundred years later must be of the most dogmatic sort to insist that they are right.

It is a fact that the Metropolitan Police, too, believed the correspondence of 25 September 1888 to be genuine. They continued to until at least 1896.

It is clear that Sir Henry Smith believed the Lusk letter to be genuine and consequently any reasonably minded person would now accept that the letter referred to by Anderson was this, and not, as previously thought, the letter signed 'Yours truly Jack the Ripper' . . .

---

[1] See Appendix 5 for Conan Doyle's remarks on the letter.

18

'YOURS TRULY, JAMES MAYBRICK'

HAVING ESTABLISHED THE LIKELIHOOD that the letter dated 25 September 1888, signed 'Jack the Ripper', was indeed sent by the Whitechapel murderer, the letters files of the Metropolitan and City Police would need careful scrutiny. As we have already seen, most authors, since the Ripper files were opened in 1976,[1] did not believe that any correspondence was written by the perpetrator of the crimes. Therefore I assumed that they had not examined these files vigilantly.

Keith Skinner informed me that Paul Begg had copies of all the letters, which he had obtained in 1987. He was sure that Paul would lend these to me. I phoned Paul and he confirmed what Keith had said. After discussing the reasons behind my request, Paul recalled reading a letter recently that intrigued him. It was the first time he had read this letter, which was apparently written by the author of the letter dated 25 September. He faxed me a copy:

Oct. 5 1888

Dear Mr Williamson,

At 5 minutes to 9 o'clock tonight we received the following letter the envelope of which I enclose by

---

[1] The Metropolitan Police and Home Office Files on the case have been open to researchers at the Public Record Office since 1976 and 1986 respectively, and had previously been seen by a number of writers – notably Douglas Browne, Donald Rumbelow and Stephen Knight – all of whom felt that they contained no material at all that would help scholars identify the murderer (*The Jack the Ripper A–Z*, 3rd edition, Headline Books 1996).

which you will see it is in same handwriting as the previous communication.

5 Oct 1888

Dear Friend

In the name of God hear me I swear I did not Kill the female whose body was found at Whitehall. If she was an honest woman I will hunt down and destroy her murderer. If she [here the words 'was an honest woman' are repeated but crossed through] was a whore God will bless the hand that slew her, for the woman of Moab and Median shall die and their blood shall mingle with the dust. I never harm any others or the Divine power that protects and helps me in my grand work would quit forever. Do as I do and the light of my glory shall shine upon you. I must get to work tomorrow treble event this time yes yes three must be ripped will send you a bit of face by post I promise this dear old Boss. The police now reckon my work a practical joke well well Jacky's a very *practical* joker ha ha ha Keep this back till three are wiped out and you can show the cold meat

Yours truly

Jack the Ripper

Yours truly

T.J. Bulling.

A.F. Williamson Esq.[1]

On 3 October 1888 a headless, limbless torso of a woman was discovered in the foundations of the New Scotland Yard building being built on the Victoria Embankment near the Palace of Westminster. The arms were found in the Thames. It became known as the 'Whitehall murder'. The press had no doubt whatsoever. This was another horrible murder by Jack the Ripper.

This was convincing. The Ripper must have written these letters. I concluded that, if you were a hoaxer and

---

[1] Mepo 3/142/491–492.

the newspapers had written that Jack the Ripper had killed again, then such a hoaxer would have claimed ownership of that murder. The police had never considered this crime to be the work of Jack the Ripper but a hoaxer could not have known that. Only two people would have known that this murder was the work of a different hand: Jack the Ripper and the murderer of the Whitehall victim!

Whether the diary was genuine or not, the letter of 5 October must, beyond all reasonable doubt, have been sent by Jack the Ripper.

I read that letter again and again. Alarm bells went off. Some of those words I had seen before. I grabbed my transcript of the diary. The letter had boasted: 'I must get to work tomorrow treble event this time'.

Astonishingly, in the very next entry after the double event (30 September), the diarist had written: 'Will visit the city of whores soon, very soon. I wonder if I could do three?' The letter also stated: 'I never harm any others or the Divine power that protects and helps me . . .'

In the diary, in the entry following the boast of 'three next time', the author wrote: 'I am convinced God placed me here to kill all whores, for he must have done so, am I still not here. Nothing will stop me now.'

In the entry following the description of the 'double event', the author of the diary had written: '. . . will send Central another . . .'

The letter of 5 October had never been published at the time that the diary was taken to the literary agent Doreen Montgomery. Therefore, if the diary had been forged, the forger had found a letter that nobody had seen in 108 years! The diary, without doubt, echoed the words of that letter. Joe Nickell, a Ripperologist, had stated that the diary was 'an amateurish fake'. Mr Nickell, with all due respect . . .

The very next day, 6 October 1888, the *Daily Telegraph* published two sketches illustrating the face of a man thought to be the Ripper. These two sketches were clearly of the same man, differing only in the fact that one had a moustache and the hats were different. The article stated:

The above sketches are presented not, of course, as authentic portraits, but as a likeness which an important witness has identified as that of the man who was seen talking to the murdered woman in Berner Street and its vicinity until within a quarter of an hour of the time when she was killed last Sunday morning . . .

This witness, Mathew Packer, has furnished information to the Scotland Yard authorities and it was considered so important that he was examined in the presence of Sir Charles Warren himself . . .

A man like the one without the moustache and wearing the soft black felt deerstalker hat, as drawn, was seen by Mathew Packer, of 44 Berner Street, two doors from the scene of the murder, late on Saturday night . . .

The article continued, probably most importantly:

Search for an individual answering to the description above detailed, but having a small moustache and wearing a black deerstalker felt hat, instead of a soft one, has been made by the police in Whitechapel ever since Saturday Sept. 1, the day following the Buck's row tragedy . . .

The sketches in the *Daily Telegraph* of 6 October and the photograph of James Maybrick show an uncanny resemblance. If the diary had been forged then the forger had been extremely lucky. Furthermore, by claiming ownership of the 25 September letter the author of the diary had, of course, indirectly associated himself with the letters dated 5 and 6 October. Had the diary been forged, this is precisely where the project would probably have fallen down.

Extraordinarily, a letter, agreed by all handwriting experts to be in the same hand as that of 25 September letter but previously unpublished, was discovered by Robert Smith of the publishers Smith Gryphon. The postmark was NW and the letter read:

6 Oct 1888

You though yourself very clever I reckon when you informed the police But you made a mistake if you though I dident see you Now I know you know me and I see your little game, and I mean to finish you and send your ears to your wife if you show this to the police or help them if you do I will finish you. It no use your trying to get out of my way Because I have you when you dont expect it and I keep my word as you soon see and rip you up. Yours truly

Jack the Ripper

Down the left-hand side was the following postscript: 'You see I know your address.'[1]

The letter is clearly not a hoax of 1888. It is certainly a threat from one man to another but would have been meaningless and pointless if not sent by the Ripper himself. The letter includes the words 'now I know you know me'. This phrase makes sense only if it is a reference to the sketch in the *Daily Telegraph* of the same date as the letter.

The phrase 'You see I know your address' suggests that the letter was originally sent to Mathew Packer.

We have established that the Metropolitan Police clearly believed that the letter of 25 September was sent by the Whitechapel murderer. The letters that recent research has uncovered, therefore, would have been just as significant. Was it for this reason that Sir Charles Warren interviewed Mathew Packer himself – the only Ripper-related interview he ever conducted?

The letter dated 5 October tied in with the diary. The letter of 6 October tied in with a photograph of James Maybrick. Was the forger of the diary enjoying inexplicable luck or was a picture beginning to emerge?

These letters were not the first time that correspondence signed 'Jack the Ripper' had shown a link to Maybrick. Admittedly tenuous, a letter was discussed by Donald

---

[1] Mepo 3/142/139.

McCormick in his book published in 1959. This letter, he said, was sent on 29 September 1888. It came from Liverpool and, as earlier stated, was signed 'Jack the Ripper'. If McCormick was right then the author had to be the same as that of the letter of 25 September 1888 as nobody was aware on 29 September of the alias 'Jack the Ripper'.

McCormick's source for this letter was Joseph Hall Richardson, a journalist with the *Daily Telegraph* at the time of the crimes. He reprinted the text in his autobiography, *From the City to Fleet Street*, in 1927:

> Liverpool,
> 29th inst.
>
> BEWARE I shall be at work on the 1st and 2nd inst. in 'Minories' at 12 midnight and I give the authorities a good chance but there is never a Policeman near when I am at work.
>
> Yours
> Jack the Ripper
> Prince William St., L'pool
> What fools the police are I even give them the name of the street where I am living.
>
> Jack the Ripper.[1]

McCormick had been inaccurate. J. Hall Richardson had not quoted a year. Most Ripper authors therefore dismissed the letter as not being relevant . . .

But, if the letter referred to had not been dated 1888, why would J. Hall Richardson have brought attention to it? He was not trying to prove who the Ripper was and could have chosen any one of hundreds of far more graphic or gruesome letters if he had not seriously considered it as being important. The letter deserved further consideration.

The Minories is a road just inside the City of London, on the border of Whitechapel about four hundred yards

---

[1] J. Hall Richardson, *From City to Fleet Street: Some Journalistic Experiences of J. Hall Richardson* (1927), p. 219.

from Berner Street, scene of the Stride murder, and less than a hundred yards from Mitre Square, scene of the Eddowes murder.

In the letter the writer said, 'I shall be at work on the 1st and 2nd'. The first and second of October in 1888 fell on a Monday and Tuesday – work days.

Our exhaustive reading of the Home Office files on the Maybrick trial led us to discover a document that left us amazed. It was a letter sent to the Home Secretary, Henry Matthews, shortly after the trial of Florence Maybrick. It transcribes, in part, as follows:

4 Cullum Street,
London August 29 1889
E.C.

Though you are no doubt more than tired of the unfortunate Maybrick affair, permit me as one of the late Mr Maybrick's most intimate friends . . . he was my partner in L'pool up to 1875 & continued to do my London firm's business up to the time of his death . . .

I remain Sir,
Your obed't servant
G.A. Witt[1]

Gustave A. Witt was a commission agent whose London office, at 4 Cullum Street, was a mere 450 yards from the Minories. This was where James Maybrick 'worked'. The diary – remarkably – stated: 'Indeed do I not frequently visit the Capitol and indeed do I not have legitimate reason for doing so.'

There is not a book written about the Maybrick Trial that contains reference to the letter from G.A. Witt. Now we had discovered that James Maybrick had not only lived in Whitechapel, but worked just a short distance from the scene of the crimes *at the time that they happened*.

No self-respecting forger could even contemplate that

---

[1] Public Record Office, Florence Maybrick file, HO 144/1638 A50678/ 629.

sort of luck, particularly when his chosen subject was believed to live and work in Liverpool.

On 10 October 1888 there was further evidence that the author of the 'Jack the Ripper' letters had a Liverpool and American connection. The following article appeared in the Liverpool *Echo*.

A LIVERPOOL FANATIC

The subjoined communication was addressed to the Liverpool *Echo* office yesterday on an ordinary postcard:-

Stafford-street

Dear Sir,

I beg to state that the letters published in yours of yesterday[1] are lies. It is somebody gulling the public. I am the Whitechapel purger. On 13th, at 3 p.m., will be on Stage, as am going to New York. But will have some business before I go. Yours truly,

Jack the Ripper
(Genuine.)   DIEGO LAURENZ

Is the connection between 'work' (in the 'Minories' letter) and 'business' merely coincidence? Maybrick and New York? Possibly. The 'Stage' is a reference to the landing stage where people get on and off a ship. The letter clearly indicates knowledge of Liverpool and the docks. What does 'Diego Laurenz' mean? I have no idea. Is it a clue?

Our work on the 'Jack the Ripper' letters was proving to be a crucial point of our investigation – it had to continue.

The next letter that caught my eye, also previously unpublished, was sent from New York in October (police

---

[1] On 9 October 1888 the Liverpool *Echo* published the following: 'THE DUBLIN POLICE AND THE CRIMES: The *Irish Times* says a number of constables have been sent to London on detective duty in connection with the Whitechapel murders. The Dublin police have received a letter purporting to be from "Jack the Ripper" stating that he intends visiting Dublin this week.'

files do not indicate which day in the month the letter was received). In all probability it was sent by the writer of the letter to the Liverpool *Echo*. The *Echo* writer would know that, if there was a Ripper murder when he was in New York, his letter would have no credibility. The writer in New York categorically says there won't be – and there wasn't. It reads:

Honorable Sir

I take great pleasure in giving you my present whereabouts for the benefit of the Scotland Yard Boys. I am very sorry that I did not have time to finish my work with the London Whores and regret to state that I must leave them alone for a *short while* I am now safer in New York and will travel over to Philadelphia and when I have the lay of the locality I might take a notion to do a little ripping there Good bye 'dear friend' I will let you here from me before long with a little more cutting and Ripping I said so and I fancy I will make it 40 on account of the slight delay in operations

Yours lovingly
'Jack'
the ripper[1]

Beside the letter the compiler of the police letter file has written: 'October 1888 Philadelphia Docket No. 1157.'

The language and spelling errors had a ring of familiarity about them. The handwriting showed great flexibility. We knew Maybrick had connections in New York. A bottle had been found in his room after his death that showed he had obtained medicine from there in 1884.[2]

There was a week between the first two murders and a fortnight between the second murder and the 'double event'. Yet nearly six weeks elapsed between the 'double event' on 30 September and Mary Kelly's murder on 9

---

[1] Mepo 3/142/90.
[2] Nigel Morland, *This Friendless Lady* (1957), Appendix 1, p. 246.

November. So when the writer of this Philadelphia letter wrote 'must leave them alone for a short while' he correctly foretold what happened. Had a hoaxer written this letter, he was certainly playing a wild card.

James Maybrick made regular business trips to the USA, usually sailing from Liverpool to New York on one of the White Star's liners. Between 1881 and 1887, in connection with his wife's claim to some land in Virginia and Kentucky, he wrote several letters to a lawyer, David W. Armstrong. In one of them, dated 19 November 1881, he wrote, in part: 'Please drop me a line with your address in Philadelphia & New York with the dates you will be there, & I will indeavor to run up to meet you.'[1]

Florence Maybrick's claim to the land continued up to 1906, so in 1888 Maybrick still had every reason to visit New York and Philadelphia on her behalf. Florence, during the case in Richmond in 1905 to determine the outcome of her claim, confirmed the regularity of her husband's trips to New York. She was cross-examined by a Mr Armstrong:

> Q. Mrs Maybrick, did Mr Maybrick pass a considerable part of each year at the City of Norfolk, Virginia?
>
> A. Yes Sir; about six months in every year – sometimes eight.
>
> Q. Was he in the City of New York at least twice in the course of each year?
>
> A. That I cannot say really.
>
> Q. Do you or not know whether in going to and from New York to Liverpool? [sic]
>
> A. Oh yes sir, for steamship purposes, in passing through from the station to the steamship dock.
>
> Q. Do you know whether on passing through New York in this way he was in the habit of seeing Mr Alfred Roe?

---

[1] Richmond Chancery, Virginia State Library and Archives, Richmond Virginia, filed under letters of Mrs Maybrick, exhibit 102, one of several letters written by James Maybrick.

A. That I could not say.

Q. Do you know whether he frequently did sometimes call upon Mr Armstrong in passing through the City of New York?

A. I have no knowledge of such fact.

Q. You were never told by Mr Maybrick of his calls upon Mr Armstrong, or upon Mr Roe, were you?

A. No sir.

Q. Who was Mr Alfred Roe of New York City?

A. He was the attorney of my grandmother.

It should be noted here that this evidence of Florence Maybrick directly contradicted the evidence of Michael Maybrick at the trial of Florence in 1889. He had said that James had not been to America since 1884.

This had been a crucial time in our investigation. Keith Skinner had been to Wyoming to photocopy the entire Christie collection. Trevor Christie's papers included a page that showed extracts from letters written by James Maybrick. His source was Richmond Chancery Court, Virginia. I contacted the court and spoke to the chief clerk. He recommended two local researchers. He, unfortunately, did not have the time to extract the necessary documents from the case files.

The first researcher I contacted was not available to work. The second, William Lindsay Hopkins, was. It was only seventy-two hours later that Bill phoned me. He had located the letters. He would have them copied and signed as true originals by the court.

We also tried to ascertain whether James Maybrick was in New York in October. I hired Marie Bierau, a wonderful seventy-seven-year-old researcher from Washington. Marie checked every shipping document for sailings from Liverpool, London and Glasgow. She did not just check October 1888, but every document from 1881 to 1889. Only once did we find the name of James Maybrick. We could not even find him when we knew he was there.

Keith Skinner had met Marie on his way to Wyoming. He also went to the National Archives in Washington and he also checked the shipping documents. Nothing. Whatever name James Maybrick travelled under, it certainly was not his own.[1]

I recalled, however, that Scotland Yard were indeed watching the ships that left Liverpool for New York and vice versa.[2] Maybe the boys in blue were closer than we have always believed. Maybe.

The *Sunday Times* of 18 November 1888 reported that a man had been arrested at Euston Station on suspicion of being Jack the Ripper, but was later released. The following day newspapers reported that detectives were watching Euston and Willesden Junction railway stations looking for any suspicious passenger from the Midlands and the North.[3] It is a fact that these stations were, in 1888, the only ones where passengers could get off the train from Liverpool.

The *Evening News* of 13 November 1888 carried this item:

ANOTHER LETTER TO THE POLICE.

Another letter signed 'Jack the Ripper,' of which the following is a copy was received last night by the police, and was published today:

'Dear Boss – I am now in the Queens Park estate in the Third Avenue. I am out of red ink at present, but it won't matter for once. I intend doing another here next Tuesday night about ten o'clock. I will give you a chance now to catch me. I shall have check trousers on and black coat and vest, so look out. I have done one not yet found out, so look out, so keep your eyes open. – Yours, Jack the Ripper.'

---

[1] Passports were not compulsory travel documents until 1913 and many people travelled under a pseudonym. Indeed Florence Maybrick travelled variously under the names Rose Ingraham and Mme F. Chaney.

[2] The *Globe*, 12 October 1888, p. 5, stated: 'The Steamers leaving Liverpool for America and other ports are now being carefully watched by the police and the passengers are closely scrutinised by detectives, there being an idea that the perpetrator of the Whitechapel murders may endeavour to make his escape via Liverpool.'

[3] The *Daily Chronicle* and the *Echo*, 19 November 1888.

The police are receiving a very large number of letters on the subject of the murder.

Philip Sugden in his *Complete History of Jack the Ripper* tells us of 'hundreds of letters' that were sent to the police after the murder of Mary Kelly on 9 November 1888. The police, however, had asked for only one to be published. This one. Only the text appeared. There was no facsimile. I remain slightly puzzled over why the police published it at all. I can only conclude that they were letting the Ripper know that of all the letters they received they knew which were the ones he had written . . .

The police were impressed by this letter. Was there any connection to the diary or James Maybrick himself?

The diary indicates that Mary Kelly was the sixth victim. So did the author of the letter. The diary claims that James stayed with his brother, Michael Maybrick, before he killed Mary Kelly. A straight line, drawn from Michael's home in Regent's Park to Willesden Junction, must take you through Third Avenue on the Queen's Park Estate.

Sir Robert Anderson had always believed that the Ripper had killed six victims. Many commentators have assumed the sixth to be Martha Tabram, who was found murdered on Bank Holiday Monday, 6 August 1888, but there is no evidence to support this. It is now reasonable to assume that, as the police did believe the correspondence, they may well have believed the author's boast of 'six after Kelly'.

This was not the only correspondence to claim six victims. At the time of the Ripper murders Dr Thomas Dutton was practising in Aldgate High Street. He held a lifelong interest in crime and claimed to have examined 128 communications from the Ripper to the police. Thirty-four of them were, in his opinion, 'definitely in the same handwriting'. In 1959 Donald McCormick published one of them, a poem:

Eight little whores, with no hope of heaven,
Gladstone may save one, then there'll be seven.

Seven little whores begging for a shilling,
One stays in Henage [sic] Court, then there's a
      killing.
Six little whores, glad to be alive,
One sidles up to Jack, then there are five.
Four and whore rhyme aright,
So do three and me,
I'll set the town alight
Ere there are two.
Two little whores, shivering with fright,
Seek a cosy doorway in the middle of the night.
Jack's knife flashes, then there's but one,
And the last one's the ripest for Jack's idea of fun.'[1]

The author of the diary also lays claim to the verse
when, on page 42, while practising his 'poetry skills', he
wrote what might have been considered the first draft:

One whore in heaven,
two whores side by side,
three whores all have died
four

The poem starts with 'eight whores'. After 'Gladstone
saved one' and 'one stayed in Henage Court' there are six
left. The diarist wrote, after describing the murder of
Kelly, that she 'ripped like a ripe peach'. The last line that
the poet wrote was 'the last one's the ripest for Jack's idea
of fun'.

The line 'four and whore rhyme aright' reflects the
diarist's preoccupation with making his poems rhyme, as
does 'It shall come, if Michael can succeed in rhyming
verse then I can do better, a great deal better he shall not
outdo me'.

The words 'set the town alight' are echoed in the diary
with the sentence, 'I believe if chance prevails I will burn
St James's to the ground.'

The author of the diary must seriously be considered as

---

[1] Donald McCormick, *The Identity of Jack the Ripper* (1959), Page 104.

the author of the McCormick poem. It was not known about until 1959. As Donald McCormick had come under heavy criticism for his book and references, it seemed strange that anyone forging the diary should choose to associate himself with McCormick. But that poem was in a similar 'language' to the other Ripper correspondence and the spelling errors were prominent.

The reference to 'Henege [sic] Court' should certainly create a debate among Ripperologists about whether PC Spicer's[1] claim to have arrested the Ripper has any validity.

For decades the original 25 September letter was missing from the official files, which had a copy only of the facsimile. In 1987 the original was returned to Scotland Yard anonymously. It arrived in a manila envelope postmarked Croydon, in south London. It was still attached to the original docket by the Victorian equivalent of modern transparent sticky tape. The docket was marked with a number 2 and was accompanied with its original envelope, also attached to its docket, marked number 3. Clearly the historical records have been missing an important document. Where was number 1 in the series? And what was it? We can reveal for the first time the following letter, discovered late in 1988 by Peter McClelland:

17th Sept 1888

Dear Boss

So now they say *I am a Yid* when will they lern Dear old Boss? You an me know the truth dont we. Lusk can look forever hell never find me but I am rite under his nose all the time. I watch them looking for me an it gives me fits ha ha I love my work an I shant stop until I get buckled *and even then* watch out for your old pal Jacky.

Catch me if you Can
Jack the Ripper.

---

[1] See Appendix 6.

Sorry about the blood still messy from the last one.
What a pretty necklace I gave her.[1]

This letter furnishes the pedigree for the 'Lusk letter':
how it came to be written and who wrote it. A journalist
looking at it could easily have copied it both in style and
content. It contains the phrase 'catch me if you can', while
the 'Lusk letter' uses virtually the same words: 'Catch me
when you can ...' Both letters are scruffy in appearance.
Both were smeared with blood. Both were badly written.
Both have silly, crude spelling mistakes. Obviously the one
is emulating the other.

The 17 September letter includes the sentence, 'So now
they say I am a Yid.'

The diary says: 'If they are to insist that I am a Jew then
a Jew I shall be.'

That sentence is inserted in the diary at the same point
as the author wrote about a cartoon in *Punch* magazine.
The publication date was 22 September 1888. These two
references tie in with historical information at precisely the
time they should do.

The diary came to public attention in 1992 and in that
year only five people in the entire world knew of the
existence of the 17 September letter.

This quintet were Peter McClelland (who discovered it),
Bill Waddell (ex-curator of the Black Museum at Scotland
Yard), Paul Begg (Ripper author), Donald Rumbelow
(Ripper author and ex-curator of the City Police Museum)
and Keith Skinner (historical researcher).

It is important to know that when McClelland found
the letter at the Public Record Office it was in a sealed
report envelope, which he carefully opened.[2]

As it was never published, begins 'Dear Boss' and is
signed 'Jack the Ripper' – the same as the 25 September
letter – both letters must have been sent by the same
person. Why? Because apart from the police and a few

---

[1] Home Office 144/221/A49301c. See Appendix 7.
[2] HO144/221/A49301c. See Appendix 7.

people at Central News no one knew about the expression 'Dear Boss' or the name 'Jack the Ripper' until the 25 September letter was first published on 1 October. No one, that is, except the journalists who copied it to create the 'Lusk letter'. And of course the man who sent it – Jack the Ripper.

The 17 September letter is informal, scruffy and badly spelt. It appears to have been written slowly and hesitantly. The 25 September letter, as already noted, is formal, neat and spelt correctly. As the handwriting styles of the two letters are so dissimilar, and we know the Metropolitan Police were impressed by the letter dated 25 September, they would have known the author's ability to disguise his handwriting.

When we acknowledged the 'handwriting' factor we decided to revisit the letters file. We focused on those letters initialled by Swanson. One such letter was received on 11 October. It read:

DSS   8/10/88
                                              Galashiels

Dear Boss,
    I have to thank you and my Brothers in trade, Jack the Ripper for your kindness in letting me away out of Whitechapel
    I am now on my road to the tweed Factories I will let the Innerleithen Constable or Police men know when I am about to start my nice Little game. I have got my knife replenished so it will answer both for Ladies and Gents other five Tweed ones and I have won my wager

    I am Yours
    Truly
    The Ripper[1]

The police docket recording the date of the postmark and place where it was posted, says, '8th October 1888 Innerleithen.'

---

[1] Mepo 3/142/149 docket number 784.

Galashiels and Innerleithen lie close together in the Scottish borders. Their main industry in the 1880s was tweed weaving. Not tweed made exclusively from wool, such as Harris tweed, but a cheaper version made from a mixture of wool and cotton. Cotton merchants such as James Maybrick would have sound business reasons for visiting the area.

The letter ends by speaking about winning a 'wager'. Our diarist had written: 'Tomorrow I will make a substantial wager. I feel lucky.'

It is a plain fact that James Maybrick was a gambling man. Florence Aunspaugh, the daughter of one of Maybrick's best friends, wrote that 'He bet on the races and played stud-poker.'[1]

This letter was extraordinary. The author indicates he is a businessman in a line of work directly connected to James Maybrick. He is a gambler like Maybrick and even uses the same words as the diarist. Was there any evidence of Maybrick's going to Scotland? Not in any book, but an article in the *New York Herald* on 21 August 1889 confirmed James Maybrick had been there. It also gave us a little more circumstantial evidence. The article was an interview with Michael Maybrick, after the trial of Florence:

'Do you think your brother used poison?'

'Indeed, I do not. I am as sure he didn't as I am of anything, almost. If he had used it I would have been certain to know of it. I was with him for weeks sometimes, up in Scotland, three years ago, for instance, often sleeping in the same bed with him and I never saw the slightest indication of his using arsenic. On the contrary, he was very particular about his medicine, and in caring for his health.'

(A fuller version of this interview is given later.)
Why was it that our modern 'forger' was so lucky?
This paragraph revealed another indicator. The author

---

[1] Trevor Christie Collection, Wyoming University.

of the diary had referred to his drugs as 'medicine'. That word had always impressed Dr Forshaw. Would a modern-day forger be aware of such detail? It is a lot easier for me to follow up on a document than it would be for someone to know where to look to create one.

Something about that letter of 8 October was bugging me. I had seen that handwriting before. It was probably on another of the Ripper letters. We checked them. It wasn't. We examined the letters written by James Maybrick. Eight of the twelve letters that we obtained from the Richmond Chancery Court were signed 'Yours Truly'. This was not a particularly common way to sign letters. 'Faithfully', 'obedient servant' and 'sincerely' were far more prevalent depending on circumstances. One such letter, written from the SS *Baltic* and signed, made the hairs on the back of my neck stand up when I laid it alongside the Galashiels letter ...

R.M.S. "BALTIC"

4th March 1881

Dear Sir — Thanks for your
letter of 27 ult. which I
just receive on the point of
sailing. On looking over
the Humm's correspondence
I do not find that Mr
Rendall has much any
[illegible] but I am
inclined to _____
to our [illegible] _____
but I will be glad to hear
from you with any
[illegible]

I enclose you a letter
from the Humm's but you
need take no notice of
the P.S. In haste

Yours tly
Jas Maybrick

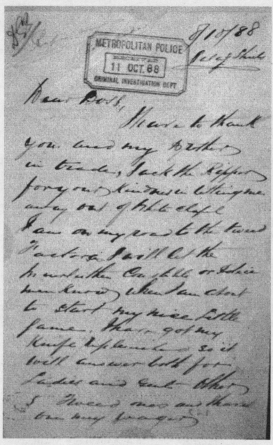

Mepo 3/142/149.   The original letter continues on its reverse side.

CHAPTER

19

'THE NURSE AT BATTLECREASE HOUSE'

IF THE DIARY AND the watch were genuine then they once were in the possession of James Maybrick. Later, they would become the property of Anne Graham and Albert Johnson respectively.

Prior to my meeting with William Graham on 1 August 1994, Anne had always assumed that the diary had been removed from Battlecrease House by Nurse Alice Yapp, and the nurse's relationship with Elizabeth Formby somehow resulted in 'ownership' being transferred to the latter.

Who was this Alice Yapp?

She had been instrumental in bringing about the downfall of Florence Maybrick, even admitting it herself: '. . . and I shall regret to the longest day I live that I was the cause of bringing about what has happened'.

That statement was made in the *New York Herald* on 21 August 1889, in an effort to defend herself following an astonishing attack by the same newspaper three days earlier. Then, in an article entitled LOOKING UP MISS ALICE YAPP, published on 18 August 1889, was the following:

FACTS FROM THE HISTORY OF MRS MAYBRICK'S
PRINCIPAL ACCUSER

Where She Has Lived and Mistresses
She Had Served – A Marriage Spoiled
by the Poison case – Mrs Owen [sic]
Thought Her a Prying Person.

LIVERPOOL, August 17 – The antecedents of the nurse, Alice Yapp, have been investigated in view of the many assertions which have been made respecting her, and of the extraordinary rumours which have obtained currency as to her condition with the Maybrick poison case. She is a native of Ludlow, Shropshire, and her parents were well-to-do. On the death of her father – she has a stepfather now – she went into service as a nurse. The age she gave when she went into the service of her employers five years ago was twenty, but it is stated by those who know her well that she is nearer thirty years than twenty-five. Her first appearance in the neighbourhood of Liverpool was at Oxton, Birkenhead, where she was in the service of a lady for about 18 months. This was nearly nine years ago. So that if Yapp's statement as to her age be true, she was then only sixteen years old . . .

After three years' faithful service with Mrs Gibson she left, about September 1887, to live with the Maybricks at Battlecrease House, Aigburth . . .

That the girl should have turned traitor is a mystery to those who know her best, for she was, or professed to be, a sincere friend of her mistress. In the witness-box she insinuated that Mrs Maybrick had not a proper motherly regard for her children. Such an allegation is emphatically denied by the other servants, who all state that Mrs Maybrick was a most affectionate mother; and these servants, it must be remembered, were the friends – almost the protégés – of Yapp. She managed so to ingratiate herself with the Maybricks, and to obtain such an all-powerful voice in the management of affairs in the servants' hall, that as soon as she settled down she began to do everything possible – no matter what became of the girls then in Mrs Maybrick's service – to get her friends about her. In this she was successful in at least two instances. She first got the witness Mary Cadwallader, who was in service with her at Mr Gibson's; and then she succeeded in getting a girl named Rosa Parker, whom she had met while she was with Mr Gibson's family at Ramsey some considerable time previously.

Before Miss Yapp went into Mrs Maybrick's employ she was courted by a man from a Lord-street watchmaker's shop, who used to go to the house to wind up clocks. They were engaged to be married and their intimacy continued until Yapp went to Battle-crease, but it was interrupted by the ardent clock winder's removal to Montrose . . .

The tongue of scandal does not leave the name of Alice Yapp alone, and it is said that if further proceedings are taken in the matter some startling disclosures will be made . . .

An interview was obtained this evening with Nurse Over, who was with Mrs Maybrick for five years, and nursed both her children. She left her to get married at the time Yapp came. She spoke of the affectionate terms upon which Mr and Mrs Maybrick were during the five years she was with them. During the course of that time she went to America with them twice, and they were always affectionate to one another, and Mrs Maybrick was devotedly attached to her two children . . . Nurse Yapp told Nurse Over some time ago that she was going to be married this July; but, of course, what occurred broke it off altogether. Nurse Over speaks of Yapp as having been of an exceedingly prying nature, and says that on several occasions the cook, Humphreys, said that she opened letters, and that as soon as Mrs Maybrick's back was turned she was prying about in her room . . . Mrs Over appears to have a very bad impression of Alice Yapp . . .

M.R. Levi, of 41, Everton-road, Liverpool, has made a statement which is interesting in view of the increasing public interest in Alice Yapp. He says: 'Last October I went to Battlecrease to see Mrs Maybrick, and found she had gone to Southport. I asked if I might write a letter to her, and was shown into a room for that purpose. I wrote the letter supposing I was alone in the room. Just as I finished something caused me to turn, and I found Alice Yapp leaning over my shoulder and perusing the letter. It made me so angry that I struck her.'

In another article, on the same day, the newspaper published a number of questions concerning the trial and many were specifically targeted at Yapp.

18. Have you observed the actions of one of the female witnesses have been somewhat remarkable?

19. Have you observed it was she who made the first accusation against Mrs Maybrick; that it was she who opened the remarkable letter given to her to post; that it was she who found all, or nearly all the arsenic; that it was she who started the fly-paper theory; and that it was she who set in motion another person, who in turn set in motion the Maybrick brothers, who in their turn deposed Mrs Maybrick and made her an object of suspicion?

20. Do you know anything about this woman?

21. Do you know whether her devotion to James Maybrick was greater or less than the average devotion of a servant to her master?

22. Do you know whether her devotion to her mistress was greater or less than the average devotion of a servant to her mistress?

23. Do you know how all that arsenic got into that house?

26. Has it ever occurred to you that if any person who knew all the intimate circumstances of Maybrick's way of living desired to cast suspicion on Mrs Maybrick it was an easy thing to do?

27. Do you believe that a woman who desired to poison her husband with arsenic would scatter it in as many directions as the evidence shows it to have been scattered?

It was from Emma (Rose) Parker's marriage to John Over that we discovered a link to Albert Johnson. Now we learn that Emma Parker, the children's nanny before Alice Yapp, had been introduced to the Maybricks by Alice herself, some six and a half years earlier. How? At the very least, we can assume that there was some sort of relationship between the Maybricks and Alice Yapp long before she was employed by them, despite the claims of Michael Maybrick.

The *New York Herald* of 21 August 1889, reported:

> Being told that one was that he had known Alice Yapp before she entered his brother's household, and that he had put her there to be a spy upon Mrs Maybrick, he replied,
>
> 'There is not a shadow of truth in such a report. I never knew or heard of her until long after she was engaged there, and do not think I ever spoke a word to her until I was summoned to my brother's bedside before he died. I never even knew her name until this trouble came. Why should I want to have a spy upon Mrs Maybrick, I should like to know?'

Michael Maybrick must have developed a relationship with Alice Yapp quickly.

During his opening speech at the trial, counsel for the prosecution Mr John Addison said, 'Now, directly he [James Maybrick] was dead, Michael Maybrick directed the nurse [Alice Yapp] and the housemaid [Bessie Brierley] to look and see what they could find.'

Alexander MacDougall, in 1891, was just as perplexed:

> Mrs Maybrick was lying in this mysterious speechless swoon on the bed in the spare room, and this pair of servant girls who had been entrusted with the search did not go into this dressing room, but went straight to a linen closet on the same landing and adjoining the death chamber, and took out a trunk, which was the only trunk which had Mrs Maybrick's initials upon it . . .
>
> . . . she [Bessie Brierley] and Alice Yapp carried the trunk into the nursery. They did not open it, and Bessie Brierley then went downstairs to the kitchen . . .
>
> . . . Alice Yapp, some few hours afterwards, about midnight, went into the nursery and opened this trunk in the presence of one of the detective-nurses – Nurse

Wilson – who was a witness of the fact, and produced from it the following articles . . .

A packet of black powder, being mixed charcoal and arsenic, open at one end and labelled on one side 'Poison' and on the other side 'Arsenic – poison for cats'; the words poison for cats in red ink, was in some handwriting which, beyond the fact that it was admitted at the trial was not Mrs Maybrick's, was not identified, but although this package had two labels no chemist's name was on the package, and the word arsenic was underlined!

A bottle labelled 'solution of morphia', but with the chemist's name erased.

A bottle with no mark on it.

A parcel of yellow powder – insect powder – but not poisonous to man.

A handkerchief with Mrs Maybrick's name on it.

Alice Yapp's evidence as to this was at the Coroner's Inquest:

I went into the linen closet for a trunk to put the children's clothes in. The closet is close to Mrs Maybrick's bedroom, and is very dark. It is not lighted except by gas. The door was unlocked.
Q. Whose trunk was it!
A. Mrs Maybrick's
Q. Has it got letters on it
A. Yes, F.E.M. at the sides . . .
   . . . At the Magisterial Inquiry, Alice Yapp said:
   '. . . I went into the linen closet to get out a trunk, *to take from it the children's clothing*.'

Why had Alice Yapp lied about why she had gone to the trunk?
Anne Graham had always said that she first saw the diary in a black trunk with letters written with white paint on the side . . .

Florence Maybrick had been found guilty on the most tenuous of evidence. A phrase in a letter written to her lover Alfred Brierley was not viewed kindly by the judge. 'He is sick unto death . . .'

As the evidence during the trial unfolded, it became apparent that on 8 May, the Wednesday before James Maybrick died, Alice Yapp had been given a letter to post from Florence Maybrick that was written in pencil and addressed to Alfred Brierley. On the way to carry out her mistress's request, Gladys, Florence's two-year-old daughter, apparently dropped the letter in some mud. Alice Yapp, being the kind and considerate person that she was, opened the letter in order to put it in a clean envelope, and just happened to read it.

When the Baroness von Roques arrived at Battlecrease House after James Maybrick had died, Edwin Maybrick told that Alice Yapp had found it 'on the floor; it fell from her dress when she [Florence Maybrick] fainted, and I carried her into the spare bedroom'.[1]

A lie has been told and, worse, manufactured. By the time the trial began, Michael Maybrick, his brother Edwin and Alice Yapp were all singing from the same hymn sheet. The letter had been dropped in the mud . . .

Of course, if it had dropped from Florence Maybrick's dress in the house, Alice Yapp might have had a much more difficult job in explaining why she had opened and read it.

MacDougall, in 1891, further made the astonishing claim that part of this letter was forged. Such a claim had not been brought up at the trial, but MacDougall's claim that Florence Maybrick's private letters had been left in his care suggests a close relationship had built up between the barrister and the convicted woman.

The letter had contained the words 'Both my brothers-in-law are here . . .'. Although Edwin was staying at the house, Michael Maybrick did not arrive until 8.30 p.m. on the Wednesday, 8 May.

---

[1] MacDougall 1891.

But the letter, apparently, had been intercepted that afternoon.

Furthermore, Florence Maybrick had returned from Flatman's Hotel in time for the Grand National on 29 March. James Maybrick first became ill on 28 April. MacDougall queried, with some justification, the words in the letter: 'Since my return I have been nursing him day and night . . .' He added, 'These are sufficient grounds to justify my doubts as to this being the letter which Alice Yapp alleges she intercepted when sent to the post with it on Wednesday afternoon the 8th of May, at three o'clock, and my doubts whether it was written on Wednesday at all.'

On 3 June, the Liverpool *Daily Post* printed the following:

ALLEGED POLICE RUSE – A FORGED LETTER

It was bruited [rumoured] abroad in the course of Saturday that the police have resorted to an extraordinary stratagem in order to procure evidence of a peculiar character which they require in the case. The story goes that in their instigation a lady was employed to write a letter to a person well known in Liverpool purporting to come from Mrs Maybrick. It is alleged that the writing so closely resembled that of the prisoner as to have deceived the person to whom the letter was addressed, and to have brought from him a response. This remarkable proceeding, we are informed, took place immediately prior to Mr Maybrick's death.

Once again, MacDougall, expresses the sentiment:

Now I cannot assume that a newspaper of such standing as the Liverpool *Daily Post* invented such a sensational story as this, and I therefore suggest that it is due to its own reputation to make publicly known the name of the author of it. There was no denial of this!! It was a direct imputation (published in a paper of the highest standing in Liverpool) of FORGERY against the

Police engaged in getting up this case against Mrs Maybrick!! And yet no denial! No attempt on the part of the authorities to call the editor of the Liverpool *Daily Post* to account for such a calumny! Why? Is it that the authorities regard such a newspaper as the Liverpool *Daily Post* as beneath contempt? Or was it because the authorities and everybody else in Liverpool had lost their heads over the Maybrick Mystery, and were unable to see that the Liverpool *Daily Post* had published a statement, which branded the police engaged in getting up the case as Forgers? Or again, Is it true? If it is true, I will ask – Do the people of this country intend to allow criminal trials to be got up in such a way?

I make no apologies for my consistent use of MacDougall throughout this chapter. The fact is that if I had made the observations that this learned gentleman did I should be accused of 'twisting the facts' to build a case to 'prove' the diary. What is important is that we are able to understand the peculiarities that surrounded the case against Florence Maybrick. MacDougall's book was published in 1891, and reflects the genuine anger felt against the establishment for the unexplained treatment of James Maybrick's spouse.

It would be reasonable to assume that, after the trial, Florence Maybrick would never wish to speak or hear of Alice Yapp again. How strange that four years later Jonathan Harris, a London solicitor employed by Florence's mother the Baroness von Roques, would place an advert in the *Daily Telegraph* of 14 November 1893:

YAPP – If ALICE YAPP (late of Liverpool) will COMMUNICATE with Jonathan E. Harris, Solicitor, Leadenhall-street, London, she will HEAR SOMETHING to her ADVANTAGE

Alice Yapp, by now, was a mother for the first time. A daughter, Margery, had been born to her in January 1892. Alice Yapp, true to form, falsified the birth certificate. She gave her name as Alice Murrin, formerly Yapp, but was not to marry Edward Murrin until June 1904 – twelve and a half years later. She was living in Rosebery Avenue in London when she gave birth but had moved to Lewisham by the time they married.

Jonathan Harris was desperate to contact Alice Yapp, and Edward Murrin did not like it one bit. On 11 January 1894 he wrote to H.H. Asquith, the Home Secretary.[1] Edward Murrin even lied to him of his marital status:

> As you are aware, no doubt, I appealed through Superintendent Bryning of Liverpool to Scotland Yard in the month of December last for protection from annoyance for my wife Alice Yapp, a witness in the above case. The authorities at Scotland Yard at the time could not see their way clear to interfere, on the grounds that not sufficient annoyance had been caused. There is no doubt they were then right in that decision. But things have assumed a different aspect since then, and I certainly think she is now entitled to some protection in having this annoyance stopped.
>
> *Mr Jonathan Harris* of Leadenhall Street, (who has the case in hand), having caused his private detective to reveal every place and abode in Liverpool and Shropshire where she has been living, and making enquiries has eventually found out my address. Hence the annoyance. This man arrives this afternoon, and finding no one at home, knocks next door and quietly enters the house. Of course I cannot say what transpired in the house.
>
> Eventually my wife came home. He knocks at the door and rudely forces his way in. Perhaps I ought not to say *force*, but anyway *invites* himself in.
>
> He commenced by telling a falsehood; – that there was a legacy awaiting her at Mr Harris if she would call. To enter into all that transpired, Sir, would, I am afraid, occupy too much of your valuable time. But

[1] HO 144/1639/A50678D/192.

here, I maintain, is the annoyance, and I might say a threat. He says 'Of course people blame you very much. *Mrs Briggs and yourself seem to have concocted facts.* You might have kept back much that you said.'

I only feel sorry that I was not at home to answer this man myself for when I arrived home my wife was thoroughly upset – As she justly says, why should the neighbours became as wise as herself. Shc has strived to keep it a secret and certainly did hope that when she had done her duty she would not be subjected to this annoyance. There is no doubt they would like to get her at Mr Harris's office and *mix her up*, so to speak.

She informed the man that what Mr Harris wanted to say he had better put in writing. But I believe he left with the intention of calling again tomorrow evening.

Finally Sir, I would ask you for advice and protection from this annoyance, for assurance of it. From my own part I fail to see why a woman, who has done her duty to the Crown should be subjected to it. If it is to ever continue I shall have to leave my abode for ever? Since my wife is continually weeping and thoroughly depressed. I should add that she would only be too willing to meet any representative of Mr Harris and answer any questions in the presence of a person appointed by yourself.

Sir, I do trust that you will see your way clear to instruct me at the earliest possible moment.

I am Sir,
Your Obedient Servant
Edward Murrin

Asquith dispatched the letter to Robert Anderson, Assistant Commissioner of the Metropolitan Police, for comments. Anderson proceeded with enquiries and a response was sent to the Under-Secretary of State on 22 January 1894:[1]

---

[1] HO 144/1639/A50678D/193.

METROPOLITAN POLICE
CRIMINAL INVESTIGATION DEPARTMENT
NEW SCOTLAND YARD
22ND day of JANUARY 1894

With reference to the attached H.O. correspondence 150678/forwarding for observations a letter received from Mr Edward Murrin (not 'Perrin', as docketed,) who married Miss Alice Yapp a witness for the Crown in the case of Florence Maybrick; I beg to report that in November last Mr Murrin wrote to the Police at Old Swan, Lancashire, complaining that enquiries to trace his wife had been made at Liverpool and Ludlow (where she formally resided,) and enclosing an advertisement from the *Daily Telegraph* of November 14th inviting Alice Yapp to communicate with Mr Jonathan Harris, Solicitor, 95 Leadenhall Street. – Mr Murrin suggested that the enquiries and the advertisement originated with the Baroness Von Roque, Mrs Maybrick's mother. Mr Murrin's letter was sent to this office by the Police at Old Swan and I said him open it [sic]. At that time it was not known to the Police or to Mr and Mrs Murrin that Mr Harris was acting for Baroness Von Roque and both Mr and Mrs Murrin declined to see Mr Harris or to enquire what he wanted. The prosecution of Mrs Maybrick having been conducted by the Public Prosecutor, the facts were laid before Mr Bernard Thomas of the solicitor's department, Treasury, who advised that it would not be expedient for either the Public Prosecutor or the Police to interfere.

I saw Mrs Murrin again on 19th inst. and her statement somewhat modifies the account of the matter given in Mr Murrin's letter to H.O. – Mrs Murrin states that on the 11th inst. a man called at no. 50 Rosebury Avenue (her address) and getting no answer, knocked at no. 49 and asked the occupier if it was known when Mrs Murrin would return. Mrs Murrin who was expecting a relative, had left word with her neighbour at no. 49 that she would be back at 6 p.m. and the neighbour, supposing the man to be the relative who was expected, asked him to come in and wait. – When Mrs Murrin returned she offered no opposition to the man's entering the house with her, and he, *after saying something about a legacy*, told her ultimately that Mr Jonathan Harris, a solicitor, wished to see her about the case of Mrs Maybrick. Mrs Murrin replied that she did not wish to see Mr Harris and that he could write and ask whatever it was he wanted to know. She invited the man to stay till her husband returned, but he declined, saying that he had another appointment. During the interview with this man Mrs Murrin states that he accused her of having 'worked up' the case against Mrs Maybrick, and said that she might, had she chosen, have kept back a great deal of her evidence.

The circumstances do not seem to justify Police interference. The only course possible would be for an officer to see Mr Harris and tell him that Mrs Murrin complains that his enquiries are a source of annoyance to her and has desired the Police to say that she does not wish to hold any communication with him. This might be effectual in stopping the annoyance to Mrs Murrin but it would also give Mr Harris the opportunity of suggesting that the authorities were taking steps to stifle enquiry.

I have told Mrs Murrin that if Mr Harris or any of his agents come to her house, she can refuse to admit him or them; and that if upon being refused admittance the person who comes creates a disturbance, he can be given into custody.

Charles F. Baker Inspector

Did Jonathan Harris's persistence reap its rewards? He wrote to the Home Secretary some four months later, in April 1894. His letter was an attempt to have Florence released from prison and contained the words: 'I have other evidence in my possession and power which (on the grounds of public policy and respect for our legal system)

I am anxious to suppress if my present application is successful . . .'

Was Alice Yapp, or had she ever been, the provider of the 'other evidence'?

Alice Murrin died in 1953, in Epsom, aged ninety-two. Her great-niece, Mrs Jo Brooks, wrote to Shirley Harrison in December, 1993:

> . . . My great aunt was Alice Yapp, the nanny in the Maybrick household. She was sister of my paternal grandmother. Consequently, from my teens I was aware of discussion in the family about the case although I only heard snippets – the subject not being deemed quite suitable for a young girl.
>
> During the war years we spent quite a few holidays in Ludlow visiting Aunt Alice and her husband, and her only daughter and son in law and her grandchild, curiously enough called Gladys.
>
> Alice would then have been in her late seventies and I remember her as tall, upright and a rather domineering woman. There must have been some discussion of the Maybrick family because I know she gave my father and mother a set of silver teaspoons engraved with the letter 'M', a locket, and a string of pearls all of which were given to her by Florence Maybrick.
>
> I remember my Mother telling her sister that they were presents for services rendered i.e. carrying letters from Florence to Alfred Brierley. It did appear that the letter which Alice had opened was by no means the first that she had been entrusted with . . .

With what we know, it does not seem a likely story, does it? James Maybrick did not let us down, however. Spoons with the letter M engraved upon them . . .

Who was Alice Yapp? Why did she lie for the brothers? What were the startling disclosures that would have been made had the proceedings been taken further, referred to by the *New York Herald*?

How was Alice Yapp known to the Maybricks six and

321

half years before she was in their employ? How were the brothers so certain of her loyalty? And what of the unusual mutual devotion between master and servant?

You may think the newspapers imply that there is 'an affair'. You may be right. After Keith Skinner visited Jo Brooks on 21 September 1994, he faxed me, saying Jo had offered her suspicion that Alice Yapp was possibly James's mistress. His fax continued:

> This was based on a feeling that there was more to Jo's mother's tight lipped attitude towards the case, that went beyond being married to somebody (Jo's father) whose Aunt Alice was involved in a famous murder trial of the late nineteenth century. Everything which Jo has since read has confirmed that feeling which Jo intuitively sensed as a teenage girl and young lady growing up.

I will float a different possibility. I was struck with the similarity of Alice Yapp to Margaret Minetta Maybrick. Could she have been another of James Maybrick's illegitimate children? Would that answer all the questions?

Perhaps it does not matter. What does matter is the role that Alice Yapp played. Fittingly, I will leave this chapter to be completed by Alexander MacDougall:

> The suspicions born in this cauldron were twins – suspicions of Arsenic and suspicions of Adultery – and the mother, or at all events the reputed mother, of them both was –
>   Alice Yapp.

'EVIDENCE HAS BEEN WITHHELD . . .'

I HAD ALWAYS UNDERSTOOD, if not agreed with, the suggestion that the diary could have been written around the known facts surrounding Jack the Ripper. Without a full investigation of the text, it would be a reasonable observation. To create a sixty-three-page document around the lives of two different people (assuming the diary is not genuine) would not just take an enormous amount of skill, but an incredible amount of luck. James Maybrick, after all, was a businessman who travelled the country constantly. Any single piece of paper could have proved him to be in a different place from London at the time of the murders. Our 'nest of forgers', however, would need to investigate all those documents before they would know whether such a piece of paper existed. If it did, all their efforts, time and money would be a complete waste. Moreover, if the idea had been dreamt up, how confident would the 'nest' be that they would not find such a document? Would you take the gamble? I would rather play the lottery – there's probably a better chance of winning!

Imagine our astonishment, when we first visited the Public Record Office to access the Maybrick trial papers, to discover that we were almost the first to have done so!

In 1985, the BBC, represented by Roger Wilkes and Rob Rohrer, initiated enquiries into papers connected with the Maybrick case. They were informed that the relevant Home Office papers were being made available for inspection. The files were opened in December 1985. Only a handful of people had seen these remarkable documents since those incredible events in the late summer of 1889.

And Mike Barrett had certainly not been there!

We knew, then, that these papers were crucial. If the diary was a hoax, then we would find the evidence here. While it was remotely conceivable that someone had researched the Ripper exhaustively to put the diary together, they had not seen the Home Office files and, of course, could not guess what might be in them. Any information about James Maybrick would have to be accessed from the books that had been written on Florence Maybrick. The source of information for those books had been, in the main, newspaper cuttings.

We did not expect what was coming.

We were disappointed to discover that all the police files that led to the arrest of Florence Maybrick had vanished. Phone calls to the police stations in Liverpool as well as the Liverpool District Register Office failed to throw any light on their current whereabouts. In all probability, they have been destroyed. There is no obligation for provincial police forces to keep such documents.

The critics of the diary had made their attacks almost entirely on the Ripper content within it. Little or nothing had been said of the references to the Maybrick household. Privately we had felt that the document would stand or fall on mistakes that might have been made in details about this mysterious family who had once resided in Aigburth, Liverpool. Paul Begg's early comment that he and his colleagues 'simply can't shake it' (the Ripper content of the diary) allowed me to feel confident that nobody else would.

From the moment I became involved with the project, I studied and read every book that I could find on the Maybrick trial. Those books did sometimes contradict what had been written in the diary. I was, nevertheless, confident that the diary was genuine, but would not be happy until I could resolve each and every anomaly.

Strangely amusing, and intriguing, was a passage in Nigel Morland's book, *This Friendless Lady*:

Christmas, 1888, held no undue emotions or unusual events. It was conventional and ordinary, distinguished by some very bad weather. The casual conversation between grown-ups, while the children played, went no deeper than to touch in passing on the terrors afflicting London and much of the country with the terrifying panic of the Whitechapel murders (as 'Jack the Ripper's' crimes were known). The police were arresting suspects on the slightest provocation and while the 'last' victim, Mary Kelly, had died horribly the month before, it was generally believed that this sadistic sexual maniac would choose Christmas Day for some particularly revolting slaughter – doors and windows in many Liverpool houses were furtively locked and bolted.

It is implied that James and Florence were in Liverpool during the Christmas of 1888. This vague insinuation is nevertheless the only reference to the whereabouts of James Maybrick during the festive period, in any book about their lives.

Our diarist contradicted this:

Christmas is approaching and Thomas has invited me to visit him. I know him well. I have decided to accept his offer, although I know the motive behind it will strictly be business.

By New Year's Eve, James Maybrick was back at home. On 31 December 1888, Florence Maybrick wrote to her mother: 'In his fury he tore up his will this morning . . .'

Our diarist was accurate once again:

The bitch, the whore is not satisfied with one whore master, she now has eyes on another. I could not cut like my last, visions of her flooded back as I struck. I tried to quosh all thoughts of love. I left her for dead, that I know. It did not amuse me. There was no thrill. I have showered my fury on the bitch. I struck and struck. I do not know how I stopped. I have left her penniless . . .

Was there any evidence that James Maybrick had been away over the festive period? The Home Office files contained a letter from Baroness von Roques to Henry Matthews, the Home Secretary. It was a response to a letter received from him 'of the 28th'.

August 4th 1892
... The December of 1888 was the first time during her married life she had been able to dance or had been out in society; and her health was then stronger. She was left unattended by her husband ...[1]

Hubby was away, that's for sure! We were hungry for more information. The whole investigation seemed to have more urgency. My team were buzzing again. We would eventually read every piece of paper in those seven large boxes at the PRO.

Our diarist had written: 'My medicine will give me strength.'

Dr David Forshaw, who holds a diploma in the history of medicine from the Society of Apothecaries, had always been impressed by the description the diarist used for his arsenic. He commented that the use of the word 'medicine' demonstrated a good knowledge of Victorian references to drugs.

Four years after the trial, when the battle to get Florence released from prison was continuing, a statement was filed by John Fleming. His home was in Halifax, Nova Scotia. He was captain of the steamship *Wanda*, which at the time was lying in Brunswick Dock, Liverpool.

He states:

I know and was well acquainted with the above named James Maybrick through his loading cotton on ships commanded by me and I was also privately with him on terms of close and intimate friendship ... I saw him deposit in his said food a grey powder resembling light colored pepper. He said to me 'you would be horrified I daresay if you knew what this (meaning the powder)

---

[1] HO 144/1639/A50678D/99.

is' – I said, 'There is no harm in pepper' and he answered, 'It is Arsenic . . . I take this Arsènic once in a while because I find it *strengthens* me'[1] (my emphasis).

While we discovered that this document proved that the diarist had used the precise word ('strengthens') that had been used to John Fleming, I was disappointed. As my footnote explains, this particular Home Office document had been transcribed at the back of J.H. Levy's book, *The Necessity for Criminal Appeal*, published in 1899. I had to accept the remote possibility that a hoaxer had used this reference to write the relevant passage. I did not believe it, but I had to accept that such an observation could not be refuted.

Keith Skinner, however, who found the transcription, made a point worthy of note. 'Firstly, a forger would have to know the book even exists. Then he would have to locate it and finally plough through the entire book to "lift" one single word – and Joe Nickell called this an amateurish fake!'[2]

As mentioned earlier, the diary had come under attack for the Ripper content alone. I had already had a little chuckle to myself that many authors who had declared themselves 'crime historians' were nothing of the sort. Either that, or they had to accept that everything that had been written in the diary about Maybrick and the family was correct.

If not, why had they not picked up on it?

That is why our research team continued to test the diary. Whether in relation to a phrase concerning the Maybrick family or the actions of Jack the Ripper. We had been concerned at an entry early on in the document. Not one critic had picked it up. We did not ignore it:

---

[1] HO 144/1639/A50678D/202. Note also that some supplemental statements made after the trial were published in J.H. Levy's book *The Necessity of Criminal Appeal*, published by P.S. King & Son, 1899. The statement by Mr Fleming was one of them.

[2] Joe Nickell in *Who Was Jack the Ripper?*, Grey House Books, 1995.

'My dearest Gladys is unwell yet again, she worries me so.'

A private letter in the Home Office files written to Florence Maybrick ended with 'I am sorry that your little girl has been ill *again*'[1] (my italics). It had been sent by Margaret Baillie, a close friend of her family whom she had met in Switzerland.[2]

Here was evidence that Gladys was frequently ill. I knew that this minor piece of detail was crucial. We had been the first to see those letters.

Did Levy publish this as well?

He did.

But he transcribed the last sentence wrongly.

Completely.

'I am sorry about your little girl.'

The letter had been written in April 1889, after both Bobo and Gladys had had a bout of whooping cough. The word 'again' was vital.

Now, if our hoaxer was using the supplemental statements transcribed in J.H. Levy, as I had to accept with regard to John Fleming's statement, then he would have used it for this letter too! He would not, therefore, have made any reference to Gladys's being ill 'again'. There was nothing else to suggest she was.

Florence, Margaret Baillie and our diarist are the only known sources for Gladys's being 'regularly' ill. Florence and Margaret because of the letter. But our diarist?

The diary had been described as an 'amateurish fake' and a 'shabby hoax'. The credibility of these 'historians' who made those statements could now be adequately described in a similar way. 'Shabby amateurs' will do. Historians had claimed that the diary 'had very little information' that could be checked. Astonishing. They had added that it was full of throwaway lines that meant nothing.

Perhaps they meant lines like 'true the race was the fastest I have seen . . .'.

---

[1] HO 144/1638.
[2] John Baillie Knight statement HO 144/1638/A50678D/11.

This entry was clearly referring to the Grand National of 1889. James and Florence Maybrick, together with their friends, had chartered an omnibus for the occasion. James Maybrick, who liked his 'little games', had perversely invited his 'friend' Alfred Brierley. Brierley, was of course, Florence's lover. The diarist . . .?

'. . . but the thrill of seeing the whore with the bastard thrilled me more so than knowing his Royal Highness was but a few feet away . . .'

But what of the race, 'the fastest . . .'? The newspapers had certainly described the race as exciting and even surprising, but we could not find detail to confirm the diarist's use of those words. My Liverpool researcher, Carol Emmas, visited Aintree. They were not able to help. Carol, like all my team, was resolute. She scoured magazines and newspapers for days on end. Her efforts were not unrewarded.

In an obscure magazine entitled the *Liverpolitan*, in an issue dated March 1939, page 27 carried the headline A STATISTICAL GUIDE TO THE WORLD'S GREATEST STEEPLECHASE. Every result since 1837 was listed. So were details of the owner, age and weight of the horse, number of horses in the race, jockey and the time. The Grand National of 1889 was won by a horse called Frigate. It was the fastest Grand National run for eighteen years!

That Grand National formed an important part of Florence's trial. James and Florence quarrelled when they returned to Battlecrease House from their day out at Aintree. Alfred Brierley had escorted Florence to the grandstand to see the Prince of Wales. It was probably this that James was referring to when Nurse Alice Yapp overheard him shouting, 'Such a scandal will be all over town tomorrow. Florrie, I never thought it would come to this.'

Then James Maybrick struck her.

The following Saturday Florence went to see Dr Hopper. He examined her black eye. Florence informed the doctor that James had dragged her around the bedroom and beaten her. Our diarist had written: 'I struck her several times an eye for an eye . . .' And on the very next line, 'Hopper will soon feel the edge of my shining knife damn the meddling buffoon.'

Although these phrases demonstrated either knowledge or an attention to detail, it was not this that impressed me. The reference to the striking of Florence by James after the race was the only known act of violence of the husband against the wife. Had the author taken another guess or calculated risk when he penned this line, earlier in the diary?

The whore has informed the bumbling buffoon I am in the habit of taking strong medicine. I was furious when the bitch told me. So furious I hit her . . .

In the Home Office papers was a statement dated 18 July 1889 sworn by John Baillie Knight of 31 Holland Park, Bayswater. Judge Stephen, during his summing up of the trial, claimed that Baillie Knight had also been her lover. He was wrong and was corrected at the time.

The statement claimed that Florence had told him in March that she had come to London to see a solicitor about a separation from her husband. Mr Baillie Knight went on to explain that the separation was desired as James Maybrick kept another woman in Liverpool. 'Tonight I shall see mine. I may return to Battlecrease and take the unfaithful bitch. Two in a night, indeed pleasure.' And he explained that he 'was cruel to her and had struck her'.

Florence had told John Baillie Knight this before the Grand National. The diarist was obviously aware of it.

The reference in the diary to 'Two in a night' suggests the close proximity between his mistress ('Tonight I shall see mine') and his wife ('I may return to Battlecrease').

Although Alexander MacDougall makes an obscure reference to a dressmaker collecting a debt for another woman, the only known mistress of James Maybrick was Sarah Ann Robertson, who was living in South London at the time. Only Florence and the author of our diary would appear to know of this woman in Liverpool.

When I first discussed the diary with Donald Rumbelow, he asked the question, 'If Florence Maybrick knew her husband was Jack the Ripper, then why did she not say so at the trial?'

First, it is important to establish why it is believed that Florence was aware of her husband's activities. The diarist had penned five words towards the end of his writings: 'My dear Bunny knows all.' I accept that Donald's interpretation of this phrase is correct. Was there any historical evidence to suggest that James had told Florence anything unusual?

A letter used as prime evidence against Florence at the trial held the answer.

Wednesday

Dearest,

Your letter under cover to John K. came to hand just after I had written to you on Monday. I did not expect to hear from you so soon and had delayed in giving him the necessary instructions. Since my return I have been nursing M. day and night. He is sick unto death.

The doctors held a consultation yesterday, and now all depends upon how long his strength will hold out. Both my brothers-in-law are here, and we are terribly anxious.

I cannot answer your letter fully today, my darling, but relieve your mind of all fear of discovery now and for the future. M. has been delirious since Sunday, and I know now that he is perfectly ignorant of everything, even to the name of the street, and also that he has not been making any inquiries whatever. *The tale he told me was a pure fabrication and only intended to frighten the truth out of me.* In fact he believes my statement although he will not admit it.

You need not therefore go abroad on this account, dearest, but in any case, please don't leave England until I have seen you once again.

You must feel that those two letters of mine were written under circumstances which must even excuse their injustice in your eyes. Do you suppose I could act as I am doing if I really felt and meant what I inferred then?

If you wish to write to me about anything, do so now as all the letters pass through my hands at present. Excuse this scrawl, my own darling, but I dare not leave the room for a moment, and I do not know when I shall be able to write to you again – in haste, yours ever, Florie.[1]

The italics in that passage are mine.

So, James Maybrick had told Florence a 'tale'. Moreover, as this letter indicates that Alfred Brierley is aware of this 'tale', we can deduce that he was told before 5 May. (Brierley is being told that Maybrick has been delirious since Sunday.) The diary's last entry is 3 May.

Whether Florence believed the tale or not, Alfred Brierley had taken it most seriously. 'On this account', he had decided to leave the country. Whatever that tale was, it was most certainly intended to frighten. Alfred Brierley clearly *was* frightened.

Philip Sugden in his book, *The Complete History of Jack the Ripper*, developed the question posed by Donald Rumbelow: 'Why didn't Florence mention it in her defence at the trial? Surely she could have argued that she poisoned Maybrick because she had learned that he was the Ripper and feared for her life?'

Oh dear! Is Mr Sugden serious?

First of all, Florence Maybrick pleaded not guilty. Secondly, although she was *found* guilty, the Home Secretary, Henry Matthews, concluded in the month she was convicted that there was reasonable doubt. Furthermore, I would not have thought poisoning her husband for fear of her life was justifiable murder. Would the police not have asked Florence why, when James had confessed to her, she had not reported the matter to them? Also, if

---

[1] Letter to Alfred Brierley from Florence (sent to be posted on 8 May but intercepted by Alice Yapp) reproduced from *Etched in Arsenic*, pp. 59–60.

you are in fear for your life, you shoot, stab, kick, punch or bite immediately – you don't slowly poison. Fortunately, Mr Sugden did not represent Florence Maybrick 107 years ago.

Assuming Florence Maybrick was the wife of Jack the Ripper, there were two bona fide reasons why the matter would not have been mentioned by her. The first is a legal one. The prosecution had struggled throughout the trial to provide a strong motive for murder. It was not money. The will of James Maybrick left her nothing to speak of. It was not her love affair. She was seeking a separation through legal channels.

As she was not guilty of his murder, her reasoning (or that of her lawyers) may have been that, if the matter of Maybrick's alter ego was mentioned, the prosecution would have been armed with the very weapon they did not have: a motive. While Florence may have won tremendous sympathy, fear is not, Mr Sugden, an excuse for murder.

W.T. Stead, in the *Review of Reviews* in 1892, confirmed that an attack on James Maybrick's moralities would have given the prosecution the motive for murder they were looking for.

The second reason concerns her children. At the time of the trial, her children, Bobo and Gladys were six and three respectively. James's younger brother Michael, otherwise the famous Stephen Adams, was to take responsibility for them. Michael was rich and very powerful. Knowledge that his brother was Jack the Ripper would have ruined him. It would have ruined all the Maybricks, including the children she loved and cherished so much.

It may surprise our cynics to learn that evidence was withheld. It was withheld before the trial, during the trial and after the trial – evidence was suppressed then, and may still be now.

After Florence Maybrick was sentenced to death, Judge James Fitzjames Stephen asked Florence if she had anything to say. She did.

'My Lord,' she told him, 'everything has been against me. I wish to say that although evidence has been given as to a great many circumstances in connection to Mr Brierley, much has been withheld which might have influenced the jury had it been told. I am not guilty of this crime.'

Well, well. Evidence *was* withheld that may have influenced the jury. Could it have been that James Maybrick was the Ripper? Even Mr Sugden implied that such a revelation would have worked in her favour, didn't he?

We can also deduce that whatever this evidence was, it was Florence's decision to withhold it. She had made a statement to the court and had every opportunity to say whatever she wanted. There were no restrictions on her whatsoever.

In the *Review of Reviews* of 30 August 1892, W.T. Stead wrote:

> When the Messrs Cleaver, her solicitors, were in consultation with her before the trial, Mrs Maybrick pathetically implored them to 'spare Jim as much as possible. I know,' she said, 'he has done many wrong things, but he is dead now, and I would be distressed if his life were to be made public.'

Clearly, what was withheld concerned her husband, James Maybrick. It was not his extramarital relationships, or his drug habits. They were public knowledge. So what had he done that could be so 'wrong', that was more important to keep quiet than to defend Florence's own life?

We then discovered a most sensational document, a letter written by Baroness von Roques to Queen Victoria.

The front page was stamped 'Returned From The Queen'.

23rd May, 1890

Florence E. Maybrick

Petition to the Queen from the Baroness von Roques in favour of setting out their family history and arguing that the Secretary of State, having admitted that there was a reasonable doubt whether James Maybrick was really murdered, he has no right to detain the convict because of a crime, for which she was never tried.

I know the many troubles she nobly and silently endured, and I am aware of matters which were suppressed during the trial, which would have thrown quite a different light on her conduct.

If, as is alleged, she deceived one within a moment of weakness and despair, and a dishonourable man took advantage of her situation and despair, at the discovery of the facts in her husband's life . . .[1]

The Baroness continued, expressing clearly her anger at British justice:

There was nothing in the indictment about 'administering and attempting to administer poison' with felonious intent, and yet I am told on authority, that the penalty your Majesty's adviser has inflicted on her is that penalty attached to that crime, a crime for which she has *not stood her trial* in any of the Crown Courts or Courts of Justice. Ought she not to be so tried and found guilty before she is thus sentenced?

Absolutely. We read on. One passage contained words that just stunned me. I read them again. And then I read them again . . .

I do not desire to say one unnecessary word against her husband, nor did she instruct her counsel to do so, hence strong evidence in her favour was suppressed, but which can now be produced if required.

Probably your most Gracious Majesty will not deem it necessary since your responsible Minister has admitted a reasonable doubt whether murder was committed on Mr Maybrick, either by my daughter or any one else . . .

Nine months later and the withheld evidence, now confirmed as pertaining to James Maybrick, is being used

---

[1] Home Office Document HO 144 1639 A50678D/667.

as a threat against the throne of Britain! The Baroness implies that this evidence is as valuable as the Home Secretary's 'reasonable doubt'. She certainly has no doubt that the Queen knows exactly what 'the suppressed evidence' is and assumes that Her Majesty would not want the information to be made public.

Now, why on earth would Queen Victoria be concerned with anything that James Maybrick did? What evidence could be so important?

We already knew that Michael Maybrick mixed with royalty. After the trial, he was to leave London to spend most of his life as Mayor of Ryde on the Isle of Wight. His home was just a short distance from Queen Victoria's privately owned Osborne House.

Queen Victoria had taken a personal interest in the handling of the Ripper case and was severely critical of those in charge. If, after his death, evidence transpired to prove that James Maybrick was the Ripper, brother of Stephen Adams, an associate of the Queen, the embarrassment to the entire establishment would have caused a potentially disastrous scandal.

Imagine discovering that Fred West played cards with Prince Andrew!

For almost a century, Jack the Ripper has been associated with royalty, Freemasonry and a cover-up. They say there's no smoke without fire. James Maybrick was a common denominator. And it did not stop there. J.K. Stephen was a Ripper suspect. He had become one, it would appear, as a result of being tutor to the Duke of Clarence, the Queen's grandson, and, according to the authors who accused him, because of his writings, which displayed certain knowledge of the crimes. How close they were! If J.K. was aware of certain facts, where did his information come from? Was it the Duke or perhaps his father – wait for it – Judge James Fitzjames Stephen, the very person who presided over the trial of Florence Maybrick?

But the links or coincidences discussed over the last few paragraphs have nothing to do with the diary, have they?

Indeed they have. These historical facts make sense only if James Maybrick was the Ripper.

I continually played devil's advocate throughout the research period. I always tried to see if anything else could make sense of the information we had other than James Maybrick's being Jack the Ripper. On this occasion, I could only conclude that if the Queen had a more intimate relationship with either Michael or James, the Baroness's letter might have meant something even more scandalous. I did not believe that, and was later able to disprove it – once again, with the help of the Home Office files.

The Baroness continued to fight for her daughter's release. She obtained the services of a solicitor, Jonathan Harris, whose offices were in Leadenhall Street.

He wrote on 11 April 1894 to Herbert Asquith, who by this time had replaced Matthews as Home Secretary. His correspondence contained 'Notes and fresh evidence', with declarations and exhibits, and he hoped that, 'after consideration of same the convict will be released'.

This letter, like the one from the Baroness to the Queen, carried a veiled threat.

'... I have other evidence in my possession and power which (on the grounds of public policy and respect for our legal system) I am anxious to suppress if my present application is successful.'[1]

This 'suppressed' evidence is clearly considered to be something that neither the Queen nor her government would want exposed. We have established that, whatever it is, it is about James Maybrick. The letter from Harris dismisses any 'fantasy' of a love affair.

What was this material? What could James Maybrick have done that would have embarrassed our establishment? By now, any doubts I had vanished. Everything seemed to fit into place. The Maybrick mystery, the Ripper crimes, the rumours over the last hundred or so years. As Colin Wilson said, 'No self-respecting hoaxer could expect

---

[1] HO 144/1639/A50678D/202.

that sort of luck.' Colin was referring to the way history 'worked' for the diary. You cannot make history work for you because you cannot change it. Of *course* history worked for the diary – the diary is genuine.

James Maybrick was Jack the Ripper. Two mysteries were solved. And, the best was yet to come.

After the Florence Maybrick trial had ended, the establishment was under attack from both sides of the Atlantic. Florence, after all, was born in Mobile, Alabama, and was from a very influential family. Nobody could understand the original verdict. Once the Home Secretary admitted publicly that there was 'a reasonable doubt' that Florence Maybrick had committed wilful murder, it just seemed to go against everything our legal system ever stood, or still stands, for that she remained in prison. As the Baroness requested from Queen Victoria in that remarkable letter in 1890:

> and therefore I humbly pray your most gracious Majesty to pardon and discharge my daughter for that offence of murder, and let her be tried on the new charge of administering and attempting to administer poison with felonious intent, that her entire innocence of that charge, as well as the other, may be made to appear.[1]

The trial of Florence Maybrick would be the last that Judge James Fitzjames Stephen would preside over. The press attacked him. The public attacked him. Sir Henry Dickens, son of Charles, wrote in his memoirs a story told by a fellow judge on circuit in Liverpool:

> He [Stephen] summed up all day, apparently in favour of Mrs Maybrick, and adjourned the remainder of what he had to say till the next morning. That night his brother judge had a somewhat startling experience. Early in the morning he was awakened by Stephen

[1] HO144/1639 A50678D/57.

whom he found walking up and down in his room, saying as he did so, 'That woman is guilty.' He opposed what he had said on the previous day.

The judge himself would later write on the Maybrick case: 'I mention it, not in order to say anything about it, but merely in order to remark that it was the only case in which there could be any doubt about the facts.'

What does all that mean?

What facts? The facts presented by the prosecution or those presented by the defence?

More importantly, what did the judge learn on the night before his final summing up that led to his directing the jury to a 'guilty' verdict? Had he learnt the truth about James Maybrick? Is that what kept him awake? He would now have the motive that had been missing throughout the trial, but the law comes before sympathy.

By January 1995 our researchers in Liverpool were reading again all the press reports following the trial. Could we find anything to connect the Baroness to 'the suppressed evidence'?

Carol Emmas called; she read me the following article from the Liverpool *Echo* dated Monday 16 September, 1889.

MRS MAYBRICK'S DIARY

Mr Stuart Cumberland, questioned as to the statement in his paper about Mrs Maybrick's diary having been offered for sale to a London publisher, said that he expected the diary would come into his own hands; if it did he would certainly publish it if he thought it to be authentic, and if he did not he would denounce the impostor who was endeavouring to palm it off as authentic. The diary, which was in three small volumes, tied together with a blue silken cord, was taken by a gentleman who declined to give his name to Messrs Triscler and Co., the Ludgate-circus publishers. He said that he was a relative of the Maybrick family, and had found the books in a box of Mrs Maybrick's at Battlecrease House. The gentleman was seen by the manager of the firm who himself examined the diary, and expresses his belief in its authenticity. He says that the writing in each of the three books is different, although it is that of the same writer. The first book contains Mrs Maybrick's childhood's reminiscences, the second those of her girlhood, and the third her married life. The manager was unable to decide what offer to make in the absence of the head of the firm, so he told the gentleman to call again, at the same time advising him that it might be worth his while to offer the books either to Mr Stuart Cumberland, who would no doubt be glad to speculate upon them, or to the Baroness von Roque, who might probably purchase them to prevent their publication. However, nothing has since been heard of the diary, so it is probable that the latter suggestion was the one adopted, and that the Baroness von Roque [sic] now possesses her unhappy daughter's diary, which will therefore never see the light.

What? An 1889 reference to a diary written by a Maybrick? Where the handwriting changes from one volume to the next? Diaries that need authenticating before publication? Another diary assumed to have come from Florence Maybrick's trunk? These were echoes of events in 1992, and the echo was very loud – too loud. This could not be a coincidence, could it?

Other questions came to mind. Was this the suppressed evidence? Why, if it was, was it being suggested that the Baroness would not want it published? Why would a publisher recommend another, on something that seemed so lucrative? Who was Stuart Cumberland?

Keith Skinner wasted no time.

Stuart Cumberland was an editor. The newspaper was Stuart Cumberland's *Illustrated Mirror*. The fact that the mysterious seller had been recommended to Mr Cumberland appeared to be very strange because, on 19 August

1889, he wrote an article in the *Mirror* from which this is taken:

MAYBRICKISM

... Personally, I take but little interest in the case; for I don't know Mrs Maybrick, didn't know her late husband, and haven't the slightest wish to become acquainted with either Mr Brierley or the mysterious 'John' ...

Even after he had become aware of the diary, Stuart Cumberland would only write on 16 September:

MRS MAYBRICK'S DIARY

A gentleman is making the rounds of the publishers, with what he claims to be the diary of Mrs Maybrick. The diary, he says, was found in a trunk after the conviction of Mrs Maybrick, and it purports to contain her impressions and confessions from early childhood up to the present year. If the diary is to be believed, the 'unhappy lady' now languishing in Woking gaol must have been of an exceedingly skittish disposition.

One passage in the diary shows that Mrs Maybrick as a young girl had some original notions with respect to Eve's temptation by the serpent.

We are not exactly convinced of the genuineness of the document, although so far as we can glean the genuineness of them is guaranteed. The object of those into whose hands the alleged diary has fallen appears to be to publish a 'shilling shocker' ...

A shocker? I could not possibly imagine what could be in it. Mr Cumberland still appears to be questioning the authenticity. I did note that this 'diary' is now also being referred to as a document.

So why on earth would anyone suggest a diary written by a Maybrick be taken to Mr Cumberland? As he states, he had no interest in the Maybricks, so what would hold his interest?

On 29 July 1889, Stuart Cumberland wrote an article under the heading MY VISION OF 'JACK THE RIPPER'.

On 5 August 1889, Stuart Cumberland wrote another article, this time with the heading IS 'JACK THE RIPPER' A MESMERIST?

On 19 August 1889, the *Illustrated Mirror* published, under the heading MAYBRICKISM, this:

Liverpool

Sir,

You call yourself a thought-reader and claim to know all about that blood-thirsty scoundrel 'Jack the Ripper'; but up to the present I have seen no sign from you respecting the innocent woman who lies in agonised suspense in Walton gaol . . .

You can have visions about the Whitechapel murderer, but poor Mrs Maybrick in your idea is apparently unworthy of a dream. It ought all to be clear to you, but perhaps you don't want it to be so . . .

A lover of justice.

A letter from *Liverpool* connecting Florence Maybrick with Jack the Ripper? Surely this means that someone at the time knew the truth about James? That person was obviously very frustrated that no one else could work it out – 'It ought all to be clear to you . . .'

On 26 August 1889, Stuart Cumberland's headline was JACK THE RIPPER AGAIN – ANOTHER DREAM.

On 16 September 1889: THE NINTH MURDER – MY VIEWS THEREON.

On 23 September 1889: THE GREAT WHITECHAPEL PUZZLE.

Without any doubt, Stuart Cumberland's prime interest was the crimes of Jack the Ripper. A diary, however, originally reported as 'Mrs Maybrick's', was recommended to be taken to him.

It is interesting to note that the diaries of 1889 ceased being referred to as 'Mrs Maybrick's Diary'. In the last-known article written by Mr Cumberland on the matter on 30 September 1889, he wrote the following:

342

> The alleged 'Maybrick Dairy' [sic], to which reference was made in THE MIRROR a fortnight ago, is still, I understand, in the hands of those who claim to have discovered it. I am not yet satisfied as to its genuineness, but those who have examined it appear to be convinced that it is all that it is represented to be. Will Mr Miller, the gentleman who holds the MS, call or communicate with me at THE MIRROR OFFICE . . .

At the very least, this indicates that diaries existed in 1889 emanating from the Maybrick household and connecting the Maybricks with the Ripper. Given that Jack the Ripper was Cumberland's great obsession, the only reason for 'Mr Miller' to have been recommended to show the diaries to Cumberland is if they concerned the Ripper. This is also the only reason for Cumberland's U-turn on these Maybrick diaries. He went from having 'little interest' in Florence in August to requesting a meeting in September with the mysterious Mr Miller.

Although we have obtained almost every Maybrick certificate since 1837, and the certificates of collateral lines for the same period, we are yet unable to determine Mr Miller's relationship to the family. Whether this is the man's real name must be doubtful.

If James Maybrick had written down everything that Florence had told him about herself, and the Baroness had acquired these 'diaries', we may have the answer to why there are several pages missing from the beginning of the document that was found in 1992.

Florence, we have learnt, had relationships with several men. There was an illegitimate child at the tender age of sixteen and, after she was married, relationships with at least three men, one of whom was James's younger brother, Edwin. Florence had also had a miscarriage of a pregnancy that was not initiated by her husband. It is also likely that she had again become pregnant after the events at Flatman's Hotel.

The Baroness or Florence or, perhaps, William Graham would not have wanted this knowledge to survive.

What exists now may just be one-sixth of what originally existed. Stuart Cumberland suggested that the diaries shed a bad light on Florence. Would Florence have been so self-critical? History suggests otherwise. Her husband was so obsessed by her that it is far more likely that James Maybrick logged all of his wife's indiscretions.

We saw earlier the curious footnote Nigel Morland wrote on page 229 of his book, *This Friendless Lady*: 'Who generously gave me these details and a number of intimacies of Florence Maybrick's which I cannot reveal.' The 'who' referred to above was a woman who accompanied Florence in a train, after she left Truro, having become acquainted with her in Liverpool.

Originally, the three books were, in all probability, a journal of Florence Maybrick's life, as told by her to her husband. The changes in handwriting are consistent with what we were told by Hannah Koren. The changes were consistent with his multiple personality. The changes were consistent with that of a drug addict.

Originally, it was said that the Baroness would not want these published. Later, she would threaten to publish them – twice. Once the background to Florence's, and perhaps her own, life had been removed, only James Maybrick's horrific crimes remained. That is why the 'diary' as we know today has pages missing at the beginning. It has been established that those pages had been cut out. Now we know why.

I am sure that, aside from the watch and the diary, there are papers and documents that show knowledge of James Maybrick's evil alias.

Perhaps the final words of this chapter belong to J.H. Levy, who wrote on page vii of the preface in his 1899 book:

When it is realised by the British public that Mrs Maybrick has been doomed to life long imprisonment on the strength of a *secret dossier* [author's italics] for a crime for which she has never been publicly tried and on a warrant for an offence of which it is admitted she may be innocent, the result will be revulsion of feeling such as has not been experienced in England for a long day.

21

'THERE SHALL BE NO MORE DEATH'

JAMES MAYBRICK'S YOUNGER BROTHER, Michael Maybrick, was, as we have seen, a famous musician. Known to the world as Stephen Adams, he was a virtuoso organist with a fine baritone voice and could be described as the Paul McCartney of his day. By his early twenties, his ability as an organist was already recognised:

> At a very early age he commenced the study of the pianoforte, and when eight years old could play tolerably well on that instrument. He then began turning his attention to the organ, and when a little older ... became exceedingly fond of the 'king of instruments', and made such rapid progress ... that at the age of fourteen he was appointed organist of St Peter's, the parish church of Liverpool ... and it was eventually decided to give the musical abilities of young Maybrick their full chance by sending him to Leipzig ... and when he was about twenty-two he took his departure for the celebrated German Conservatoire.[1]

His voice, too, was celebrated:

> Mr Maybrick's popularity is now so assured that we hardly need point out those characteristics of voice and style that have earned him such striking favour wherever he has sung. There is great sympathetic quality in his fine baritone voice; and added to this, is

---

[1] Touchstone; Or The New Era, 14 September 1878, p. 3.

an excellent method of production and complete control of the organ. His phrasing is artistic and he knows how to lend unusual expression to his tones.[1]

Among Michael's popular songs, written under his *nom de plume*, were 'The Warrior Bold', 'True Blue', 'True To Last', 'The Tar's Farewell', 'Alsatian Mountains' and, most famously, 'Nancy Lee'. Ironically, he also wrote a nautical ditty called 'We All Love Jack'.

At the time of the Ripper murders Michael Maybrick lived in Wellington Mansions, Northbank, close to Regent's Park in London. Under the title CELEBRITIES AT HOME – MR MICHAEL MAYBRICK IN WELLINGTON MANSIONS, *The World* wrote:

> There are few houses between Portland Place and Hampstead Heath which command a finer view from the upper windows than the provokingly angular brick buildings at the north-west corner of Regent's Park, dignified by the name of Wellington Mansions ... Dwellers in Wellington Mansions are accustomed to regulate their clocks by Big Ben, and a tradition exists among them that on exceptionally clear days they can catch a glimpse of Windsor Castle. 'Pleasant melodies must have pleasant surroundings' was a favourite axiom of Stephen Adams ... The Maybricks of Liverpool have been musicians for at least three generations.[2]

Later, Michael was ensconced in even more 'pleasant surroundings' where he could write his 'pleasant melodies'. This was 6 Cornwall Terrace, a palatial, stuccoed Nash crescent, part of the Regent's Park Outer Circle at the Clarence Gate entrance. He still held this property when he died on the Isle of Wight, where he had five times been the Mayor of Ryde.

Intriguing. *Jack the Ripper: The Final Solution*, written

---

[1] Ibid.
[2] *The World*, 15 January 1890.

by Stephen Knight and published in 1976, was written on information from a Joseph Sickert, who claimed to be the son of Walter Sickert, an English impressionist of the late Victorian and Edwardian periods.

Joseph Sickert had always claimed to know the true story of Jack the Ripper. Whether he did or not, there can be no doubt that his stories had been embellished.

Most authors have ridiculed him and his 'knowledge' of the Duke of Clarence theory. Paul Begg and Keith Skinner were to tell me, quite early on in our relationship, that they felt there 'was something there'.

Recent research, discussed later in this book, revealed support for Sickert's story before Joseph was born.

When Stephen Knight was writing *The Final Solution*, he 'obtained' copies of the BBC's research notes on Joseph Sickert's story.

Wendy Sturgess and Ian Sharp, researchers for the BBC, visited Nigel Morland on 11 March 1973. They wrote in a memo:

> We asked if Morland had any knowledge of a woman imprisoned against her will, or unjustly; he quoted the Maybrick Trial, where a Mrs Maybrick was sent to jail, and condemned to death by James Fitzjames Stephen for murdering her husband (a Liverpool Cotton Merchant).[1]

Clearly, the question directed at Morland reflected Joseph Sickert's original story before contamination.

Stephen Knight, however, deduced that the woman was Annie Elizabeth Crook, Sickert's grandmother. As Annie had not spent any time in prison (bar a day or two), the story was rubbished.

Sickert had also talked about a coach driver who was murdered for his part in the murders. That man was John Netley, who purportedly drove the coach with the Royal Crest on it and Jack the Ripper in it.

John Netley died in 1903, under the wheels of his own

---

[1] Stephen Knight Collection.

cart, at Clarence Gate, outside Michael Maybrick's front door.

Incidentally, the 'Maybrick Arms', the family crest granted to James Maybrick on 4 July 1881, was also used by Michael Maybrick 'on the door of the carriage', as Amy Maine, daughter of Edwin, tells us in a recorded in an interview in July 1985.

Curious, indeed.

According to *The Freemason*, a magazine published by authority of the United Grand Lodge of England, Michael Maybrick was a man in a very powerful position, almost at the very pinnacle of this secret society's hierarchy. In a memorial to him, published four days after his death in 1913, they wrote:

> A wide circle of Brethren ... will regret to learn of the death of Bro. Michael Maybrick ... [he] was initiated in 1876, in the Athenaeum Lodge, No. 1491. In the following year he became a founder of the Orpheus Lodge, No. 1706, formed for members of the musical profession ... He was exalted in the Mount Sinai Royal Arch Chapter, No. 19, in 1878 ... In the Ancient and Accepted Rite he was perfected in the St George Rose Croix Chapter, No. 42 ... In 1889 he was appointed Grand Organist of England, and also Grand Organist of Grand Chapter ... in 1890 [he] was admitted a member of the 30th Degree.[1]

Thirtieth Degree! Michael Maybrick was indeed very powerful, as well as very famous. Thirtieth Degree was just three degrees below that of the highest Freemasons in the land – a maximum number of seventy-five men who made up the Supreme Counsel – Thirty-third Degree – which included royalty, peers and other eminent and powerful men.

Michael Maybrick's power, and position, did not end there.

Florence Aunspaugh remembered:

---

[1] *The Freemason*, 30 August 1913, p. 140.

Michael Maybrick realised over a million dollars on that song [Holy City]. He had been courted by royalty, the Pope and all the celebrities of the world and it had 'turned his head'. My father did not like or admire him at all. He said his success had endowed him with the 'superiority complex' and thought he had forgotten more than anybody else ever did know . . .

These English cotton brokers literally despised Michael. After he wrote the 'Holy City', the popularity of that song made an absolute fool of him and classed himself with the nobility and peerage . . .

Michael had the idea, especially after he wrote 'The Holy City', that he was floating on the Celestial plains and did not belong to earth . . .

He [Michael] thought he should be classed with Shakespeare, Byron, Milton and Tennyson. My father often laughed and said 'Michael had already engaged a tomb in Westminster Abbey . . .'

Amy Maine, daughter of Edwin, recalled being taken to Osborne House, home of Queen Victoria, as a little girl. Michael Maybrick clearly mixed with royalty.

Michael married Laura Withers, his housekeeper. Laura's great niece, Gay Steinbach, currently lives in Connecticut. In her possession is a picture of Laura Maybrick with Queen Victoria outside Osborne House as well as an invitation to Michael to attend the coronation of King Edward VII.

Jack the Ripper had been associated with royalty and Freemasonry for years.

A cover-up was another popular belief.

By researching the diary, we seemed to have stumbled into a pothole of Ripper folklore, or was everything just starting to make sense? Our investigation had reminded me of a huge jigsaw. At the beginning we would find a bit here and a bit there. As we would near the end, the pieces just started to fall into place.

Did Michael Maybrick know who James was and, if so, when did he find out?

Is the 'habit' being referred to in the next piece of text from the diary James's drug-taking or his more violent habits?

I suspect the latter, as James is already well aware that Florence had written to Michael in respect of his 'white powders':

> My dear Bunny knows all. I do not know if she has the strength to kill me. I pray to God she finds it. It would be simple, she knows of my medicine, and for an extra dose or two it would be all over. No one will know I have seen to that. George knows of my habit and I trust soon it will come to the attention of Michael. In truth I believe he is aware of the fact. Michael will know how to act he is the most sensible amongst us all I do not believe I will see this June, my favourite of all months.

If Florence did not kill James, who did?

Michael certainly had a motive. Knowledge of James's alter ego would have horrified him. If it were to become public, he would lose everything he had achieved. Wealth, power and position. The risk of James's surviving, and returning to Whitechapel, this time to be caught, was too great for Michael to have contemplated.

James Maybrick's death was shrouded in mystery.

As MacDougall wrote:

> So that the CONFLICT OF MEDICAL OPINION amounts to this, that both as regards the symptoms during life and the appearances after death, the balance of medical opinion is that James Maybrick did not die of arsenic at all . . .
>
> Upon some points there is no conflict of medical opinion.
>
> 1. That the one-tenth of a grain of arsenic found in the body was not sufficient to cause death.
>
> 2. That the cause of death was gastro-enteritis; or, in other words, congestion or acute inflammation of the stomach and bowels.
>
> 3. That gastro-enteritis may be set up by a vast variety

of things – impure food, excessive alcohol, getting wet through, or arsenic.

Florence Maybrick's defence counsel had a problem. She had been charged with murder by administering arsenic. However, Florence knew that James was a drug addict. A self-confessed arsenic eater. How could that be proved when only less than one-tenth of a grain of arsenic was found in his body?

Irrespective of whether Florence murdered her husband, why wasn't more arsenic found in James Maybrick's body? I was surprised to find that, while authors have debated how James did die, that question has not been put forward.

The diary answered the conundrum: 'I no longer take the dreaded stuff for fear I will harm my dear Bunny, worse still the children.'

James Maybrick had stopped taking arsenic, which is why so little was found in his body. As Dr Thomas Stevenson said, 'less arsenic was found in the viscera of Maybrick than in any previous case of arsenical poisoning.'[1]

For unknown reasons, Florence's counsel found it necessary to bring witnesses from Richmond, Virginia, to try to prove James's habit. The various statements in the Home Office files that support this fact were all forthcoming only after Mrs Maybrick was convicted.

Whatever killed James Maybrick was not arsenic. We decided to take a closer look at the facts of his death after discovering the following document in the Home Office files.

H.M. Prison – Lewis

27 Jan 1894

Statement by Robert Edward Reeves, a prisoner in the above prison

What I heard one night as I was standing under a place

---

[1] HO 144/1638 A50678D/16.

they call the Royal Exchange, near Dale Street in Liverpool. There was two young men talking by themselves ~~near~~ not far from where I was standing. They could not see me as I was behind a pillar. I drew as near as I could to hear what they were talking; then one said to the other 'how will you manage this.' The other said 'I will manage that allright with the servant. I will get her to put a bottle of laudanum in Mrs Maybricks drawers and leave one on the table just as if it had been used and we can get Mr Maybrick to go to have some drink with us tomorrow and you can engage him in talking about the business and I will slip a strong dose into the drink that will settle him by tonight.' Then the other said 'the blame will fall on our sister.' The other said 'what do that matter, you know she dont like Mr Maybrick and she is keeping in with that other fellow that she seems to like best. She will be glad to get him out of the way, you know that they can't prove it was her poisoned him if they do send her away the whole business will fall to us you know and we shall be two lucky fellows then it don't matter about getting rid of one or two ~~fellows~~ out of this world will you agree with me about it.' The other said 'yes you will scc that that will manage this business alright.' Then the other said 'It is settled.' The other said 'Yes.' They then left their hiding place and went as far as the Merchant Tavern close by I followed thcm. I could not go in as I had no money with me at the time I was a deserter at the time else I should have gone to Dale Street police Court I was afraid of getting taken back to my regiment. I belonged to the Eight of Kings Liverpool regiment. My regimental number was 2955 I was at the depot at Warrington and I went home to my young girls house number 5 Vaughan Street Park Street Toxteth Park and I told her brother John Crane all I had heard them two young men say. He said 'don't you have anything to do with it, you might get caught and taken back to your regiment.' So I said nothing about it. Soon after I was taken by Detective Wilson in Manchester

Street one night so soon after I heard how Mrs Maybrick poisoned her husband and was sent for trial. I didn't think it worthwhile to say anything about it but it has been on my mind ever since I even think of it at night when I lay awake such a thing could be done against a lady that is innocent.[1]

I am certainly not the first person to have been suspicious of Michael Maybrick. Shortly after the trial on 15 August 1889, the *Manchester Courier and Lancashire Advertiser* published the following letter:

TO THE EDITOR OF THE 'MANCHESTER COURIER'

Sir, – There remain yet a few circumstances in this case that have had very little airing, and which at least admit of some notice from those who have a penchant for reflection and the solution of conundrums.

1. Who had a great antipathy to Mrs Maybrick?
2. Who had as much or more access to Mr Maybrick about the period of his violent attacks than anybody else?
3. Who had as much chance as anyone else of adding extra 'condiments' to Mr Maybrick's food or medicine?
4. Who, on one occasion, administered a pill to Mr Maybrick, causing him illness?
5. Who made a mistake in stating that the pill administered was 'written upon' by a doctor?
6. Who administered a pill that was not written upon by a doctor to Mr Maybrick, which pill caused illness?
7. Who takes charge of the bulk of the deceased's property? Query: Why is Mrs Maybrick charged with murder any more than he whose name forms an answer to all the above questions – Why? – Yours &c.,

R.F. MUCKLEY,
Hope-road, Sale, August 14, 1889

The 'who' referred to is clearly Michael Maybrick. Unfortunately, Mr Muckley could not add:

---

[1] HO 144/1638 A50678/298.

8. Who would stand to lose his wealth, power and position if it was known that his brother was Jack the Ripper?

The public were angry at the outcome of the trial, and the heat was on Michael. The *New York Herald* of 21 August 1889, two weeks after Florence Maybrick had been sentenced to death, reported the following interview with Michael Maybrick:

No one is awaiting more anxiously the decision of the Home Secretary relative to Mrs Maybrick than are Mr Michael Maybrick and Mr Edwin Maybrick, brothers of the man for whose death she stands condemned to be hanged ... 'Nothing would please me more now,' said Michael Maybrick ... 'than to hear that the Home Secretary's decision is that Mrs Maybrick shall go free.'

Mr Maybrick declined at first to be interviewed, or to say anything for publication, but upon being told that reports had been sent from Liverpool reflecting severely upon him, he changed his mind and talked freely.

'What are the reports?' he asked.

Being told that one was that he had known Alice Yapp before she entered his brother's household, and that he had put her there to be a spy upon Mrs Maybrick, he replied, 'There is not a shadow of truth in such a report. I never knew or heard of her until long after she was engaged there, and do not think I ever spoke a word to her until I was summoned to my brother's bedside before he died. I never even knew her name until this trouble came. Why should I want to have a spy upon Ms Maybrick, I should like to know? It has been published that I never liked her – that I avoided her house, and said once that I would never darken her door again. All this is untrue. My relations with her were always pleasant. She has come to me time and again for money and one thing and another, and she always got it. Only three weeks before my brother died – the day after she was with Brierley in London, in fact – I took her to dine at the Cafe Royal, in Regent

Street, and took her to the theatre. Does that look as if I disliked and distrusted her? I never spoke but one [word] harshly to her, and that was when I told her I had grave suspicions of poisoning in my brother's case. I was excited at the moment, and spoke harshly, but I tried instantly to remove the effect of the words by telling her that she was not strong enough to care for my brother, and ought to have help. I did nothing against her. My sole desire was to save my brother's life, not to get her or anyone into trouble. Since his death my chief desire has been to save his good name for the sake of his children. For their sake I hoped she would not be convicted, and am now anxious for her release. I have no enmity against her, and do not want to be understood as making any charge against her.'

'Did you think during her trial that she would be convicted?'

'No I did not. I said to my brother after the case was closed that I believed she would be acquitted, and so sure was I that she would be that I packed my things, so that I could catch the first train to London. As for my deposing her in caring for my brother, and scheming with Mrs Briggs and Miss Yapp against her, that is all nonsense. Why, after my brother's death Mrs Maybrick thanked me for being so kind to her.'

'Did you see nothing in the actions or manner of Mrs Briggs or Miss Yapp that suggested to you that they might be hostile to Mrs Maybrick?'

'No I did not. Mrs Briggs came to the house only when she was invited to come. She got up at four o'clock in the morning to come. Miss Yapp seemed to me to be a straightforward, honest sort of woman.'

'Another report is that your brother's clothes disappeared rather mysteriously, and that the real reason was that the pockets contained evidence of his having been an habitual arsenic user. Do you know anything about it?'

'That is nonsense. His clothes were in the hands of the police for two or three weeks after they were told of the case. They searched them thoroughly, and no such evidence was found . . . The clothes are now at my brother's office. They are not even locked up. Anyone can examine them. There was no concealment at all.'

'Was it not important for the prosecution to show that no arsenic was found in your brother's clothes? Would not that have sustained the theory that he was poisoned?'

'One would think so. But the truth is, I thought that no one connected with the case tried very hard to have Mrs Maybrick convicted. I know I tried my best to have the physician give a death certificate, but he refused to do so, and when the trial came I assure you I was a most unwilling witness. I do not think that the prosecution even desired Mrs Maybrick to be found guilty or expected that she would be. No one seemed to desire it.'

'Not even the judge in his summing up?'

'Oh, I wouldn't want to say anything on that.'

'Do you think that your brother used arsenic?'

'No, I do not. I am as sure he didn't as I am of anything, almost. If he had used it I would have been certain to know of it. I was with him for weeks sometimes, up in Scotland, three years ago, for instance, often sleeping in the same bed with him and I never saw the slightest indication of his using arsenic. On the contrary, he was very particular about his medicine, and in caring for his health. He was not a man to use poison. Besides, he was always very confidential with me, told me everything, and he would have been sure to tell me if he had any habit of that kind. The chemist, Heaton, who said he sold him pick-me-ups, was simply mistaken in the man, that's certain. He did not know his name, you remember, but recognised him from a newspaper cut. That cut was unrecognisable as a likeness. When shown my brother's photograph Heaton said, 'Yes; he looked like that, only whiter.' Now my brother was scarcely grey at all, and he did not have the pale complexion arsenic-users are understood to have. If he used arsenic he must have bought it somewhere.

Where did he get it? He used to buy medicines of McGuffie, in Castle Street, and Clay & Abraham's, in Bold Street, Liverpool, and of John Bell, in Oxford Street, in London. If they should say they used to sell him arsenic I would think it might be true. No member of the exchange in Liverpool has been found who ever saw my brother even go into Heaton's shop, although it was right across the street.'

'It is said that you violated the conditions of your brother's will in selling off the furniture and household effects.'

'The facts about that are these:- Of course neither Mrs Maybrick nor any of us wanted to go on paying the expensive rent of the house. Of course something had to be done with the furniture. She consented to its being sold. She and her counsel consented to its being sold. An inventory was made and the list given to Mrs Maybrick to check off the articles which were her private property. Afterwards it was thought better to pay her a given sum for such articles as were hers. That was done with the full agreement of Mrs Maybrick and her counsel, and she gave her receipt for the amount, which was £300. A large part of the proceeds was used paying the debts of the estate, chiefly bills for household expenses and tradesmen's bills, which she had allowed to accumulate, although her allowance for such things was large. There was nothing connected with the sale that was not straight and above board, and done with the full knowledge and consent of herself and counsel.'

'Where are Mrs Maybrick's clothes and private effects now?'

'They were delivered to her counsel and were by them stored at Woolright's in Bold Street. There were three or four great trunks full of her things, including dresses and jewellery.'

So Michael Maybrick's version was that his brother was 'very particular about his medicine and caring about his health'.

As MacDougall in 1891 pointed out:

In fact the house and the office were like apothecaries shops, and yet Michael Maybrick swore at the trial he had never heard of his brother having a habit of 'dosing himself'! Well, to be charitable, either Michael Maybrick is not a man of any observant or enquiring turn of mind, or he really knew very little about his brother.

Michael Maybrick would also appear to have overrated his relationship with James. On 1 May 1889 James had dined at home with his brother Edwin, Florence, and a friend, Captain Irving, of the White Star Line. James had met Irving when travelling from England to America in 1878, on a boat called the *Republic*, which was under the command of the captain.

Irving would later give a statement to the Home Secretary. It told of a meeting he had with Edwin, shortly before James's death.

Captain Irving had asked Edwin, 'What on earth is a matter with Jim?'

Edwin replied, 'Oh, he's killing himself with that d – – – – d strychnine.'

So Edwin clearly had knowledge of James's use of poisons, even if Michael did not. Or did he?

During the trial, Sir Charles Russell for the defence put the following questions to Michael Maybrick in cross-examination:

Q. Have you never heard about his dosing himself?
A. I never heard, except in a letter from Mrs Maybrick.
Q. I should like to see that letter.
A. Well, unfortunately, I destroyed it. I did not think it of any importance . . .

Florence was concerned. So much so that she had written to Michael in March 1889. Although Florence was married to James, and clearly was worried, Michael did not feel her letter was 'of any importance'.

Clearly Michael was not too concerned either, when he

received the following letter from James himself, in April. He certainly did not rush to Battlecrease House.

Liverpool 29th April 1889

My Dear ~~Michael~~ Blucher[1]

I have been very very seedy indeed. On Saturday morning I found my legs getting stiff and useless, but by sheer strength of will shook off the feeling and went down on horseback to Wirrall Races and dined with the Hobsons.

Yesterday morning I felt more like dying than living so much so that Florry called in another Doctor who said it was an acute attack of indigestion and gave me something to relieve the alarming symptoms, so all went on well until about 8 o'clock I went to bed and had lain there an hour by myself and was reading on my back. Many times I felt a twitching but took little notice of it thinking it would pass away. But instead of doing so I got worse and worse and in trying to move round to ring the bell I found I could not do so but finally managed it but by the time Florry and Edwin could get up stairs, was stiff and for two mortal hours my legs were like bars of iron stretched out to the fullest extent but as rigid as steel. The Doctor came finally again but couldn't make it indigestion this time and the conclusion he came to was the Nuxvomica I had been taking under Dr Fuller had poisoned me as all the symptoms warranted such a conclusion I know I am today sore from head to foot and played out completely.

What is the matter with me none of the Doctors so far can make out and I suppose never will until I am stretched out and cold and then future generations may profit by it if they hold a postmortem which I am quite willing they should do.

I don't think I shall come up to London this week as

---

[1] Blucher was Michael's nickname used by the family, and there was obviously a change of mind here over which salutation to use. HO 144/1639/A50678D/29.

I don't feel much like travelling and cannot go on with Fullers physic yet a while but I shall come up and see him again shortly. Edwin does not join you just yet but he will write you himself. I suppose you go to your Country quarters on Wednesday.

I have not seen Dickinson yet

With love your affectionate Brother.

Jim

Of this letter, Alexander MacDougall wrote:

> Now Michael Maybrick had already given evidence at the Coroner's Inquest on the 28th of May, and he certainly said nothing about having received any such letter ... If Michael really did have such a letter, he suppressed the fact when giving his evidence at the Coroners Inquest, notwithstanding the statement to which his solicitor, Mr Steel, pledged himself that Mr Michael Maybrick 'wished to disclose everything he knew.'

Actually, it appears that almost everyone close to James knew of his drug habits, except Michael. Charles Ratcliffe wrote to John Aunspaugh, telling him:

> James attended the Wirral races April 27th and came home sick. He began dosing himself as usual, but did not seem to improve, so called in Dr Humphrey. Humphrey doctored him for several days.

And later, in the same letter:

> If they had only found the arsenic in Mrs Maybrick's room, as James was such an arsenic dope I don't think they could have proven anything on her, but finding all those love letters as a motive it is going hard with her ...

During the trial, Michael Maybrick told the court how he came to arrive at Battlecrease, three days before his brother died.

'On Wednesday, the eighth of May,' he said, 'I received

three telegrams – one from Mrs Briggs, and in consequence of the contents of these messages I left London the same day for Liverpool . . .

'I was much shocked at my brother's condition, and could hardly remember what I said then. Afterwards, downstairs, I told Mrs Maybrick I had very strong suspicions about the case. She asked me what I meant, and I replied that she ought to have called in professional nurses, and also another doctor, earlier. At that time I had heard that Dr Humphreys was in attendance and a professional nurse had been procured that day. I also learnt that Dr Carter had been called in as a consulting physician. Mrs Maybrick said that no one had a better right than a wife to nurse her husband, and I agreed with this. I reiterated that I was not satisfied with the case, and that I would go and see Dr Humphreys, which I did.'

Edwin Maybrick had returned from America on 25 April. James had first become ill on 27 April, and Edwin had been staying in the house for that entire time. He said that Mrs Maybrick had been nursing his brother with the utmost solicitude and assiduity, sitting up night after night with him, and had got him to send Dr Carter out as a second doctor, and a professional nurse; and that there had been no lack of nursing and medical attendance; indeed, if there had been, he himself ought to have seen to it . . .

Within a few hours of arriving, Michael told Florence he was suspicious of her, a woman with whom his meetings had always been 'very pleasant'. What was he suspicious of? It was not until forty-eight hours later that Dr Humphreys did not believe his patient would recover.

Maybe Dr Carter could throw some light on it. In the following, he is quoted from MacDougall:

'Saw Mr Maybrick for the first time at 5.30 p.m. on Tuesday 7th May 1889 in consultation with Dr Humphreys. Dr Humphreys conducted me to Mr Maybrick's bedroom, the patient being in bed and a young lady sitting on a low seat at the window. I was

362

introduced to Mr Maybrick, but not to the lady whom I did not know to be Mrs Maybrick until shortly before I left the house . . .

'I did not see Mr Maybrick again till 4.30 p.m. His brother Mr Michael Maybrick, Mrs Maybrick and a nurse (I think nurse Callery) were present with Dr Humphrey's and myself in the bedroom . . . When Dr Humphreys and I left the bedroom we were followed closely by Mr Michael Maybrick who before we had had any further consultation said to me abruptly "Now what is the matter with my brother Doctor?" I replied "acute dyspepsia." "But what is the cause of it?" he asked. I said that this was by no means clear to us . . .

'He [Michael] then turned sharply round to Dr Humphreys and said "Have you told Dr Carter of my suspicion?" He replied "No." Mr Maybrick then told me that he had reason to suspect that his brothers wife was administering something to him that caused his illness. I replied that that was a very serious imputation to make against a wife. He seemed to take this as a reproof and said "God forbid that I should lightly suspect anyone, but if I think that I have good grounds for entertaining such a suspicion don't you think it is my duty to mention it to you." I said that it was and that it would be our duty to surround his brother by such safeguards as to prevent the possibility of his being tampered with by any one, but that it was not our duty to allow our minds to be biased against any individual until we had some good reason given to us. He then stated to us the following reasons:

'1. That his brother was able to eat any ordinary food a very short time previously while on a visit to him at London, but that soon after returning home he began to suffer from sickness and that a similar contrast between his condition when away from and at his own home had been observed before.

'2. That on his, Mr Michael Maybrick's, arrival at his brothers house on the previous day he discovered that there were a good many fly papers in the house.

'3. That he had certain proof of his sister-in-law's adultery . . .'

Michael Maybrick was evidently 'suspicious' about the fly papers, even though '. . . arsenic in quantities sufficient to poison fifty men was found in the house, all in his and none in her apartments or belongings'.[1]

Wait a minute. Who was in the bedroom with James? Surely not Florence, whom Michael was so suspicious of. How thoughtless of him. And he must have overlooked all that arsenic – unlike his younger brother:

> . . . that Edwin Maybrick, his brother, after Mr Maybrick's death had found a pill box containing arsenic pills in his brother's washstand drawer, but kept it concealed, saying nothing, notwithstanding the peril of his brother's wife, until her solicitor, Sir Charles Russell, hearing of it, dragged the admission from him during the later stages of the trial . . .[2]

Of course, I am sure that Michael Maybrick knew nothing about this at all. Dr Carter had diagnosed 'acute dyspepsia', but somehow Michael knew he was wrong.

On Saturday 11 May 1889 James Maybrick died.

Jack the Ripper was also dead. There would be no more murders by his hand in Whitechapel or anywhere else.

On Sunday 12 May 1889 Michael instigated a search of the house for 'the keys'. But in the Liverpool *Echo*, on Wednesday 21 August 1889, Michael said, 'Nothing of the kind happened, I never mentioned the word "keys" and had absolutely nothing to do with the search.'

Michael, but you said at the inquest, 'On Sunday morning we were searching for the keys in the little dressing room of my late brother's.'[3]

And before the Magistrates you said, 'On Sunday

---

[1] Mr Call, Document No.224, in the Senate of the United States, 20 April,1896.
[2] Ibid.
[3] MacDougall 1891.

morning the 12th I searched for keys in my brother's bed-room.'[1]

What were they looking for? Whatever it was, the search was completed before the police arrived in the evening. Neither Dr Humphreys or Dr Carter would issue a death certificate, and perhaps it is best commented on by Charles Ratcliffe, in his letter to John Aunspaugh of 7 June 1889:

> Old Dr Humphreys made a jackass of himself. After James died he and Dr Carter expected to make out the death certificate as acute inflammation of the stomach. After Humphreys had a conversation with Michael he refused to make a certificate to that effect, but said there was strong symptoms of arsenical poisoning, though Dr Carter still insisted that it should be inflammation of the stomach ...
>
> Michael wanted a post-mortem examination. Humphreys and Carter assisted by Dr Barron performed it. They found no arsenic. Michael was still not satisfied and after James had been buried ten days his body was exhumed and all organs sent to a chemist ...

It is almost as if Michael knew that arsenic would be found. In fact he had a remarkable sixth sense as far as this substance was concerned, except of course with regard to his brother. He had given a bottle of Valentine's Meat Juice to Dr Carter on Thursday 9 May for examination.

During the trial, Mrs Martha Hughes, a close friend of the Maybricks, was under cross-examination from Sir Charles Russell:

SCR   Do you recollect hearing that arsenic was traced, and that it had been found in a bottle of Valentine's Meat Juice?

MMH   Yes ...

SCR   ... When did you learn about Valentine's meat juice? Did you learn that on Saturday or Sunday?

---

[1] MacDougall 1891.

MMH   I heard it on the Saturday.
SCR   Was it from Dr Carter that you heard it?
MMH   No.
SCR   From whom?
MMH   Mr Michael Maybrick.

Remarkable. As MacDougall explains:

Now how came Michael Maybrick to know that arsenic had been found in the meat juice on Saturday? Dr Carter had certainly not told him so; on the contrary, he had told him on that Saturday that all he had found up till then in the meat juice was 'a metallic deposit upon the copper' and he had taken the bottle back with him on Saturday night to test – make further tests, and ascertain what the metallic deposit was.

And we must not forget that pill. A pill that made James Maybrick ill and about which Dr Fuller, Michael's own doctor, said, 'Deceased told me he had been taking a pill which he said I had prescribed for his brother. This, however, was not the case. I had not prescribed it. That pill contained powdered rhubarb, extract of aloes, and extract of camomile flowers, and was a mild aperient. He told me of nothing else he had been taking.'[1]

In fact, not one doctor who was attending to James had voiced any concern for his life until after the arrival of Michael Maybrick to Battlecrease House.

The Dover Street Institute – Attached to the Royal Liverpool Infirmary – from where the nurses were sent to Battlecrease House, recorded as late as 10 May 1889 that James was being treated for gastroenteritis. By that date, Florence was no longer being allowed to nurse her husband.

Michael Maybrick certainly had a motive to ensure his brother never recovered. Florence was also a problem. Would she talk? If she had not been arrested, she would have retained custody of the children and been able to

---

[1] H. Irving, *Notable English Trials*, William Hodge & Co., 1912.

reside in Battlecrease House. Free to say whatever she wanted to whomever she wanted.

The children were under the care of Michael, and Florence, even after the trial, would have been aware of the consequences for her children should Michael be ruined through scandal and shame.

So have we proved conclusively that Michael Maybrick killed his brother? Perhaps not, but the evidence against him is far stronger than the evidence that resulted in Florence Maybrick's being condemned to death.

Michael had the motive, method and opportunity.

It would have been in the best interests of many if Florence Maybrick had been hanged for the murder of her husband. But having been given a reprieve due to 'a reasonable doubt', she was kept in prison for a further fifteen years. If that 'reasonable doubt' had been acknowledged in court, Florence would have walked away a free woman.

Now we know why Florence Maybrick was kept locked up for a crime she had never committed. Then again, James's closest friend, George R. Davidson, may also have known the truth about James's Whitechapel visits, if my interpretation of the 'Bunny' passage (page 315) is correct. So what happened to him? On 9 March 1893, the Liverpool *Echo* published the following:

THE DISAPPEARANCE OF A COTTON BROKER
BODY FOUND

Private information to hand enables us to say that the body of Mr Davidson, who has been missing just four weeks to-day was found yesterday at Millom, where the body had been cast on the shore. A very great friend of the deceased recognised the body, and at the inquest held to-day a verdict of 'Found drowned' was returned. The interment takes place in Cumberland to-morrow (Friday).

The *Millom News*, on Saturday, 11 March 1893, carried a statement given at the inquest by Davidson's close friend, James Stewart:

. . . I was an old friend of the deceased, and have known
him for 23 years. I identify him by his shirt; I believe it
was the one he bought in my presence at the Bon
Marche, Liverpool, because it has the name of Bon
Marche on it, and it is the same kind of shirt as I then
saw him buy. The trousers are similar to the ones which I
have seen the deceased wear, and the scarf also. The
eye-glasses found on the body were bought from Knott
and Co., where I know deceased used to deal. The
deceased has been missing since about February 10th,
and a reward of £10 has been offered for information
about him. I last saw deceased alive about four o'clock
on the afternoon of February 9th, in the Liverpool
Exchange. For about two or three weeks he had
complained of being unable to sleep. He frequently got
up during the night and went for a walk and a smoke
round the square. He dined at 6.30 on the evening of
February 9th, and afterwards went to bed, but his
landlady thought she heard the front door close about
12.30 on the morning of the 10th, and about 10 a.m. he
was found to be missing, and has not since been heard of.
The deceased's watch was found under his pillow, and
his clothes that he had taken off contained his papers and
keys except his latch key, which he took with him. It was
a wild stormy night, and it is supposed that this is the
reason why he put on the old clothes. The deceased was a
strong minded man, and not one at all likely to commit
suicide, and as far as I know, there was nothing in the
state of his affairs which would lead him to do so. The
deceased lived about one and a quarter miles from the
docks. We cannot account in any way for his getting in
the water. I have often seen the deceased wear a brown
overcoat similar to the one found on the body.

One for the Ripperologists . . .
Michael Maybrick must have been terrified that the
truth about his brother would come out at the trial.
During the two months after his brother's death and the
trial, he may have even been prepared for such an event.

Not that I am suggesting that Michael would have dirtied his own hands.

If Jack the Ripper killed *after* the death of James Maybrick, a suggestion that they were one and the same person is, of course, ludicrous.

Alice McKenzie was found murdered in Castle Alley, Whitechapel, on 17 July 1889, just fourteen days before the trial began.

> Blood was flowing from two stabs in her throat, and her skirt was pulled up, revealing blood over her thigh and abdomen. Post mortem examination showed that this came from a long but not unduly deep wound running from below the left breast to the navel, seven or eight superficial scratches from this wound towards the genitals, and a shallow cut across the mons veneris ... Her clay pipe and an old farthing were found under the body, leading to the belief that the murderer might have repeated the deception it was suspected had been practised on Annie Chapman of offering a polished farthing as a sovereign, or an old farthing as a sixpence.[1]

A murder that appeared, at first, to be by the same hand as killed Nichols, Chapman, Stride, Eddowes and Kelly.

Food for thought.

On 26 August 1913 Michael Maybrick died. *The Times* claims he was born in 1844. That claim was repeated in *Who's Who*. It is repeated on his death certificate, which shows him aged sixty-nine when he died. Michael Maybrick even lied about his age. He was in fact seventy-two when he died, as his baptism records show his date of birth as 31 January 1841.

The census return of 1861, at 77 Mount Pleasant, Liverpool, supports his birth year of 1841. He is listed as a 'Professor of Music', aged twenty.

His obituary was printed in *The Times* on August 27, 1913:

---

[1] Paul Begg, Martin Fido and Keith Skinner, *The Jack the Ripper A–Z*, 3rd edition, Headline Books, 1996.

The death took place at Buxton yesterday of Mr Michael Maybrick, the composer. Mr Maybrick had been staying at Buxton for some weeks for the benefit of his health. He was apparently well on Monday night, when he visited a place of amusement, but he did not come down to breakfast yesterday morning, and when his room was entered he was found dead in bed.

Mr Maybrick was born in Liverpool in 1844. He received his early education in that city, and then proceeded first to Milan and afterwards to Leipzig for the study of music. On his return to this country Mr Maybrick soon became popular as a baritone singer, and for many years he figured in the programmes of the principal concerts in London and the provinces. He also made several appearances in English opera. But it is as a song-writer, under the name of 'Stephen Adams,' that Mr Maybrick will best and always be remembered . . .

For over a quarter of a century Mr Maybrick had resided at Ryde, and he took a prominent part in the public and social life of the island. He was five times Mayor of Ryde, being unanimously elected from outside the council. He was for several years president of the Isle of Wight Conservative Association, and was largely instrumental in extending and improving the Royal Isle of Wight County Hospital, of which he was chairman.

Mr Maybrick was one of the witnesses at the trial in Liverpool in August, 1889, of Florence Elizabeth Maybrick for the murder of his brother, Mr James Maybrick, the Liverpool cotton Broker.

The funeral will take place at Ryde.

Michael had not 'engaged a tomb at Westminster Abbey', as Florence Aunspaugh remembered her father saying, but the procession to his place of rest was reminiscent of a state funeral. The streets of Ryde were crammed with people. The whole occasion was extremely elaborate.

Yet the epitaph on his headstone was very simple: 'There shall be no more death.'

22

'THE RIPPER WAS NEVER CAUGHT BUT HE SHOULD HAVE BEEN . . .'

SO WHAT OF THE other suspects? And other Ripper folklore? Can we make any sense of it?

The title of this chapter are the words apparently said by Metropolitan Police Commissioner James Monro in the presence of one of his grandsons after his retirement. He also left some papers on the subject of Jack the Ripper with his eldest son Charles, who subsequently told a younger brother, Douglas, that the theory was 'a very hot potato', without revealing what it was.

The words suggest to me knowledge with hindsight. It could be argued that they simply mean that it would have been 'desirable' if the Ripper was caught, but that is true of any crime. No, I am fairly sure that Monro's words reflect that the Ripper's identity became known to the establishment at some time after the Whitechapel murderer's death.

The more I learnt about James Maybrick, the more impressed I became with the FBI profile. James Maybrick had the motive, the opportunity and the method. He was a drug addict, frequented brothels often and knew the area of Whitechapel well.[1] He came from a middle-class

---

[1] This fact was not well known until our research discovered it. Melvin Harris claimed in his document entitled 'Maybrick, Mayhem and Moonshine' that James Maybrick, at an early point in his life, had once lived in the East End of London. Harris claimed that this made Maybrick an obvious candidate to whom any forger could attribute the diary. He failed to point out the extensive and detailed research – problematic for any forger – which was necessary to establish the East End link.

background (not upper-class as the cynics suggested), and he was *not* successful, compared with those closest to him: his brothers. He was even borrowing money from his mistress in order to keep up appearances. It is a total fabrication that James Maybrick was a wealthy and successful businessman.

The Duke of Clarence, royalty, the Freemasons, J.K. Stephen, Sir William Gull and even M.J. Druitt had a common denominator in James Maybrick. The 'rumours' had clearly developed from their association with Maybrick and the acquired knowledge of those speculating about the identity of the Ripper – it was not 'luck' or 'coincidence'.

The suspect who fell outside of the above category was 'the poor Polish Jew', whether that be Aaron Kosminski, David Cohen or whoever. So I will deal with this first.

Personally, I never liked this theory. Whoever the Ripper was, Mary Kelly entertained him in her room for some considerable time. Mary Kelly did not need to pay for a bed for the night, which indicated that her payment was more than normal and, therefore, was more likely to be from a moneyed gentleman. There would have been no need for Mary Kelly to entertain a 'poor Polish Jew' in her own home.

To some avid Jack the Ripper enthusiasts, it may come as some surprise that it was Paul Begg who was convinced that the evidence given at the inquest of Elizabeth Stride proves that whoever pushed her to the ground could *not* have been the murderer. Why would the enthusiasts be surprised? Because, if Paul Begg has shown any preference for a suspect, it has been Aaron Kosminski.

Elizabeth Stride had been pushed to the ground outside Dutfield's Yard in an incident seen by a witness, Israel Schwartz. Sometime later her body was found in Dutfield's Yard. It was established that Elizabeth Stride was clutching cachous at the time of her death.

Are we expected to believe that a man assaulted Elizabeth Stride and dragged her into the back of the yard while managing to keep her quiet, and that she made no attempt to struggle? There was no doubt that Elizabeth Stride was killed at the spot where she was found. I find it unbelievable that she would willingly go to the back of the yard with a man who had just assaulted her, or that she would go with no attempt to protect herself. Her murderer, in all probability, was the supplier of the cachous.

Israel Schwartz had spoken of a second man outside a pub. It was far more likely that this was Elizabeth Stride's murderer. He could not be sure whether it was this man, or the one who assaulted Stride, who cried 'Lipski'[1] out to him.

It must be remembered that Elizabeth Stride was killed by a different knife from the one that killed the other victims. There was, however, no doubt at the time that she was a victim of Jack the Ripper, and this was accepted without question by Abberline, Anderson, Macnaghten, Smith and Swanson.

So how did Elizabeth Stride die?

The following may be a theory, and only a theory, but it does make sense of all the known facts:

- Elizabeth Stride is waiting for James Maybrick to come out of the pub.
- She is approached by Kosminski.
- Communication results in her being assaulted; Schwartz witnesses.
- As Stride falls, she withdraws her own knife.
- Maybrick comes out of pub at time of assault, cries 'Lipski' to the assailant.
- The assailant runs. Schwartz does also, assuming he is being chased.
- Maybrick goes to Stride, helps her up, hands her cachous, consoles her and takes her knife.
- Maybrick takes her into the yard. Stride leans against wall to be taken from behind with one of her hands clutching the cachous.

---

[1] A murderer whose name was allegedly used as an anti-Semitic insult at that time.

- Maybrick cuts her throat with her own knife, but because of its bluntness the penetration is slow, allowing time for Stride to clutch at her throat with her free hand, and scream briefly. Schwartz hears the scream.
- Maybrick is disturbed, but escapes with the knife. When he sends the 'Saucy Jacky' postcard, he throws the knife into a doorway.

Authors who have written about J.K. Stephen could not have been closer really, could they? His father, James Fitzjames Stephen, presided over the trial of Florence Maybrick. It was the only case of which the learned judge felt it necessary to state in his memoirs that 'the facts should have determined a different result from the jury'. That comment, despite the judge's extraordinary summing up, has been criticised by all.

The Ripper Legacy by Martin Howells and Keith Skinner had been written exploring a possible relationship among J.K. Stephen, M.J. Druitt and the Duke of Clarence.

Macnaghten was reported in the *Daily Mail* as saying that 'the greatest regret of his life was that he joined the force six months after "Jack the Ripper" committed suicide', and continuing:

> Of course he was a maniac, but I have a clear idea who he was and how he committed suicide, but that, with other secrets, will never be revealed by me. I have destroyed all my documents and there is now no record of the secret information which came into my possession at one time or another.

The Scotland Yard version, first described by Donald Rumbelow in 1975, comprises seven foolscap sheets in Macnaghten's own hand, headed 'confidential'.

> . . . No one ever saw the Whitechapel Murderer: many homicidal maniacs were suspected, but no shadow of proof could be thrown on any one. I may mention the cases of 3 men, any one of whom would have been more likely than Cutbush to have committed this series of murders:-

(1) A Mr M.J. Druitt, said to be a doctor & of good family, who disappeared at the time of the Miller's Court murder and whose body (which was said to have been upwards of a month in the water) was found in the Thames on 31st Dec. – or about 7 weeks after that murder. He was sexually insane and from private info I have little doubt but that his own family believed him to have been the murderer.

(2) Kosminski, a Polish Jew, & resident in Whitechapel. This man became insane owing to many years indulgence in solitary vices. He had a great hatred of women, specially of the prostitute class, & had strong homicidal tendencies; he was removed to a lunatic asylum about March 1889. There are many circs connected with this man which made him a strong 'suspect.'

(3) Michael Ostrog, a Russian doctor, and a convict, who was subsequently detained in a lunatic asylum as a homicidal maniac. This man's antecedents were of the worst possible type, and his whereabouts at the time of the murders could never be ascertained ...

Sir Melville's daughter, Lady Aberconway, had a slightly different version from that of Scotland Yard. These handwritten notes of Sir Melville's were discovered by the writer Daniel Farson in 1959.
They read:

No one ever saw the Whitechapel murderer (unless possibly it was the City P.C. who was a beat [sic] near Mitre Square) and no proof could in any way ever be brought against anyone, although very many homicidal maniacs were at one time, or another, suspected. I enumerate the cases of 3 men against whom Police held very [A pencilled addition in Lady Aberconway's hand reads 'reasonable suspicion'.] Personally, after much careful & deliberate consideration, I am inclined to exonerate the last 2, but I have always held strong opinions regarding number one, and the more I think the matter over, the stronger do these opinions become.

The truth, however, will never be known, and did indeed at one time lie at the bottom of the Thames, if my conjections [sic] be correct.

The last sentence suggests that Sir Melville Macnaghten was not given the name of M.J. Druitt, but had deduced his suspect from the 'private information' given to him. '... If my conjections [sic] be correct' is a comment that is critical in understanding how the name of M.J. Druitt was added to the list of suspects. Time for theory number two.

- Sir Melville and J.K. Stephen are known to each other. J.K. Stephen is Sir Melville's 'private info' (see footnote 2, page 6).
- J.K. Stephen, from knowledge he has obtained from his father, informs Sir Melville that Jack the Ripper is dead, and that the murderer's own family believed him to be sexually insane.
- Sir Melville trusts J.K., and considers the 'clues' offered to him. Perhaps they included references to Wimborne, Dorset. He lists acquaintances of J.K. Stephen. M.J. Druitt is one, through knowing J.K. from the Cambridge Apostles,[1] but the only one who is dead.
- Sir Melville then reviews the Ripper files, the J and M on the envelope found at the scene of Annie Chapman's murder, the inverted Vs carved on Catharine Eddowes's face. Two and two make five. '... And the more I think the matter over, the stronger do these opinions become.' One can easily see how these clues would lead Sir Melville to suspect.

As far as Ostrog is concerned the January 1996 issue of *Ripperana* reported that Philip Sugden had 'uncovered the record of Ostrog's 1888 conviction in France'. On 14 November 1888 Ostrog had been convicted in Paris of theft under the alias of Stanistan Sublinsky and sentenced

---

[1] A theory advanced by Martin Howells and Keith Skinner in *The Ripper Legacy* (1987).

to two years' imprisonment. If Sugden has discovered that Ostrog was in the custody of the French police prior to 9 November 1888, then he could not have murdered Mary Kelly in London on that date.

The case against Dr Francis Tumblety[1] further supports the argument for James Maybrick. Tumblety was an American, with Liverpool and Whitechapel connections. Maybrick was a Liverpudlian with American and Whitechapel connections. The police had sent the CID to Liverpool and were watching the docks there. They were, without doubt, on the right track. As for Tumblety, Mark King's[2] discovery that Tumblety was arrested in London on 7 November 1888 and brought before the magistrates nine days later was difficult for Stewart Evans and Paul Gainey to explain. They tried, suggesting that Tumblety, 'must have been released on an unrecorded Police bail'. Hardly likely.

And Sir William Gull? How did he enter the frame?

Probably through displaying some detailed knowledge, perhaps aquired through his position as Physician-in-Ordinary to Queen Victoria. The Queen was kept up to date with all of the latest developments in the Ripper investigation and Sir William may have picked up some snippets of information during his conversations with Her Majesty. Repeating such tit-bits in company could easily lead others to speculate about how he came by otherwise unpublicised inside information. Or maybe he obtained fragments of information from a man who was to become his best friend in later life, the surgeon Sir James Paget.

At the trial of Florence Maybrick, in the opening speech for the prosecution, Mr Adamson said, 'The reason she gave her husband for going to London was that she had an aunt who was going to undergo an operation under the

---

[1] Introduced as a suspect following the discovery of a letter by Stewart Evans that was written by Inspector Littlechild, who was head of Special Branch at the time of the Whitechapel murders.

[2] A researcher who has made impressive contributions to Ripperana – mentioned in *The Jack the Ripper A–Z*, 3rd edition, Headline Books.

care of Sir James Paget and the aunt wanted her niece to be present . . .'

Paget attended Gull's funeral in 1890 and he held the position of Sergeant Surgeon to Queen Victoria.

Frank Spiering, author of *Prince Jack*, published in 1978, claimed to have seen 'a copy of Dr William Gull's notes, bound in an ancient portfolio, kept in, of all places, the New York Academy of Medicine'.

In a letter mistakenly dated 4 January 1994 (it should have read 1995), Melvin Harris claimed that Spiering 'invented' this.

In Nigel Morland's private collection was an unpublished manuscript by Mr Spiering. Contained within it were the details of Gull's notes. Frank Spiering wrote that he found a single index card, numbered S115 and headed 'Acland, Theodore Dyke'. On it was:

See:
Gull, Sir William Withey
A collection of the public writings of . . . Edited . . . by
Theodore Dyke Acland.
Medical Papers
London, New Sydenham Soc, 1894 1X2 p. 3-609 p.19
pl.80

The New York Academy of Medicine Library confirmed to us that the above reference was legitimate, but that Gull's notebook was now 'missing'. Frank Spiering had not perpetrated a hoax after all.

Joseph Sickert had also been heavily criticised, and perhaps, from a historical point of view, justifiably. Keith Skinner, in particular, had always felt that there was 'something there'. He was right.

In December 1992, before I was involved with the diary, Ellen May Lackner, a cousin of Joseph Sickert, granted an interview to Paul Begg, Melvyn Fairclough and me. She confirmed that a story of the Ripper and royalty had been in the family since before Joseph was born.

Ellen's aunt was Annie Crook, purported to have had an affair with the Duke of Clarence and to have secretly married him, according to Joseph Sickert. Annie was Joseph's grandmother. What became clear was that it was not Annie but her daughter Alice who appeared to be the 'link' to the Ripper. While Annie was always welcome in Ellen's home, Alice was not, because she reminded Ellen's mother of Jack the Ripper.

Apparently, Annie Crook, who had conceived the child by the Duke of Clarence, had given the child to Mary Kelly to bring up.

Let us suppose for the moment that Annie Crook and Mary Kelly were friends. At least that does get support from Jean Overton-Fuller.[1] This time, let us suppose that Mary Kelly as opposed to Annie Crook was the woman pregnant. Mary used her friend's name when entering the workhouse to give birth, and gave that child to Annie Crook to bring up.

Alice would be the daughter of Mary Kelly, and Joseph the grandson. Ellen May Lackner's mother would have understandably referred to Alice as 'reminding me of Jack the Ripper'.

What had surprised me was that even one of the most notable of our crime writers believed that Joseph Sickert had 'invented' the Duke of Clarence theory. I shall not embarrass him by naming him, as he was quick to acknowledge that it was Dr Thomas Stowell who was the original proponent of that theory when he published his article in *The Criminologist* in November 1970. The article was entitled 'Jack the Ripper – a solution?:

We were to discover information that would give further support to Joseph's story. In February 1996 I received a telephone call from Stuart Thomson, as a result of my video, *The Diary of Jack the Ripper*, which had recently been networked on television.[2] Mr Thomson lived in Hastings with his ninety-year-old mother, Freda, who in 1915 was told a story about the Duke of Clarence being associated with the Ripper murders. Elements of Freda's story closely reflected Joseph's, but Freda had recently

---

[1] Author of *Sickert and the Ripper Crimes*, 1990.
[2] Transmitted 20 February 1996.

been upset and deeply vexed by one Ripper author who, when promoting his book on the radio, dismissed Joseph Sickert's story and the royal connection as a manufactured hoax, claiming that people were just cashing in on sensationalism. As a consequence of this, Freda's son, in 1995, wrote down his mother's recollections, and deposited the manuscript with a local solicitor.

Freda's original story is reproduced here for the first time and Stuart maintains that it has never varied since he himself learnt about it in the 1950s.

The story that I am about to tell you is a part of history and is a bit more to a story that has never been told before. It has been passed down to the family by my grandfather to my mother [her father].

It started with the Duke of Clarence and was the story at that time that he had met a girl who was a working prostitute, they fell in love and in time got married.

They had a house in Fitzroy Square off the top of Tottenham Court Road.

He was one of the sons of Queen Victoria and at the time it was said and understood that she did not like her children very much, and maybe she was not very happy with the choice of her son's wife as there was no doubt in her eyes that there would have been a scandal and therefore it would have to be covered up at all costs to protect their names ...

The story at that time was that his wife had been removed very quietly and put away into a mental home and one can only think she died there. It was said she went mental but she was never heard of again.

He may have been so upset with grief that it turned his brain, and by going after her friends he saw her face in theirs and turned to murdering them because in his mind's eye she had gone away and left him.

Then maybe he only wished to silence her friends for what they knew about their marriage. This way, in his mind, it would stop any more scandals. He may also have been ordered to end the marriage by his mother.

I will now give you the names of the people in this story. They were my great-grandmother, also both my great-grandfathers and my grandfather. My great-grandfather and grandfather were called Lythel, and my other great-grandparents name was Talor.

Great-grandfather Talor was working at the Royal Mint goods yard and my other great-grandfather was a Detective Sergeant in the police. My great-grandmother was a housewife at the time.

And so on with the story. It started the night before the last murder. My great-grandfather Talor was at work at the Royal Mint goods yard on night work. My great-grandmother Talor was walking through Mitre Court for a short cut to her husband's works. She had her husband's evening meal in her basket, when out of the shadows stepped a man. The figure stepped in front of her, he looked into her face, then he looked down into her basket, then he just stepped round her and went back into the shadows and into the night again.

As in those days the gas lamps did not give out much light and there were many shadows, it was easy to merge back into the safety of the dark streets and alleys. She always said to the family he was dressed in a long black cloak and had a big black hat (like the Sandyman port advert).

When my great-grandmother arrived at the goods yard she was as you might expect very upset and frightened.

My great-grandfather therefore sent for his friend, my other great-grandfather Detective Sergeant Lythal. There was a complete check all round the streets around Mitre Court but no sign was found of the man that had stepped in front of my great-grandmother. How long they went on looking my grandfather never said.

Then the next morning my great-grandfather, Detective Sergeant Lythel was called out by the Police Station. It was before six o'clock, and it was to go to Mitre Court again. My grandfather went with his father, at that time he was 14 year old boy. He was working for Reuters as a news boy before he was himself to go into the police force. When they arrived in the court there were three men already there (toffs), well known to his father as belonging to the royal household.

My grandfather never forgot about what he had seen. He was in his nineties when he passed away.

He always said that the blood and water were running in the gutter all round the court. The three men had knocked on the doors and called all the people that were living in the court out to wash the blood away. He always said there was no body there as far as he could see.

Then he was sent to Reuters News offices to break the news to the world that there had been another murder the night before or in the early morning.

So how was it those men were in the court before the police even got there if they were not aware that something was wrong. Maybe he was followed and someone had kept an eye on what he was doing, or, maybe when he got back he had told somebody about what he had done to the girls. Maybe someone was with him all the time.

Why did those men do what they did to try and clean up. Did they have orders to try and cover it all up to stop any more getting out about him and at the same time stop the scandal about the royal household.

The story was that the police knew that it was the Duke. It was also said at the time that the head of the investigation had his orders not to do anything about the Duke.

These orders must have come from the very top even though he had been having a bad time from the public, as they were concerned that no one had ever been arrested.

So nothing could be done. This was a well known fact down the police ranks.

Here are some of the background details to the story to make up your own minds.

My mother was first told about these events when she was eight years old living in Liverpool. Her father would relate the story many times to her.

It was not until she was eighteen years old when she was told the rest of the story by the rest of the family when she had moved back to London to live with her grandmother Talor.

Her aunts used to joke about the fact that he may have smelt their father's dinner and wondered if it had made him hungry.

My mother also said that in the seventies she had a letter from the grandson of the man in charge of the investigations thanking her for helping in clearing his grandfather's name for not having done anything to catch Jack the Ripper. This was after she had sent a letter to one of the papers but this letter has unfortunately been lost.[1]

After what had happened my great-grandmother and great-grandfathers just got on with their lives of bringing up their families.

Something else my mother has talked about was that her grandfather Talor's funeral stopped all the traffic all round the streets around Aldgate as his funeral coaches passed by in the year 1912.

Her other grandfather died in 1898 at Barnes after being retired on ill health grounds due to damage from a punch when he was involved in his police duties.

Seven detective inspectors attended his funeral.

We have to this day his shield which was given to him on retirement on January 4th 1894.'[2]

In March 1996 Keith Skinner went to Hastings to talk

---

[1] Freda's letter detailing her story was written to Dr Peter Warren, grandson of Sir Charles Warren, as a result of an article which appeared in the *Sunday Express* of 12 August 1973. The newspaper had forwarded Freda's letter to Dr Warren. What is of interest to note here is that Freda's letter predated Joseph Sickert's appearance on BBC television, when his story was given its first public exposure.

[2] An embellished version of this story by Marjorie McConnell Smith appeared in the April/May 1996 issue of *Family Researcher*.

with Freda and Stuart. As with Billy and Anne Graham, Keith was immediately struck with how unpretentious these people were and, in particular, how little they knew about the subject of Jack the Ripper. They had neither heard of Joseph Sickert nor read Stephen Knight's best-selling book, *Jack the Ripper: The Final Solution*, which had developed Joseph's story. Neither had they seen the 1973 BBC drama documentary, *Jack the Ripper*. When Keith returned to London he sent them Knight's book and Stuart later wrote back to Keith informing him that Freda insisted that some of the historical claims in the book were wrong.

Keith Skinner was able to confirm that Freda Thomson's grandfather was a detective sergeant with the City of London Police at the time of the Ripper murders and most certainly could have been called out to the murder scene of Catharine Eddowes in Mitre Square.

As we know that James Maybrick was the Ripper, why the concern with the Duke of Clarence?

I feel that continued research will prove a relationship between Michael Maybrick and the Duke. Indeed, it is probable rather than possible. It may not have been the Duke that the police were watching, but the people who were closely associated with him.

And Joseph Sickert?

I met Joseph several times, and got to know him fairly well. There was no doubt that he had embellished his stories, or others had done so for him, but I did not get the impression that he had ever done any proper research to find support for the stories he told. Hence his reference to a 'Roofer Castle', which does not exist.

The Cornwallis West family owned Ruthin Castle. We researched the family. Was it just a coincidence that Major William Cornwallis West had three illegitimate daughters while painting in Italy? And was it another coincidence that we discovered that Lady Cornwallis West was, as Mrs Patrick Campbell in her first marriage, a lover of Edward VII?

It should be noted that both of Joseph's parents were

deaf; Joseph himself is partially so. I doubt many of the 'facts' that Joseph has told – but he has been told *something*, and, whatever it was, it was important. He has tried to put the jigsaw together with what has been written by others and what he can remember.

I put it to Joseph that he had not descended from royalty as he had claimed, but that his grandmother, Alice, born in 1885, was the daughter of Mary Kelly, the prostitute. Joseph wept. 'She was not a prostitute,' he yelled back. He later denied the conversation.

Joseph had told Melvyn Fairclough that it was not Mary Kelly who was killed in Miller's Court on 9 November 1888.

There is, without doubt, support for that possibility. If Mary Kelly did not die, then we would have an understanding of why the police allowed Joseph Barnett and George Hutchinson to be released as quickly as they were, and in the case of the latter, why the police attached importance to his description.

Mary Jane Kelly apparently died at 2 a.m. Maurice Lewis, a tailor who lived in Dorset Street, told the press he had known her for about five years. He said he saw Kelly drinking with 'Danny' and 'Julia' in the Horn of Plenty on the night of the murder. He also claimed to have seen her leaving her room at 8 a.m. the day her body was found, and that he saw her later, in the Britannia, at about 10 a.m. (i.e. several hours after her death).

Caroline Maxwell, who had known Kelly for about four months, claimed at the inquest that at 8 a.m., while going on an errand in Bishopsgate, she not only saw Kelly, standing at the corner of Millers Court, but spoke to her. Kelly was wearing the maroon shawl that Mary Ann Cox saw her in the night before. Maxwell saw her again at 9 a.m., talking to a man 'about 30, height about 5ft 5in., stout, dressed as a market porter',[1] outside the Britannia public house. The time and day of the errand was later verified.

---

[1] Coroner's papers at the Greater London Records Office.

On 10 November 1888 *The Times* reported an unnamed woman seeing Kelly between 8.30 and 8.45 a.m.

Time for theory number three.

- George Hutchinson is drinking with Mary Kelly and a friend of hers (unknown). James Maybrick is in the Horn of Plenty also.
- Maybrick leaves first, and stands on the other side of the road.
- George Hutchinson leaves with the two women and stands talking to them outside the pub, where he is seen by Sarah Lewis.
- George Hutchinson goes off with Mary Jane Kelly, her friend returning to Miller's Court with a key that used to belong to Joseph Barnett.
- As George and Mary go off in one direction, Maybrick crosses to talk to Kelly's friend, whom he saw in the pub. The friend is wearing borrowed clothes from Mary Kelly, and so Mary Ann Cox, who follows the couple back to Miller's Court, assumes, reasonably, that the woman *is* Mary Kelly. The man has a carroty moustache and a blotchy face.
- It is Mary Kelly's friend who is murdered by Jack the Ripper.
- Mary Kelly returns home at about 8 a.m. and enters the room, this time using her own key. She immediately leaves, after seeing the revolting mess that awaited her. Maurice Lewis sees her come out.
- She has to go back in to collect some personal belongings, which Maurice Lewis also witnesses. Mary Kelly has no intention of returning.
- Mary stands in shock on the corner of Miller's Court. She throws up at the thought of what she had just seen. Caroline Maxwell sees her, and asks why she is ill. Mary uses an excuse that she has been drinking.
- Mary waits outside the Britannia for Joseph Barnett. She has nobody else to talk to. Joseph arrives. Mary tells him what has happened and Caroline Maxwell witnesses them.

- Joseph Barnett tries to calm her down, taking her into the pub for a drink. She is seen again by Maurice Lewis.
- Mary tells Joseph that she is leaving Whitechapel and going home. She wants the police to think that it was she who was killed, as she always had a fear that Jack the Ripper wanted to get her.
- Barnett gets Mary a change of clothing. He takes Mary's key and her neatly folded clothes and places them at the bottom of the bed. He locks the door as he leaves.
- When the police finally arrive, they are unable to unlock the door. The only way to gain entrance is to smash the door down, which they do.
- Police note the neatly folded clothes are not covered with blood and this may have led to the thought that the murderer had an accomplice.[1]
- George Hutchinson reads about the inquest and realises that Sarah Lewis saw him talking to Kelly. He decides to volunteer a statement.
- The police do not believe Hutchinson's statement. The interrogation intensifies until Hutchinson tells the 'truth' i.e. that Mary Kelly left him shortly before 8 a.m.
- The police question Joseph Barnett. He 'creates' the story of the lost key when questioned about it. He has panicked as the key is in his pocket. The police know that he is lying. Joseph Barnett then tells the truth. Mary Kelly was with him between 9 a.m. and 10 a.m. He put her clothes back in the room.
- Inspector Abberline now knows why he could not break Caroline Maxwell's story. She had been telling the truth. So had Maurice Lewis. Mary Jane Kelly was not the victim. Whoever her friend was had taken her place.

---

[1] Accomplices of Jack the Ripper were alleged by the Home Secretary, Henry Matthews, to exist. On 23 November 1888, Matthews observed when answering a Parliamentary question on the offer of a reward for information, 'In the case of [Mary Jane] Kelly there were certain circumstances which were wanting in the earlier cases, and which make it more probable that there were other persons who, at any rate after the crime, had assisted the murderer.' (*The Jack the Ripper A–Z*, 3rd edition, Headline Books.)

• None of Mary Jane Kelly's family attend the funeral.

If Mary Jane Kelly lived, then what happened to her? you may ask. Sorry, but that is another story, another time.

Jack the Ripper was described as between thirty and forty by the eyewitnesses who were supposed to have seen him. James Maybrick was fifty in October 1888. I have been asked whether the discrepancy bothers me. The short answer is no.

A man living and working in Whitechapel would look far older for his years than a man who lived the way James Maybrick did. How old does Cher look, for example? Or Diana Ross? Roger Moore? I also had the privilege to meet Paul Daniel, editor of *Ripperologist*, and I defy anyone to tell me he looks a day over forty-five. Paul will not be offended when I say that he was sixty in 1997.

The last photograph taken of James Maybrick was in 1887. He had a fair complexion and red hair. He did not have a heavy five o'clock shadow.

Without doubt, he would have appeared younger than his years to the locals from Whitechapel.

As we saw in Chapter 18, Donald McCormick published a poem entitled 'Eight Little Whores' in 1959. He claimed that it was contained within Dr Thomas Dutton's diaries. This doctor had allegedly been engaged by Inspector Abberline to look at correspondence written by Jack the Ripper.

Whether supporters or critics of James Maybrick's diary, the 'experts' were unanimous: the poem was clearly 'echoed' in it.

Melvin Harris (again) claimed that Donald McCormick made the poem up.

I found that accusation quite odd. Donald's book has been based on a theory of eight murdered women. The poem clearly suggests that only six were. Donald, should he have intended to, surely would have concocted a poem that at least supported his theory.

Melvin Harris went further. He claimed that the Dutton

diaries were 'sheer fiction'. My research team were to prove him wrong, once more.

The *Daily Express* of 13 November 1935 published the following:

One of Britain's cleverest bacteriologists yesterday entered the West London surgery of Dr Thomas Dutton, the aged specialist who was found dead on the floor beside his bed on Monday, and looked at his old colleague's quarters with grief in his eyes.

Every room was littered with books, papers, and unpaid bills. Many had not been used for months. Dust lay thick on floors and furniture.

In extreme old age, Dr Thomas Dutton, friend of princes, brilliant physician, once wealthy, had lived on the borderline of poverty. He had cooked his own food, looked after his rooms and himself, scorning help. Few of his friends knew.

Two pounds was all the money he possessed. No banking account can be traced.

In death he faced a 'parish burial.' The friend who stood in his rooms yesterday has saved him from that. He had undertaken to pay all funeral expenses.

Unmethodical though he was in all that pertained to the mechanical side of living, there was one habit Dr Dutton never lost. A diary has been found that he kept faithfully for more than fifty years.

DUKE OF CLARENCE

It tells not only of his own medical activities, but records events of importance in the lives of the Royal family.

It goes back to the days when the Duke of Clarence (the King's older brother) was his friend; to the days when he himself was the possessor of a substantial fortune keeping his own hunters, playing an active part in the colourful social life of the Edwardians and the late Victorians.

In his diaries Dr Dutton revealed himself as an enthusiastic race-goer and backer, a keen student of crime and one intensely interested in the affairs of the greater world.

Such names as those of Sir Robert Perks, the engineer and Lady Cathcart figure in its pages.

The case of Mrs Rattenbury and her young chauffeur-lover, George Stoner, who killed her husband in their Bournemouth villa early this year, is commented on at length.

That Duke of Clarence, he pops up everywhere.

On November 17 1935, the *Empire News* carried the following:

TRAGIC LAST DAYS OF A BRILLIANT DOCTOR

A few days after the last murder committed by that fiend in human guise, 'Jack the Ripper,' and at a time when the scared but infuriated people in the Whitechapel district were crying out for the life of the assassin, there passed down the Whitechapel-road a man, carrying a small, black bag.

At once he was surrounded by a mob of people and violently hustled, and it required the united efforts of several police officers to save him from the crowd and take him along to Leman-street Police Station amidst cries of 'Jack the Ripper – Jack the Ripper.' Once inside the police station, however, a few minutes sufficed to prove that far from being the man who had murdered and mutilated no fewer than six women of the unfortunate class, the victim of this outcry was none other than a doctor working in the district who had endeavoured to assist the police by a little amateur detective work in connection with the crimes.

The man was Dr Thomas Dutton, and this week his dead body was found, lying on the floor beside his bed . . .

The *Daily Express* of 12 November 1935 published a curious article under the headline:

Detectives visited a surgery in Uxbridge Road, Shepherd's Bush W. last night and took away documents belonging to seventy-nine year old Dr Thomas Dutton . . .

No attempt is made by the newspaper to explain the reasons behind the detectives' visit.

Knowing that the diary is genuine helps us solve two Ripper conundrums.

On the night of the 'double event', a chalked message was found written on a wall in Goulston Street, just off Middlesex Street. On the floor, underneath the message, was a torn piece of Catharine Eddowes's apron, thereby convincing the authorities that the message had been written by the perpetrator of the crimes. The message read: 'The Juwes are The men That Will not be Blamed for Nothing . . .'[1]

The 'Juwes' spelling has been constantly debated, but it is worth noting that 'James', written with the letter 'a' open, can be read as 'Juwes'. Maybrick had written: '. . . if they are to insist that I am a Jew then a Jew I shall be'.

I do not believe that James was contemplating instant circumcision or planning a late bar mitzvah, but had merely devised another use for his name.

Knowing that the diary is genuine helps us solve another Ripper conundrum. The chalked message was discovered at 2.55 a.m. It was not there thirty-five minutes earlier. PC Edward Watkins had discovered the body of Catharine Eddowes at about 1.45 a.m. in Mitre Square, which is no more than two or three minutes from Goulston Street just off Middlesex Street. The 'missing' forty minutes has led to debate about whether the Ripper double-backed on himself. The answer is simple. James Maybrick goes back to his lodgings in Middlesex Street. He cleans himself up, collects all his belongings and waits for the commotion to die down. As he leaves, forty minutes later, he enters

---

[1] Mepo 1/48/5 (Commissioner's letter books).

Goulston Street, disposing of the piece of apron, the one piece of evidence that links him to the murder. He then chalks his 'funny Jewish joke'.

Even though Jack the Ripper has been identified as James Maybrick, I am sure that Ripperology will continue. I hope that, when so-called voices of authority start shouting hoax every time something is written that they don't like or agree with, they will be seriously questioned about what proof they have for such an attack. Proof, as we have seen, does not equal opinion.

23

'WHEN YOU HAVE ELIMINATED THE IMPOSSIBLE . . .'

THE DIARY OF JACK the Ripper *is* genuine and it *was* written by James Maybrick. However difficult it is to accept. It is a fact.

There is no other possibility? Let's see . . .

Even when the evidence told me that this leather-bound book, signed by the notorious Whitechapel murderer, was real, it was hard to believe. Very hard.

I do not blame or knock anyone who, after first reading it, believed this document to be a fake, a hoax or a forgery. I would not have blamed anyone alive in 1888 who thought that a man landing on the moon was nothing more than the crazy fantasy of a madman.

It was a safe bet to state that it was a fake. The Hitler diaries were; this must be.

Surely?

When I interviewed Dr David Forshaw in the early days of our investigation, he told me, 'When the experts start moving the goalposts, then you will know the diary is real.'

Even Manchester United would be banned from the Premier League if they moved the goalposts as often as the experts did.

Remember Kenneth Rendell? He moved from 1920 to 1991, despite the evidence of the team of scientists working for him.

Melvin Harris? Someone 'schooled in the 1920s or 30s' became a man or woman born in the 1950s.

At first, I could not understand how my heroes were

not, at the very least, prepared to examine this document in a serious and professional way.

I first felt the diary was a genuine document when, much to my horror, Hannah Koren said that it was 'impossible' to forge it. I had trusted Hannah's impartiality. Hannah knew one thing only: that, if the document was genuine, then I had to spend time and money on a long-term investment. It had been Michael Marx, a very close friend, who recommended Hannah. Michael knew that by doing so I would not make a mistake. Michael was right.

Hannah's statement that it was 'impossible' to fake such a document had been based on the complexities of the characteristics of the handwriting, which had been written fluently and naturally. Almost a year later, Hannah was to be filmed repeating her views.

Predictably, the detractors attacked Hannah's credibility. Unfairly. Even the debunkers must have realised that Hannah's integrity was beyond doubt.

I had told her, 'You say the diary cannot be forged. The author suggests he wrote this letter [the one dated 25 September and signed 'Jack The Ripper']. He must have. Prove he did.'

Hannah did not, because she could not. Hannah could not prove he did not, either. Hannah told the truth.

Hannah was asked to compare James Maybrick's will to both the diary and the Jack the Ripper letter of 25 September 1888. Hannah could not prove or disprove a connection. Hannah told the truth.

The debunkers were happy to accept all but her first report because it did not work for them. Fair? Consistent?

The handwriting of a sick, drug-addicted, sexual serial killer was highly complex. When you become 'two people' it is far too complicated for the majority of us to understand.

It is necessary to emphasise that Hannah Koren *never* said the diary *was* written by James Maybrick and/or that he was Jack the Ripper. She simply said that the diary was written 'spontaneously' and the characteristics displayed could not be re-created even by herself, and she knew what she was looking for. Remember those characteristics?

- Disturbed, possibly mentally
- Very strong imagination
- Fluctuating self-esteem. Varying from domineering to deprived
- Sexual problems – lack of satisfaction
- Problems with mother image
- Ambivalent feeling about father
- Much aggression – also towards self
- Multiple personality
- Lack of stability
- Changes his mind
- Dramatic sense – me as 'victim'
- Has ideas, is imaginative – but can't always execute
- Likes games – sees people as pawns
- On the outside he can control himself – inside is like a volcano which sometime will burst out
- The crosses – possibly there's a religious link
- No trust for others
- Hypochondria
- Stubborn
- Has had disappointments in the emotional area
- Very strong guilt feelings
- Compulsive thoughts – neuroses – repetitive
- Drugs or alcohol? Something physiological

There is no doubt that several, if not all, of the above would fit into the character and personality of Mr James Maybrick.

It would be fair to question whether the 'forger' could have had these characteristics as well, particularly as Michael Barrett claimed the handwriting was that of his ex-wife Anne Graham, who certainly does not fit Hannah's profile.

Paula Adamick, the journalist whose work was *not* published by the *Evening Standard*, once told me, 'If the diary had been "perfect", with the handwriting matching the will or the "Dear Boss" letter, and contained *specific* detail, I would not have believed it.'

Think about that. The author of the diary clearly knew the will and the letter sent to the police and dated 25 September existed. If it *was* a forgery, then the forger could have traced the will and the 'Dear Boss' letter in order to construct the diary. At the very least, wouldn't a forger have reconstructed the signature on one of the documents to sign off his masterpiece?

The detractors rest on the handwriting argument to insist that the diary is a 'modern forgery'. They make no attempt to explain why anyone would go to the trouble of producing such a document without attempting to reproduce, at the very least, a signature that exists in the public domain!

Furthermore, the 'forger', having written sixty-three pages, could have written just one more, in the same hand, on another sheet of paper. He could have signed it 'James Maybrick', passed it on to any one of his 'team', who could have then come forward to 'prove' the handwriting.

But the document is not forged.

I went to primary school in the late 1950s. I was taught italics to write a formal letter. My italic handwriting won me competitions, but it bore no resemblance to my natural hand. My ex-father-in-law, over ninety now, is able to write the most beautiful copperplate, but it bears no resemblance to any betting slip he may fill out! Even relatively normal, well-adjusted individuals will use different handwriting styles for different purposes.

There was no need for the author of the diary to 'forge' a signature that resembled those known to be either Jack the Ripper's or James Maybrick's. The author of the diary did not need to prove who he was to anyone. He knew. He was Jack the Ripper. He was James Maybrick.

Yes. It was Hannah's review of the diary which convinced me that I had to write off the financial investment already made on Jack the bloody Ripper, and conclude a deal with Robert Smith.

I studied Jack. Paul Begg was a first-rate tutor. So, later, were Martin Howells, Keith Skinner and Melvyn Fairclough.

Melvyn Fairclough has been underrated by other Ripperologists. Melvyn's knowledge of general history, the Bible, royalty and Freemasonry has proved invaluable. Melvyn's instinct to follow up Joseph Sickert's story, for which he was much criticised, will ultimately be shown to be right. I will add here, before my desperate co-authors try to suggest otherwise, that I do *not* believe the Abberline diary[1] was written by anyone other than someone very close to Joseph.

During my investigation, I met many of the Jack the Ripper authors. Donald Rumbelow, Colin Wilson, Martin Fido, Richard Whittington-Egan, Paul Begg ... The list could go on for ever. I asked each and every one, 'If the diary is a fake, tell me how it was done. Tell me who did it. Tell me when. *You* are the experts. Where did the information *within* the document come from? How was the watch forged?' And so on.

I even gave these learned gentleman creative freedom. 'Make it up,' I said.

I am sorry to disappoint the supporters of any previous author's theory, but not one of them could even suggest a scenario that made any sense.

After I had interviewed Anne and Billy Graham, it became even more difficult for the critics to knock the diary, particularly those who said it was a modern forgery written after 1987 or 1989. Anne claimed she first saw it in 1968 or 1969. Her dad said he saw it in 1943. If they were not telling the truth, then they were accepting that they might be charged with fraud.

The debunkers did not think about this at first. When they did, they would not address the obvious problem of Anne and Billy exposing themselves to possible prosecution.

---

[1] Three leather-bound diaries owned by Joseph Sickert which came to light in 1988 and were purported to be the diaries of Inspector Abberline. The diaries are widely believed to be forgeries.

Should it not now be understood why J.K. Stephen, royalty, Freemasonry and an official cover-up were always associated with Jack the Ripper? Why those Liverpool connections were really there? Why the Florence Maybrick trial was such a mystery to so many learned people? Why Mrs Maybrick spent fifteen years in prison for a crime for which she had never been tried?

On 7 February 1998, I was interviewed by Keith Skinner during an evening of debate at the Cloak and Dagger club in Whitechapel. It was nearly six years after the diary had become public knowledge. It was still being debated. Its authenticity was still being questioned. The attendance at the club was almost twice the average.

Keith stated that, of the Ripper experts, Melvin Harris, Martin Fido, Richard Whittington-Egan, Philip Sugden and Stewart Evans all still believed the diary to be a 'modern fake'.

Well. Knock me down and blow me over. Four of the five individuals in the previous paragraph have had a book published *since* Shirley Harrison's publication. The fifth, Martin Fido, went public on national radio to state his disbelief in the diary's authenticity some considerable time ago.

Although the room at the Cloak and Dagger that evening housed many notable historians, *not one* challenged the diary on any of the text contained within it.

Donald Rumbelow questioned whether the diary had had its paper scientifically analysed.

Martin Fido argued the handwriting of the diary versus the will.

Donald Rumbelow is not a scientist. Martin Fido is not a handwriting expert. They are competent historians and experts on the Whitechapel murders of 1888.

Why are notable authors on the subject of Jack the Ripper resorting to debating matters outside their own areas of expertise? Why are they not demonstrating to the world that this remarkable document contains historical information that *proves* it cannot be written by Jack the Ripper? Or, as historians, why won't they tell us where the diary contains information that *proves* it could not have been written by James Maybrick?

Why? Because they can't. They never will. They have shot their bullets. Shirley Harrison and I have repelled them. Competently, with historical documents to support our findings. We would not have been able to do so if the diary were a fake. We were able to because it is not. Whenever the diary has conflicted with historical belief, research has shown that it is the historians who are left wanting.

That night, 7 February 1998, Martin Fido made two statements that clarified how he continues to address the diary.

First, he claimed that the handwriting I discovered in Richmond, Virginia, belonging to James Maybrick was very 'similar' to the will purportedly signed by James Maybrick but nothing like the diary. According to Martin Fido, this 'proved' the diary was a modern fake.

What Mr Fido did not comment on:

- Whether the handwriting of one of those Virginia letters (reproduced in this book) bore any similarity to a letter signed by Jack the Ripper, sent to the Metropolitan Police and initialled by Chief Inspector Donald Swanson. The initials of Chief Inspector Swanson clearly indicate his serious interest in these letters, a fact that was discovered by me but disbelieved by most modern Ripperologists.
- Whether the handwriting of the Richmond, Virginia, letters does not match that of the 'natural' handwriting of James Maybrick that we discovered in the Bible that belonged to Sarah Ann Robertson.

Why did Mr Fido not address these questions?

Why do the detractors continue to answer only the questions that suit them?

Mr Fido's second point was to tell the audience that I was avoiding the issue of the authenticity of the diary by requesting that experts tell us how, when and why the diary was forged.

We will return to that point shortly.

In the meantime, let us play 'forgery' . . .

Our team of 'conspirators' must comprise at least Anne Graham, Mike Barrett, Billy Graham, eleven-year-old Caroline Barrett, Albert Johnson, Tony Devereux, Richard Bark-Jones (Barrett's solicitor), and Tom Cobbly and all.

One day, one of them suggests that a diary should be written, and signed 'Jack the Ripper'. As they come from Liverpool, James Maybrick seems a good candidate.

Someone must have also decided that, instead of a watch being 'found' with the diary, Albert would have purchased it a 'year ago'.

Now, they have to make sure that one of them understands Victorian English to the extent that they can even prove the *Oxford English Dictionary* wrong. Someone else has to learn the art of metallurgy in order to implant a piece of copper that is decades old into scratches that they make using a complex process. (Then the same people have J.O. engraved on the back instead of J.M.)

Another reads up on the psychopathology of serial killers. Another becomes an arsenic addict to convince doctors that they understand the effects of such a habit. Of course, knowledge of graphology is required, whether the public believes in it or not. Graphology experts interpret letters in a particular way, and our forgers have to ensure that they interpret them in the way they want them to.

Maybe it was Anne, or Billy, who suggested that a crash course in 'How to write in a way that an ultraviolet test does not detect recent writing' might be useful.

Who was going to learn how to speed up the transfer of ions from ink to paper? Oops! Someone had also better find out where to buy a Victorian ink that is still usable. If they could not, of course, it did not matter. Just make one up from an old formula using tap water. That will do.

Our team of geniuses achieves all this very quickly. Then they decide that perhaps it would be a good idea to look at the case histories of James and Florence Maybrick and Jack the Ripper. If James is in New York or Liverpool or anywhere at the time of Jack's crimes then their efforts so far would be a waste of time. Still, that's the way the cookie crumbles. They read every book, newspaper and Home Office file on the Whitechapel murderer. They have to achieve this without being seen. Perhaps that is not true. They may have collectively read and absorbed everything in one day, thereby not really being noticed.

To get to the Maybrick files before anyone else, our team of evil, greedy forgers arranges with someone on the inside to get material out. That way, nobody will know they have read them. Data is computerised.

As the team has the ability to absorb everything they read instantly, they are able to know which books have references that are wrong (like *The Jack the Ripper A–Z*), and avoid only that information.

Billy, having read, and become an expert in, all local history while doing shifts at Dunlop, is aware that James Maybrick's wife came out of prison and, by sheer fluke, called herself Mrs Graham. Although that is Billy's surname, the team decides not to reveal this to the world immediately, simply implying that there is a relationship in order to keep everyone in suspense. Instead, Tony Devereux agrees to die so that Mike can say the diary came from someone who could not be questioned.

Billy is perceptive. He considers that people may still not believe the diary, and also agrees to die. He does, of course, on his deathbed, tell the world a blatant lie in order to protect his daughter from any implication of a hoax.

Now, having gained enough scientific knowledge so that scientists would not be able to prove that the ink was put to paper between 1989 and 1992, and confirmed their tactics, they agree to start collating everything they can about the Ripper and James Maybrick.

Fortunately, although James Maybrick travelled all over the country, and visited his doctors something like twenty times in the autumn of 1888, and prescribed drugs were found all over the house, and he lived in Liverpool, none of his movements seemed to prove that he could not be in London at the time of the crimes.

This team of forgers were not just good: they were lucky, very lucky.

While they researched unnoticed at Colindale Library and the PRO, they discovered things that no other author had noticed:

That the letters FM were on the wall in the room where Mary Kelly was murdered. Write it into the diary. It fits, too. Lucky.

That the inverted Vs cut into Catharine Eddowes's face could look like an M. Write it into the diary. That fits, too. Lucky.

That an empty tin matchbox had been excluded from the list of Eddowes's belongings given to the media. Write it into the diary. Observant.

That a J as well as an M was on the envelope found at the scene of Annie Chapman's murder. Lucky. Write it into the diary.

And so on. And so on.

They must have met regularly to consolidate their research. It must have been a secret location, as nobody seems to have ever seen them together.

Imagine how happy they were when they realised that the first two letters and last two letters of James Maybrick make Jack. When they realised that evidence at the Florence Maybrick trial was suppressed – about James. And he had lived on the edge of Whitechapel. And worked there. And a drawing in the *Daily Telegraph* on 6 October 1888 looked just like him.

Somehow, Billy arranges for his sister and father to bear a striking resemblance to Florence Maybrick, and for his father to be born in a year that Florence was in England.

OK, so our nest of forgers are clever and lucky. They want to convince the world that the document is genuine, and make lots of money, so they make a reference to a letter and a will, one signed Jack the Ripper, the other James Maybrick.

And they decide not to attempt to copy the handwriting or even the signature. (Fortunately for our forgers, a letter signed Jack the Ripper, and another, found in Norfolk,

Virginia, signed James Maybrick show – shall we say – similarities.)

Then they decide to take their manuscript not to the *News of the World*, which might have offered them a great deal of money, but to a literary agent, who sells it to a publisher for a much smaller sum that they will have to share between them. That sum, divided amongst the 'nest of forgers', could not buy each a new Mini, so Mike decides to keep the lot, and nobody points the finger.

It was easy to say 'fake, modern forgery'. How transparent that not one person, not even the self-acclaimed 'King Hoaxbuster' Melvin Harris, has been able to explain how the diary was forged or expose the forgers.

Strange, also, that the critics did not accept the diary because the handwriting within it did not appear to match that of James Maybrick, but were prepared to accept that any of the 'nest of forgers' mentioned above wrote it, even though it did not match theirs either.

Almost every scientist, psychologist and handwriting expert was criticised during our investigation – by historians.

The Ripperologists knew, very early on, that there were details in the diary which have only been discovered since 1987. The information relating to Mary Kelly's heart was not published until 1989. If they accepted the scientific evidence, they would not have been able to explain the historical content and would have been forced to accept that the diary may be genuine.

So, the diary 'became' modern, and the scientists incompetent.

The information and wide range of knowledge required to construct both the diary and the watch was just not available to the people involved.

The 'forgery' scenario that I constructed above is not acceptable to Martin Fido. Nor is it acceptable to anyone with a basic understanding of this subject. Unfortunately, Martin Fido cannot create a scenario that answers *all* the questions. Neither can Melvin Harris, nor Philip Sugden, nor Richard Whittington-Egan nor Stewart Evans. That is why they made no attempt to do so in their books.

No, Mr Fido. It is not I who evade the issue of authenticity. I have openly debated all known criticisms of the diary. You, Mr Fido, and some of your colleagues, must sit down and discuss the document in a serious historical context.

Cynics Inc. will continue to find fault with the experts who disagree with them, and to hide behind the comparison of James Maybrick's will with the diary. Worse, they will not acknowledge that other samples of Maybrick's handwriting do not match the will either.

I have stated publicly that Messrs Fido, Harris, Sugden, Whittington-Egan and Evans (amongst others) are 'frightened' of the diary. Keith Skinner asked me why I think that. I will explain to you as I explained to him.

All the gentlemen referred to in the above paragraph have, one way or another, publicly stated that they believe the diary to be a modern forgery. All made that observation before the first edition of my book was published. Before all the evidence had been examined. Many (not all) of those gentlemen had made the same observation before Shirley Harrison's book was published. At least two publicly debunked the diary before they had seen it, or even a photocopy of it.

Then again, they had their own books to be published.

The cynics are angry about this diary. They do not debate. They scream and bellow 'fake', 'hoax' and 'a waste of time'. Whether my investigation was going to prove a forgery or not, it was never, as Paul Begg identified early on, going to be 'a waste of time'. Who, when, how and why were all questions that needed to be answered.

The debunkers are frightened because there is nobody hiding any more. Therefore, they have nobody to hide behind. If they had been right and the diary is a forgery, then we know who the forger is, don't we?

Anne Graham. With or without the help of her ex-husband, Mike Barrett, and Albert Johnson and so on.

Ms Graham, however, has *never* said that the diary is genuine. Nor has she said it was written by James Maybrick. Only that she first saw it in 1968 or 1969. Her father said he first saw it in 1943, just two years after Florence Maybrick died.

If Billy and Anne were lying, the former on his deathbed, then they must have forged it.

On 7 February 1998, I told the attendees that the historians must accept that, *if* the diary was forged, then Anne Graham, her father and Albert Johnson forged it somehow.

Therefore, for six years at least, Anne and Albert have outwitted scientists, graphologists and tens of authors who have written on both Jack the Ripper and the Florence Maybrick trial. How about linguists? Experts in the fields of ion migration and infrared, and so on?

OK, experts, if it is a forgery: you know the players, so go prove it! Anne Graham's, her father Billy's and Mike Barrett's handwriting all exist. Go check it. At the same time, perhaps you will take to the forensic handwriting expert of your choice the letters published on pages 306–307 in this book.

Anne Graham and Albert Johnson are not scientists; nor are they historians. They are hard-working people, and both care deeply about their families.

They had never met until after the diary and watch had become public.

Tell us, cynics, how and when Anne accessed the information needed to construct this document. Tell us, cynics, how and when Albert learnt enough about metallurgy to know that two scientists would be fooled.

Richard Whittington-Egan once said to me, 'There comes a time when circumstantial evidence is no longer circumstantial.'

The circumstantial evidence that we have discovered to support the authenticity of both the watch and the diary is overwhelming. Perhaps, for some, it is not enough.

For those, I ask this:

Why did a security report on Anne Graham, sent to me in June 1994, state: '. . . we are able to confirm that all medical records (with regards Anne Elizabeth Graham) were officially destroyed in 1976. On inquiring into the reason we discovered that this was "due to the security risk associated with the subject"'?

The report continued: '. . . all other records relative to the maiden identity of this subject have been deleted from all public records. We can confirm that only government officers would have the authority to destroy such records.'

Anne does not have a criminal record. She was shocked when I showed her the report. To confirm its authenticity, she visited her doctor shortly after her father died and asked him if he could obtain the records. He could not. They no longer existed.

I had wanted to publish this information in the hardback edition of this book but, due to my respect for Anne and her family, I requested her permission to do so. Anne asked to think about it, but the delay prevented publication.

The Ripperologists who shouted 'modern fake' too early can never admit the diary is genuine as their reputations as historians would be tarnished for ever. They would rather have the world believe the inconceivable and illogical scenario that various families in Liverpool and Whittlesey have conspired to deceive the world.

However, it is simple logic that gives us the undeniable proof that both artefacts, the diary and the watch, are genuine.

It is impossible for the diary to have been written since 1989.

It is impossible that the marks in the watch owned by Albert Johnson were made after 1989.

It is impossible for anyone to have access to the detailed knowledge contained in the diary before 1989.

Unless you were Jack the Ripper.

Unless you were James Maybrick.

... when you have eliminated the impossible,
whatever remains, however improbable,
must be the truth.

Sir Arthur Conan Doyle

APPENDICES

Appendix 1

The following is the full text of the statement given by Ronald Murphy on 20 October 1993.

I RONALD GEORGE MURPHY am the Proprietor of STEWARTS, Jewellers of Liscard, Wallasey, Wirral. [Private address and telephone number have been withheld.] I sold the MAYBRICK watch to ALBERT JOHNSON on or about the 14th July 1992 for a sum in the region of £250.00. There is nothing unusual that I can recall about the watch, other than the fact that it was hallmarked 1846. I had owned the watch for a couple of years prior to selling it. It had been given to me by my father-in-law, who had a Jewellers Shop himself in Lancaster. At first it did not work, so I kept it in a draw [sic] and then eventually some time before selling it, I sent it through to MR DUNDAS, a Watch Repairer at The Clock Workshop, 4 Grange Road, West Kirby, Wirral. Mr Dundas fixed the watch and sent it back to me. The watch case was then cleaned and the watch put in the window – and Mr Johnson purchased it. Having now seen the watch for the first time since selling it, I am almost certain that the markings were present when the watch was sold but they were not markings that I would have taken notice of. I have been given the impression by certain people in the Press that there were engravings in it, which I had not noticed – but this is not the case.

Appendix 2

Letter from Charles Ratcliffe to John Aunspaugh (7 June 1889). Reproduced from the Trevor Christie Collection.

Dear friend John,

I know it was a crushing blow to you when you received my cable that poor James Maybrick had passed on to the 'other shore', you and James always had such a mutual admiration society for each other, and I know how you will miss him.

I am sure you have read from the different papers throughout the country that his wife was arrested and is now in jail, charged with poisoning him with arsenic, which caused his death.

This was a great shock to me. I had been expecting a tragedy in the family, but was looking for it from the other party. James had gotten wise to the Flatman Hotel affair, and I was expecting him to plug Brierley at any time.

Well here is a resume to date. James attended the Wirral races April 27th and came home sick. He began dosing himself as usual, but did not seem to improve, so called in Dr Humphrey. Humphrey doctored him for several days.

James seemed to grow worse then better until May 6th he seemed very sick with vomiting and badly coated tongue. Humphrey then called in Dr Carter for consultation, but the next day James seemed much better. However, the next day he grew steadily worse, and at 8.30 p.m. May 11th he died.

Now for the female serpents. Of course old lady Briggs had to make her appearance at Battlecrease, as soon as James got sick. Yapp saw some fly papers soaking in a bowl in Mrs Maybrick's room. She told Mrs Briggs fly paper had arsenic in it and she believed Mrs Maybrick was poisoning James with arsenic.

Two days before James died, Mrs Maybrick gave Yapp a letter to mail addressed to Brierley. This was too good a thing for Yapp to miss so she opens it and reads to Mrs Briggs. Mrs Briggs at once sent for Edwin and shows him the letter.

Edwin, deep in the mire himself, pays no attention to it and returns to Liverpool. When Mrs Briggs finds Edwin will do nothing she telegraphs to Michael in London and he comes at once. She shows him the letter Mrs Maybrick wrote to Brierley.

Old Dr Humphreys made a jackass of himself. After James died he and Dr Carter expected to make out the death certificate as acute inflammation of the stomach. After Humphreys had a conversation with Michael he refused to make a certificate to that effect, but said there was strong symptoms of arsenical poisoning, though Dr Carter still insisted that it should be inflation of the stomach.

Now wouldn't that cork you? A musical composer instructing a physician how to diagnose his case.

Michael wanted a post-mortem examination. Humphreys and Carter assisted by Dr Barron performed it. They found no arsenic. Michael was still not satisfied and after James had been buried ten days his body was exhumed and all organs sent to a chemist. The chemist found no arsenic in the stomach, very small amount in the intestines, but a good bit in the liver and the kidneys.

Michael, the son-of-a-bitch, should have his throat cut. Mrs Maybrick was sick in bed when James died. He had only been dead a few hours when Michael forced her to get up and go with Tom to Liverpool on a trivial affair which he represented to her as being most important. While she was gone Michael and two policemen searched the house, and in her room they claim to have found quantities of arsenic, thirteen love letters from Edwin, seven from Brierley, and five from Williams.

I always knew the madam was dumb, but I must frankly admit I did not consider her that dumb as to leave her affairs accessible to any who choosed to penetrate.

I am sure Yapp and Mrs Briggs had gone through everything at any time. When Mrs Maybrick returned from Liverpool she was completely prostrated and went to bed, was at once arrested and placed under guard in her own room. No one knew anything about this. Michael then took possession of Battlecrease and put Mrs Briggs in charge.

My wife and myself called and was told by Mrs Briggs that Mrs Maybrick was too sick to receive any company. Sutton and his wife called, Holloway and his wife, Hienes and his wife and numerous others. They were all told the same thing. No one could see Mrs Maybrick.

Six days after, Liverpool was thunder struck by the announcement that Mrs Maybrick had been arrested and jailed on suspicion that she had poisoned her husband with arsenic which caused his death. Mrs Sutton and Mrs Holloway came to my house in Mrs Suttons carriage.

My wife and I got into the carriage and we four at once went to the jail. Mrs Maybrick presented a most pitiful and deplorable picture. She showed she had been very ill and was yet a sick woman, eyes were sunken, hair dishevelled, dirty and filthy.

She told a most pathetic story and her appearance surely did substantiate the proof of her statement. She said when Michael took possession and put Mrs Briggs in charge she was subjected to all kinds of insults and ill treatment by Mrs Briggs and the servants.

She was not allowed to have any communication with her friends. She was cursed and given impudent answers whenever she made a request of them. That she would lay in bed all day with only being given a cup of cold coffee and cold dry toast.

They would not help her out of bed when she needed attention. She was not able to get out of bed alone and she just layed there in her own filth and they would not change her bed. Filth was all over her and she smelled horrible.

Mrs Sutton went home at once, got a tub and some clean clothes. She and my wife gave Mrs Maybrick a good hot bath and put clean clothes on her. We got her a good soft mattress for the jail bunk and clean bed clothes.

The cotton broker's wives take it turn about to go every day to the jail, carry her a good meal and see that she is kept clean.

If they had only found the arsenic in Mrs Maybrick's room, as James was such an arsenic dope I don't think they could have proven anything on her, but finding all those love letters as a motive it is going hard with her.

Edwin is in bed with 'nervous prostration.' Tom and Michael are seeing to it that he leaves England, and Michael says Edwin's letters will never be produced in court. Brierley immediately evaporated from England when it was made public Mrs Maybrick's arrest. Williams says his letters to Mrs Maybrick will never be brought into court.

Sutton tells me he is sailing for the US in three weeks. He can give you as much better verbal account that I could write.

Regards to all the firm
Chas Ratcliffe

Appendix 3

Hannah Koren has an impressive armoury of qualifications (see Chapter 16, Impossible):

EDUCATION

B.Sc. in Management, Touro University, New York (1985)
Certified Graphologist, USA (1978)
AAHA – American Association of Handwriting Analysts
Certified Graphologist, HAI, USA (1977)
Certified Graphologist, ABA, USA (1978)

EXPERIENCE

- Professional graphologist since 1973.
- The active Director of the Graphology Institute since January 1976. The institute has branches in Haifa, Tel-Aviv, London and Sydney.
- Vice president of AAHA, since 1990, and in charge of the Israeli branch of AAHA.
- A member and guest speaker to the Graphology Association of the National Society for Graphology in New York and to the AAHA.
- A member of NADA – National Association of Document Examiners (1990).
- A member of and a guest speaker to the Graphological Society of San Francisco (1990).
- A guest speaker for BIG – the British Institute of Graphology (1991).
- A member of and a guest speaker for the Graphology Society, England (1991).
- Advanced and refresher courses in the USA regarding forgery and comparative handwriting.
- A lecturer on graphology in courses, workshops and

seminars for various institutions and graphological associations in Israel and around the world. Among them are the Israeli Defence Ministry, Israeli Police and Defence force.

- Congresses: Chicago 1989, Cambridge 1991.
- A lecturer in graphology in the Popular University and in the Institute of Psychology in Haifa from 1975 until 1981.
- A regular contributor to the Israeli IDF radio programme on graphology.
- Author of *Graphology*, Massada Books, 1983.
- Author of *The Secret Self*, NY, Adams Books, 1987.
- A forensic document examiner for the Israeli Ministry of Justice and the Israeli Social Security Services since 1985.
- Appears frequently in court as an expert graphologist since 1980.
- More than 250,000 handwriting samples from Israel and all over the world have been assessed in Hannah Koren's institute of graphology, at various levels, from preliminary screening and up to executive level analysis.

Appendix 4a

THE WILL held at Somerset House

Liverpool 25th April 1889 In case I die before having made a regular & proper will in legal form, I wish this to be taken as my last will & testament.

I leave & bequeath all my wordly possessions, of whatever kind or description, including furniture, pictures, wines, linen & pleats, Life Insurances, cash, shares, property, in fact everything I possess in trust with my Brothers Michael Maybrick & Thomas Maybrick, for my two Children James Chandler Maybrick and Gladys Eveleyn Maybrick. The furniture I desire to remain intact & to be used in furnishing a home which can be shared by my widow and children but the furniture is to be the childrens. I further desire that all moneys be invested in the names of the above Trustees (Michael & Thomas Maybrick) & the income of same used

for the childrens benefit & Education such education to be left
to the discretion of said Trustees.

My Widow will have for her portion of my Estate the
Policies on my life, say £500 with the Scottish Widows Fund
and £2000 with the Mutual Reserve Fund Life Association of
New York, both Policies being made out in her name. The
Interest on this £2500 together with the £125 a year which
she receives from her New York property will make a
provision of about £125 a year, a sum although small will yet
be the means of keeping her respectably.

It is also my desire that my Widow shall live under the same
roof with the children so long as she remains my Widow.

If it is legally possible I wish the £2500 of Life Insurance
on my life in my wifes name to be invested in the names of
the said Trustees, but that she should have the sole use of the
interest thereof during her lifetime, but at her death the
principal to revert to my said Children, James Chandler &
Gladys Eveleyn Maybrick.

Witness my hand & seal this
twenty fifth day of April 1889.

Signed by the Testator in the presence of us who at his
request in his presence and in the presence of each other have
herunto affixed our names as Witnesses

Geo R Davidson
Geo. Smith
James Maybrick

Appendix 4b

Extracts from MacDougall, pages 203–4

MacDougall's extract is headed 'The Will' and is dated
Liverpool 25th April 1889:

> In case I die before having made a regular and proper will in
> legal form, I wish this to be taken as my last will and
> testament. I leave (*1)[1] all my worldly possessions, of what

---

[1] I shall use this convention of an asterisk and a number to point out
differences between the two wills, which are listed below.

(*2) kind or description, including furniture, pictures, wines, linen, and plate, life insurances, cash, shares, property – (*3) in fact, everything I possess, in trust with my brothers Michael Maybrick and Thomas Maybrick for my two children, James Chandler Maybrick and Gladys Evelyn (*4) Maybrick. The furniture I desire to remain intact, and to be used in furnishing a home which can be shared by my widow and children, but the furniture is to be the children's. I further desire that all moneys be invested in the names of the above trustees (Michael and Thomas Maybrick), and the income of same used for the children's benefit and education, such education to be left to the discretion of said trustees. My widow will have for her portion of my estate the policies on my life, say, £500 with the Scottish Widows Fund, and £2,000 with the Mutual Reserve Fund Life Association of New York, both policies being (*5) in her name. The interest on this £2,500, together with the £125 a year which she receives from her New York property, will make a provision of about £125 a year, a sum which, (*6) although small, will yet be the means of keeping her respectable (*7). It is also my desire that my widow shall live under the same roof with the children so long as she remains my widow. If it is legally possible, I wish the £2,500 of life insurance on my life, in my wife's name, to be invested in the names of the said trustees, but that she should have the sole use of the interest thereof during her lifetime, but at her death the principal to revert to my said children James Chandler Maybrick (*8) and Gladys Evelyn (*9) Maybrick.

Witness my hand and seal this

Twenty-fifth day of April, 1889, JAMES MAYBRICK

Signed by the testator in the presence of us, who, at his request and (*10) in the presence of each other, have hereunto affixed our names as witnesses, Geo. R. Davidson, Geo. Smith

The affidavit of due execution filed T.E. Paget, District Registrar at Liverpool on the 29th July, 1889.

Administration (with the will annexed) of the personal estate of James Maybrick, late of the city of Liverpool, and of

Riverdale Road, Aigburth, in the county of Lancaster deceased, was granted to Michael Maybrick and Thomas Maybrick the brothers, the universal legatees in trust named in the said will; they have been first sworn, no executor being named in the said will.

Personal Estate, gross	£5,016 1 0
Personal Estate, net	£3,770 16 0¾

LAYTON, STEEL AND SPRINGMAN,
Solicitors, Liverpool

There are a number of significant differences between the will referred to by MacDougall and the will currently filed at Somerset House (marked with a *)

- 1. The word 'bequeath' is missing from the Mac-Dougall transcript.
- 2. 'What' in MacDougall becomes a 'whatever' in will at Somerset House.
- 3. '-' in MacDougall becomes a ',' in Somerset House will.
- 4/9. In will at Somerset House 'Evelyn' is spelt incorrectly, as 'Eveleyn'.
- 5. The words 'made out' are missing from MacDougall.
- 6. The word 'which' is missing from Somerset House will.
- 7. 'Respectable' becomes 'respectably' in Somerset House will.
- 8. 'Maybrick' is missing from Somerset House will.
- 10. The words 'in his presence' are missing from MacDougall.

Appendix 5

In the *Portsmouth Evening News* of 4 July 1894, Arthur Conan Doyle, creator of Sherlock Holmes, wrote of the 25 September letter:

> I remember going to Scotland Yard Museum and looking at the letter which was received by the police and which

purported to come from the Ripper. Of course, it may have been a hoax, but there were reasons to think it was genuine, and in any case it was well to find out who wrote it. It was written in red ink in a clerkly hand ... The most obvious point was that the letter was written by someone who had been in America. It began 'Dear Boss', and contained the phrase, 'fix it up', and several others which are not usual with Britishers. Then we have the quality of the paper and handwriting, which indicate that the letters were not written by a toiler. It was good paper, and a round easy, clerkly hand. He was, therefore, a man accustomed to the use of the pen.

The 25 September letter does not contain the words 'fix it up'. It does contain the words 'they wont fix me just yet'. Was he, too, relying on his memory? Did he see the actual letter or one of the many Ripper letters in the Scotland Yard files? Conan Doyle also uses the phrase 'the letters'. The plural use suggests he might have been looking at several letters at the time. But clearly there is some confusion here.

It should be noted here that Americanisms in the 25 September letter were under discussion long before Conan Doyle's comments. In a letter sent to the *Daily Telegraph*, published 4 October 1888, a reader made the following observation:

The writer is probably an American or an Englishman who has mixed with our cousins on the other side of the Atlantic. 'Boss', 'Fix me', 'Shant quit', and 'Right away' are American forms of expression.

Appendix 6

Pray For Me

A flash of light on my fates night,
Sent me tumbling down a cloudy stairway,
Buffeting down as a windlass kite,
On to a rainbow fairway.

Snow white down, Snow white down,
Everything silent and still,
Snow white down engulfs my surround,
I shudder with inner chill.

I hear the beat of the drum,
And the hum of the angel choir.
A ghostly hand beckons me to come,
With the sounds of a roaring fire.

White misty path drawn along,
To my left the shudder of fear.
To my right the angle song,
As demon shapes appear.

Blues and blacks swirling around,
Inside my hovering soul.
Demons Black, Angels blue so bound,
As the frisky tethered foal
Dressed in hooded stoles,
Clearing turning a brilliant hue.
A Jury on Golden Thrones,
Or Ten fold few.

Surrounded by rainbow cloud,
Brilliant stars and radiant flowers.
Mystic colours all around,
Is the Lord that is ours.

The book before him on table gold,
He stares at with eyes so blue.
The book of a Forty Five year old,
That his eyes pierce right through.

Trying to find what is due,
The Lord already knows what goes.
The flickering pages of black and blue,
All my highs and lows.

Pictures of my Life on every page,
My past Good, My past Shame.
The Calm and the Rage,
The Aim of my Life Stain.

The Jury, Ten fold few stood,
The pages flickered, Nothing to hide.
No face could be seen under the dark black hood,
As the last page flickered to when I Died.

Thundering votes they did take,
Five for Heaven, Five for Hell.
As before me my hovering soul began to shake,
A Hung Jury at the Judgement bell.

Bright Blue eyes stared into mine,
I would hear his Judgement soon.
But those eyes filled me with heavenly Divine,
That I may hear Heaven Gardens Tune.

Demons hold my left hand,
Angels hold my right.
The Roaring fires of Hells Band,
And the glory of Heavens Garden sight.
Then came the Peals of Prayer,
From those I love.
Echoing down my cloudy stairs,
For my Soul, from above.

The smile was Radiant, From Him so Divine,
My Shadows depart to Brilliant Sunshine.
Powers of Prayer has won the day,
That has pointed My Soul the Heavens Way.

A.E. Johnson
(Reproduced with the kind permission of Albert Johnson)

Appendix 7

In March 1931 a former police constable, Robert Spicer, alleged in the *Daily Express* that on the night of the murders of Stride and Eddowes he arrested a man he firmly believed was Jack the Ripper. The man was caught in Heneage Court off Heneage Street, off Brick Lane, talking to a prostitute called Rosy. He had blood on his shirt cuffs. Spicer claimed that he took the man back to the police station, where there were eight or nine inspectors working on the Ripper case. The man said he was a Brixton doctor, but the bag he was carrying was not searched and, to the utter amazement of Spicer, he was allowed to go free with no more ado. Spicer was ticked off for arresting a respectable man and was thereafter so disappointed and disillusioned with the police that his heart was no longer in his job. If the man arrested was Jack the Ripper he must have left the police station wearing a grin. What fools he must have thought the police were, which is exactly what the author of the diary wrote: 'They remind me of chickens with their heads cut off running fools with no heads *ha ha*. It is nice to laugh at bastards and fools they are indeed.'

The Heneage Court reference makes it clear that the author of the poem is claiming to be the man Spicer arrested. The author of the diary also penned 'The Doctors and the Jews will get all the blame'.

Appendix 8

Peter McClelland was given permission by Mr Odell of the PRO at Kew (now dead) to look through the original Home Office Ripper files. Although the files are now on microfilm, Mr McClelland was having difficulty in reading the microfilmed documents and was allowed access to the originals. He found the 17 September letter in a report folder that had become stuck over the years. He gently opened it with his thumbnail. The letter is in blue ink. This led McClelland to conclude that because it was never made public the writer, believing that he had made no impact on the Home Office, sent his next letters in red ink to the news agency.

Although highly unlikely, it is possible that this letter was placed in the files by a modern-day hoaxer, making its connection to the 25 September letter and the Lusk letter a complete fabrication. At the time of going to print the PRO were investigating the matter but it has not been possible for us to interview Mr McClelland about his discovery.

GLOSSARY

Aunspaugh, Florence Daughter of John Aunspaugh. She stayed with the Maybricks in the summer of 1888. She was about eight at the time.

Aunspaugh, John Close friend and business associate of James Maybrick.

Baillie, Margaret Family friend of Baroness von Roques. Florence claimed that she stayed at her home while meeting Alfred Brierley at Flatman's Hotel in London.

Baillie Knight, John Nephew of Margaret Baillie. In his summing up of the trial, Judge Fitzjames Stephen wrongly accused Florence of also having an affair with him.

Bancroft, George Close friend of James Maybrick. He provided an affidavit after the trial that confirmed Maybrick's habitual use of drugs.

Bark-Jones, Richard Solicitor representing Michael Barrett at the time of his 'confession'. Mr Bark-Jones claimed he had evidence in his possession that proved Barrett's claim of forgery was untrue.

Barrett (née Graham), Anne Elizabeth The (illegitimate) great-granddaughter of Florence Maybrick. Anne first saw the diary in 1968 or 1969 when her father was moving house after having decided to marry for a second time. The diary returned to her in 1989, when her father moved into sheltered accommodation following the death of his second wife.

Barrett, Caroline Daughter to Michael Barrett and Anne Elizabeth Graham.

Barrett, Lynne Sister to Michael Barrett. After Mike and Anne had separated, it was Anne who Lynne called to ask her to stop the 'hounding' of the Barrett family. This was confirmation that there was family knowledge that the diary did emanate from Anne.

Barrett, Michael ('Bongo') The man responsible for taking the diary to a literary agent, Doreen Montgomery. After Anne left him, he claimed that he forged the diary. This was either an attempt to discredit Anne or a last attempt to display his love for her. (It is possible that Mike, at this stage, believed Anne *had* forged the diary. Was his confession an attempt to take the rap?)

Barrett, Susan Sister to Michael Barrett.

Bills, Alice The informant of Sarah Ann Robertson's a.k.a. Maybrick's death in 1927.

Bills (later Parkinson), Barbara Daughter of Alice Bills. Barbara has in her possession a Bible inscribed by James Maybrick to Sarah Ann Robertson and dated 1865. The transcription begins 'To My Darling Piggy'. Although the Bible has impeccable provenance, the handwriting does not match (visibly) either the diary or the will purported, in both cases, to be written by James Maybrick.

Blackiston ('otherwise Conconi'), Gertrude Probably an illegitimate daughter of Sarah Ann Robertson, who witnessed Gertrude's marriage in 1895. The birth and death certificates of Gertrude Blackiston cannot be traced.

Bond, Alan Living great-grandson of Richard Ellison, whose family was inextricably linked to the Maybricks.

Borrows, Elizabeth (Illegitimately) related to Henry Stanley Flinn. Anne Graham's grandfather, William, was the informant on her death certificate as 'cousin'.

Brierley, Alfred A business associate and friend to James Maybrick who 'turned'. His well-known affair with Florence Maybrick, and in particular the events that took place at Flatman's Hotel in March 1889, probably led to the guilty verdict given against Florence Maybrick at her trial later that year. Alfred Brierley is almost certainly the second 'whoremaster' referred to in the diary.

Bromilow, Irene Mother of Anne Elizabeth Graham.

Brooks, Mrs Jo Living great-niece of Alice Yapp.

Case (née Robertson), Christiana a.k.a. Christiana Conconi According to census records, the aunt of Sarah Ann Robertson. Sarah appears to have lived with Christiana almost her entire life. The fact that neither Sarah's birth certificate nor baptismal records can be found suggests that maybe she was the illegitimate daughter of Christiana.

Cheeseman, Muriel The last known informant of the Flinn family.

Conconi, Thomas David Husband to Christiana, who was Sarah Ann Robertson's 'aunt'. It was from his will that we learnt that James Maybrick and Sarah Ann Robertson were considered man and wife, even by their own family. There is no known record of such a marriage taking place.

Coney, Edward Second husband to Margaret Minetta Maybrick. Married in 1942.

Crawley, Elizabeth Grandmother of Albert Johnson, owner of the Maybrick watch. Suspected illegitimate daughter of James Maybrick and Emma Parker (Mrs John Over).

Davidson, George R. James Maybrick's best friend. Found dead in suspicious circumstances.

Dean, Alice Stepdaughter of William Graham.

Devereux, Tony Friend of Michael Barrett. Handed the diary to Mike, with the words 'Do something with it'.

Dodd, Paul Living owner of Battlecrease House, the home of James and Florence Maybrick at the time of the Whitechapel murders.

Du Barry, Madam a.k.a. Baroness von Roques (née Caroline Elizabeth Ingraham) Mother of Florence Maybrick. Reported to have possibly bought a Maybrick diary in 1889. Pursued Alice Yapp for at least five years.

Dundas, Timothy The man who apparently repaired the Maybrick watch. He has, however, described it as both 'black and white' and 'gold' on different occasions.

Eastaugh, Dr Nicholas Examined the ink in the diary and concluded that 'there was nothing in the ink inconsistent with the Victorian date'.

Ellison (née Daniels), Ada Grandmother of Norma Meagher. Married Richard Maybrick Ellison.

Ellison (later Maybrick), Elizabeth Grandmother of Brian Maybrick, married to John Maybrick. Daughter of Richard Ellison.

Ellison, Florence Ridehalgh Great-aunt to Norma Meagher. Her son, Arthur, is the nephew of Boris Karloff. Daughter of Richard Ellison.

Ellison, Martha Maybrick The first Ellison to be born with the curious middle name of Maybrick. Daughter of Richard Ellison.

Ellison, Norman Father of Norma Meagher. Son of Ada Ellison and Richard Maybrick Ellison.

Ellison, Olga Maybrick Claimed to be the illegitimate descendant of Michael Maybrick. Daughter of Richard Maybrick Ellison. Aunt to Norma Meagher.

Ellison, Richard 'Father' of the first Maybrick Ellisons. Married Jane Whalley.

Ellison, Richard Maybrick First male Ellison given the middle name Maybrick. Son of Richard Ellison. Grandfather of Norma Meagher.

Ellison, Vincent Maybrick Uncle to Norma Meagher. Family tradition claims that Vincent was angry when Olga Maybrick Ellison's headstone was carved without 'Maybrick'. Son of Richard Maybrick Ellison.

Flinn, Henry Stanley Suspected lover of Florence (née Chandler) Maybrick in or around 1879. His family were wealthy ship owners. Anne Graham's father would visit his grave frequently, often taking Anne with him. 'He is family . . .' Billy would tell Anne.

Formby, Elizabeth William Graham's mother-in-law from his second marriage. Affectionately remembered as 'Ganny' by Billy Graham.

Grady (née Cooper), Jeanette A Whittlesey Maybrick. Daughter of Rose Ellen Maybrick.

Graham, Adam Officially the father of William Graham. This is highly unlikely according to the testimonies of both Billy and Mary Graham, Adam's 'paper' grandchildren.

Graham (née Spence), Alice Wife of Adam Graham.

Graham, Billy Father of Anne Graham. In all probability the illegitimate grandson of Florence Maybrick and Henry Stanley Flinn. Billy first saw the diary in 1943, when returning for three weeks from the war. It was the first time he had been home since 1938. Billy's personal recollections alone make nonsense of the claim that the diary was a modern forgery.

Graham (née Formby), Edith William Graham's second wife. Step-mother to Billy and Mary Graham.

Graham, Harry Billy Graham's older brother who died aged seven.

Graham (née Grimes), Maggie Billy's second wife. It was when Anne Graham was packing up her father's belongings just prior to the marriage that she saw the diary for the first time.

Graham, Mary Billy Graham's (living) sister.

Graham, Rebecca William Graham's first wife. Rebecca had been married before. Her first husband was killed. She married William as Rebecca Jones.

Graham, William The illegitimate son of Florence Maybrick and Henry Stanley Flinn. William was asked to leave home by his 'paper' parents when he was eleven years old. He was told 'the money had run out'. William first went to Ireland but returned to Liverpool to be educated. Father to Billy and Mary, grandfather to Anne.

Hamer, T. A. Attended the funerals of both James Maybrick and Henry Stanley Flinn.

Hartnett, Ethel Daughter-in-law of Hannah Reed. Ethel was able to identify the picture we discovered of Sarah Ann Robertson as Sarah had attended Ethel's wedding. Ethel also identified the actual address the photograph was taken. The picture positively linked the Whittlesey Maybricks with Sarah Ann Robertson.

Hartnett (née Reed), Hannah Lived with Sarah Ann Robertson.

Hartnett, Nellie Daughter of Hannah Hartnett.

Hartnett, William Husband to Ethel. Son of Hannah Hartnett.

Jepson (née Maybrick), Annie A Whittlesey Maybrick. The youngest of the five girls, Annie has never believed that Margaret Minetta was her true mother. Indeed, her birth certificate claims her mother's name was Shelgrave.

Jepson, Peter Son of Annie Jepson (née Maybrick).

Johnson, Albert E. Owner of the Maybrick watch. Grandson of Elizabeth Crawley. Albert no longer denies he is a descendant of James Maybrick.

Johnson (née Somers), Dora Mother of Albert Johnson. Suspected (illegitimate) granddaughter of James Maybrick.

Johnson, Robert ('Robbie') Brother of Albert Johnson.

Johnson, Tracey Daughter of Albert Johnson.

Johnson, Valerie Wife of Albert Johnson.

Lefevre, George and John Registrars of the Whittlesey Maybrick's births and deaths. Clearly aware of the discrepancies, they have recently been criticised by the OPCS.

McKay, William Witness to the marriages of both Elizabeth Taylor (née Crawley) and Bessie Jane Over.

Maine (née Maybrick), Amy Daughter of Edwin Maybrick. Her daughter was last known to be alive and living in Australia, but attempts to contact her through solicitors proved unfruitful.

Mattin, Charles First husband to Margaret Minetta Maybrick.

Maybrick, Brian Grandson of John Maybrick, who was first cousin to James Maybrick.

Maybrick, David William Walsall, West Midland Maybrick. No records exist of either his birth or death. Father to Leonard Maybrick.

Maybrick, Edwin Younger brother of James Maybrick. According to a letter from Charles Ratcliffe to John Aunspaugh, Edwin was Florence Maybrick's lover before Alfred Brierley. Edwin was also James's partner in the cotton business. Edwin was in the United States during the Autumn of Terror and returned on 25 April 1889.

Maybrick, Elizabeth Susannah ('Lizzie') A Whittlesey Maybrick. Lizzie was the eldest of the children born to Margaret Minetta Maybrick. Lizzie is the young woman photographed alongside Sarah Ann Robertson. Born Woolerson.

Maybrick, Emily Minetta A Whittlesey Maybrick. Born Woolstone.

Maybrick (née Chandler), Florence a.k.a. Mrs Graham ('Bunny') Wife of James Maybrick. Born in Mobile, Alabama, USA. Florence was twenty-six, James forty-nine, at the time of the Ripper crimes. Historical evidence supports the fact that she had at least three lovers during the seven years she was married to James.

Florence Maybrick was arrested in May 1889 and charged with murdering her husband. The jury found her guilty and she was sentenced to death.

The evidence against her was almost nonexistent, and the subsequent support that she received from both sides of the Atlantic led to her death sentence being commuted to life imprisonment, on the grounds that 'she had attempted to murder her husband'.

Florence spent fifteen years in prison for a crime that she had not even been tried for. On release from prison she used the pseudonym 'Mrs Graham'.

Maybrick, Gladys Evelyn Daughter to James and Florence Maybrick. The second of two children from the marriage. She was not known to have any children, although she adopted Fergus Hugh Graham Kell. Mr Kell was alive at the time the hardback edition of this book went into print.

Maybrick, Jack A Whittlesey Maybrick. Died aged eight. There is no known birth certificate for him.

Maybrick, James Purported author of a diary brought to the public's attention in 1992. The diary was signed Jack the Ripper. The detailed information within the document convinced historians that it was a post-1987 forgery. Evidence uncovered by the author of this book has negated that argument.

James Maybrick was a self-confessed drug addict and frequently visited brothels. He certainly had a motive and the opportunity to have committed the Ripper crimes.

Maybrick, James Chandler ('Bobo', 'Sonny') The first-born and only son of James and Florence Maybrick. Died in mysterious circumstances in Canada, after having apparently drunk potassium cyanide instead of water. He was engaged at the time of his death, and had no known offspring.

Maybrick, John First cousin to James Maybrick. Their fathers were twin brothers. Chief mourner at James Maybrick's funeral.

Maybrick (née Withers), Laura Married Michael Maybrick. They had no known children.

Maybrick, Leonard William David Walsall, West Midland Maybrick. Son of David William Maybrick.

Maybrick, Margaret Minetta a.k.a 'Elizabeth', a.k.a Margaret Edges, Edgis, Egges A Whittlesey Maybrick. Although most of her children were born with the name of Woolstone, she was to have them all baptised Maybrick at Saint Mary's, Whittlesey, in November 1917. Her 'paper' father, James Edges, does not appear to have any connection with the Maybricks. Descendants of the Edges family have no knowledge of Margaret.

Maybrick, Mark a.k.a. Mark Woolston(e) 'Father' to the 'Whittlesey Maybricks. Although Mark Woolstone appears on several birth certificates as Mark Maybrick, and husband of Margaret Minetta Maybrick, oral tradition in the family insists he had nothing to do with the Maybrick family at all. There is no known record of his birth.

Maybrick, Michael ('Blucher') James Maybrick's younger and most successful brother. Michael Maybrick was an accomplished musician. He wrote music as Stephen Adams.

His Masonic career was also paved with success, and he achieved 'thirty degrees'. He was well known to Queen Victoria.

After the trial of Florence Maybrick ended in 1889, Michael went to live in Ryde, Isle of Wight, where he became mayor.

Michael had power and money. He had the most to lose if James Maybrick had ever been caught. Nicknamed 'Blucher' by Florence Maybrick.

Maybrick, Naomi A Whittlesey Maybrick. Born Naomi Woolston, she died aged eight months as Naomi Maybrick. The same registrar recorded both events.

Maybrick, Rose Ellen A Whittlesey Maybrick. Mother of Jeanette Grady.

Maybrick, Ruth Mary A Whittlesey Maybrick. The only one of the girls registered illegitimately by Margaret.

Maybrick, Sheppard Shalgrave A Whittlesey Maybrick. Although born in 1913, he was no longer with the family when they were admitted to the workhouse in December 1915. There is no known record of either a marriage or his death.

Maybrick, Thomas Younger brother of James Maybrick. Neither of Thomas's children are known to have had any offspring. The author of this book does not believe that this Thomas is the one referred to by James Maybrick in the diary.

Maybrick, Ursula Grace a.k.a. Sister Mary Joachim Granddaughter of John Maybrick, and therefore first cousin, twice removed, to James Maybrick. Sister Mary was to state that she 'knew Albert Johnson was a Maybrick the first time [she] set eyes on him'.

Maybrick, William James Maybrick's only older brother.

Maybrook, William Maybrick Connection to James Maybrick unknown. He did, however, have his will witnessed in 1874 at 3 Jamaica Street, the precise address where Sarah Ann Robertson had once lived.

Maybury, Francis John Married Jane Margaret Sumner. Original owner of Nestlé shares.

Meagher, Norma Great-granddaughter of Richard Ellison and Jane Whalley. It was interviewing her that led us to discover that the Maybrick watch was known about within the family long before 1987, when the historians believe it was forged.

Miller, Mr The name of the person reported, in 1889, to be selling a diary that had come from the Maybrick household. It has been suggested that his name was a pseudonym of Mr Murrin, who became Alice Yapp's husband.

Murphy, Ronald George Owner of the jewellery shop in which Albert Johnson 'acquired' the Maybrick watch. However, like George Dundas, Mr Murphy described the watch as 'white-faced with black numbers'. Mr Murphy also claimed that nothing could have been engraved on the back, as the ornate design left no room for engraving.

Murrin (née Yapp), Alice Nurse to the Maybrick children at the time of the Whitechapel murders. She claimed to have arranged for her predecessor, Emma Parker, to be employed by the Maybricks. Her testimony at the trial of Florence Maybrick was suggested by the media to have been tantamount to leading to Florence's conviction. The newspapers clearly suggested a more 'intimate' relationship between James Maybrick and Alice Yapp.

Murrin, Edward Married Alice Yapp.

Nicholas, Richard Solicitor of Albert Edward Johnson.

Over, Bessie Jane Daughter of John Over.

Over, Mrs John (née Emma Parker) Possibly the true mother of Elizabeth Crawley. Emma Parker was the Maybrick's nanny before Alice Yapp. It is her husband's initials that are engraved on the back of the Maybrick watch. .

'Read, Mrs' Annie Jepson (née Maybrick) remembered this to be the name of the woman who her oldest 'sister' often used to visit. Hannah Hartnett, who lived with Sarah Ann Robertson, had the maiden name of 'Reed'.

Riley, Irene Adopted granddaughter of Olga Maybrick Ellison. In possession of various artefacts and information that made us aware that the Maybrick watch was known within the family long before 1987.

Robertson, Sarah Ann a.k.a. Sarah Ann Maybrick ('Piggy', 'Old Auntie') Lover of James Maybrick for more than twenty years. James and Sarah met in London in or around the early 1860s and lived in Bromley Street, off Commercial Road, in Whitechapel. According to various sources, they had five children. Reports vary as to how many lived or died.

Roughton, Janice A Whittlesey Maybrick. Daughter of Annie Jepson (née Maybrick) and in possession of Elizabeth Susannah Maybrick's belongings.

Samuelson, Christina Another apparent lover of James Maybrick.

Somers, Mary ('Auntie May') Aunt of Albert Johnson. Elder sister of Dora Somers (later Johnson). Although born Mary Somers, she was married 'Mary May . . .'. Mary had a very close relationship with her nephew and it has been mooted that she passed the watch to Albert Johnson.

Somers, Patrick Second husband of Elizabeth Crawley.

Sumner, Jane Margaret Margaret Minetta's 'paper' grandmother.

Steele (née Devereux), Nancy Daughter of Tony Devereux.

Nancy inadvertently confirmed Anne Graham's version of events.

Stephen, Sir James Fitzjames Presided over the trial of Florence Maybrick. He was never to sit before a court again.

Sir James's own son, J.K. Stephen, tutor to the Duke of Clarence, was later to become a Ripper suspect.

Taylor, Charles First husband of Elizabeth Crawley.

Taylor, William Son to Charles Taylor and Elizabeth Crawley.

Wadham, Albert John Married 'Auntie Wadham' (née Knight). His family originated from Wimborne in Dorset, the home of M.J. Druitt.

Wadham (née Knight), Elizabeth ('Auntie Wadham') Known to the five Whittlesey Maybrick sisters as Auntie. The relationship would appear to be 'blood'. There is no birth registered for Elizabeth Knight, but she is probably the sister of Margaret Minetta Maybrick, and also, therefore, an illegitimate descendant of James Maybrick and Sarah Ann Robertson. Attempts to contact the informant of her death proved fruitless.

Whalley, Jane Married Richard Ellison.

Wilson, Janet Only living descendant of the Walsall, West Midland Maybricks. Janet was not aware of any connection to the Maybrick name at all.

Witt, Gustave A. Employer of James Maybrick at the time of the Ripper crimes. His offices in Cullum Street were just a short distance away from the Minories.

BIBLIOGRAPHY

Jack the Ripper

Anderson, Sir Robert, *The Lighter Side of My Official Life* (1910)

Begg, Paul; Fido, Martin; and Skinner, Keith, *The Jack the Ripper A–Z*, Headline Book Publishing plc (1996)

Begg, Paul, *Jack the Ripper: The Uncensored Facts*, Robson Books Ltd (1993)

Dew, Walter, *I Caught Crippen* (1938)

Evans, Stewart and Gainey, Paul, *Jack the Ripper: First American Killer*, Arrow Books Ltd (1996)

Fairclough, Melvyn, *The Ripper and The Royals*, Gerald Duckworth and Co. Ltd, second impression, (1992)

Farson, Daniel, *Jack the Ripper*, Michael Joseph Ltd (1972)

Fido, Martin, *The Crimes, Detection and Death of Jack the Ripper*, George Weidenfeld and Nicolson Ltd (1987)

Harris, Melvin, *The True Face of Jack the Ripper*, Michael O'Mara Books Ltd (1994)

Harrison, Michael, *Clarence: the Life of HRH the Duke of Clarence*, Harrap (1965)

Harrison, Paul, *Jack the Ripper: The Mystery Solved*, Robert Hale (1993)

Harrison, Shirley, *The Diary of Jack the Ripper*, Smith Gryphon (1994)

Howells, Martin and Skinner, Keith, *The Ripper Legacy: The Life and Death of Jack the Ripper* Warner Books (1992)

Kelly, Alexander, with David Sharp, *Jack the Ripper: A Bibliography and Review of The Literature*, AAL Publishing (1995)

Knight, Stephen, *Jack the Ripper: The Final Solution*, Grafton (1977)

Macnaghten, Sir Melville, *Days of My Years* (1914)

McCormick, Donald, *The Identity of Jack the Ripper*, Arrow Books Ltd (1959)

Paley, Bruce, *Jack the Ripper: The Simple Truth*, Headline Book Publishing plc (1995)

Rumbelow, Donald, *The Complete Jack the Ripper*, Penguin Books (1988)

Smith, Lt-Col. Sir Henry, *From Constable to Commissioner*, Chatto and Windus (1910)

Spiering, Frank, *Prince Jack: The True Story of Jack the Ripper*, Jove Publications, Inc. (1978)

Sugden, Philip, *The Complete History of Jack the Ripper*, Robinson Publishing Ltd (1994)

Whittington-Egan, Richard, *The Casebook of Jack the Ripper*, Wildy (1976)

Wilding, John, *Jack the Ripper Revealed*, Constable-Volcano (1993)

Wilson, Colin and Odell, Robin, *Jack the Ripper: Summing Up the Verdict*, Bantam (1987)

Winslow, L. Forbes, *Recollections of Forty Years*, John Ousely Ltd (1910)

Wolff, Camille, *Who Was Jack the Ripper?*, Grey House Books (1995)

Woodhall, Edwin T., *Jack the Ripper: Or When London Walked in Terror*, Mellifont Press Ltd (1937)

Fiction based on Jack the Ripper

Belloc Lowndes, Mrs, *The Lodger*, Methuen (1913)

West, Pamela, *Yours Truly, Jack The Ripper*, St Martin's Press (1987)

Florence Maybrick

Christie, Trevor L., *Etched in Arsenic* (1968)

Densmore, Helen, *The Maybrick Case* (1892)

Irving, H.B., *Trial of Mrs Maybrick*, William Hodge and Company (1912)

Levy, J.H., *The Necessity For Criminal Appeal, As Illustrated By The Maybrick Case*, P.S. King and Son (1899)

MacDougall, Alexander W., *Treatise on The Maybrick Case* (1891)

Hartman, Mary S., *Victorian Murderesses*, Robson Books (1985)

Maybrick, Florence, Elizabeth *My Fifteen Lost Years* (1909)
Morland, Nigel, *This Friendless Lady*, Frederick Muller Ltd (1957)
Ryan, Bernard, *The Poisoned Life of Mrs Maybrick* (1977)

Fiction based on Florence Maybrick

Florence Maybrick: A Thrilling Romance, Purkiss (1889)

American sources

American Heritage Center, Wyoming University, Wyoming
Bureau of Vital Statistics
Library of Congress, New York
Manchester Reference Library, Manchester, New Hampshire
National Archives and Records Administration, Washington DC
Richmond City Court House, Richmond, Virginia
Virginia State Archives, Richmond, Virginia

British sources

British Telecom Archives, London
Business Archive Council
Cambridgeshire County Records Office
Central Chancery of the Orders of Knighthood, St James's Palace
Cheshire Arts and Archives
Convent Community of the Epiphany, Truro, Cornwall
Corporation of London Records Office, Guildhall
Freemasons Hall
General Register Office, Edinburgh
General Register Office, St Catherine's House, London
General Registry, Isle of Man
Greater London Record Office
Hammersmith and Fulham Archives and Local History
Hand Hotel, Llangollen, Wales
Huntingdon Coroner's Office
IGI Registers, Public Record Office, Chancery Lane
Kensington and Chelsea Local Studies Centre
Kensington Palace (for dating clothing from old photographs)
Lancashire County Constabulary
Lancashire County Records Office, Preston
Law Society
National Army Museum

National Museum of Film and Photography, Bradford
National Register of Archives
Northamptonshire Records Office
OPCS, St Catherine's House, Kingsway, London
OPCS, Southport
Public Record Office, Kew
Public Record Office, Chancery Lane for the Census – 1841,
    1851, 1861, 1871, 1881, 1891
Register of Wills, Family Division, Somerset House
Royal London Hospital Archives
Royal Mail Archives and Records, London
Ruthin Archives, Ruthin, North Wales
Ruthin Record Office, Ruthin, North Wales
Society of Genealogists
Sotheby's
Scottish Record Office
Surrey Records, County Hall, Kingston
Tower Hamlets Local History and Archives
Turner Home (Liverpool)
Tyne and Wear Archives
Victoria and Albert Museum
Walton Prison, Liverpool
Wellington Barracks
Westminster Archives Centre

Libraries

Amersham Reference Library, Birmingham Central Library,
British Library, British Library Newspaper Library Colindale,
Bodleian Library Oxford, Chester Reference Library, Durham
Reference Library, Guildhall Library London, Harrogate
Library, Hartlepool Reference Library, Huntingdon Local
History Library, Huntingdon Reference Library, Lancaster
Reference Library, Lewisham Local History Library, Liverpool Record Office and Local Studies, Marylebone Reference
Library, Peterborough Reference Library, Newham Local
History Library, Northampton Local History Library,
Reading Local History Library, Southwark Local History
Library, Whittlesey Library, Wirral Archives Service, Woking
Reference Library.

INDEX

177n; knife used 63, 373–4; screams 277–8

Sugden, Philip 47, 72, 277–8, 299, 332–4, 376, 398, 403–4

Sumner, Jane Margaret 136n, 429

Sunday Express 383n

Sunday News 191–2

Sunday Times 1, 22–4, 179, 217, 298

Swanson, Chief Inspector Donald 46, 52–3, 277, 279, 280–81, 284, 303, 373, 399

Tabram, Martha 299

Taylor, Charles 250, 430

Taylor, William 250, 430

Thick, Sergeant 59n

This Friendless Lady 118n, 163–4, 167, 185, 202n, 211, 295n, 324–5, 344

Thomas, Bernard 319

Thompson, Freda 379–84

Thompson, Stuart 379, 384

Thompson, William 85

Tidy, Dr 89

Time-Warner Books 25, 91, 96, 98

Times, The 50n, 59n, 68, 70, 73, 207n, 369–70, 386

True Face of Jack the Ripper, The 103–4, 274n, 275n

True Identity of Jack the Ripper, The 47

trunks, metal: Billy Graham's 199–200, 313; Florence Maybrick's 312–13, 340

Tumblety, Dr Francis 280, 377

Turgoose, Dr Stephen 34–5, 37–9, 238

Uncensored Facts, The 144

Underwood, Peter 103

Verity of Lancaster 31n

Victoria, Queen 204, 334–8, 350, 377–8

von Roques, Baroness (*née* Caroline Elizabeth Ingraham) 77, 78n, 314, 423; ancestry and background 75, 203, 204; engages Jonathan Harris 319, 337; letter to Home Secretary 62, 116, 326; and 'Mrs Maybrick's diary' 340, 343, 344; petitions Queen Victoria 204, 334–6, 338

Waddell, Bill 71, 282, 302

Wadham, Albert John 135n, 430

Wadham (*née* Knight), Elizabeth ('Auntie Wadham') 135, 135n, 430

Ward, Leonard 132

Warren, Commissioner Sir Charles 6n, 291, 383n

Warren, Nick 256

Warren, Dr Peter 383n

Washington Post 25

watch, Verity: acquisition by Albert Johnson 29–33, 39–40, 239–40, 242–3, 246–51, 408; acquisition by Ronald Murphy 33–4, 408; description 28–9, 241–2; doubts about provenance 200, 246–51; Timothy Dundas's account 240–42; engravings 28–33, 35–6, 37–9, 242–5, 248, 251, 408; jeweller's receipt 30–31, 243; Norma Meagher's account 236; Ronald Murphy's account 30–31, 33–4, 242–4, 408; Richard Nicholas's account 238–9; Turgoose report 34–5, 37–9, 238; Wild report 244

Watkins, PC Edward 55, 391

West, Acting Superintendent 48n

West, Pamela 137n

Whalley, Jane 236, 430

Whitechapel (in 1888) 42–3

Whitechapel murders 43

Whitehall murder 288–9

Whittington-=gan, Richard 18, 46–7, 155, 397, 398, 403–4, 405

Whittlesey 122, 123, 124, 131; workhouse 127, 129, 131, 135n

Who was Jack the Ripper? 104, 105, 327n

Wickes, Gary 4, 7–8, 244

Wild, R.K. 244

Wilkes, Roger 105, 106, 323

Wilson, Colin 91, 101, 249, 258, 270, 337–8, 397

Wilson, Janet 227, 430

Wilson, Nurse 312–13